HORROR FILMS

HORROR FILMS

HORROR FILMS

James Marriott

This edition published in Great Britain in 2007 by
Virgin Books Ltd
Thames Wharf Studios
Rainville Road
London
W6 9HA

First published in Great Britain in 2004

A catalogue record for this book is available from the British
Library.

ISBN 978 0 7535 1253 1

Typeset by TW Typesetting, Plymouth, Devon
Printed in the UK by CPI Bookmarque, Croydon, CR0 4TD

CONTENTS

ACKNOWLEDGEMENTS

Many thanks go to Ed Maidment, Kerri Sharp, John Coulthart and Pan Pantziarka for loans of resources and ideas, Harvey Fenton of FAB Press for services to horror fandom, Simon Whitechapel and Simon Fowler for incisive comments on the text, and my editor Kirstie Addis for editorial help and extending my deadline! Thanks also to my parents, for their continued support.

I am grateful to the following individuals and organisations for permission to use quotations: Donato Totaro, *Sight & Sound*, *Harper's Magazine* and the *Texas Monthly Reporter*.

ACKNOWLEDGMENTS

INTRODUCTION

Horror is the madwoman in the attic of cinema. Professing a liking for or interest in the genre tends to provoke shudders of distaste in many circles, but for fans its disreputableness just adds to its charm. If we agree with Robin Wood's famous argument that horror's 'true subject is the struggle for recognition of all that our civilization represses or oppresses', it's hardly surprising that the genre is considered unsavoury. As David Cronenberg puts it: 'If you accept, at least to some extent, the Freudian dictum that civilisation is repression, then imagination – and an unrepressed creativity – is dangerous to civilisation'; and for all of horror films' often formulaic nature, the genre throws up a kind of wild creativity that just isn't seen anywhere else.

This is partly due to its guaranteed box-office appeal – horror is a perennial favourite – and also to the fact that it has traditionally attracted independent, low-budget filmmakers. Many of the films covered in this book are early efforts by young directors without much money to spend, but low budgets mean low risks, encouraging a formal innovation missing from most other genres, and horror has traditionally been one of the only areas in film where small investments can yield extremely high returns.

Horror acts as a kind of test lab, allowing experimentation with ideas and technologies that will eventually filter through to the mainstream. This works in a number of ways. Thematically, *The*

Silence of the Lambs (Jonathan Demme, 1991) is a sanitised, cosy take on the genre's slashers and serial killers, and *The Accused* (Jonathan Kaplan, 1988) puts a user-friendly gloss on the stark harshness of *I Spit on Your Grave* (Meir Zarchi, 1978). Film directors, actors and technicians often hone their skills on horror, one of the easiest ways to break into the mainstream: A-list directors like Peter Jackson and Sam Raimi started out making sick zombie splatter movies, and 80s slashers chopped and stabbed their way through a long line of up-and-coming stars. And effects technology tested on horror audiences percolates into the mainstream too, in subtler, self-disguising adaptations of horror's unabashed displays.

The genre acts as a fertile ground for experimentation for viewers as well. Part of the appeal of horror is that it allows audiences to feel scared or shocked in an environment that does not otherwise allow room for such responses; as critic Charles Derry argues in *Dark Dreams*:

> In an era where death – in the form of Vietnam killing, live riots, and assassinations – is watched daily over a long period of time on the evening news, and our responses to death have become complacent and anaesthetised, going to *The Exorcist* and throwing up reaffirms man's ability to be revolted, his ability to feel; thus the viewer's vomit almost becomes a valid artistic response to the world around him.

Hitchcock had a similar idea, claiming that 'The only way to remove the numbness [of civilisation] and revive our moral equilibrium is to use artificial means to bring about the shock. The best way to achieve this, it seems to me, is through a movie.'

But for all the critical theorising about horror's social or political implications, at its best the genre speaks directly to the unconscious, bypassing our rational defences entirely. If cinema has a privileged position among media because of its relationship to dreams, horror's nightmares remain some of its most powerful and effective statements. While zombies or psychos may open the door, horror's true interest is in providing a set of oblique strategies for dealing with anxieties about everything from isolation, transformation, disfigurement, madness and death, to traumas we have already experienced (witness the popularity of birth imagery and 'no exit' womb panic scenes, most clearly visible in *The Shining* (Stanley Kubrick, 1980) and **Alien**) and those we may have to face in the future.

According to critic Leonard Wolf, 'the cinema of horror provides its highly secularised audience with their last – perhaps their only – opportunity to experience mystery and miracle ... Priests of the horror cinema still recite incantations that count.'

Camille Paglia makes a similar point when she describes horror films as 'rituals of pagan worship. There western man obsessively confronts what Christianity has never been able to bury or explain away ... The horror film uses rot as a primary material, part of the Christian west's secret craving for Dionysian truths.'

All this makes the genre sound a bit grim and serious, but the experience of actually watching horror films can be a lot of fun. Horror isn't just about confronting fears, but also channelling aggression: the genre often takes irreverent swipes at such hallowed institutions as the family, the church and authority in general, and characteristically presents displays of shockingly anti-social behaviour that are invigorating to watch. If we are taught to revere social norms through our moral conditioning, horror recognises our resentment at being oppressed in this way, and allows us to revel vicariously in the violation of taboos surrounding everything from socialisation to toilet-training.

It's impossible not to mention censorship, at least in passing, in a book on horror films. The UK, until recently, has had probably the most repressive film censorship laws in the West, and the country has been swept by periodic moral panics focusing on horror films, most notoriously in the 'video nasty' clampdown that resulted in 1984's Video Recordings Act (VRA), leaving a number of the films in this book unavailable to the law-abiding viewer in the UK for decades.

Happily censorship in the UK has slackened off considerably in the past few years. Previously banned films like **The Texas Chain Saw Massacre** and **The Exorcist** have graced cinemas recently, although the revival of both is directly attributable to ex-director James Ferman's retirement from the British Board of Film Classification (BBFC), taking his twin bugbears of pre-teen religious hysteria and the inappropriate use of power tools with him; and many previously shredded 'nasties' have on recent resubmission to the BBFC been passed uncut. The censors have probably realised they are fighting a losing battle: with real-life atrocities readily available on sites like rotten.com and films like the notorious *Guinea Pig* series a click away on eBay, snipping a couple of seconds from a zombie film must look like even more of a waste of time than it used to. Fortress Britain has finally started to crumble.

What's important in a genre is less individual films than the accretion of images and themes over time; yet certain films are milestones in the history of horror, and the twenty titles selected here have been chosen because they all represent a different key strand in a genre spanning everything from the SF leanings of **Alien** to the poetic Surrealism of **Eyes Without a Face**. The films are not necessarily the best of their type nor indeed personal favourites, but are either the most influential in their field or give the broadest scope for a discussion of important issues.

The structure of each chapter should be fairly self-explanatory. Key crew and full cast listings are followed by:

SYNOPSIS: a brief account of the film's events.

ORIGINS AND INSPIRATION: where did the idea for the film come from? What were its key influences?

DIRECTOR: a brief account of the director's career, focusing specifically on his work within the horror genre. Auteur theory tends to obscure the industrial and collaborative nature of film production, but some directors, particularly Cronenberg, Romero and Argento, have written most of their own scripts and returned to the same obsessions again and again, making them clearly the prime movers behind their films.

CASTING: a brief look at some familiar horror faces and their work within the genre.

PRODUCTION: how the film was made, and interesting stories related to the production.

SOUNDTRACK: sound is a crucial element in successful horror. Whose music is featured on the soundtrack? What sound effects were used, and how were they made?

'IT'S ONLY A MOVIE ... ONLY A MOVIE ...': what marketing gimmicks were used to sell the film? Did the ticket come with a vomit bag or 3-D glasses?

RELEASE: how the film did at the box office, what the papers said and how the censors reacted.

CRITICAL EYE: an in-depth analysis of the film, spanning both other critics' ideas and personal observations.

INDUSTRY IMPACT: film producers around the world try to cash in on successful ideas for films, with mixed results. From British **Alien** rip-off *Inseminoid* to remakes and spin-offs, this section shows what kind of splash the film made in the global industry.

FINAL WORD: a brief summing up of the above which justifies the film's inclusion in this book.

I have restricted myself to coverage of genre horror in this book and, even then, have focused on those films that seem particularly worthy of attention. While avoiding detailed descriptions of *Spookies* or *Ghoulies* may be no great loss, films like Fred Wiseman's *Titicut Follies*, Gaspar Noé's *Irréversible* and the work of David Lynch contain scenes as horrifying as anything in this book, but are outside its remit. Finally, a word of warning: watching horror films tends to encourage a morbid sense of humour, a new sense of aesthetics that prizes high weirdness above all else, and an overdraft fed by creaking shelves full of books, magazines and films. But it won't, despite what you may have heard, turn you into a drooling blood-crazed killer or make you dabble with occult forces beyond your control. Just as long as you remember: don't answer the phone, don't go in the basement, and never, ever wander around the woods on your own ...

THE SILENT ERA

Nosferatu, A Symphony of Horrors (1922)

Germany, Prana Film, b/w, 81 mins

Directed by F W Murnau
Produced by Enrico Dieckmann, Albin Grau
Script: Henrik Galeen, based on *Dracula* by Bram Stoker
Sets and Costumes: Albin Grau
Camera: Fritz Arno Wagner
Original Music: Hans Erdmann

CAST: Max Schreck (*Graf Orlok*), Alexander Granach (*Knock, an Estate Agent*), Gustav von Wangenheim (*Hutter, his Assistant*), Greta Schröder (*Ellen, Hutter's Wife*), Georg H Schnell (*Harding*), Ruth Landshoff (*his Sister*), John Gottowt (*Professor Bulwer*), Gustav Botz (*Dr Sievers*), Max Nemetz (*Captain of the Demeter*), Guido Herzfeld (*Proprietor*), Fanny Schreck (*Nurse in Hospital*), Albert Venohr (*1st Sailor*), Hardy von Francois (*2nd Sailor*)

SYNOPSIS: Knock, an estate agent, wants his clerk, Hutter, to go to Transylvania to sell a house to Count Orlok. Hutter is overjoyed at the chance to advance his prospects, but his wife Ellen is less enthusiastic.

In the Carpathians, villagers in an inn are alarmed to discover that Hutter is travelling to Orlok's castle. They warn him not to continue that night, so Hutter stays, and in his room finds a book about vampires that mentions Nosferatu.

Late next day his coachman refuses to go any further, and Hutter crosses a river alone. He is soon picked up by another coach, and taken to the castle, where he meets Orlok. While eating that evening, Hutter cuts his finger. Orlok, who has been reading a letter sent by Knock, tries to suck the blood, then convinces Hutter to stay up late with him.

In the morning Hutter finds holes in his neck, and tells his wife in a letter that he has been bitten by a mosquito. While he shows Orlok the papers for the house on sale – opposite his own – the count is impressed by a picture of Ellen. That night, Hutter reads more about Nosferatu, and hides under his sheets when he sees the count approaching.

In the morning Hutter finds Orlok's body in a coffin in the basement. He runs away, terrified, and later, locked in his room, sees the count leaving with a consignment of coffins. He escapes and later wakes up in a hospital, suffering from a fever.

The coffins are loaded onto a ship – one is opened, and a rat leaps out of the soil inside and bites a crew member. Meanwhile Knock is in an asylum, where he eats flies and attacks a doctor.

Hutter and Orlok race back to Wisborg, all on Orlok's boat falling prey to a mysterious fever, until the count kills the captain, who has lashed himself to the wheel. A plague is decimating vast regions of central Europe.

Both Hutter and Orlok arrive in Wisborg, and go to their homes. The ship is found to have been carrying the plague, and the town is put on alert. Knock overpowers his guard and escapes.

The town is ravaged by the plague, and blame is placed on Knock, who is chased into the fields. Ellen reads Hutter's book on vampires, and discovers that a sinless maiden can destroy a vampire by offering herself to him willingly.

Ellen opens her windows to the count, who feeds on her and is still there in the morning; he perishes in the light of the sun. When Hutter visits her, Ellen is dying, and the plague has ended.

ORIGINS AND INSPIRATION: *Nosferatu* was the first film to feature what has become one of horror cinema's most enduring figures, the vampire. There had been plenty of vampire fiction, of course – Stoker's novel came as the culmination of a century of fanged chillers, rather than inaugurating the genre – and a number of other silent films had already dealt with supernatural themes. *Dr Jekyll and Mr Hyde* was a popular story – Murnau directed a version himself – and various Frankenstein's Monsters and Golems had found their way onto the screen. *The Cabinet of Dr Caligari/Das Cabinet des Dr Caligari* (Robert Wiene, 1919) seemed to many to define the imaginative potential of film, and Scandinavian director Victor Sjöström, who showed how landscape could be used as a narrative character in *The Phantom Carriage/Körkarlen* (1920), proved a powerful influence on Murnau.

But the Germans seemed more than any other nationality to latch on to supernatural films. Critic Lotte Eisner has explained 'the weird pleasure the Germans have in evoking horror' in terms of 'the excessive and very Germanic desire to submit to discipline, together with a certain proneness to sadism'. But there are other reasons too: the frustration and despair felt in the wake of the First World War, for instance, with the attendant popularity of spiritualism and an influx of debilitated and disfigured war cripples; or the rich national heritage of black Romanticism and demonic folklore; and the Expressionist movement, an exploration of the inner life through external representations of emotional conditions, lent itself well to the styles of acting and set design demanded by the silent tale of terror.

Germany in the early 1920s was also recovering from other traumas reflected in Murnau's film: high inflation and an economy crippled by France's insistence on immediate war reparations, which led to a resentment and distrust of foreigners; and a Spanish flu epidemic and famine that ravaged the country in 1920–1, killing more than the Great War itself.

Nosferatu's production company, Prana Films, was set up by two German businessmen who announced that it would release a series of supernatural or mystical films. Sadly the company soon became bankrupt, and *Nosferatu* is all that remains of their output.

Murnau asked the estate of Bram Stoker for permission to adapt *Dracula*, but was turned down. He and scriptwriter Henrik Galeen, who had directed the 1914 *Der Golem* and *The Student of Prague/Der Student von Prag* (1920), pressed on anyway:

maybe if they transferred the action from London to Wisborg, changed the names of the characters (Harker became Hutter, Dracula Orlok), and reduced the scope of the sprawling novel, they could avoid any copyright issues.

While Galeen retained some traditional vampire beliefs – the count cannot cross moving water unaided, nor cross a threshold uninvited, and must nest in the soil in which he was buried – he also discarded a substantial portion of Stoker's vampire lore. Stoker's vampires could cast neither shadow nor reflection, but could safely be exposed to sunlight: Orlok, by contrast, casts both shadow and reflection, and is killed by contact with the sun, an innovation that was largely retained in future vampire stories. Galeen's script also dispensed with any suggestion that religion can combat vampires; and science and rationalism don't help much either, with the script's Van Helsing character, Bulwer, relegated to an impotent role. In a Wagnerian twist, only the sacrifice of a sinless maiden can prevent the vampire from continuing his dark work.

Set and costume designer Albin Grau was a member of the OTO (Ordo Templi Orientis), a magical group concerned with spreading tantric sexual magic throughout Europe, and corresponded briefly with Aleister Crowley. Grau was responsible for the arcane correspondence between Knock and the count, which uses a combination of cabalistic and astrological symbols that are repeated later on Knock's cell wall – the symbols in the letter, seen on screen only for a couple of seconds, provide favourable auguries to the count for the purchase of the house.

Grau was also responsible for the look of Count Orlok, whose make-up, which has been memorably described as 'a disturbing combination of a rat and a penis', grows progressively uglier as the film unfolds. The animalistic terms in which the count is viewed here couldn't be further from Christopher Lee's suave egotist in the Hammer series, and it's even suggested at one point that the count has shape-shifted into a hyena. Animal imagery is rife throughout the film, with repeated references to spiders and flies, and images of horses, rats, hyenas and hydras: these serve the double function of reminding us that vampires fit into nature's scheme of exploitation – everything feeds on something – and to anchor the tale of the supernatural in reality. If nature is this fantastic, why should vampires not also exist?

DIRECTOR: FW Murnau, described by critic Lotte Eisner as 'the greatest film-director the Germans have ever known', directed over twenty films, but almost half have been lost. His most famous works are probably his supernatural films *Nosferatu* and *Faust* (1926), a far more lavish production that lurches from spectacular imagery to rank sentimentality, and his other silent classics *The Last Laugh* (1924) and *Sunrise* (1927).

Murnau is widely considered to be an Expressionist director, and the heightened emotional states, dreamlike quality and use of characters to represent personality principles in his films can all be attributed to the movement's influence. But the use of location shooting in *Nosferatu* prevents it from being a true Expressionist film, and Murnau's influences are drawn at least as much from the Romantic movement, especially painters like Caspar David Friedrich.

Other distinctive features of the director's work include his allusions to off-screen space, drawing on the viewer's imagination to extend the scope of his narratives; his sparse use of objects, a theatrical innovation that lends an ominous and dreamlike quality to film scenes; and his subtlety, most clearly apparent if *Nosferatu* is compared to a film like *The Cabinet of Dr Caligari* (1919), which by contrast seems at times hysterical.

CASTING: While other members of *Nosferatu*'s cast appeared in several other films, only Max Schreck's name has lived on, his bat-like head and etiolated frame marking him out as one of the silver screen's most memorable vampires. Despite rumours that he appeared only in this role, he was a member of Max Reinhardt's theatre troupe and worked as a character actor in plays and films until his death. He does not, as suggested in *Shadow of the Vampire* (E Elias Merhige, 2000), appear to have been a vampire himself, and nor is there any record of him devouring members of the film's cast and crew.

Schreck (the word means 'terror' in German) brings a certain dignity to the role of the count, who is described by André Gide as 'dashing, venturesome, and even very pleasingly bold'. Boris Karloff was said to have been influenced by Schreck for his performance as Frankenstein's Monster; and ironically enough one of Karloff's final screen roles, in *Targets* (Peter Bogdanovich, 1968), was as an actor whose surname is Schreck.

PRODUCTION: Most of the shooting, unusually for a German film of the time, took place on location, principally the Baltic cities of Lubek and Wismar, and the Tartra mountain range on the border between Poland and Slovakia, in the summer of 1921. Although the location shooting was probably mainly due to budgetary concerns, Murnau chose the locations carefully, and ensured that images were framed for the maximum sinister impact; the whole film is shot through with a wild Romantic beauty, aided by non-narrative sequences of clouds scudding across the sky or waves crashing on a beach. When the director still didn't have the effect he wanted, he would alter the framing by adding shadows using matte cut-outs: one is visible on the right of the screen when Hutter first meets Orlok.

As well as location shooting, Murnau's other innovations included trick photography, with stop-frame used in a number of sequences, and negative photography for part of Hutter's carriage ride to Orlok's castle – the count himself eerily remains black in this sequence, while everything else is inverted, Schreck having been dressed for the shot in a white robe. Murnau also tinted the film: the night skies were dark blue, and elsewhere the film was tinted yellow, sepia, rose and blood red.

The intertitles (the cards that provide information for the viewer in silent films) were played off against the images, and vice versa, one subverting the other; and Murnau used cross-cutting to create a powerful psychic continuity to scenes separated by time and space, a technique later described by German critics as 'creative geography'. The count usually appears in the same part of the screen where he'd last been seen, and when he menaces Hutter, the count seems to see and pace towards Ellen, although he is separated from her by hundreds of miles.

SOUNDTRACK: As the film is itself a 'symphony of terrors', it is constructed in a self-consciously symphonic way, with motifs (mirrors, windows) repeated throughout and fluctuating tempos building up to periodic crescendos. The original soundtrack was written by Hans Erdmann but is now lost; for the German 1929 re-release for the sound market a new soundtrack was commissioned, from Georg Fliebiger, which is also now lost. Both composers were relatively unknown, and are not noted for any other work.

'IT'S ONLY A MOVIE ... ONLY A MOVIE ...': The film was marketed using a series of Expressionist posters and publicity pieces in magazines, warning the unwary that 'Nosferatu is not just fun, not something to be taken lightly'; the publicity costs eventually exceeded those of making the film, surely a contributing factor to Prana Films' short life. Some of these pieces carried a story about vampires by Albin Grau, told in an appropriately gothic style: in Serbia during the winter of 1916 Grau, then in the army, was billeted with an old peasant, who told the soldiers how his father, who had died without receiving the appropriate sacraments, had haunted his village as a vampire.

The storyteller showed the soldiers an official document describing the exhumation of a corpse. The body, which showed no signs of decomposition and had long, sharp teeth protruding from the mouth, was staked through the heart, and the Lord's Prayer was read over it, whereupon it groaned and expired.

RELEASE: Nosferatu barely survived its initial release: the favourable critical responses when the film came out in Germany were soon overshadowed by press attacks on the debt-ridden Prana Films, and when Florence Stoker found out about this unauthorised adaptation, the impoverished widow sued the company for breach of copyright. As Prana Films was already bankrupt, she settled for a court order of the destruction of all prints of the film; but fortunately a couple survived.

In 1929 the film was re-edited for the German sound market and re-released as Die Zwoelfte Stunde (The Twelfth Hour). Outtakes from Murnau's film were introduced, along with additional footage, principally scenes of peasants and a Mass for the Dead. The film seems to have had a more Christian feel than the original, and features the extra character of a priest; rather than finding a book on vampires in the inn, Hutter reads a Bible, and Ellen survives her encounter with Orlok, the transposition of an earlier scene showing her with Hutter giving it a happy ending.

This may have been the version shown in the US as Nosferatu the Vampire the same year; at least, this film featured different character names from Murnau's original, with Orlok now 'Count Nosferatu' and Knock 'Vorlock'. Most American reviewers, perhaps now familiar with John Balderston's theatrical adaptation of the novel, were unimpressed, the New York Times noting that it was 'more of a soporific than a thriller' while the Herald

Tribune thought it 'jumbled and confused', its visual beauty unsupported by a story that 'flopped woefully due to inexpert cutting or bad continuity'. The *New York Post* was the only paper to acknowledge the qualities of the film, which was not widely considered a classic until after the Second World War: 'Not since Caligari has this reviewer been so taken with a foreign horror film ... Mr Murnau's is no momentary horror ... but a pestilential horror coming from a fear of things only rarely seen.'

CRITICAL EYE: *Nosferatu* has divided critics from its release to the present day. Bela Balazs, a German film critic, in 1924 described the 'chilly draft from doomsday' that passed through the film, and Lotte Eisner rated it as the finest example of its type: 'Never again was so perfect an Expressionism to be attained, and its stylisation was achieved without the aid of the slightest artifice.' Detractors included Theodore Huff, who in 1946 complained that it was crude and too 'Teutonic', with poor acting and a shoestring budget that made the trick photography ridiculous rather than impressive; and noted horror historian Carlos Clarens had similar points to make: 'It is crude, unsubtle, and illogical, whereas the book is perfectly logical within the boundaries of fantasy. The film's ending, in particular, reeks of Nordic mysticism and betrays the genuine horror of the original.'

Novelist André Gide was also critical of the film, pointing out that too often the actors' terror got in the way of that of the audience. He had a point – Schreck aside, the principals are unconvincing, and some parts (notably that of Harding's sister) were given as favours rather than in recognition of acting merit. Gide also objected to the bestial portrayal of a vampire, and presciently described how the count should have looked – 'not as terrible and fantastic but on the contrary in the guise of an inoffensive young man, charming and most obliging'.

The film's supporters argue that the lack of depth to the characters is by design rather than otherwise: that they represent fragments of a personality, or personality types, rather than whole people. To them *Nosferatu* is an allegorical tale of an inner conflict, one that takes place in the psyche of the individual rather than the mountains and towns of the Baltic.

The theme of doubling is central to the film, which opens with an image of Hutter staring at himself in a mirror and closes with the reflection of the count; Orlok's choice of the house opposite

Hutter's further suggests that he is in a sense Hutter's double, or alter ego. So what part of Hutter's personality does the count represent? Like vampires past and present, Nosferatu – bald, stiff and springing up from his coffin like an erection – personifies sexual potency. Indeed the name 'Nosferatu' itself has sexual connotations, being in Romanian a type of vampire that specialises in making husbands impotent. Not that Hutter needs any help: he is a weak figure, an immature child who perpetually shirks his marital duties. His marriage appears to be unconsummated: when he brings Ellen some flowers, she is distraught that he has killed these symbols of fertility, and she recognises herself as a 'sinless maiden' able to destroy the vampire at the end.

Hutter seems to be more interested in furthering his career than in meeting his wife's needs – while he lacks financial security, she lacks a sexualised relationship, and their desires are the key drivers to the film. Even towards the end, when they are seen in their bedroom, she is in the bed while he sleeps in a chair; and when she dies, he leans over her body to console himself but always keeps one foot on the floor.

The count, by contrast, represents animalistic sexual energy, displaying a kind of fertility – the ship he travels on is named the Demeter in the script, after the Greek goddess of fertility, and he travels with coffins full of soil – in contrast to Hutter's barrenness. His sexual desire is focused at first on Hutter, whose bleeding finger he attempts to suck, and then, when he sees a photo of his wife, on Ellen; and as soon as he leaves the castle his power seems to grow, with the ship, finally propelled solely by his supernatural energies, bursting through the frame to leave Murnau focusing on an empty sea.

Of course, Orlok also brings death. This could be seen in terms of the Freudian ideas popular at the time, an intermingling of the eros and thanatos drives; but the death is at least partly one of sexual repression, visible not least through Knock, who turns into a Pan-like figure causing havoc in the town and leaping around the fields. If *Nosferatu* is to be read as an allegory, it is an allegory of sexual awakening – unsurprisingly, given the stated aims of Grau's beloved OTO.

Ellen's recognition of the count's potency is marked by a mixture of horror and desire. When an intertitle reveals that she is pining for her beloved, she is seen on a beach, staring out to sea. But her husband left by land, and would presumably return that way, which suggests that she is waiting for the count; similarly, after she sleepwalks along a parapet then calls out 'He's coming, I must go to meet him', Murnau cuts to an image of Orlok's ship rather than Jonathan.

Ellen shows an almost erotic pleasure on reading Hutter's book on vampires – a text he forbids her to look at, recalling perhaps the contemporary status of pornography or the psychosexual works of writers like Krafft-Ebing; and the advice she reads there – to give herself willingly to the vampire, and to keep him occupied until sunrise – might be that given to a virginal bride on her wedding night, as well as suggesting Christian self-sacrifice. In this sense the count is a projection of Ellen's desires – desires that bring ruin on the town.

This was hardly a new idea. The popularity of vampire tales at the end of the nineteenth century can be related to a new awareness of female sexuality and its political implications, and the focus of Stoker's novel and virtually every adaptation since is less Dracula himself than the effect he has on women. One of Murnau's coups is to present a count who is a fascinating figure in himself, rather than simply a catalyst for desire.

INDUSTRY IMPACT: The vampire is one of the most iconic and popular figures in cinema: only Sherlock Holmes has appeared as a fictional character on film more often than Dracula, and the vampire genre beats others in terms of sheer volume hands down, appearing everywhere from Japan (*Lake of Dracula/Chi o Suu Me*, Michio Yamamoto, 1971) to Mexico (*World of the Vampires/El Mundo de los Vampiros*, Alfonso Corona Blake and Paul Nagle, 1961). There are conventions to the genre, but they have been toyed with so often that it's difficult to pin down exactly what they are – some modern vampires use syringes and straight razors rather than fangs, and a few don't drink blood at all – even if they are still instantly recognisable.

So why are they so popular? Part of the appeal lies in their symbolic flexibility: vampires have variously been interpreted as representing exploitation, financial or otherwise (Marx referred to 'vampires' frequently in his writings), class structure (the count is an aristocrat), the dangers of foreign property ownership, colonialism, pestilence, invasion and sex, as well as the more recent themes of AIDS, drug addiction and teenage angst. They also, perhaps more powerfully than any of the other figures in this book, represent our desires as well as our fears: they are superhuman, powerful and seductive, and to many their dubious charms are irresistible. Given the popularity of screen vampires, this account will be restricted to Stoker's best-known character, to avoid being overwhelmed by plastic fangs, black cloaks and syrupy blood.

Only three films have followed *Nosferatu*'s animalistic characterisation of the vampire, with fangs at the front and a bald head. They are the Czech fairy tale *Valerie and her Week of Wonders/ Valerie a týden divu* (Jaromil Jires, 1970), Larry Cohen's TV movie *Salem's Lot* (1980) and Werner Herzog's 1979 remake of *Nosferatu*. While the Czech film simply has a Nosferatu lurking in the background, a projection of sinister sexual fears, *Salem's Lot* takes *Nosferatu*'s geographical transposition from London to the Baltic a step further, and reimagines it as an all-American tale.

Herzog's haunting and elegiac remake, one of the most visually impressive of all vampire films, follows the plot of the original faithfully, but humanises its count (a startling Klaus Kinski) as a pathetic and lonely figure, cursed by immortality; and in a reluctance to provide an ending in which good triumphs over evil that is typical of the decade, it adds a coda in which an ineffectual Van Helsing stakes the count and is arrested for his murder, whereupon a fanged Jonathan Harker rides off to spread the vampire curse.

The first authorised version of *Dracula* moved far away from the feral Orlok. A stage adaptation, written by Hamilton Deane, had travelled to the US in 1927, following a successful London run. The actors engaged to play Dracula and Van Helsing, Bela Lugosi and Edward Van Sloan, were later taken to LA to reprise their roles in the 1930 Universal film of Deane's play.

Although Tod Browning's *Dracula* is seriously flawed – after an impressive opening sequence, much of the film is stagy and dull, and most of the action happens off screen, including the count's death – Lugosi made the part his own in a way that ensures his spectre still lingers over adaptations today, informing everything from Hammer horror to *Sesame Street*.

Lugosi never played the part again, save for an inglorious appearance in *Abbott and Costello Meet Frankenstein* (Charles Barton, 1948) – as with their other monsters, Universal quickly hammered the count into the ground – but when he died in 1956 he was buried in a full Dracula costume. He did, however, appear in two other non-Universal vampire films, *Mark of the Vampire* (Tod Browning, 1935) and *The Return of the Vampire* (Lew Landers, 1944), playing a similar role. In the former he is eventually revealed to be an actor pretending to be a vampire, an early example of the self-reflexive strain in horror that dates back far further than Wes Craven's *Scream* (1996).

When Hammer produced their version of **Dracula** in 1958, it gave the world Christopher Lee as the most iconic count since Lugosi, and restored the sex and violence of Stoker's novel to the cinema; after the studio's riot of bare breasts and overwrought acting, the next two notable *Dracula* adaptations, a 1973 production starring Jack Palance as the count (*Dracula*, Dan Curtis), and the 1979 Frank Langella vehicle, seem positively restrained.

Until the release of *Bram Stoker's Dracula*, *Love at First Bite* (Stan Dragoti, 1979) was the highest-grossing vampire film ever released, and between 1972 and 1992 many if not most vampire films had their tongues at least gently in their cheeks. As with the Frankenstein films, caricatures often proved more insightful than straight renditions, and Polanski's underrated *The Fearless Vampire Killers/Dance of the Vampires* (1967) and Paul Morrissey's *Blood for Dracula* (1974) supplied a richly gothic feel alongside their digs at the genre.

Bram Stoker's Dracula (1992) often plays like a parody but isn't, with director Francis Ford Coppola taking elements from many disparate *Dracula* adaptations to produce a symbolically overloaded tale that is as much a tribute to one of the twentieth century's most enduring screen icons as it is an adaptation of Stoker's novel. The film is almost hobbled by Keanu Reeves's ghastly acting as Jonathan Harker, but its splendour and extravagance finally redeem it, and the film became the highest-grossing *Dracula* in history, prompting Coppola to turn his eyes, Universal-style, to *Frankenstein*.

FINAL WORD: The richness of *Nosferatu*'s imagery gives it a quality few other interpretations of the vampire legend have matched. The film may be unlikely to scare modern viewers who are more used to sophisticated techniques of manipulation and slick production values, yet it still boasts a dreamlike intensity: it's one of the only vampire films to use central European locations, rather than a studio backlot or the countryside around Bray, and it is filled with iconic images of desolate beauty, from the shot of the raft being taken down river to the ruined castle seen at the end. *Nosferatu* achieves a genuine eeriness that is still palpable today, and remains one of the most powerfully nightmarish vampire films ever made.

UNIVERSAL MONSTERS

Bride of Frankenstein (1935)

'Warning! The Monster demands a Mate!'

USA, Universal, b/w, 75 mins

Directed by James Whale
Produced by Carl Laemmle Jr
Assistant Directors: Henry Mancke, Fred Frank, Joseph McDonough
Screenplay: William Hurlbut, suggested by the novel *Frankenstein, or, the Modern Prometheus* by Mary Wollstonecraft Shelley
Adaptation: William Hurlbut, John Balderston
Script Contribution: Tom Reed
Photography: John J Mescall
Music: Franz Waxman
Editor: Ted Kent
Art Director: Charles D Hall
Photography Effects: John P Fulton
Make-up: Jack Pierce, Otto Lederer

CAST: Boris Karloff (*the Monster*), Colin Clive (*Henry Frankenstein*), Valerie Hobson (*Elizabeth*), Ernest Thesiger (*Dr Pretori-*

ous), Elsa Lanchester (*Mary Wollstonecraft Shelley, the Bride* [uncredited]), Gavin Gordon (*Lord Byron*), Douglas Walton (*Percy Bysshe Shelley*), Una O'Connor (*Minnie*), EE Clive (*Burgomaster*), Lucien rival (*Albert, the Butler*), OP Heggie (*Hermit*), Dwight Frye (*Karl, the Hunchback*), Reginald Barlow (*Hans*), Mary Gordon (*Hans's Wife*), Ann Darling (*Shepherdess*), Ted Billings (*Ludwig*), Joan Woodbury (*Miniature Queen*), Arthur S Byron (*Miniature King*), Norman Ainsley (*Miniature Archbishop*), Peter Shaw (*Miniature Devil*), Kansas DeForrest (*Miniature Ballerina*), Josephine McKim (*Miniature Mermaid*), Robert A'Dair, Frank Terry (*Hunters*), Brenda Fowler (*Mother*), Helen Parrish (*Communion Girl*), Walter Brennan, Rollo Lloyd, Mary Stewart (*Neighbours*), Gunnis Davis (*Uncle Glutz*), Tempe Pigott (*Aunt Glutz*), John Carradine, Jack Curtis (*Hunters at Hermit's Hut*), Nell Fitzgerald (*Rudy, Second Graverobber*), Sarah Schwartz (*Marta*), Edward Peil Sr, Frank Benson, Anders Van Haden, John George (*Villagers*)

SYNOPSIS: Byron recaps the events of *Frankenstein* to the Shelleys, then complains that it ended too abruptly. Mary tells him it has not ended, and proceeds to tell the rest of the story.

The windmill set on fire at the end of *Frankenstein* has burned down. Hans, the father of Maria (killed in the first film), wants to see the corpse of the Monster for himself. He falls into the windmill's flooded cellar, where the Monster drowns him, then escapes. He throws Hans's wife into the cellar and scares the Frankensteins' housekeeper, who flees to the castle; nobody believes her story.

Henry Frankenstein, convalescing, debates the ethics of science with his wife Elizabeth. The housekeeper introduces Dr Pretorious, who asks Henry for help in continuing his experiments; he threatens to reveal him as the person responsible for the killings of the first film and tells him that some of his own experiments have been successful.

Henry accompanies Pretorious to his lab, where he is shown some homunculi. Pretorious has grown these himself, but wants Henry's help in grander experiments.

In the woods the Monster terrifies a shepherdess, who falls into a pool. He helps her out, but her screams attract the attention of hunters, who shoot him in the arm.

The burgomaster gathers a hunting party, who soon track the Monster down and put him in a dungeon. He escapes and hides in the house of a blind violinist, who teaches him to say a few words. Two hunters enter the hut and fight with the Monster, who takes refuge in a crypt.

There he meets Dr Pretorious, who has found a suitable corpse for his experiments. Pretorious tells him that he will make him a female friend. When Pretorious visits Frankenstein, Henry is adamant that he will not help him – Pretorious has grown a brain, but needs Frankenstein's help in creating a body – but when the Monster kidnaps Elizabeth he agrees to help.

Pretorious sends Karl, the hunchbacked assistant, to a hospital for a fresh heart; Karl simply kills the first young woman he sees for the specimen.

When the body is ready it is winched up to the roof, where kites are being flown to conduct the lightning of a storm. The Monster climbs to the roof and throws Pretorious's other assistant off the edge. Finally lightning strikes, and the body is lowered.

The Bride is alive. She stares at Henry, then sees the Monster and screams. The Monster advances on the Bride, as Frankenstein and Pretorious try to protect her. Elizabeth arrives, and Henry reluctantly joins her. She begs him to leave, and the Monster encourages him to go, before blowing the laboratory up, killing them all except Henry and Elizabeth.

ORIGINS AND INSPIRATION: Mad scientists have been a staple of the horror genre since its inception. Mary Shelley's Dr Frankenstein, Robert Louis Stevenson's Dr Jekyll and HG Wells's Dr Moreau represent an unholy triumvirate of men driven by the thirst for scientific knowledge unrestrained by ethical concerns. The theme of mad science – whether explored through unethical scientists, the accidental consequences of scientific development (the nuclear and eco-horrors of the 1950s) or bungled experiments (the fly in the teleporter in both versions of *The Fly*) – represents one of this characteristically radical genre's most popular and reactionary concerns. If elsewhere horror deals favourably with idiosyncratic beliefs and eccentricities, here it is profoundly conservative, mistrusting not only scientific endeavour but knowledge and intelligence themselves.

This conservatism is further reflected in a theme that, while less important in Shelley's novel, has been developed through the many film adaptations. Frankenstein is playing God, and is duly punished for daring to question Christian views of creation and the place of humanity. In a line cut from *Frankenstein* (James Whale, 1931), Colin Clive calls out, 'Now I know what it feels like to be God!' upon animating his creation, anticipating a theme very much at the forefront of Universal's *Moreau* adaptation *Island of Lost Souls* (Erle C Kenton, 1932).

That a mistrust of science should strike such a chord in the 1930s is unsurprising: the mechanised slaughter of the Great War had led many to question their belief in the inexorable progress of rationalism, and the Scopes monkey trial of 1925, in which a Tennessee schoolteacher was prosecuted for teaching evolution, had reminded the public of Darwin's dethroning of humanity as being uniquely made in God's image. Many films of the period feature scientists attempting to bridge the gap between ape and man, transplanting brains from one to the other.

And yet not all science is mistrusted: in what would become a staple of the mad scientist film, many versions of *Frankenstein* feature benevolent scientists to whom the doctor unsuccessfully pitches his ideas; and his work, essentially necromancy, or raising the dead, can be considered black magic rather than science, or a branch of science that, like alchemy, has long since fallen into disrepute.

Whale's *Frankenstein* was far from the first adaptation. The novel's huge success had led to numerous stage versions; one which Shelley herself went to see in 1824 introduced a new character to the story, Fritz, the deformed assistant, and further stage and screen adaptations continued to provide new details to accrete around the myth, allowing it to grow in patchwork fashion much like the Monster himself. In Whale's *Frankenstein* the Monster is given an 'abnormal' or 'criminal' brain (a development credited to co-screenwriter Francis Faragoh); while in Shelley's novel the Monster becomes monstrous through being rejected and reviled by humanity, here he is criminal, or evil, from the outset, providing a eugenic subtext that was more thoroughly explored in Hammer's *Frankenstein* cycle.

Such accretions often provided an ironic commentary on the original tale: Shelley's novel carried the subtitle 'The Modern Prometheus', but here the doctor's creation is afraid of fire; and the story of Burke and Hare, the infamous Edinburgh body-snatchers, became another reference point when Fritz started to kill people for fresh body parts.

One of the first film adaptations was produced by the Edison Manufacturing Company in 1910 (*Frankenstein*, J Searle Dawley), and the first full-length version of the story was released five years later, entitled *Life Without Soul* (Joseph W Smiley). Other films of scientists creating life were also early hits, including various versions of *Alraune*, a German story in which a mad doctor impregnates a prostitute using semen from a dead man; at least three versions of *The Golem*, the Jewish tale in which a rabbi creates a man from clay; and *The Magician* (Rex Ingram, 1926), an adaptation of Somerset Maugham's novel about Aleister Crowley, in which the titular character creates a number of homunculi. The 1920 *Golem* (Carl Boese, Paul Wegener)and *The Magician* were influences on Whale's films, with sequences from both reworked for the Universal series, and Karloff's performance as the Monster was allegedly inspired by Paul Wegener's perform-ance as the man of clay.

The first great cycle of horror films was heralded by Universal's 1930 adaptation of *Dracula* (Tod Browning). The company's fortunes had been flagging since the birth of the talkie, although they had already developed a reputation in the nascent horror genre with Lon Chaney vehicles like *The Hunchback of Notre Dame* (Wallace Worsley, 1923) and *The Phantom of the Opera* (Rupert Julian, 1925). Their punt in adapting Stoker's novel for the screen proved so successful that they turned to Shelley's creation, and went on to film *The Mummy* (Karl Freund, 1932), *The Invisible Man* (James Whale, 1933) – starring an invisible Claude Rains as the greatest mad doctor of them all – and *The Black Cat* (Edgar G Ulmer, 1934), before descending into a mire of second-rate sequels.

Originally Robert Florey was asked to direct a test reel for *Frankenstein*, featuring Bela Lugosi as the Monster under Jack Pierce's make-up, but producer Carl Laemmle Jr was unhappy with the result, and Florey was moved on to other projects. Lugosi didn't want the part anyway – there was no dialogue, after all – and nor did John Carradine, the studio's second choice.

James Whale, then riding high on the success of his first Universal film, *Waterloo Bridge* (1931), selected *Frankenstein* from a pick of the studio's properties: it wasn't something he was particularly interested in, but it was the best of a bad bunch, and at least it wasn't a war film like the others he'd been given. Working from a screenplay based on Peggy Webling's 1927 *Frankenstein* play, he picked Karloff, whose 'queer, penetrating personality' had impressed him in a gangster film, *Graft* (Christy

Cabanne, 1931), to test as the Monster. Whale wanted the film to share the look of the German Expressionist classics, and screened Robert Wiene's *The Cabinet of Dr Caligari* (1919) and Paul Leni's *The Cat and the Canary* (1927) for the art director.

When the film opened it caused a sensation. American newspapers refused to run ads for it, Kansas censors ordered 32 cuts and the British censor excised a hanging scene – but the fuss pulled in the punters, with the film earning over $1,000,000 during its initial release, twice the earnings of *Dracula*.

The publicity department made the most of the controversy, naming and defining a genre by dubbing the film 'a horror picture', and offering 'a friendly warning' advising the faint-hearted not to watch it. No cases of heart failure were recorded, but several fainting spells were latched onto by the hugely effective marketing campaign, which revolutionised film advertising: studios now realised that audiences could be scared into seeing a film.

After releasing several other horror films, Universal decided on a sequel, which they wanted Whale to direct. Unfortunately the original film ended not only with the Monster being killed but also with an epilogue featuring the Baron toasting his son's recovery after some time had passed. Universal recalled circulating prints and excised the scene, although the film's commercial run had by no means ended, and the epilogue was lost until 1957, when it was restored for the film's American TV release.

Whale rejected the first version of the script he saw, which may have been an early treatment featuring Henry and Elizabeth running away to join a circus and becoming puppeteers; his response was 'it stinks to high heaven . . . I never want to work on *Frankenstein* again'. Other early treatments for the sequel involved Frankenstein trying to sell a death ray to the League of Nations, and Elizabeth being killed and her brain put into the body of the Bride; all were eventually rejected, and Hurlbut's screenplay started again from scratch.

The studio toyed with the idea of using a young German director, Kurt Neumann, but Whale eventually accepted the project, possibly because other pet projects had been turned down by the studio, and proceeded to subvert everyone's expectations. He insisted on a framing device introducing the film, presenting it clearly as a fantasy narrated directly by the author; it was also to be set in a kind of mythic neverland, out of time and space. This allowed him to get away with far more than he could have if he'd had to stick to the stark realism of the first film: as long as he could make the sequel work as a horror film, he could make sure that elements of sly fantasy were there to be appreciated by sophisticated viewers.

DIRECTOR: James Whale left his native England for Hollywood in 1928, to work on a movie of his successful stage production of *Journey's End*. He went on to direct four horror films for Universal: *Frankenstein* (1931), *The Old Dark House* (1932), adapted from JB Priestley's *Benighted*, *The Invisible Man* (1933)– 'We've got a terrible responsibility: he's mad and he's invisible' – from HG Wells's novel, and *Bride*. He made seventeen other films, but it is for his horror classics that he will be forever remembered.

He arrived in Hollywood feted as a cultured English gentleman of the theatre, and the theatrical and eccentric gesture soon became a hallmark of his films, with Henry Frankenstein staging the animation of the Monster in *Frankenstein* as a demented theatrical *mise en scène*, and his old friend Ernest Thesiger employing an enjoyably overblown style in both *The Old Dark House* and *Bride*.

Following the success of *Frankenstein*, Whale was lauded as Universal's 'Master of Horror'; he may well have aspired to higher things, but used his power as a director to enjoy a near-total creative autonomy over his subsequent horror films, hiring respected writers to rework his scripts and filling the films with an excellent British backing cast.

As well as his superb eye for casting – he picked both Karloff and Clive from relative obscurity – Whale's films are notable for their innovative use of tilted camera angles and their quicksilver changes of mood. The tone in *Bride* moves from grotesque humour through terror to pastoral idyll without stumbling once, and his other genre films, bar *Frankenstein*, are similarly sophisticated mixtures of horror and comedy.

They're also full of small domestic details that root his characters in the audience's sympathy, as well as providing an air of credibility to otherwise outlandish tales. Dr Pretorious asks the Monster, 'Do you like gin? It's my only weakness', an in-joke reference to Thesiger's character in *The Old Dark House*; and central to *The Invisible Man* are the mundane difficulties of invisibility, whether wearing clothes, eating or becoming dirty.

But the mundane was mixed with the mythic – all of Whale's horror films, and particularly the *Frankenstein* films, are studded through with iconic moments. That Whale was conscious of his role as mythmaker is clear: during the filming of *Frankenstein*, members of his team wanted a certain scene to end differently. He told them that it could not: 'It has to be like that: you see, it's all part of the ritual.'

CAST: Boris Karloff, born William Henry Pratt, took his stage name from a family name on his mother's side. Originally from London, he developed a reputation as a stage villain in an American touring theatre company before trying to break into the movies. After a number of bit parts he landed the role of killer Ned Galloway in Howard Hawks's *The Criminal Code* (1930), and was then spotted by Whale in *Graft* (1931).

Karloff's name only appears in the end credits of *Frankenstein*, and he was considered so dispensable that he was not even invited to the premiere. But after seeing the audience reaction to the Monster, Universal put Karloff under contract, prompting him to tell his agent, 'After more than twenty years of acting, for once I know where my next breakfast is coming from!' He was 44 years old.

While he disapproved of the term 'horror', and bemoaned directors' increasing reliance on ramped-up levels of sex and violence, Karloff worked steadily in genre films until his death in 1969, starring in films ranging from Columbia's 'Mad Doctor' series of the 1930s to Val Lewton's atmospheric and understated 40s horror classics and Roger Corman's 60s Poe adaptations. At the end of his career he even starred in such minor classics as Peter Bogdanovich's *Targets* (1968) and Michael Reeves's *The Sorcerers* (1967). He played Frankenstein's Monster, possibly his most famous role, once more in *Son of Frankenstein* (Rowland V Lee, 1939), and also appeared as Dr Frankenstein in *Frankenstein 1970* (Howard W Koch, 1958).

Dwight Frye's most famous role is probably the fly- and scenery-chewing Renfield in Tod Browning's *Dracula*, although he appeared in many other ghoulish films throughout the 30s, including *The Vampire Bat* (Frank R Strayer, 1933) and *The Invisible Man*. His role as Karl in *Bride* – in which two of his major scenes were cut before release – is a virtual reprise of Fritz, his character from the first film, who is killed by the Monster, and the actor came to resent playing only 'idiots, half-wits and lunatics'. Soon he wouldn't even get these roles: his performance in *Son of Frankenstein* was removed, and he was reduced to bit parts as villagers in *The Ghost of Frankenstein* (Erle C Kenton, 1942) and *Frankenstein Meets the Wolf Man* (Roy William Neill, 1943). By the time of his death his acting career had reached such a low point that his profession was listed as 'tool designer'.

The scene-stealing Ernest Thesiger played against Karloff in *The Old Dark House* and *The Mummy* (James Whale, 1932), as well as appearing in over fifty other films in the UK and US. According to Elsa Lanchester he was 'a weird, strange character! Very acid-tongued – not a nasty person at all, just *acid*!' Claude Rains had originally been slated by the studio to play Pretorious, but prior commitments prevented him from taking the part; Whale had wanted Thesiger in the role anyway, to maximise the script's comic potential.

Colin Clive had been picked by Whale from a chorus line for the lead in his theatrical production of *Journey's End*, and when the opportunity arose to film the production (1930), Whale insisted Clive retain the part. He went on to appear alongside Elsa Lanchester in *The Stronger Sex* (William Watson, 1930) before being again selected by Whale for the part of Dr Frankenstein. Clive turned down the offer of a part in *The Invisible Man*, but was reunited with the director in Universal's *One More River* (1934). His final genre role was playing Stephen Orlac in Karl Freund's delirious *Mad Love* (1935), opposite Peter Lorre's magisterially demented Dr Gogol.

PRODUCTION: Filmed under the titles *The Return of Franken-stein* and *Frankenstein Lives Again!*, the sequel took 46 working days to shoot and cost just under $400,000, $100,000 over budget. *Bride* reunited some members of the original cast – the twitchily neurotic Clive, Karloff and Frye – while replacing Mae Clarke with Valerie Hobson as Henry's wife, discarding the weakest characters of the original film, the Baron and Henry's friend Victor, and bringing in Ernest Thesiger and Una O'Connor for their camp humour value.

Another newcomer was Elsa Lanchester, who Whale had seen nine years before on the stage; he had also worked with her husband Charles Laughton on *The Old Dark House* (1932), and she seems to have been his first choice for the Monster's mate. All of the main characters were to be played by British actors, a feature exploited by the publicity department's endless photographs of the cast drinking tea.

More use was made of Kenneth Strickfaden's lab equipment, comprising Tesla coils, Van der Graaf generators and unique items dubbed by Strickfaden a 'bariton generator', a 'nucleus analyser' and a 'vacuum electrolyser': the look became the classic mad scientist lab arrangement, and was re-created in its entirety for Mel Brooks' spoof *Young Frankenstein* (1974).

Jack Pierce's make-up for the Monster had taken three hours every evening for three weeks to perfect before the shooting of *Frankenstein*; for both films, it took three and a half hours every morning to put on and two hours every evening to take off. To create the look, Pierce had done extensive research into anatomy, surgery and ancient and modern burial customs, as well as taking Whale's own sketches as an inspiration. The make-up was slightly different from the first film, at the end of which the Monster had been burned; some of his hair was missing, revealing the metal staples holding his skull together.

Karloff's arms were made to look longer by shortening his sleeves, and his legs were stiffened with steel struts; the actor himself suggested adding mortician's wax to his eyelids, something he later regretted as 'painful'. Elsa Lanchester also suffered under her make-up, which was designed by Whale.

Whale's interpretation of the script met with some resistance, both from Karloff, who felt that allowing the Monster to laugh, eat, drink, smoke and speak was a mistake, and from Universal, who similarly disapproved of Whale's efforts to humanise the Monster; for the next sequel, *Son of Frankenstein* (1939), the Monster was mute again. The script also had to be passed by the Production Code Administration, who censoriously objected to the number of murders and some of the religious imagery in the film, although Whale's irreverent equation of the Monster with Christ – he is tied to a mock cross when captured by villagers, and a cross lights up in the background when the Monster sheds a tear – seems to have passed them by. Before the film was released they insisted on trims of a scene of Elsa Lanchester in a low-cut gown, a shot of the Monster laughing as Hans drowns and another of a mother carrying her child's dead body.

Another fifteen minutes were cut from the film after it was test screened: deleted sequences included references to the scandalous behaviour of the three writers in the prologue; a speech from Pretorious attacking Frankenstein for his bungled attempts to create life; and a long sequence in which the Monster beats up the burgomaster, prompting the village idiot to murder his uncle, steal his savings and blame the killing on the Monster; this was replaced by the scene in which the Monster attacks a gypsy family, the only scene not accompanied by Waxman's score.

The ending originally had Henry and Elizabeth perishing in the castle's explosion; this was replaced by a happy ending in which they survive, although keen-eyed viewers can still spot Henry being crushed by debris in the lab.

SOUNDTRACK: In contrast to the almost music-free *Frankenstein*, there is barely an unscored moment in *Bride*. The influential soundtrack, which features leitmotifs for all the central characters and is scored for a symphony orchestra, was written by Franz Waxman, who had left Germany in 1934 to escape Nazi persecution. *Bride* was his first major US score, and was so successful that it secured him a contract as Head of the Music Department at Universal Studios; he went on to score major hits like *Rebecca* (Alfred Hitchcock, 1940), *Sunset Boulevard* (Billy Wilder, 1950) and *Rear Window* (Alfred Hitchcock, 1954).

The success of *Bride* owes a good deal to Waxman's score, which underlines the film's shifting moods with a musical accompaniment ranging from cheesy organ music when the Monster sheds a tear to the demented bells of the Bride's animation. The film received an Academy Award Nomination for Best Sound Recording, and parts of the score were reused for Universal's *Buck Rogers* and *Flash Gordon* serials, as well as for B features including *Tower of London* (Rowland V Lee, 1939), in which *Bride*'s 'Monster motif' is used as the signature music for Karloff's entrances.

This highlights a feature of horror actors that was consciously encouraged by studio star systems: the accretion of roles around their screen personae, so that the audience would bring knowledge of their former characters to each new film. Karloff thus became 'Karloff the Uncanny' on promotional posters, his entrance heralded by the theme for his most famous character, the Monster; and Dwight Frye was able to virtually reprise his role as laboratory assistant here, despite having been killed in *Frankenstein*.

While this applies to all films – few viewers will watch a new Clint Eastwood film without a recognition that he brings the history of *Dirty Harry* (Don Siegel, 1971) and the Man with No Name with him – it is rare to find horror's fluid approach to casting elsewhere. Thus Karloff could play not only Frankenstein's Monster but Frankenstein himself, shifting smoothly from mad scientist's creation to mad scientist; Peter Cushing could play a villainous Frankenstein and a heroic Van Helsing without seeming cast against type; and Christopher Lee could shift from villain to hero with similar ease.

RELEASE: *Bride* didn't quite re-create the massive box-office success of the first film, although it has come to be regarded as its superior. Whale's films forever conflated the names of Frankenstein and his Monster in the public imagination; the title of *Bride of Frankenstein* is confusing, although its taglines are rather clearer. The confusion continued throughout the many subsequent film adaptations, although in some the doctor himself is at least as monstrous as his creation: by the time of Hammer's *Frankenstein Must be Destroyed* (Terence Fisher, 1969), the public is in no doubt that it is the doctor himself who deserves such a fate.

The film ran into trouble with censors, rejected altogether by Trinidad, Palestine and Hungary while Sweden and Japan made swingeing cuts; but reviews, in the US at least, were generally positive. *Variety* noted Karloff's 'subtleties of emotion that are surprisingly real and touching' and the 'excellent camerawork coupled with an eerie but lingering musical score', while the *New York Times* called it a 'first-rate horror film', and added that 'Karloff's makeup should not be permitted to pass from the screen. The Monster should become an institution, like Charlie Chan.'

But Graham Greene, writing in *The Spectator*, was less impressed: 'the breeding of monsters can become no more exciting than the breeding of poultry ... This is a pompous, badly acted film, full of absurd anachronisms and inconsistencies.'

CRITICAL EYE: While contemporary reviewers tended to focus on the tour-de-force animation sequence or the Bride's electrified hairdo, modern critics have been more concerned with the film's play on themes of sexual deviance. Necrophilia, for instance, is suggested by Pretorious wining and dining the corpses of the crypt, as well as by his insistence that the Monster and his mate should procreate and bring forth a new race. There is also the suggestion that the Bride has been created as a sexual playmate for Frankenstein himself: she is, after all, the Bride of Franken-stein, and it is to the doctor she turns upon her animation. The suggestion is one made more explicit in later adaptations of the story, whether in the creation of *The Rocky Horror Picture Show*'s (Jim Sharman, 1975) sex toy Rocky or *Flesh for Franken-stein*'s (Paul Morrissey, 1973) oversexed Monster – as Franken-stein puts it there, 'To know life, you must first fuck death in the gall bladder!'

More important than necrophilia is the theme of homosexuality in the film, which is widely regarded as a camp classic. The novel can be read as dealing with this theme too, with the creation's monstrousness a projection of Frankenstein's own guilt and self-loathing at his deviant sexuality, or a feminist writer's fear that women were being written out of the biological equation by male science; but it is far more marked in *Bride*. There have even been suggestions that Whale only agreed to film a sequel when he realised how subversive he could make it, encouraging a largely unwitting mainstream audience to endorse a deviant sexual outlook in the clearest way possible – by buying tickets to see the film.

Firstly there is the issue of cast and crew: aside from Whale himself, whose homosexuality was explored in the biopic *Gods and Monsters* (Bill Condon, 1998), Colin Clive's career was blighted by rumours of bisexuality; Whale's favourite camp interpreter, Ernest Thesiger, was a married gay man; and Elsa Lanchester was married to Charles Laughton, another gay man.

The prologue features two men who are heavily made up and act in an outlandishly effeminate manner – one is Lord Byron, famously bisexual – and from this point on, the Bride aside, women are sidelined throughout the film. The comic-relief maid Minnie shrieks and fusses like a caricatured drag queen, and domestic harmony between Frankenstein and his wife Elizabeth is blocked repeatedly through the film.

Early on Elizabeth tries to quell Henry's fiery Romantic rhetoric with lines like 'Don't say those things – don't *think* those things – it's blasphemous and wicked', then screams at the spectre of death she claims to see approaching; the sequence portrays her as both blandly conservative and hysterical, shrieking at imagined fears while her husband dispassionately soldiers on, elbow-deep in grue. Even the animation of the Bride contains a sly touch: in the first film the final addition to the male Monster is the brain, while here the Bride is finished with a heart.

Frankenstein repeatedly ignores Elizabeth's requests, and replaces her in the marital bedchamber with Pretorious, who is introduced by the maid as a 'very queer-looking old gentleman'; the two then discuss the business of creating life without feminine input or interference. Pretorious tells Henry with an arched eyebrow that 'I grow my creatures . . . as nature does, from seed', possibly a reference to masturbation, and is scathing on the subject of heterosexual love: he even points to his king and queen homunculi and says 'Royal amours are such a nuisance.'

The only successful relationship in the film involves two male outsiders, the Monster and the blind violinist. In a parody of the nuclear family, intimacy and affection here are available only to cripples and monsters – as society would have viewed homosexuals – while their intelligence and sensitivity goes ignored and unseen.

In the light of what has gone before, the happy ending with Henry in Elizabeth's arms seems forced and unnatural; but before the married couple are finally united, the viewer is treated to a grotesque parody of marriage in which the Bride, in her wedding dress of tattered bandages, is given away by father substitute Pretorious to the lurching groom, Franz Waxman's wedding bells providing a suitably over-the-top accompaniment.

Yet the film is far from didactic, and works as a particularly sophisticated horror comedy whatever the viewer thinks of the subtext. While *Frankenstein* contained several iconic images – the first view of the Monster, and the sequence of him playing with a little girl by the lake, for instance – it seems humourless and flat compared to its sequel, and is marred by two weak characters (the Baron and Victor), a lack of musical accompaniment and a predominantly static camera. The sequel, by contrast, has a ghoulish sense of humour, a fantastically baroque look and a more fluid and experimental use of camera; it also provides the template for every mad scientist scene to follow, especially in the animation sequence, a dazzling set-piece full of sparking coils, crazed angles and forced perspectives.

If the story itself is essentially conservative – there are some things man is not meant to know – Whale creates a tension by introducing subversive elements and anti-establishment jibes, giving Dr Pretorious all the best lines ('Sometimes I wonder if life wouldn't be much more amusing if we were all devils, and no nonsense about angels, and being good') and allowing us to exult with Frankenstein, rather than simply damn him, as he succeeds in creating a mate for the Monster.

INDUSTRY IMPACT: While *Bride* was Whale's last horror film, and Karloff only appeared in one more film as the Monster, *Son of Frankenstein*, Universal were not about to allow this hot property to cool down. When they found Lon Chaney Jr to replace Karloff as the Monster, they tried to maximise their returns by producing films featuring as many monsters as possible, with *Frankenstein Meets the Wolf Man* (1943), *House of Frankenstein* (Erle C Kenton, 1944) and *House of Dracula* (Erle C Kenton, 1945); and any dignity left to the studio's monsters was annihilated when they were introduced to Abbott and Costello in a series of unfunny parodies.

The Monster fared little better even after Universal had finished with him, appearing only in teen schlock like *I was a Teenage Frankenstein* (Herbert L Strock, 1957) – 'Body of a Boy! Mind of a Monster! Soul of an Unearthly Thing!' – until Hammer kicked off a new horror cycle with 1957's *The Curse of Frankenstein* (Terence Fisher). The Hammer films added new levels of viciousness, gore and sex to the formula, with the Baron, played by Peter Cushing as a cold, scheming man who embraces death over sex, becoming the real villain.

Apart from the Hammer cycle, the Monster appeared only in nudie comedies, Mexican wrestling films and the TV series *The Munsters* through the 1960s; most 1970s interpretations, such as Jess Franco's incomprehensible Frankenstein films, just ladled on more sex and violence, although Paul Morrissey's *Flesh for Frankenstein* and Mel Brooks' *Young Frankenstein* (1974) were amusingly insightful takes on the Hammer and Universal films, respectively.

The special-effects explosion and boom in home video led to some exceptionally gruesome adaptations of the legend in the 1980s, with *Re-Animator* (Stuart Gordon, 1985) (see **ORIGINS AND INSPIRATION, Evil Dead 2**) leading the field. Its sequel, *Bride of Re-Animator* (Brian Yuzna, 1989), was less inspired, and a straight remake of Whale's sequel, *The Bride* (Franc Roddam, 1985), failed on every count.

The 1990s, as well as giving us Frank Henenlotter's lurid *Frankenhooker* (1990), also gave us the first major studio outing for the Monster since Universal ran out of mortician's wax. *Mary Shelley's Frankenstein* (Kenneth Branagh, 1994) was probably the most faithful cinema adaptation of Shelley's novel to date, which is also where it falls down: the novel is symbolically overloaded, with its various themes proving too much for one film to deal with. Yet the Monster's symbolic flexibility is also his strength, and ensures that he has not yet hung up his boots altogether. Given contemporary concerns about cloning and organ theft, it is only a matter of time before the doctor unleashes another Monster upon the world.

FINAL WORD: It is Whale's films, rather than Mary Shelley's novel, which now provide the definitive account of this modern myth. The symbol of Frankenstein's Monster is enormously flexible, incorporating everything from the themes of abandonment and rejection to the act of artistic creation: Whale's films fix this meandering symbol by paring down Shelley's novel to a simpler exploration of the ethics of science.

But while Whale's *Frankenstein* is static and grim, lumbered with inappropriate comic relief, *Bride of Frankenstein* is one of the few horror sequels to actually improve on the original, shot through with a deliciously irreverent humour that resonates perfectly with the film's mythic glow. Without Whale, Universal's monsters would have been little more than a gallery of shambling grotesques, and *Bride*'s sophistication was decades ahead of its time; few other films from any era have reached such a delirious pitch of self-parody while retaining a powerful poetic charm.

KILLER Bs AND 50s PARANOIA

Invasion of the Body Snatchers (1956)

'... there was nothing to hold onto – except each other'

USA, Allied Artists, b/w, 80 mins

Directed by Don Siegel
Produced by Walter Wanger
Screenplay by Daniel Mainwaring from the *Collier's* serial by
Jack Finney, *The Body Snatchers*
Director of Photography: Ellsworth Fredericks
Art Director: Edward 'Ted' Haworth
Assistant Directors: Richard Maybery, Bill Beaudine, Jr
Editor: Robert S Eisen
Music: Carmen Dragon
Special Effects: Milt Rice

CAST: Kevin McCarthy (*Dr Miles Bennell*), Dana Wynter (*Becky Driscoll*), King Donovan (*Jack Belicec*), Caroline Jones (*Teddy Belicec*), Larry Gates (*Dr Danny Kaufman*), Everett Glass (*Dr Ed Pursey*), Jean Willes (*Sally*), Virginia Christine (*Wilma*), Ralph Dumke (*Nick Grivett, the Police Officer*), Whitt Bissell (*Dr Hill*), Richard Deacon (*Dr Harvey Bassett*), Tom Fadden (*Uncle Ira*), Kenneth Patterson (*Mr Driscoll, Becky's Father*), Guy Way (*Sam*

Janzek, the Police Officer), Guy Rennie (*Proprietor of the Sky Terrace Night Club*), Beatrice Maude (*Grandma Grimaldi*), Bobby Clark (*Jimmy Grimaldi*), Sam Peckinpah (*Charlie Buckholtz, the Gas Meter Reader*), Dabbs Greer (*Mac, the Gas Station Attendant*), Marie Selland (*Martha, his Wife*), Jean Andren (*Aunt Aleda*), Eileen Stevens (*Mrs Grimaldi*), Pat O'Malley (*Baggage Handler*)

SYNOPSIS: Psychiatrist Dr Hill is called to hospital to interview a man the police think is insane. The man, Miles Bennell, tells Hill the following story.

Miles, a doctor, returns to Santa Mira after a trip. Sally, his secretary, tells him that many people have abruptly cancelled appointments they'd booked in his absence. Miles is visited by Becky, an old flame. He visits her cousin Wilma, who thinks her uncle has been replaced by an impostor. Another patient, Jimmy, thinks his mother has been replaced as well.

Miles and Becky run into Kaufman, a psychiatrist, who describes the beliefs as mass hysteria. They then visit Miles's writer friend Jack Belicec, who shows them a body he's found with a 'vague' face and no fingerprints. Jack drops a glass and cuts himself.

Miles takes Becky home, and meets a panicked Jack and Teddy Belicec at his house. Teddy saw a cut on the body's hand. Miles calls Kaufman, then goes to Becky's house and breaks into the cellar, suspicious that something is wrong; in a chest he discovers Becky's double.

He carries Becky out of the house. Back at Miles's, Kaufman is sceptical. They go to the Belicecs', where they find the body gone; Becky's double has also vanished. Becky's father calls a policeman, who tells them that the body they'd found at the Belicecs' had turned up in a burning haystack.

Jack and Teddy stay with Miles, and they have a barbecue. But they find giant seed pods in the greenhouse, with their doubles spilling out. They realise that the pods replace people in their sleep, and that the police cannot be trusted. Miles calls the FBI, but cannot get through. Jack and Teddy leave, as Miles pitchforks his own double.

Miles and Becky head for Sally's house, but find the pod people there. They hide in Miles's office, taking pills to stay awake. Next morning they see trucks spreading pods around the state. They open the door to Jack, but he has turned into a pod person; Kaufman is with him, and argues the case for being a pod.

Miles tranquillises their captors and he and Becky escape, but when Becky screams they are chased into the hills by a mob. They hide in a mineshaft, and later hear music; Miles investigates, only to find it's the radio from a truck full of pods.

When he returns to the cave Becky has changed. When she fails to persuade him to join them, she calls out to the others. He runs to the highway, but no cars will stop for him; a lorry he climbs onto is full of pods.

Back at the hospital, Dr Hill hears about an accident involving a truck loaded with giant seed pods. He believes Miles, and calls the FBI.

ORIGINS AND INSPIRATION: Much as anxieties about the Bomb informed the creature features filling 50s drive-ins, Cold War anxieties lay at the root of a host of films about alien invaders intent on brainwashing the US public. Christian Nyby's *The Thing from Another World* (1951), in which an emotionless vegetable alien – 'An intellectual carrot – the mind boggles!' – drained humans of their blood, inaugurated the horror/SF cross-over that was to dominate US genre product throughout the 1950s, and anticipated the evolutionary fears that would underlie everything from *Invasion* and *The Quatermass Xperiment* (Val Guest, 1955) to *Day of the Triffids* (Steve Sekely, 1963) and **Alien**.

The Thing's shifty scientist, Carrington, helps to keep the 'super-carrot' alive, hiding it from the military men who want to destroy it; according to him 'There are no enemies in science . . . only phenomena to study', and he is awed by the creature's evolutionary perfection: 'No pain or pleasure as we know it. No emotions. No heart. Our superior . . . in every way', although the compliment clearly isn't returned.

Other alien invaders also foreshadowed Siegel's film: Robert Heinlein's 1951 story *The Puppet Masters*, itself filmed by Stuart Orme in 1994, described giant alien slugs attaching themselves to US citizens and zombifying them; and Philip K Dick's story *The Father-Thing* (1954) introduced a theme the author would return to repeatedly throughout his career – how can humans be distinguished from impostors? William Cameron Menzies' *Invaders from Mars* (1953) explored the idea too, showing a boy's family looking normal but acting suspiciously, their minds centrally controlled by a malign alien force.

But there was something about Jack Finney's serial *The Body Snatchers* that struck a chord with independent film producer Walter Wanger; he read the first instalment in *Collier's* magazine in late 1954 and was so impressed that he began negotiations for the film rights before even reading the rest. Wanger's enthusiasm was shared by Don Siegel, who'd directed *Riot in Cell Block 11* (1954) for the producer and Allied Artists, and Siegel in turn showed the serial to Daniel Mainwaring, an old friend who'd scripted *The Big Steal* for him to direct in 1949. Wanger, Siegel and Mainwaring visited Jack Finney to discuss the screenplay, and Mainwaring's first draft was finished by the time Finney's revised and expanded version of the story was published as a novel.

Mainwaring stuck fairly close to Finney's tale, although he left out some explanatory material concerning the pods' origins, and made the key change that Becky eventually turns into a pod. In the original story, Miles and Becky fight together throughout, and it is only with Becky's help that he is able to score even small victories against the pods. The screenplay also finishes with Miles trying to stop passing motorists on the highway, while Finney's tale has our hero rescued by the FBI – an ending the studio finally reinstated.

DIRECTOR: Don Siegel's films, principally B pictures shot within the studio system, are notable for their fast pace, documentary realism and taut direction; recurring themes are a celebration of the individual and an exploration of the conflict between control and instinct. The director is probably most famous for his work with Clint Eastwood, notably *The Beguiled* and *Dirty Harry* (both 1971), although the latter suggested to some that Siegel had succumbed to the lone wolf vigilantism implicit in the individualist genre.

Siegel described *Invasion* as 'my favorite film, which doesn't mean that it's my best work but that it's the most interesting subject I've ever filmed'. His personal stake in the film may have come partly from his insomnia, which informs its theme of sleep deprivation: 'when people suffer from chronic insomnia . . . they are afraid to go to sleep. One reason for this is that they fear they won't wake up.'

The director used the term 'pods' liberally after shooting the film, which he felt 'exposed what a large group of people are doing to us culturally. They are pods. They have no soul and I'm sorry to say most people are that way. I think the pods outnumber us, if indeed we ourselves are not pods.' But he recognised that pods had their good side too:

> Well, I think there's a very strong case for being a pod. These pods, who get rid of pain, ill health, and mental disturbance are, in a sense, doing good. It happens to leave you with a very dull world, but that . . . is the world that most of us live in.

Siegel didn't make any other horror or SF movies after *Invasion*: he was put off by the genres' reliance on special effects, as he preferred to focus on character and plot. In light of this, it's worth noting that the weakest parts of *Invasion* are those that show the pods being handled or opening. Siegel did one other favour for the horror film, though – he gave English director Michael Reeves (*The Sorcerers* (1967), *Witchfinder General* (1968)) his first break in the industry as a runner, after the seventeen-year-old Reeves travelled to Hollywood to profess admiration for Siegel's work.

CASTING: Wanger considered a range of well-known actors for the lead roles: for Miles he thought of casting Joseph Cotten or Dick Powell, while for Becky Anne Bancroft and Vera Miles were in the running. At this stage, the film was budgeted at over $450,000, but when the studio cut the budget to just $350,000 Wanger was forced to rely on a relatively unknown cast. Kevin McCarthy had starred in Siegel's *Annapolis Story* (1955); Dana Wynter had appeared on TV but never before in a film.

McCarthy's other genre roles include parts in Joe Dante's *Piranha* (1978), *The Howling* (1981), *Matinee* (1993) and *Looney Tunes: Back in Action* (2003), a cameo in which he is still screaming 'You're next!' in the 1978 remake of *Invasion*, *Twilight Zone: The Movie* (Joe Dante and John Landis, 1983), *Addams Family Reunion* (Dave Payne, 1998) and, less auspiciously, *Ghoulies 3: Ghoulies Go to College* (John Carl Buechler, 1991).

PRODUCTION: Shooting took place over 23 days in late March and early April 1955, and cost around $382,000. Cast and crew were impressed by the idea of the pods as a metaphor for conformist, passionless society, and Siegel took to playing tricks on them:

> One night, I broke into Dana Wynter's house and slipped a pod under her bed. By this time, the pods had become a scary, realistic, believable possibility to cast and crew. The next morning, when Dana found the pod, she was in a state of near hysteria.

Director Sam Peckinpah did uncredited work on the film as Siegel's assistant, and also appeared in a cameo role as the gasman; Peckinpah's other contributions to the genre include upping the stakes for mainstream cinema violence with *The Wild Bunch* (1969) and directing *Straw Dogs* (1971), a powerful rape-revenge movie that anticipates Wes Craven's favourite theme – the apparently civilised driven to savage violence – and sleazy shockers like *I Spit on Your Grave* (1978).

While Siegel and Mainwaring were happy with what they'd shot, the studio, 'bursting with pods' according to Siegel, was not, and most of the humour was cut from the film. Siegel fought to have these scenes restored, feeling that 'the idea of pods growing into a likeness of a person would strike the characters as preposterous. I wanted to play it that way, with the characters not taking the threat seriously.' But according to the studio, horror and humour didn't mix.

Wanger was worried that the film wouldn't reach the audience it deserved, and tried unsuccessfully to have Orson Welles, in a nod to Welles's famous 1938 *War of the Worlds* radio broadcast, or Ray Bradbury introduce it. He also wanted to have a Churchill quotation inserted at the beginning of the film, but his suggestions were rejected by the studio. After a preview screening that Wanger thought went particularly badly, he tried to recall the film for further amendments, at which point the studio insisted that a framing device was shot. They wanted an introduction, and a happy ending in which the FBI were called in, as well as a voiceover from Kevin McCarthy explaining events as they happened.

Although Siegel was opposed to the framing device, because it showed the audience right away that something unusual was going on, he and Mainwaring agreed to script and shoot the required scenes, presumably worried that if it was taken further from their hands the film would be butchered even more badly.

There were also wrangles over the title of the film. They wanted to avoid confusion with Robert Wise's 1945 film *The Body Snatcher*, and the studio suggested *They Came from Another World*. Siegel protested against the title, suggesting *Better off Dead*, which recalled the Cold War slogan 'Better dead than red'; McCarthy favoured the Shakespearean *Sleep No More*, and Wanger came up with *World in Danger*. The studio, unimpressed by these, settled on the release title, which Siegel considered an 'absurd' suggestion that 'cheapened the content of the story'. The film was finally released in late February 1956, some ten months after shooting was finished.

SOUNDTRACK: The pounding score by Carmen Dragon is not one of the film's best features; Siegel, among others, found it inappropriate.

'IT'S ONLY A MOVIE ... ONLY A MOVIE ...': Wanger wanted the studio to promote the film using badges with slogans like 'I don't want to be a pod', 'I'm not a pod' and 'Are you a pod?' It didn't happen.

RELEASE: *Invasion* opened in the US on a double bill with *The Atomic Man* (Ken Hughes, 1956), a slow British SF effort. It was sold as a trashy exploitation picture, despite Wanger's efforts to have it marketed as a serious film, and deemed too disreputable for a *New York Times* review. But the papers that did review it had generally positive things to say: the *LA Examiner* called it an 'almost terrifying science-fiction yarn', warning readers to 'Watch out there! You too may become a potted plant.' *Weekly Variety* noted that despite the film being 'occasionally difficult to follow due to the strangeness of its scientific premise', this 'tense, offbeat piece of science fiction ... looks headed for stout box-office returns'.

The *Hollywood Reporter* felt that the film 'seems to be saying that modern man, tired of facing the mental problems of our intricate age, is prone to welcome the irresponsible life of a human vegetable. This is a sobering and shocking thought'; while the London *Daily Film Reviewer* described the film as a 'brilliant and unusual science shocker for the countless thousands who enjoy being chilled to the marrow'.

Despite a desultory marketing campaign, the film was popular with moviegoers and did reasonably well, although it was hardly a runaway success. According to Siegel, it was often shown in Europe and on the US underground circuit with the prologue and epilogue edited out, as the 'Siegel version'.

CRITICAL EYE: *Invasion* has been interpreted as both a damning indictment of McCarthyite witchhunts and a piece of hysterical anti-Communist propaganda, and there's evidence to support both readings.

Miles refers to the pods as a 'malignant disease', recalling Adlai Stevenson's campaign speech of 1952, in which Communism was described as 'a disease which may have killed more people in this world than cancer, tuberculosis, and heart disease combined'; and the focus on staying awake recalls the Cold War's imagery of wakefulness versus sleep.

Conversely, Mainwaring came from a leftist background, and his scripts were consistently concerned with social justice, making him more likely to have been anti-McCarthy than anti-Communist; and Siegel's individualist ethos, while occasionally veering into right-wing radicalism, seems similarly opposed to whistle-blowing suspicion.

But these political readings derive as much from the film's Cold War context as anything in the film itself; more important (and common to both interpretations) is an understanding of the film's fear of conformity and the resulting loss of self. While the US enjoyed new heights of prosperity in the 1950s, many social commentators showed a growing concern with the depersonalisation that accompanied it. Society was regulated and controlled as never before; work and leisure were managed for maximum efficiency, with dissenters medicated back into line. Processes of consumption as well as production were rationalised and controlled, with advertising techniques ensuring that people made the sanctioned choices. Books like David Riesman's *The Lonely Crowd* and William Wyte's *The Organization Man* rang a warning bell – the bureaucratic, government-dominated and conformist America of the 1950s was growing too close to its totalitarian mirror image of Red Russia.

The characters in *Invasion* do not trust their own feelings, but rely instead on experts – doctors, or psychiatrists – to explain anomalous events to them. Miles is a doctor too, but is asked by Jack to 'forget you're a doctor'; Jack is a writer, and thus inhabits the realm of the imagination that provides the final refuge from thought control. Indeed all three of the people seen being initially suspicious of the pod people – a child, a woman and a writer – traditionally represent the irrational and intuitive.

Dr Kaufman, the psychiatrist, by contrast rationalises the fears of Miles and Jack – they have been seeing things, and should not trust their senses; he has tranquillisers to calm them down. Psychiatry is here equated with brainwashing, a popular fear of the time after stories about the mistreatment of American prisoners in Korea. Kaufman is also, tellingly, the spokesman for the pod people, and makes a strong case for their superiority, perhaps playing on a fear that conformity – even Communism – might be an evolutionarily higher social condition.

After all, the characters conform even without the interference of the pods – as Miles points out, 'In my practice I see how people have allowed their humanity to drain away', and the response of Miles, Jack, Teddy and Becky to the threat posed by the pods is to have a barbecue, each of them slotting smoothly into their predefined gender role. This is not necessarily a bad thing – conformity has its appeal in providing a structure to disguise the painful uncertainties of social existence – and this is exactly why the pods appeal. A threat – in the 1950s nuclear Armageddon, or Communist invasion – inspires a desire for security, an urge to group together; but this longing to merge is a profound threat to the self.

Yet the film strikes a deeper chord, one that can't be explained away in simple social or political terms. The fears it represents are closer to our hearts – the fear of identity loss, of sleep and death, fears that our friends may not be the people we believe them to be and fear of ourselves. *Invasion* is in a sense a *doppelgänger* narrative: references are made to characters' 'doubles', and perhaps these represent our fears of our own repressed qualities, our tendency to become pod-like in search of security.

Critic David Seed has pointed out that this theme is grounded in the film's lighting scheme:

Many shots are lit from below so that characters project huge shadows. They emerge as double entities at some points; at others back-lighting reduces them to silhouettes, emphasising the pods' function of duplication and erasure respectively.

And other techniques are also used to sustain a pitch of free-floating anxiety: three 'emergency' signs are seen in the hospital at the start, and police sirens recur throughout the film; clocks are a repeated image, stressing the theme of time running out; and Becky and Miles seem to be perpetually running. The film's setting is important too in this respect: Santa Mira is a small town in which Miles, as the local doctor, would know everyone; and much of *Invasion*'s power comes from familiar settings and encounters becoming slowly untrustworthy and unfamiliar, in a textbook example of Freud's definition of the *unheimlich* or uncanny.

Some critics have aligned the fear of identity loss in the film with a fear of female sexuality. The pods resemble female genitals – one of these slit ovals is even seen giving birth – and Miles's anxiety about what is happening in Santa Mira is mirrored in his growing attraction to Becky; perhaps his fear is simply that of falling in love and the attendant loss of control and identity. His moment of greatest horror comes when he kisses Becky, then pulls away from her seductive yet mocking look, realising that she has 'turned': women, here, seem to represent passivity, giving up, sleep, loss of self and death. Yet while this may be one of *Invasion*'s themes, it hardly defines gender in the film: qualities that are usually defined as masculine, such as rationality, are closest to the pods, and it is the 'irrational' or feminine qualities, like emotion, feeling and intuition, that are distinctively human.

The framing device insisted upon by the studio provides an altogether different reading for the film. Miles insists that he is 'not crazy', but he certainly looks wild, and has by his own admission been popping pills to stay awake – amphetamines, known to produce hallucinations and psychotic delusions after protracted use. All of the events that take place in Santa Mira – including things he could not have known – are narrated by him, and there is only the unconvincing truck accident to support his story. The framing device, then, puts *Invasion* squarely in the realm of paranoid movies. Miles asks Becky, 'What's wrong with madness?', and the question loops back into the fear of conformity at the film's heart: to subscribe to consensus reality is to conform at a most fundamental level, while to go mad is to embrace an entirely personal universe.

In fact, the symptoms shown by *Invasion*'s characters are classic examples of Capgras Syndrome, a psychological condition in which individuals believe that their close relatives – sometimes their pets or even themselves – have been replaced by sinister doubles. Other 50s science-fiction films use the theme too, notably *I Married a Monster from Outer Space* (Gene Fowler Jr, 1958) and *Invaders from Mars* (1953). This is how Finney saw his story; rejecting any political subtext, he was 'simply intrigued by the notion of a lot of people insisting that their friends and relatives were impostors'.

INDUSTRY IMPACT: While the original *Invasion* wasn't considered worthy of a *New York Times* review, the paper considered Philip Kaufman's 1978 remake 'dazzling . . . brilliantly unsettling'.

Kaufman's film provides a more likeable and convincing group of protagonists – the character of Becky in the original is a little insipid, unlike the remake's Elizabeth – who come across as genuine individuals; as Pauline Kael pointed out in a glowing review in the *New Yorker*, the film champions the rights of freaks to be freaks, rather than norms to be normal. It's helped by a quirky cast: Jeff Goldblum, Donald Sutherland, Veronica Cartwright and Brooke Adams play the freaks, while a hilarious Leonard Nimoy takes the psychiatrist role, as a sleazily untrustworthy counsellor brimming with encounter-group bullshit. But he's a star in the San Francisco setting, a city inhabited by narcissistic therapy addicts whose personalities are so dulled by their self-absorbed quests that, as in the original film, the arrival of the pods only exaggerates a trend that was already there. This setting loses the claustrophobic feel of the first film, but Kaufman makes up for it by showing us in graphic detail how the pod people grow, with grotesque birth sequences, and introduces a new pod trait: when alarmed, they emit a banshee-like wail.

The first suggestion that anything is wrong comes when Elizabeth's slobby sports-fan husband, who keeps an eye on the game while giving her a kiss, takes the rubbish out in the morning: she's far more alarmed by his change of character than pleased by his new sense of duty. In Abel Ferrara's second remake, entitled simply *Body Snatchers* (1993), one of the characters is similarly worried when her alcoholic mother stops drinking and takes up bridge: to be human, with all its foibles, is still preferable to being an automaton. Ferrara's film relocates the action to an Alabama military base – the perfect setting for exercising metaphors of conformity – and makes still more of Kaufman's developments, with splashy effects showing the pods snaking tendrils into their victims and an even more alarming eerie shriek.

Invasion also shows distinct plot similarities to *Quatermass 2* (Val Guest), by far the best of Hammer's forays into SF, although as the British film was also released in 1956 *Invasion* is unlikely to have been a direct influence. But it did influence two 60s films, *Creation of the Humanoids* (Wesley Barry, 1962) and **Night of the Living Dead**, and was given a feminist spin in the 1970s with *The Stepford Wives* (Bryan Forbes, 1975).

The astonishingly visceral *Shivers* (1978) combines Heinlein's slugs, **Night of the Living Dead**'s zombies and *Invasion*'s ambivalent view of sex in one of David Cronenberg's first forays into body horror. Dr Emil Hobbes, understandably deranged by the sterile surroundings of a Canadian apartment complex, becomes convinced that 'man is an animal that thinks too much ... an over-rational animal that's lost touch with its instinct and its body', and unleashes a brace of phallic slugs which turn their victims into sex-crazed drones. The film was retitled *They Came from Within* by American Independent Pictures (AIP) for the North American market, a twist on Allied Artists' original title for *Invasion*, *They Came from Another World*, and a reflection of Cronenberg's insistence on home-grown horrors: no aliens from outer space need apply. Here, as in *Invasion*, the climactic moment of horror comes when the hero's girlfriend has 'turned' – but this time a kiss proves far more dangerous.

In its guise as paranoid nightmare, *Invasion* anticipates the conspiracy theories that have informed popular political thought since the 1960s. Its cinematic descendants in this respect include Brian Yuzna's *Society* (1989), a deliciously comic if often unsubtle fable about the exploitation of the poor by the rich. *Society* shares *Invasion*'s basic distrust of authority, with another psychiatrist ('I don't like giving you drugs, Billy!' he claims as he plunges a hypodermic into the hapless hero's arm) acting as spokesman for the 'others', and cops who cannot be trusted. Bodies, in both films, are not always what – or whom – they seem.

Unlike Siegel's film, however, here Billy is not encouraged to join 'society' – they simply want to use him to their own ends – and the principal locus of anxiety is the family, with Billy convinced that his blood relations are a bit too hands-on when he's not around. Although occasionally marred by Screaming Mad George's rubbery 'surrealistic special effects', *Society* is the necessary inverse to American celebrations of elitist mediocrity like *Beverly Hills 90210* and *Baywatch*, and features one of the slimiest finales in film history.

1998 saw *Invasion* receive the *Scream* treatment courtesy of *The Faculty*, written by the recursive slasher's Kevin Williamson and directed by Robert Rodriguez. The film, which features an unlikely group of high-school students battling against the aliens who have taken over their school, refers not only to Siegel's film but also *The Puppet Masters*, as the characters jockey for position as premier pop-culture pundit; there's even a verbatim repetition of the pod people's argument from Siegel's film. *Invasion* isn't the only film it borrows from – one of the best sequences parodies the alien test from *The Thing* (John Carpenter, 1982) – but *The Faculty*'s neither scary, tense nor particularly interesting, and only makes sense if you want to join in with spotting its self-conscious cultural references. Otherwise, it's a perfect example of the redundancy of most modern genre product.

FINAL WORD: For all of *The Faculty*'s flaws, it demonstrates, along with Kaufman and Ferrara's remakes, that *Invasion of the Body Snatchers* remains relevant today, and is indeed unmatched in its depiction of the unease that lies beneath the surface of modern life. And with America reeling under fears of another abstract enemy within with the War on Terror, and medicating itself into a vapid ignorance of depression, rage and adolescence, the battle against the pod people is clearly far from won.

HAMMER HORROR

Dracula (1958)

'The chill of the tomb won't leave your blood for hours ... after you come face-to-face with DRACULA!'

US: The Horror of Dracula

UK, Hammer Studios, colour, 82 mins

Executive Producer: Michael Carreras
Producer: Anthony Hinds
Associate Producer: Anthony Nelson Keys
Director: Terence Fisher
Screenplay: Jimmy Sangster, based on the novel by Bram Stoker
Photography: Jack Asher
Supervising Editor: James Needs
Music: James Bernard
Editor: Bill Lenny
Assistant Director: Bob Lynn
Special Effects: Syndey Pearson

CAST: Peter Cushing (*Dr Van Helsing*), Christopher Lee (*Dracula*), Michael Gough (*Arthur Holmwood*), Melissa Stribling

(*Mina Holmwood*), Carol Marsh (*Lucy Holmwood*), Olga Dickie (*Gerda*), John Van Eyssen (*Jonathan Harker*), Valerie Gaunt (*Vampire Woman*), Janine Faye (*Tania, Gerda's Daughter*), Barbara Archer (*Inga*), Charles Lloyd Pack (*Dr Seward*), George Merritt (*Policeman*), George Woodbridge (*Landlord*), George Benson (*Official*), Miles Malleson (*Undertaker*), Geoffrey Bayldon (*Porter*), Paul Cole (*Lad*)

SYNOPSIS: Jonathan Harker takes up a position as librarian at Count Dracula's castle; he knows Dracula to be a vampire, and has arrived to kill him. In the castle Harker meets a girl who begs him to help her until the count introduces himself, but falls silent when the count appears. Later that night Harker wanders around the castle, and meets the girl again. She repeats her plea for help, then tries to bite him. Dracula intervenes. Next day Harker discovers the vampires' hiding place. He stakes the female vampire, but the sun sets before he can stake the count.

Van Helsing visits an inn near Dracula's castle, and is given Harker's diary by the barmaid. He then visits the castle, and sees a coffin being driven off in a carriage. He finds Harker, now a vampire, where Harker had found Dracula.

Van Helsing explains to a suspicious Arthur and Mina Holmwood that Harker has died. Harker's fiancée, Lucy, is ill in bed; she has already been bitten by Dracula. The doctor cannot help her, and Mina asks Van Helsing to look at her instead. Van Helsing sees her bites, and orders that her windows be closed and the room filled with garlic. Lucy asks the maid to open the windows and remove the garlic, and duly dies that night.

Van Helsing gives Harker's diary to a sceptical Arthur. Tania, Gerda's daughter, says she's seen Lucy. Arthur visits Lucy's grave and finds the body missing; he then sees Lucy returning to the graveyard with Tania, and Lucy tries to bite him. Van Helsing appears and drives her away with a crucifix, then stakes her.

Van Helsing and Arthur visit a border post – Dracula's castle is in a neighbouring country – to find out where his hearse was going. Meanwhile Mina is told by a messenger to meet the men at an undertakers': the same address that Van Helsing receives. She descends into the basement to find Dracula's coffin.

When Arthur and Van Helsing visit the undertakers', they find that Dracula's coffin has gone. Arthur gives Mina a cross to wear, but it burns her skin: she is infected with vampirism. Arthur and

Van Helsing keep watch outside that night, but Dracula still feeds on Mina. Arthur gives Mina a blood transfusion.

They discover Dracula's coffin in the basement of Holmwood's house, but he escapes with Mina. They travel to the castle, where Dracula tries to bite Van Helsing, but the doctor drives him into the sunlight with a pair of candlesticks held like a cross – Dracula dissolves into dust, and Mina is saved.

ORIGINS AND INSPIRATION: Before Hammer, the British film industry had never really taken to horror. There had been the occasional Tod Slaughter melodrama, and a number of British films featured horror stars Boris Karloff and Bela Lugosi, but for the most part the censors' disapproval held sway: American films like *Freaks* (1932) and *Island of Lost Souls* (1932) were banned in the UK for decades, and other horror films were rendered incomprehensible through the efforts of scissor-happy defenders of English morality. One of the few important early home-grown genre films was Ealing's *Dead of Night* (Alberto Cavalcanti, Charles Crichton, Basil Dearden and Robert Hamer, 1945), a portmanteau collection of ghost stories with a profoundly unsettling sequence featuring a ventriloquist's dummy; but all this inspired, apart from nightmares, was a rash of weak imitations. It would take Hammer's gothic cycle to inaugurate the British horror boom.

Hammer had existed, in name at least, since the 1930s, but the company as it is known today was started in 1947. This small production company distinguished itself from the outset in two ways: its preference for using characters and scenarios already familiar to the public, whether through television or other media, and its use of country homes rather than studios to film its productions. In 1951 Hammer started using Bray Studios, a country house near Maidenhead which formed the company's home until they were obliged to sell it in 1968. The location gave Hammer films a distinctive look, and also gave the company a head start in making period films.

In the early 1950s a deal with the independent US producer Robert Lippert allowed them to feature fading US stars in their productions, which helped secure US distribution. The US studio system had been broken up by anti-trust legislation at the time, which meant the major studios were making principally big-budget glossy fare; but cinemas needed more material, and so exploitation movies were born: low-budget independently produced shockers taking advantage of relaxed censorship laws and aimed squarely at teenagers. The Lippert deal allowed Hammer's early thrillers to compete in this market, and the studio's high production values and professionalism ensured their films looked far glossier than many of their rivals'; this attention to quality would soon become one of the studio's defining characteristics and enduring selling points.

In the mid-1950s, with the Lippert deal drawing to a close, Hammer reinvented itself again. *The Quatermass Xperiment* (1955) had some similarities to previous Hammer fare: it was based on a TV series (written by Nigel Kneale), featured an imported US star (Brian Donlevy) and wasn't the studio's first SF picture. But it was the first to receive an X certificate (hence the title), and became a runaway success. Hammer promptly dropped ten of its planned films for 1956 and looked around for new material of a fantastic nature, filming a sequel and another SF movie, *X – The Unknown* (Leslie Norman).

But the follow-ups didn't do as well as the original film, and Hammer's flirtation with fantastic cinema seemed over before it had really begun. Enter US producer Milton Subotsky, who went to Associated Artists (AA) with an idea for making a new Frankenstein film. AA passed the idea to Hammer, Subotsky dropped out, and with backing from the American studio and a distribution deal with Warner Bros, Hammer started work on *The Curse of Frankenstein* (1957).

Nothing could have prepared them for the film's success. There was no indication that the British public would enjoy a new wave of classic horror, a genre that was thought to have died decades ago. But the film broke house records wherever it was shown, its cynical villainy, lurid colour and unprecedented gore – amounting to little more than Frankenstein wiping his bloodied hand on his smock – ensuring delighted audiences. Most critics were less impressed, one reviling the studio as a 'sick way to make a living' and another considered the film 'among the half-dozen most repulsive films I have encountered', but what shocked the critics pulled in the punters, and on the strength of the film's success the studio signed a deal with Columbia to make three films a year.

For *Curse*, Hammer had gone to great pains to distinguish their monster from Universal's creation, a copyrighted image; but by the time they started work on *Dracula* (reversing the original

Universal order), Universal had given the studio permission to remake its horror backlist. It might seem strange in retrospect that this large American studio should trust a small British company with such potentially lucrative products, but home-grown US gothic only returned to the screens with Roger Corman's Poe cycle for AIP, some of which was shot in the UK: most US genre product was set in the present day and, above all, aimed at teenagers. An American Dracula film, *The Return of Dracula* (Paul Landres, 1958), opened simultaneously with Hammer's first vampire film but couldn't have been further from the British period piece, full as it was of wisecracking teens pitted against the count in a contemporary setting.

For *Dracula* Hammer retained the tight team from *Curse*, reuniting the director, cinematographer, production designer, screenwriter, editor, composer and much of the cast, giving the studio a factory feel it would retain until its demise in the 1970s. To save money, screenwriter Jimmy Sangster pared Stoker's novel down, compressing its geographical scope and giving the count a small, homely castle, contributing to the domestication of Dracula taking place elsewhere in 50s popular culture. The character of Renfield was dispensed with altogether; Jonathan Harker was a vampire hunter, in one of many reversals of audience expectations; character names were shuffled around; the team of young men who help Van Helsing in the novel was reduced to just one man, Arthur Holmwood; and, ironically for the first British film adaptation of *Dracula*, the count would not travel to England.

Rather than the pestilential invasion of **Nosferatu**, this time the count was merely interested in finding another bride, his own having been killed; Dracula's aims throughout his film history can be easily deduced by seeing how many coffins he takes with him on leaving the castle – here it is just one, in the 1931 Universal film it is three, and in **Nosferatu** it is half a dozen.

Sangster also tampered with vampire lore: here a vampire could not turn into a bat, and given the appearance of the bats in *The Brides of Dracula* (Terence Fisher, 1960) the decision was probably wise. Sunlight would be fatal, as it was in **Nosferatu** but not Stoker's novel; vampires were to be re-fanged, for the first time since **Nosferatu** – this time with canine fangs – and this would be the first period adaptation of the story since Murnau's film. It would also be the first vampire film in colour, using a muted palette that ensured the appearance of blood – and Lee's scarlet contact lenses – was even more lurid and shocking.

DIRECTOR: Terence Fisher, one of the best-known directors to work for Hammer, didn't start directing films until he was 43, and didn't make his first horror picture until he was 52. He went on to helm almost all of the important early Hammer horror films, including *The Mummy* (1959), *The Revenge of Frankenstein* (1959), *The Hound of the Baskervilles* (1959) and *The Curse of the Werewolf* (1960), until the box-office failure of *The Phantom of the Opera* (1962) prompted the studio to rely more heavily on other directors. But he still continued to make films for Hammer – the relatively late *The Devil Rides Out* (1968) is considered by some his best film – until his last, *Frankenstein and the Monster from Hell*, in 1974. It was his fiftieth film.

Fisher's work tends to divide critics, who have referred to it variously as 'trite and reactionary, his style turgid and stagey' or containing a 'powerful atmosphere augmented by an underlying sexuality'. It's certainly true that compared to other directors specialising in gothic fare, whether James Whale or Fisher's Italian contemporaries Mario Bava and Riccardo Freda, his style comes across as flat and inexpressive, and the success of his films has often been put down to his screenwriters, but his best work – and *Dracula* is one of his finest films – has a rigorously symmetrical structure in which the tension between the surface attractiveness of evil and a dualistic condemnation of it erupts in scenes of sudden kinetic violence.

Dracula also provides a perfect illustration of the director's idea of the 'beast within' – the potential corruption lying dormant in innocent flesh – with the count being harboured in the Holmwoods' house. The director considered the film to be 'just about the best thing I have ever done for Hammer', and maintained that if his films reflected a personal vision, it was 'in their showing of the ultimate victory of good over evil'.

CASTING: Much of the success of Hammer's horror films can be attributed to the iconic figures of Christopher Lee and Peter Cushing. Lee's association with the count remains strong, despite the fact that after *Dracula* he refused to play the role again for seven years. Worried about being typecast, he appeared in a wide variety of other material to ensure he became a star in his own right before returning to his most famous role. It is a testament to the way in which Lee had made the role his own that Hammer did not even consider casting anyone else, developing instead the character of Baron Meinster (played by David Peel) for the first sequel, *Brides of Dracula* (1960).

Lee decided to become an actor after leaving the RAF at the end of the Second World War. His big break came when he was asked to play the part of Frankenstein's Monster in *The Curse of Frankenstein* (1957), a role for which his 6′ 5″ height fitted him perfectly. According to the actor his height had served him poorly in his career until then, with most British stars refusing to have him on set for fear his presence would upstage them.

The actor was a great fan of Stoker's novel, and was disappointed by Hammer's move away from the source material in subsequent Dracula films, although that didn't stop him from appearing in the execrable *Dracula AD 1972* (Alan Gibson, 1972) and *The Satanic Rites of Dracula* (Alan Gibson, 1973).

Lee was always at pains to express the vulnerability of the count – 'I think he's a very sad person. He's not a hero, but an anti-hero in many ways. He has tremendous ferocity and power, but he doesn't always have it under control' – and noted his roots in the historical figure of Vlad 'The Impaler' Tepes:

> Above all, I have never forgotten that Count Dracula was a gentleman, a member of the upper aristocracy, and in his early life a great leader of men ... you never see me get out of a coffin or resting-place – it would look ridiculous.

As well as playing a variety of villains for Hammer, from the Mummy to Fu Manchu, Lee's memorable roles include the transvestite Lord Summerisle in *The Wicker Man* (Robin Hardy, 1973), Scaramanga from *The Man with the Golden Gun* (Guy Hamilton, 1974) and Saruman from Peter Jackson's *Lord of the Rings* trilogy.

Peter Cushing's acting career started in Hollywood, where he appeared in small roles in a number of films including James Whale's *The Man in the Iron Mask* (1939) and *They Dare Not Love* (1940). On the outbreak of war he returned to the UK, and continued to take minor parts until his performance in a BBC adaptation of *1984* drew the attention of Hammer's Michael Carreras, and the actor was duly offered the role of Frankenstein.

Cushing was forty years old, and had been on the verge of giving up acting to design scarves for a living, but the role made his career, even more so than that of Van Helsing. Before his semi-retirement from the screen in the mid-80s, he also played Dr Who in two 1960s cinema adaptations, and Grand Moff Tarkin in *Star Wars* (George Lucas, 1977), as well as starring in numerous non-Hammer British genre films.

Dracula also features a number of other actors who routinely reappeared in Hammer productions, notably Miles Malleson as the undertaker, in a typical light comedy role, and Michael Gough, who also featured in non-Hammer British horrors like *Horrors of the Black Museum* (Arthur Crabtree, 1959), *Dr Terror's House of Horrors* (Freddie Francis, 1965) and *Horror Hospital* (Antony Balch, 1973).

PRODUCTION: Production started on 11 November 1957 and concluded on 3 January the following year. The budget had been increased from *Curse*'s £64,000 to £81,000, and the shooting schedule was slightly longer. By all accounts *Dracula* – and indeed the subsequent Hammer films – was very much a team effort. Fisher saw his role purely in terms of adapting the script for the screen, and does not seem to have imposed a personal vision on cast and crew. He welcomed suggestions for changes, and the idea for Van Helsing's run down the count's dining table and use of candlesticks for a cross came from Peter Cushing – they are not in the shooting script.

The team made the most of their scant resources: the set design and camera movements were arranged to make the sets appear far larger than they really were, and Fisher delighted in shooting scenes to undercut audience expectations. The entrance of Dracula is a key moment in the film, as the director recalls:

everybody was ready to laugh their bloody heads off – I've seen it in cinemas again and again – they thought they were going to see fangs and everything. They didn't, of course. Instead they saw a charming and extremely good looking man with a touch, an undercurrent of evil or menace.

Lee's urbane and civilised count – his suave introduction, 'I'm Dracula', is far removed from Lugosi's r-rolling 'I am Dracula' – recalled the Byronic anti-hero of late 19th-century vampire lore, and the eroticism and sheer physicality of the film brought it closer to Stoker's novel than previous adaptations. Where Dracula's brides had before been ethereal, ghostly figures, here his victims were voluptuous, the depth of cleavage often showing how far they were under the vampire's thrall; the bite became an explicitly sexualised act that the predominantly female victims awaited with barely suppressed glee; and where the count would glide, apparently untouchable, in previous films, here he was ready to fight, and showed considerable strength.

SOUNDTRACK: Hammer's approach to soundtracks was fairly innovative, as the studio routinely gave opportunities to classically trained composers to score films, even when they had little or no experience in the industry. *Dracula* features a distinctive score from James Bernard, with a signature theme for the count's appearance that recalls Waxman's signature for the Monster from **Bride of Frankenstein**, and an eerily shimmering build-up as his victims expectantly await his bite.

Following this and other Hammer films music would be viewed as far more important to the success of a horror film than it had been previously, with such signatures increasingly common. Bernard was Hammer's most prolific composer, and was responsible for the scores of such key films as *The Quatermass Xperiment* (1955) and *The Curse of Frankenstein*, as well as eighteen other titles for the studio and the BFI DVD release of **Nosferatu**.

'IT'S ONLY A MOVIE ... ONLY A MOVIE ...': Hammer's posters for *Dracula* stressed the eroticism of this new vampire film, with an illustration of a fanged Lee leaning over a prone woman's chest and the strapline 'The terrifying lover – who died – yet lived!'

The studio's success soon meant they could promote films simply on the strength of their being Hammer products; once they even promoted a number of films abroad as Hammer films, with no indication of their content, and takings were as high as for any of their other films.

RELEASE: On its release *Dracula* was even more successful than *The Curse of Frankenstein*. This was probably partly due to the critical drubbing it received: audiences couldn't wait to see why the opinion-formers were so outraged.

The shock wouldn't last for long. Critical responses to *Dracula*, and to the Hammer horror boom in general, shifted through three stages: initial shock at the films' disreputability, followed quickly by establishment acceptance – the studio won the Queen's Award to Industry in 1968, after three years of production in which they had brought £1,500,000 into the UK each year – and a desire on the part of younger British filmmakers to distance themselves from the studio's 'moralistic' stance, and finally a critical re-evaluation of the films as reactionary.

The film did receive some positive reviews on its release, notably from industry papers which were mainly concerned with its commercial potential. *Variety* praised the art direction and production, while the *Daily Cinema* felt the 'lavish settings and the magnificent use of backgrounds give the production a commanding appearance', and even the *Star* felt it 'probably the best acted, directed and photographed horror film ever made'.

But the reaction in most papers was one of appalled bemusement. CA Lejeune, writing in the *Observer*, described it as a 'singularly repulsive piece of nonsense', while Nina Hibbin in the *Daily Worker* noted that although she'd been 'prepared to enjoy a nervous giggle' she 'came away revolted and outraged ... Laughable nonsense? Not when it is filmed like this, with realism.'

Hibbin seems to be taking the film to task for being too effective, and *Dracula*'s harshest critics tended to rely either on a similar sense of outrage that it had managed to affect them or a critical superiority over this lowbrow genre. In some ways the British press's attack on Hammer was just as much a response to the X certificate itself, and a perceived slackening of public morals, especially among the 'lower' classes, the principal market for horror films: the popularity of Hammer was symptomatic, it was reasoned, of an American crassness invading the UK.

CRITICAL EYE: Today Hammer films are viewed as predominantly reactionary rather than radical. The lower social orders are routinely depicted as stupid, a mindless mob or the impotent victims of cruel aristocrats: here the patronising middle-class figure of Van Helsing must help those incapable of helping themselves, even if his efforts are thwarted by bumbling figures like Gerda, the maid who gets rid of the garlic and opens Lucy's windows.

More importantly, the film is charged with taking a dim view of women, who are punished for expressing their sexuality or asserting their independence instead of accepting that they are the property of men. This fits *Dracula* well enough, but it doesn't mean that the viewer is encouraged absolutely to take the side of Van Helsing and Arthur Holmwood.

Fisher uses various techniques to draw parallels between Dracula and the other male characters, from the use of screen space to plot dynamics. Most of the film is set either at Dracula's castle or Arthur Holmwood's house, and in many ways they are strikingly similar: like Holmwood, Dracula has one wife, and lives in a well-kept house (not really a castle) not too far from town. When his bride is killed, he seeks first Harker's fiancée then Arthur's wife, and Harker takes the place of Dracula in his tomb.

Both Harker and Holmwood are weak figures: Harker fails miserably in his attempt to dispatch the count, and Arthur is similarly ineffectual, a drab patriarch who receives scant respect from his wife. Their sexuality is buttoned-down, repressed, although at least they have partners, unlike Van Helsing, whose skeletal rigour appears to have long lacked a female touch. If Van Helsing is strong and authoritative, he is also dour, thin-lipped, prim and unexciting – an overbearing puritan, much like the witchfinder character Cushing plays in *Twins of Evil* (John Hough, 1972). He's convinced that the victims 'consciously detest' being vampires, but Lucy and Mina don't look too upset by the count's arrival: in fact they seem positively to welcome it.

Dracula himself is by contrast a suave, commanding presence, holding each woman he meets in a sexual thrall expressed by a burgeoning voluptuousness. Would the viewer rather be the count, enfolding his victims in a black cloak as he sinks his fangs into a bared female neck, or Van Helsing as he goes about the grim task of staking a good (male) friend? Good ultimately triumphs over evil here, but only really by way of a cheat: while the audience may identify with virtuous forces in principle, in practice it's behind the count all the way, and when his ring is seen at the end the viewer suspects and hopes that it won't be too long before he is seen again.

In this sense the accusations of patriarchal and reactionary concerns levelled at the film rely on an overly simple reading: *Dracula* can just as well be seen as a criticism of stuffy repression, a warning that sensuality needs to be acknowledged before it boils over into violent desire. Rather than an assertion of patriarchal power, it is an exploration of male weakness, of men's lust and fear over women's sexual satisfaction – fears that also relate to gender shifts in the 1950s, expressing male anxiety about women's departure from traditional social roles – and the possibility of being rejected for another lover.

And not just any other lover, but a foreign one: the Holmwoods live in a different country from Dracula. Sexual energy is here, in a typically British way, located in a foreign country; and the Holmwoods' home, although ostensibly in Carlstadt, looks more like a parody of Victorian England. The fear of foreign men stealing women is primal and powerful – according to biologist Matt Ridley it is the original source of war – and is explored further in the activities of Emile, the dusky vampiric Lothario of *Vampire Circus* (Robert Young, 1972).

Sangster's script tightens the range of Stoker's novel so that everyone bitten is related to the Holmwoods either by blood or marriage. This, along with the parallels drawn between the count and Arthur Holmwood, demonstrates Hammer's recognition of the family as a key source of horror, anticipating by a few years the generic shift to familial horror generally associated with **Psycho**. Elsewhere in Hammer's vampire cycle *Countess Dracula* (Peter Sasdy, 1972) threatens to feed on her own daughter, while 1960's *The Brides of Dracula*'s Baron Meinster bites his own mother; even 'normal' families can be characterised by monstrous relationships, as in *Taste the Blood of Dracula* (Peter Sasdy, 1970).

Dracula also foreshadows other horror developments with its open ending, a feature that would not become common until the late 60s, and its equation of vampirism with drug addiction. But probably its most important contribution to horror is a kinetic energy, a dynamism shown in its rapid plot development, the physicality of the characters' actions and the roving camerawork, all contained within a powerfully symmetrical structure. David Pirie has described *Dracula* as 'a dashing metaphysical detective story with a strong diagrammatic structure in terms of image, colour and landscape', and it is this balance of tightly controlled form with explosions of energy that make the film still look fresh today.

INDUSTRY IMPACT: The unprecedented success of Hammer's two gothic chillers led the studio to throw almost all its energies into making similar material. The results weren't always successful – their 1962 remake of *The Old Dark House* (William Castle) was particularly ill-advised – and the studio diversified into exotic prehistoric epics (*One Million Years BC*, Don Chaffey, 1966), Hitchcockian psycho-thrillers (*Fanatic*, Silvio Narizzano, 1965) and apocalyptic SF (Joseph Losey's astonishing *The Damned*, 1961); but it is for a selection of true horror classics that the studio will be remembered.

The studio was always at its best when working with new material, and Hammer's Dracula cycle much resembled its Frankenstein films in their diminishing returns. *The Brides of Dracula* replaced the count with Baron Meinster, who actually manages to bite Van Helsing, while *Kiss of the Vampire* (Don Sharp, 1963) suffered from a lack of both Cushing and Lee; but the series returned to form with *Dracula – Prince of Darkness* (Terence Fisher, 1966), which saw Lee back as the count (albeit with no dialogue, just a series of bestial growls) and Fisher again at the helm. It also featured a particularly nasty staking which many critics equated with a gang rape, a burst of violence given an uneasy tone by Fisher's 'declared stance on the subjugation of wanton sexuality'.

Dracula Has Risen from the Grave (Freddie Francis, 1968) upped the stakes in both the extreme religious iconography – Dracula was increasingly equated with the Antichrist – and sexual content, with the count explicitly seducing his victims before putting the bite on them. By 1970's *Taste the Blood of Dracula* the count had moved to England, and his transformation into the Antichrist was complete: from now on, Satanic rituals would mark fealty to the vampire. *Scars of Dracula* (Roy Ward Baker), released the same year, reversed the trend of giving the count increasingly less screen time, and allowed him to indulge in bouts of uncharacteristic violence, including administering a whipping!

In a misguided effort to match what was happening with revisionist vampire films elsewhere, Hammer now dragged the count into contemporary London for *Dracula AD 1972*, and gave him high-level political contacts as a property developer in its sequel, *The Satanic Rites of Dracula* (1973). Here the films' Satanic trend reached its logical conclusion, as the count, wearing a crown of thorns, was positioned in an inverted cross before being killed. Hammer's last few vampire films look like increasingly desperate attempts to mix genres, whether horror and kung fu (*The Legend of the Seven Golden Vampires*, Roy Ward Baker,

1974) or horror and paranoid thriller (*The Satanic Rites of Dracula*): but the count was happiest at home.

The Karnstein trilogy – *The Vampire Lovers* (Roy Ward Baker, 1970), *Lust for a Vampire* (Jimmy Sangster, 1971) and *Twins of Evil* – benefited from their voluptuous casts, including the unforgettable Ingrid Pitt, and the second film achieves a dream-like intensity at times; but they suffer from having no viable adversary, no Van Helsing against whom the oversexed vampires can pit themselves. Still, they push the fear and lust that inform *Dracula* to their limits: here lesbian vampires are both the focus of a lustful gaze and the source of fears that men are, ultimately, expendable.

While Frankenstein and Dracula proved Hammer's biggest box-office stars, the studio attempted to revive other monsters in films like *The Mummy* (1959) and *The Curse of the Werewolf* (1961), and invent new ones, such as *The Gorgon* (Terence Fisher, 1964) and *The Reptile* (1966). The latter was directed by John Gilling, who also made *Plague of the Zombies* (1966); both are set in 19th-century Cornwall, and are among the most interesting Hammer products, with a bleak pessimism that prefigured horror's harder edge in the 1970s.

Hammer's other notable successes include *Dr Jekyll and Sister Hyde* (Roy Ward Baker, 1971), a perverse exploration of RL Stevenson's story that throws Jack the Ripper and bodysnatchers Burke and Hare into the mix; 1972's *Demons of the Mind* (Peter Sykes), an unusually intelligent look at early psychiatry and madness; and *The Devil Rides Out* (see **ORIGINS AND INSPI-RATION, Rosemary's Baby**).

The gothic revival exemplified by Hammer was not restricted to the UK – Roger Corman's Poe cycle for AIP in the US and the opulent productions of Italians Riccardo Freda (*The Terror of Dr Hichcock/L'Orribile segreto del dottor Hichcock*, 1962) and Mario Bava (*Mask of Satan/La Maschera del demonio*, 1960) provided foreign competition, although some Italian gothic film-makers took to using English pseudonyms to cash in on the taste for Anglo horror. There were also gothic gems emerging from Eastern Europe: Wojciech Has's *The Saragossa Manuscript/Rekopis znaleziny w Saragossie* (1965) is a sprawling period epic of tales nested within tales, shot through with beautiful phantoms and lavish visuals, while Juraj Herz's *Morgiana* (1971) brings a hallucinatory richness to its decadent fairy story.

Hammer also had home-grown competitors: Anglo-Amalgamated made three films loosely related by the theme of voyeurism, *Horrors of the Black Museum*, *Circus of Horrors* (Sidney Hayers, 1960) and *Peeping Tom* (Michael Powell, 1960, see **INDUSTRY IMPACT, Psycho**); Robert Baker and Monty Berman produced shockers like *Corridors of Blood* (Robert Day, 1962), *Grip of the Strangler* (Robert Day, 1958) and John Gilling's *The Flesh and the Fiends* (1959); Amicus made a series of fun portmanteau films like *Dr Terror's House of Horrors* and *Tales from the Crypt* (Freddie Francis, 1972); and Tigon produced *Blood on Satan's Claw* (Piers Haggard, 1970) and Michael Reeves's *Witchfinder General* (1968), both of which had a psychological intensity lacking in most Hammer fare and made a more innovative use of the English landscape than the studio was able to with Bray.

By the 1970s Hammer's grip on the market was loosening. Other filmmakers were able to make Hammer-style films with more panache: the parodic gothic horrors of Paul Morrissey's *Flesh for Frankenstein* (1973) and *Blood for Dracula* (1974), for instance, or Tigon's period horrors; and while the studio continued to ramp up the sex and violence in their films, they were never able – and perhaps never wanted – to go as far as the gruelling relentlessness of a film like **The Texas Chain Saw Massacre**.

Horror audiences were also more reluctant to accept the rigid dualism and optimistic endings of most Hammer films, although the studio did move towards an overt criticism of patriarchal structures in some of its 70s films, notably *Twins of Evil* and *Hands of the Ripper* (Peter Sasdy, 1971); but it was probably too little too late. Authority was now distrusted, and British horror fans expressed a preference for the downbeat tone and stark realism of films from Michael Reeves and Pete Walker (*Frightmare*, *House of Whipcord*, both 1974), who responded quickly to the harder edge of US horror cinema in the early 70s.

The studio's final genre feature, *To the Devil ... a Daughter* (Peter Sykes, 1976), was a disaster, and apart from a couple of forays into television with the popular *Hammer House of Horror* series, the studio crumbled. Various attempts to revive Hammer failed, and while some of the British horror films that followed – *Frightmare* (1974), *The Wicker Man* (Robin Hardy, 1973), *Death Line* (Gary Sherman, 1973) – may have been more interesting and powerful than most of the studio's productions, none had the influence or commercial impact of the company's first forays into gothic horror.

FINAL WORD: The past in Hammer is an overly familiar place, populated by surly bartenders, buxom serving girls, decadent aristocrats who prey on ignorant peasants and nubile virgins who turn into voluptuous nymphs at the sight of a black cape. Hammer rearranged stock characters and scenarios so often that their films often seem like an amorphous self-parodic mass, a full-blooded version of Carry On, or a funhouse portend of the heritage industry's costume dramas, a sense encouraged by the studio's own marketing tactics.

The presentation of the films after their initial theatrical runs has encouraged such a view: while other horror classics are available in their original aspect ratio on video and DVD, Hammer films are almost always seen panned and scanned, denying fans the chance to see them in their full glory, and are more usually considered as part of a series than as individual features. Needless to say, the films are not best served by such treatment, which can obscure the fact that their best efforts, such as *Dracula*, stand on their own as some of the finest gothic films ever made.

EURO-HORROR AND SURGICAL PANIC

Eyes Without a Face (1959)

US: The Horror of Dr Faustus (dubbed version)

France/Italy, Champs Elysées Lux, b/w, 90 mins

Directed by Georges Franju
Produced by Jules Borkon
Screenplay by Jean Redon, from his own novel, adapted by
Georges Franju, Jean Redon, Claude Sautet, Pierre Boileau,
Thomas Narcejac, with dialogue by Pierre Gascar
Photography: Eugen Shuftan
Special Effects: Henri Assola, Georges Klien
Editor: Gilbert Natot
Art Director: Auguste Capelier
Music: Maurice Jarre
Sound: Antoine Archaimbaud

CAST: Pierre Brasseur (*Professor Genessier*), Alida Valli (*Louise*), Edith Scob (*Christiane*), Francois Guerin (*Jacques),* Juliette Mayniel (*Edna Gruber*), Beatrice Altariba (*Paulette*), Alexandre Rignault (*Inspector Parot*), Réné Génin (*Bereaved Father*), Claude Brasseur

SYNOPSIS: Professor Genessier is an eminent Parisian plastic surgeon whose daughter, Christiane, has vanished. He is called in by police to identify a corpse that may belong to his daughter, and tells them that it is indeed hers. But Christiane is still alive, and is hidden away at Genessier's home. She wears a mask, having been horribly disfigured in a car accident with Genessier at the wheel; the corpse he identified had been dumped into the Seine by his secretary, Louise, after a botched attempt by Genessier to graft the victim's face onto Christiane. Louise is one of Genessier's plastic surgery success stories, and will do anything to serve him.

Louise seeks more women for Genessier's experiments, and lures one, Edna, back to his house in the suburbs with the promise of a cheap room. Edna is chloroformed and operated on, her face removed and put on Christiane. At first the graft appears to take, but it deteriorates rapidly. At this Christiane protests that she wants to die, and that Genessier is more interested in his experiments than in providing her with a new life: she is a guinea pig, much like the dogs he keeps for experimentation. She phones her former boyfriend, Jacques, who works with Genessier, and whispers his name.

Genessier and Louise abduct a third girl, Paulette, who has been planted at the clinic by the police in response to Jacques's suspicions. The police investigate her disappearance, but find nothing suspicious, and the imminent removal of the girl's face is prevented only when Christiane frees her. Christiane then stabs Louise in the throat, and releases a cage of doves and Genessier's dogs. Genessier hears them barking and goes to investigate, but they run out of the compound, knock him to the ground and tear off his face.

ORIGINS AND INSPIRATION: The operating theatre has long been recognised as a zone of profound anxiety by filmmakers. While Dr Frankenstein's Faustian attempts to cheat death involve experiments on corpses alone, a slew of mad and obsessive doctors have honed their surgical skills on living bodies, as they attempt to graft skin, organs and life-forms, or gratify their sadistic urges through their victims' shrieks of pain. The mad surgeon is a staple of the 30s horror film, with Charles Laughton's Dr Moreau in *Island of Lost Souls* (1932) and Peter Lorre's gleeful turn in *Mad Love* (Karl Freund, 1935) highlights among the seemingly endless appearances of Karloff and Lugosi hamming it up as twitchy psychos handy with a scalpel.

By the late 1950s, you could have been forgiven for assuming that there was little more the mad surgeon had to offer the silver screen: the eye-rolling and delirious boasts of previous incarnations had long since lapsed into farce, as with most of the early horror tropes. Franju's skill, then, came in taking the most hackneyed plot elements and rejecting any Hitchcockian narrative sophistication in favour of a concentration on imagery and the dubious, Sadean pleasures of watching.

But first there had to be a native demand for a horror film. Henri-Georges Clouzot's *Diabolique/Les Diaboliques* (1955) told the story of a woman's attempt to murder her husband with the help of his mistress, and succeeds in mounting levels of tension to a fever pitch by the climax. The screenplay for the film was written by the team of Boileau and Narcejac, from their novel: Clouzot had pipped Hitchcock to the post in securing its film rights, and the international success of the film led Hitchcock to prepare a stripped-down psychological thriller of his own (see **ORIGINS AND INSPIRATION, Psycho**), while Boileau and Narcejac wrote *Vertigo* when they heard of the portly director's interest in their work.

One filmmaker who was less impressed by Clouzot's efforts was Georges Franju, who maintained that 'The trouble with Clouzot is that he tries to knock the audience's head off. That's wrong: you should twist it off.' It wasn't long before Franju was given a chance to demonstrate his thesis.

When producer Jules Borkon asked Franju to make a horror film from Jean Redon's novel *Les Yeux sans Visage*, he gave him several restrictions, as he didn't want any problems from the censor or the church. No animals were to be cut up, to avoid offending the English market; there was not to be too much blood, as this would make the film unsuitable for younger audiences; and there should be no mad doctors, as this would upset Germans with perceived allusions to concentration-camp experiments.

Franju, rather than rejecting the project at this stage, welcomed the strictures, which acted as a spur to his imagination. Dr Genessier was not to be a mad genius but rather an ordinary man, performing extraordinary deeds: this both increased the tension of the film and made it more believable; and the unearthly figure of Christiane would act as the audience's point of identification, providing a poetic beauty in contrast with the sordid horrors of the surgical table, and helping us to feel sympathy for the villains of the piece as they try to help her. The team of Boileau and Narcejac were recruited to work on the adaptation, their skills lying in expertly mixing rational and irrational fears and telling a story from the victim's point of view, as opposed to that of detective or criminal.

Eyes dispensed with the gothic/historical concerns that had dominated the horror genre to date for a thoroughly modern film, one intimately concerned with the present day and blackly comic in a way that pointed out the juvenility of Hollywood horror from most of the early Universal classics to AIP's 50s teen transformation movies. It also took an important cue from Hammer's *The Curse of Frankenstein* (1957), which had acknowledged for the first time the sheer bloodiness of surgery. The stakes had been upped, and Franju was not the man to back down: the removal of a young woman's face was the centrepiece of the film, with a long lead-up and no cutting away. Audiences had never seen anything like it before.

DIRECTOR: Georges Franju is often considered a *nouvelle vague* director, but he really belongs to an older generation, with more in common with Clouzot than Godard, and ultimately stands alone in the history of French film. As with many other directors of the period, he started off as a critic, publishing a short-lived magazine then screening films at a cine club, before turning his hand to the documentaries with which he would make his name.

One early documentary, *Le Sang des Betes* (1949), detailed the day-to-day running of a slaughterhouse, and foreshadowed the stark realism shot through with poetic images and subversive intent that later characterised the director's feature work. He was to direct six features in all, returning to the fantastic only once more after *Eyes*, with *Judex* (1963), an adaptation of an early film serial by Louis Feuillade that was based loosely on the exploits of Fantomas, an arch-villain whose exploits were cherished by the Surrealists among others. The Surrealists were a key influence on Franju – 'I have always been in full agreement with the Surrealists. I have learned a great deal from them' – and his tastes in literature ranged from Fantomas to de Sade and Freud, a heady set of influences that was mixed to devastating effect in his films.

Franju took only projects offered to him by producers, rather than generating his own material, but still demonstrated a very marked style. The Surrealist influence can be seen in his films' startling juxtaposition of objects and moods – *Eyes*, memorably described by novelist Christopher Petit as 'Hammer films meets Georges Bataille', has moments of beauty and horror vying with each other for intensity of impact as the film progresses. This juxtaposition is never arbitrary, but always designed to expose the true nature of things, providing a startling freshness that reveals the poetry of the everyday. For Franju '. . . the fantastic is above all realism. I detest fiction . . . I love what is realistic because I think that it is more poetic . . . Dreams, poetry, the fantastic must emerge from reality itself. Every film is a documentary, even the most poetic.'

The director was reluctant to see his work in genre terms, and disapproved of the term 'horror' for *Eyes*: 'It's an anguish film. It's a quieter mood than horror, something more subjacent, more internal, more penetrating. It's horror in homeopathic doses.' But he loved Murnau's **Nosferatu**, 'the most beautiful horror film', and owed something to the German director's technique: Expressionism is usually seen as a rejection of realism, but Murnau's Expressionism took real places and used them for Expressionist ends, through a powerful evocation of place and an obsessive attention to detail. These are central to Franju's films too, with the emptiness of the suburbs and the curious atmosphere of the surgical theatre providing unsettling backdrops to the story of *Eyes*, and an almost fetishistic attention paid to the paraphernalia of surgery.

At his cine club Franju showed many science films, which also influenced his style, peeling back with surgical dispassion the assumptions an audience brings to a film; their legacy can be most clearly felt in *Eyes* when Christiane's facial deterioration is displayed in its varying stages of decay. One of the films Franju showed was particularly memorable, and sheds further light on his ideas:

Dr Thierry de Martel's *Trepanation pour crise d'epilepsie Bravais-Jacksonnienne* . . . was an authentic horror film, twenty people were out flat, I've never seen anything so drastic. It was an atrocious film, but a beautiful and poetic one, because it was also realistic . . . plastic values, the macabre, and poetry, have never been sparked off in unison together with all the efficacy of realism and the beauty of surrealism, as, by pure chance, in a film in which no-one even wanted them . . .

But Franju's sympathy for the cold truths of science is tempered by humanism. His films never slip into sentimentality, but show a repeated evocation of purity and innocence, whether in the doves of *Judex* or *Eyes*, or in the person of Edith Scob, part bird, part child, who for Franju 'gives the unreal reality'. For the director the tenderness of his films is inseparable from the brutality of science: indeed the intensity of one encourages the growth of the other. His most violent films are the most tender, 'because the more tender you are the more you feel the violence, and it's in the face of violence that tenderness is most extreme'.

Sadly Franju's films are difficult to see today: the notoriety of *Eyes* has overshadowed his other work, which – ironically, considering his enthusiasm as a film archivist – has missed out on the archival mining that makes the work of many of his peers readily available.

CASTING: Franju used the same principals in most of his films, with Pierre Brasseur and Edith Scob particularly well favoured. Alida Valli also stars as the governess of the ballet school in Dario Argento's *Suspiria* (1977), as well as appearing in its follow-up, *Inferno* (1980), Mario Bava's distinctive *Lisa and the Devil* (1973), and a couple of trashy Euro-horror films: *Exorcist* rip-off *The Tempter/L'Anticristo* (Alberto De Martino, 1974) and *Killer Nun/Suor Omicidi* (Guilio Berruti, 1978).

PRODUCTION: Cinematographer Eugen Schüfftan, who had done the special visual effects on Fritz Lang's *Metropolis* (1926) and also worked on Franju's *La Tête Contre Les Murs* (1959), provided the icy black and white photography, fetishising the processes of surgery; he went on to win an Oscar for his work on *The Hustler* (Robert Rossen, 1961).

SOUNDTRACK: Maurice Jarre's soundtrack provides an effective counterpoint to Franju's images, with demented fairground music accompanying Alida Valli's angel of death as she patrols the streets in her 2 CV, and an echoing lilt providing a signature theme for Christiane.

Franju used Maurice Jarre as composer for almost all of his features. Jarre is still a prolific scorer, and has provided the soundtrack for everything from genre-tinged material like *Ghost* (Jerry Zucker, 1990) and *Jacob's Ladder* (Adrian Lyne, 1990) to major hits like *A Passage to India* (David Lean, 1984), *Fatal Attraction* (Adrian Lyne, 1987) and *Dead Poets Society* (Peter Weir, 1988).

'IT'S ONLY A MOVIE ... ONLY A MOVIE ...': For the US release the promoters vainly attempted to draw an arthouse crowd, using the following lines to promote the film:

Selected for special showings at the Edinburgh Film Festival

A ghastly elegance that suggests Tennessee Williams

Worthy of the great horror classics of our time

The punters, principally a drive-in crowd looking for monster movies, were unimpressed.

RELEASE: The producers hoped that Franju's film would find a welcoming audience in the UK, the home to Hammer and a long, rich tradition of the gothic and macabre. *Eyes* was duly presented at the Edinburgh Film Festival, where seven people fainted, and the film was greeted with outrage; Franju didn't help matters by saying that now he knew why Scotsmen wore skirts. The press in England were similarly scathing, focusing on the violence of the film as decontextualised from its poetry, although they disagreed over whether the film was too incompetent or too horrifying to find favour; the only reviewer to give the film a positive review in a national daily almost lost her job for breaking with such a vehement critical consensus.

Dilys Powell, reviewing the film in the *Sunday Times*, thought it 'deliberately revolting', the *Birmingham Evening Despatch* attacked it with the headline 'WHY did they let this film come in?' and *Monthly Film Bulletin* felt that:

When a director as distinguished as Georges Franju makes a horror film as fundamentally trite as *Les Yeux*, one cannot but feel tempted to search for symbols, an allegory, layers of interpretation. Unhappily, there is practically nothing in this inept work to offer any encouragement for doing so.

The film met a similar response in France: audiences were shocked, and Paris daily *L'Express* noted that at the notorious facelift scene 'the spectators dropped like flies'. The scandal that met the film was similar to that of Michael Powell's *Peeping Tom* a year later: nobody could understand why a highly respected filmmaker should sully his hands with such a trashy genre. Many French critical appreciations of Franju's work still either ignore the film or gloss over it quickly, despite the fact that it eclipsed the director's other films commercially; and some French critics, such as *Cahiers du Cinema*'s Michel Delahaye, could only appreciate *Eyes* by reconfiguring it as film noir.

If critics were shocked, artists were more receptive towards Franju's vision. Jean Cocteau praised the film – 'The more you touch on mystery, the more important it is to be realistic . . . The ancestors of this film live in the Germany of the great cinematic epoch of *Nosferatu*' – and Franju went on to adapt his *Thomas L'Imposteur* in 1964.

For its inglorious US release, *Eyes* was trimmed of the facelift, dubbed and retitled *The Horror Chamber of Dr Faustus*, then put on a double bill with shlocky Japanese mutant romp *The Manster* (George P Breakston and Kenneth G Crane, 1962). But most audiences were disappointed by the film's pace, and the film was not a commercial success, although some viewers enjoyed it; Pauline Kael was shocked to find a packed cinema 'pleased and excited by the most revolting and obsessive images'.

CRITICAL EYE: 'Even dubbed, *Eyes* . . . is perhaps the most austerely elegant horror film ever made . . . It's a symbolist attack on science and the ethics of medicine, and though I thought this attack as simple-minded in its way as the usual young poet's denunciation of war or commerce, it is in some peculiar way a classic of horror . . . even though I thought its intellectual pretensions silly, I couldn't shake off the exquisite, dread images.'

Kael was one of the first critics to give the film a favourable review, and her praise – tempered as it is – was eventually shared by many critics in the UK and US. In the wake of Franju's other films, which were easier to appreciate critically, and due to the enthusiasm of a new wave of younger critics, *Eyes* was quickly rehabilitated, and became a darling of some sectors of the critical community.

But Kael's view of the film as a simple-minded 'attack on science and the ethics of medicine' is in itself rather simple-minded; perhaps she was put off by the 'excited' audience. There

71

is an attack on science and medicine in the film, but it isn't the traditional conservative horror attack, a Frankenstein-style punishment for overreaching and attempting to dethrone God; it's more of an attack on the dehumanised callousness of science, a drive which disregards the wishes of everyone else for its own ends. But Dr Genessier isn't like this simply because he is a doctor or scientist; it comes from his strong will to power, which caused his crash in the first place, and it is this sense, threatened by failure, that leads him to murder.

Critic Raymond Durgnat has argued that the conservatism of the family is also here under attack. This idea has a stronger resonance in France than it would, for instance, in England: in Franju's native country the cult of the family has long had right-wing connotations, and in this analysis Christiane, 'ravaged by Genessier's familial egoism ... can oppose to it, finally, only her sense of obligation to utter strangers, a sense of indiscriminate solidarity which here becomes a left-wing attitude'.

Other critics have seen Genessier's activities as recalling Nazi concentration-camp experiments – the indulgence of sadism under the mantle of dispassionate science – and point to his use of the term 'ton vrai visage' (a phrase used by French Nazi sympathisers during the Occupation to describe French racial and national purity) as an indication of the film's political subtext. It has also been seen as an indictment of France's treatment of its colonies, with Genessier as colonial oppressor, exploiting his poor, homeless charges in an attempt to maintain a surface beauty that can end only in despair; or as a religious allegory, with Genessier recalling a megalomaniac God, Christiane as the suffering child who is finally able to sacrifice herself through a selfless act and Louise as the dark angel, tempting innocents towards a certain death.

But such readings serve more as elaborate critical baubles than inspired readings of the film, whose central themes are looking and appearances. Christiane's limpid pools aren't the only eyes without faces here: the corpse found at the start, Genessier and Louise in their surgical masks, and Edna's bandaged face and wild eyes all confirm the primacy of the gaze in the film, which moves from one display to the next with teasing build-ups – Genessier climbs endless flights of stairs before the viewer first sees Christiane. And the theme of looking is grounded so deeply in the film that Louise even gives a guilty start when a plane passes overhead as she and Genessier dispose of a body, as though scared that she is being watched.

Ironically, for a film so concerned with appearances, Christiane's flayed face is only seen briefly, and even then it is so blurred that it's impossible to make out much detail. But elsewhere the film's focus on appearances give it a startlingly tactile quality: Christiane complains about the reflective surfaces in which she can still see her face, and the camera lingers lovingly on the textures of fibrous bandages, sheer silk, shiny PVC or the sweat beading on Genessier's brow.

Such an obsessive concern with surfaces gives the film a fetishistic sheen, and while there is little overt sexual content in the film, many of the details seem imbued with a perverse eroticism: Christiane's white satin housecoat, Louise's shiny black raincoat, the loving attention to detail given to the surgical procedures, and Louise's choker, which recalls the studded collars of the dogs and reminds the viewer that both are slaves to Genessier's desires.

Of course, appearances also drive the plot itself: Genessier wants to give his daughter a new face, Louise will kill for the man who rescued her own features, Edna commits suicide rather than live without a face, and Paulette is more worried that her head will be shaved than she is about the 'severe pain' she claims has brought her to the clinic.

At the start of the film Genessier gives a presentation in which he claims that 'man's greatest new hope is the recapture of physical youth', and he is applauded by a cabal of overdressed elderly women: the obsession with appearances is nothing but vanity. Franju's target here seems to be specifically the vanity behind cinema, and he shows the rottenness and fakery that lie behind the screen's obsession with beautiful faces: plastic surgery had been a staple of the Hollywood dream factory since the early 1930s, and producers and casting directors had long been keen to have their starlets' faces surgically rearranged to fit standardised models of glamour by the time Franju's film was made.

Some critics have accused the film of pessimism, which misses its rich vein of black humour. When Christiane, having been given what appears to be a successful facelift, asks how she can re-enter society, her father tells her he will arrange everything, and encourages her to smile – 'Smile, smile! But not too much' – the doctor quickly replacing the parent as he worries about her graft. When the police discuss the open wound of a face on the corpse found at the start, one interrupts 'And the rats – don't forget about the rats!'; and Genessier's 'how many fingers?' test of a young boy is just as darkly comic.

Some of these scenes resemble outtakes from an unintentionally humorous grade-Z movie like *Doctor of Doom* (René Cardona, 1963), and images like Christiane's calming of Genessier's savage dogs seem similarly almost unbearably trite: but the film's relationship to crass and generic exploitation fare is an essential part of its power. The formulaic story allows Franju to focus on his true interests, screening startling images that stay in the mind long after the complex characterisation and plots of other films have faded away.

INDUSTRY IMPACT: *Eyes*, which was widely seen and highly influential, opened the floodgates to an increasingly wild style of Euro-horror that mixed sex, horror and poetic imagery with barely comprehensible plots through the 60s and 70s. The explosion of hardcore in the mid-70s effectively killed off this mutant strain of Eurotrash, but until then the boundaries between the sex and horror genres became increasingly blurred; a number of filmmakers who, like Franju, were enamoured of Feuillade and early film classics and keen to pursue their own idiosyncratic visions, churned out a seemingly inexhaustible supply of low- to no-budget quickies.

One of the filmmakers most enthusiastic about following Franju's vision of surgery and sex, albeit in an altogether more debased mode, was Jess Franco. Franco's first major film, *The Awful Dr Orlof/Gritos en la Noche* (1961) took its plot wholesale from Franju's film, and kickstarted the Spanish horror film industry, soon to bring the world such delights as Paul Naschy's werewolf cycle, Jorge Grau's *The Living Dead at Manchester Morgue/No profanar el sueño de los muertos* (1974) and Amando de Ossorio's Blind Dead series.

Franco took the sexual hints of Franju's film and the coy titillation of Hammer product and made the sex explicit; he returned to Franju's theme repeatedly over his career, which encompassed over 150 films and almost as many pseudonyms, and eventually directed a straight remake of *Eyes* with *Faceless* (1988), his biggest-budget film to date.

With so many films, it's hardly surprising that Franco's work runs the gamut of exploitation themes: from women in prison

(*Ilsa, the Wicked Warden*, 1977) and vampire films (*Dracula vs Frankenstein*, 1972) to obsessively filmed girl-on-girl action. Such a prolific output is predictably variable, and while Franco's best films are characterised by a wild energy, moments of uncanny dream logic and a powerful sense of verve, many are torturously slow and painful to watch.

Another low-budget European filmmaker working in the erotic horror field of the 60s and 70s was Jean Rollin, whose dreamlike vampire films, occasionally entirely improvised, at their best – *Requiem for a Vampire/Requiem pour un Vampire* (1971), *Fascination* (1979) and *The Living Dead Girl/La Morte Vivante* (1982) – reach a dizzy pitch of unearthly intensity.

The theme of facial skin grafts and demented plastic surgeons remained a horror staple immediately after the release of *Eyes*, with films like *Circus of Horrors* (Sidney Hayers, 1960) a step back from the savage beauty of Franju's film or the psycho-sexual dynamics of its peer *Peeping Tom* (1960). More recently, the theme has been explored in films as diverse as *Batman* (Tim Burton, 1989), *Face/Off* (John Woo, 1997) and *Suture* (Scott McGhee and David Siegel, 1993), while Genessier's use of his daughter as a human guinea pig has echoes in the disreputable Italian Nazi exploitation cycle, with films like *SS Experiment Camp* (Sergio Garrone, 1976) resisting any attempts to be rehabilitated as 70s cinetrash chic.

Hospitals and clinics have provided the settings for *Horror Hospital* (Anthony Balch, 1973), *Visiting Hours* (Jean-Claude Lord, 1982), *X-Ray* (Boaz Davidson, 1983), *Flatliners* (Joel Schumacher, 1990) and *Dr Giggles* (Manny Coto, 1992), while Brian Yuzna's *The Dentist* (1996) and *The Dentist 2* (1998), recall Jack Nicholson's demented pain-freak dentist from Roger Corman's *The Little Shop of Horrors* (1960). Innovative organ transplants are also still the source of horror they were at the time of *Mad Love*, with the terrors of *The Eye/Jian gui* (Oxide Pang Chun and Danny Pang, 2002) following a radical eye transplant.

David Cronenberg has made surgical fears something of a stock-in-trade. *Rabid* (1977) features a gory skin transplant early on, as Dr Hal Keloid attempts to graft morphogenetically neutral tissue onto Rose's (Marilyn Chambers) side following a motorbike accident. But after the experiment Rose can feed only on blood, which she absorbs through a penile appendage in her armpit; and her victims contract a rabies-like disease which spreads rapidly through Montreal.

The casting of porn star Marilyn Chambers in this typically apocalyptic 70s genre offering, which owes a clear debt to **Night of the Living Dead**, is not only commercially savvy but also feeds back into the story. The attacks on her victims are explicitly sexualised, and the film is constructed around a series of set-pieces resembling nothing so much as porno set-ups – Rose visits an adult cinema, Rose meets another girl in a Jacuzzi, and so on. If her own forays for food are parodic of porn staples, her victims' attacks are hilarious explosions of antisocial behaviour in inappropriate situations: one of the most shocking comes when an infected Keloid tells a nurse that 'I need something to cut with' during surgery, then proceeds to snip the end off her finger with the scissors she supplies.

The director's *Dead Ringers* (1988) also features unorthodox surgical techniques: loosely based on the real-life story of the identical Marcus twins, New York gynaecologists found dead in their apartment, the film continues the foray into claustrophobic chamber pieces that Cronenberg began in **The Fly**. Jeremy Irons plays Beverly and Elliott Mantle, subtly differentiated gynaecologists who share everything from their work to their women. Their relationship is threatened when they have an affair with an actress, Claire Niveau (Genevieve Bujold), with whom Beverly falls in love. Introduced by her to the recreational use of prescription drugs, he descends into addiction and madness, finally developing a series of tools for operating on mutant women that he uses in his surgery; Elliott's efforts to synchronise with him lead to an increased lack of differentiation between the twins, and ultimately to their inevitable death.

Here gynaecology is, as plastic surgery is for Genessier, a means of relating to, or rather controlling, women, and, again like Genessier, Beverly's unusual experiments bear little relation to the Hippocratic Oath. The surgical procedures are if anything more stylised than in Franju's film, a mixture of Catholic and medieval imagery that has the surgeons in scarlet robes and Beverly's hospital bed shrouded and womb-like in the centre of a large room. While the film doesn't feature any images as show-stopping as the facelift in *Eyes*, Beverly's drug-addled attempt to use his specially designed tools on a patient, surrounded by increasingly concerned professionals, is one of the most concise expressions of surgical unease ever filmed.

FINAL WORD: Franju's film took plot elements familiar to horror fans – the obsessed doctor, beautiful female victims, disfigurement, skin grafts and the mechanics of surgery – and recombined them to make a film limned with unremitting grisliness, poetry and sexual energy.

The formulaic nature of the plot freed Franju from worrying about narrative complexity and allowed him to focus instead on a succession of startlingly evocative images: *Eyes* demonstrates not only Franju's dictum that the poetic is found most often where it is least expected, but also the paradoxical freedom offered by genre horror, in which certain images and scenarios take on semi-mythic qualities that work their irrational magic on the viewer's mind.

The importance of the unflinching gaze in *Eyes* only helped to revitalise this decadent tradition of looking, of a cinema less concerned with plot and narrative than with pure imagery, that had been neglected in Hollywood's obsession with narrative coherence. Sex and surgery may be one of horror's most popular – and perverted – themes, but nobody else would do it quite as well as Franju.

HORROR HITS THE MAINSTREAM

Psycho (1960)

'We All Get Crazy Sometimes'

USA, Shamley Productions/Paramount, b/w, 109 mins

Directed and Produced by Alfred Hitchcock
Screenplay: Joseph Stefano, based on a novel by Robert Bloch
Director of Photography: John L Russell, ASC
Art Direction: Joseph Hurley and Robert Clatworthy
Title Design: Saul Bass
Editor: George Tomasini, ACE
Special Effects: Clarence Champagne
Sound Recording: Waldon O Watson and William Russell
Assistant Director: Hilton A Green
Pictorial Consultant: Saul Bass
Music: Bernard Herrmann

CAST: Anthony Perkins (*Norman Bates*), Vera Miles (*Lila Crane*), John Gavin (*Sam Loomis*), Martin Balsam (*Milton Arbogast*), John McIntire (*Sheriff Chambers*), Simon Oakland (*Dr Richmond*), Vaughn Taylor (*Mr Lowery*), Frank Albertson (*Cassidy*), Lurene Tuttle (*Mrs Chambers*), Pat Hitchcock (*Caroline*),

John Anderson (*'California Charlie'*), Mort Mills (*Highway Patrolman*), Janet Leigh (*Marion Crane*)

SYNOPSIS: Marion Crane prepares to return to work after a tryst with Sam Loomis in a Phoenix hotel room; they want to start a new life together, but Sam is still paying his dead father's debts, as well as alimony to his ex-wife.

At the real-estate office where she works, Marion is asked to deposit Mr Cassidy's $40,000 cash in the bank. She tells her colleague that she'll go straight home after the bank, but doesn't visit the bank at all. Instead she packs and drives off to Fairvale, where Sam lives. On her way out of town she is spotted by Mr Lowery, her boss.

She spends the night by the roadside, and is woken up by a traffic policeman, who asks to see her ID. Worried by his attention, she part-exchanges her car at a used car dealership, but the policeman sees her.

Later on she finds it difficult to drive in the rain, and when she sees a motel sign she pulls in. She signs in using a false name, and the proprietor, Norman Bates, offers to share a meal with her. She hears Norman's mother, who lives with him in the house behind the motel, berating him for spending time with a strange woman. As they eat, Marion tells him she has made a mistake and plans to set it right.

She undresses for a shower; Norman watches through a peephole. Suddenly she is stabbed to death. Norman finds the body and disposes of it, along with the car and the undiscovered $40,000, in the swamp behind the motel.

Marion's sister Lila visits Sam and asks him if he knows where Marion is. He doesn't; private detective Milton Arbogast, who has been hired by Cassidy, is also interested. The police have not been involved: Cassidy just wants his money back.

Arbogast visits the motels along Marion's route to Fairvale, and finds that she was staying at the Bates Motel. He tells Sam and Lila he plans to go back there, but when he does he is killed. Lila and Sam go to the sheriff, but he is convinced nothing is wrong, so they go to the motel themselves. In one of the bathrooms they find a slip of paper with Marion's calculations on it, and Sam distracts Norman while Lila investigates the house.

There she finds Norman's mother – a dessicated corpse – and is attacked by Norman in his mother's clothes. Sam saves her. A psychiatrist explains that Norman had poisoned his mother and her lover after becoming jealous of their relationship, and had been so traumatised by guilt that a separate persona, 'Mother', periodically took over. Norman has now been fully absorbed by his mother persona.

ORIGINS AND INSPIRATION: Everyone in Ed Gein's home town of Plainfield, Wisconsin, thought the old man a harmless eccentric until the eviscerated body of a local woman was found strung up in his barn like a deer in 1957. A look around Gein's house revealed an appalling collection of artefacts, ranging from a skull used as a soup bowl to human body parts in the freezer, a skin vest with breasts intact and a selection of rouged and made-up faces hanging on nails. Gein had progressed from robbing graves, initially restricting himself to those around his mother's burial place, to killing, and was implicated in the deaths of up to ten women, although he was convicted of killing only two. He was found criminally insane.

The local community was devastated: how could they not have known what Gein was up to? The press avoided covering the grislier findings, but the rumour mill worked overtime, and Gein quickly became one of America's most fabled bogeymen.

One person who could not shake off his fascination with the killings was novelist Robert Bloch, who was captivated by the idea of such horrors continuing unnoticed in a small town; he'd been interested in writing a novel based on Freudian ideas for some time, and slowly the story of *Psycho* began to form.

Bloch's novel contains most of the elements that would later be credited as the film's innovations – the early death of Mary Crane in the shower, the disposal of her body and car in the swamp, the shock ending – but his Norman Bates was an older man, envisaged by Bloch as being played by Rod Steiger rather than Anthony Perkins.

Psycho was considered quirky enough for a film script, but was rejected by some studios: a Paramount script reader thought it 'too repulsive for films'. Bloch eventually sold the film rights for $9,000, of which he saw $5,000 once his agent's fee and taxes had been taken care of. It was only after he'd accepted the deal that he discovered who had bought the rights: Alfred Hitchcock.

Hitchcock had recently completed *North by Northwest* (1959), a slick star vehicle, and was said to be so scared of slipping into a rut that he had asked his script readers to look for a typically un-Hitchcock idea. Stories vary as to why, of these, the director chose *Psycho*. The most mundane explanation is that he had a commitment to Paramount to make a film, and that *Psycho*, a small project, would fulfil it; the director's last two projects had failed to get off the ground, and Bloch's novel would be an easy way for him to get back into his stride.

He also resented paying large salaries for big-name stars, and had been checking the box-office returns for low-budget shockers from studios like AIP and Hammer: a recent big-budget project of his, *Vertigo* (1958), had been panned by critics and public alike, and he wanted to prove that he could make a successful film on a low budget. He had grown critical of his 'glossy Technicolor baubles', and recognised that cinema audiences wanted something grittier, more adult.

There was the issue of competitors, too: home-grown talent like William Castle, a low-rent master of suspense and the marketing gimmick whose *Macabre* (1958) and *House on Haunted Hill* (1959) had been pulling in the punters; and Henri-Georges Clouzot, whose *Diabolique/Les Diaboliques* (1955) proved profoundly influential on both Castle and Hitchcock (see **ORIGINS AND INSPIRATION, Eyes Without a Face**).

The similarities between *Psycho* and Clouzot's film are legion. Both are shot in black and white; both share a sordid milieu of dead-end jobs and rented rooms; the principal shocks in both films occur in bathrooms; both have a second act in which a grubby detective harasses the lead characters; and both rely on a twist ending.

Hitchcock even took Clouzot's publicity campaign: French newspaper ads had discouraged viewers from missing the beginning of *Les Diaboliques*, while cinema doors were closed at the start of each screening, and the end titles requested viewers: 'Don't be diabolical yourself. Don't spoil the ending for your friends by telling them what you've just seen. On their behalf – thank you!' The techniques were emulated for the film's American release.

Paramount were unimpressed by Hitchcock's idea, and refused to finance it. The director decided to put up the money himself, waiving his director's fee for 60 per cent ownership of the film on the condition that Paramount distributed it. The studio reluctantly agreed, but stressed that there would be no Technicolor for the film, nor any big-name stars, which fitted the director's aims perfectly.

Screenwriter James P Cavanagh was hired but dismissed after an unsuccessful first draft; Joseph Stefano, a relative novice to film, was then taken on after impressing the director with his insistence on making Mary Crane the story's principal character. But the name had to be changed: studio researchers found two Mary Cranes in the Phoenix phone book, and Mary duly became Marion.

Production designers Joseph Hurley and Robert Clatworthy were hired, and developed the look of the Bates Motel and the old dark house behind it. The architectural style has been referred to as 'California Gothic', and is according to the director fairly common in North California, as well as featuring in Edward Hopper's painting *House by the Railroad*; but the house also bears a passing resemblance to the Addams Family property from Charles Addams's *New Yorker* cartoons.

The look and feel of Phoenix and the route to Fairvale were meticulously researched, with scouts reporting back to the director about exactly what people – from used-car dealers to real-estate secretaries – wore and looked like; this verisimilitude was reflected in Leigh's clothes and hair for the film, with her dresses bought from cheap local shops and the star required to do her hair herself, as Crane would have done.

DIRECTOR: Hitchcock is one of the few directors to achieve near-universal name recognition among Western audiences. His view of filmmaking as an industry rather than an art form, and his insistence that his first duty was to entertain the audience, meant that his films were immensely popular with the general public before he received the critical acclaim he enjoys today. The French *Cahiers du Cinéma* critics, many of whom went on to become filmmakers themselves, were among the first to consider Hitchcock a master of the form, rather than just the popular entertainer he was seen as in the Anglophone critical community. Truffaut's book of interviews with Hitchcock, published in 1966, cemented his position as darling of the *Cahiers* crowd, and since then he has become one of the postwar period's most acclaimed directors.

Hitchcock's films are characterised by a repetition of certain themes and techniques. His characters tend to be 'normal', ordinary people drawn into extraordinary circumstances, with whom an audience can easily empathise: this, we feel, could easily happen to us. Similarly, traumatic acts can occur anywhere, including the most mundane settings; and the director's villains are often likeable, sympathetic characters, with whom the audience can also empathise even as they carry out their grim work.

The director famously developed the idea of the 'MacGuffin' – a device that sets the plot in motion and keeps it going. The MacGuffin is the characters' chief concern, while our concern is for their safety. *Psycho*'s MacGuffin is the \$40,000 stolen by Marion Crane.

The tension in Hitchcock's films is often leavened by moments of black humour, and the director delighted in appearing in each of his features: the keen-eyed viewer will spot him as a man wearing a Stetson and standing on the kerb as Marion returns to the office in *Psycho*.

Psycho was the director's 47th film, and its overwhelming success seems to have bewildered him. He was said to have been hurt by the way audiences embraced this small film when more personal projects like *Vertigo* had failed at the box office, and even considered employing a market-research firm to discover the film's secret, although he balked at the cost. The film revitalised his career, but also left him uncertain what to do next.

It took three years before the director's next feature, an adaptation of Daphne du Maurier's *The Birds* (1963), was released. The film, another 'offbeat shocker', was not nearly so successful as *Psycho*, although it features a number of striking images and was itself highly influential: its siege sequence informs films from **Night of the Living Dead** to *Straw Dogs* (Sam Peckinpah, 1971), and the revolt of nature theme kept audiences out of the water in *Jaws* (Steven Spielberg, 1975), as well as playing on fears of insects (*The Swarm*, Irwin Allen, 1978), rats (*Willard*, Daniel Mann, 1970), worms (*Squirm*, Jeff Lieberman, 1976), *Frogs* (George McCowan, 1972), cats (*The Uncanny*, Denis Héroux, 1977) and *Dogs* (Burt Brinckerhoff, 1976).

The director then returned to more traditionally Hitchcockian fare. He was now working with Universal, but it was an unhappy relationship; he had far from the same amount of creative control he'd enjoyed previously, and some of his later films are pale shadows of his former work. Ironically, as his new films failed to impress critics or audiences, *Psycho*'s status grew and grew, and it was routinely placed on critics' top ten lists.

One of his better late films was a return to *Psycho* territory: *Frenzy* (1972) was based on the exploits of real-life murderer Neville Heath, and shows a seedy London bristling with drunks, down-and-outs and psycho-sexual murders. The strangulations here are far more brutal than anything in *Psycho*, and once again the film's set-piece, in which the murderer breaks a dead victim's fingers in an attempt to retrieve a tie pin while in the back of a lorry loaded with potatoes, encourages the audience to identify with a killer.

CASTING: Hitchcock's dismissive attitude towards his actors, who he once referred to as 'cattle', is well documented. He did not as a rule give actors much room to interpret parts: his films were so well prepared before he started shooting that he knew exactly what he wanted them to do, and he may also have resented the way they drew attention away from the main star of his films – the director himself.

Anthony Perkins was the first actor to be hired for *Psycho*, and took the part before even reading the script. He was 27, and already being groomed as a teen idol; taking the part of a transvestite murderer was a bold move, but he was convinced it would make his career. Unusually, the director welcomed Perkins' suggestions for dialogue and characterisation for Bates, allowing him freer rein than most of the other actors; he also allowed him to attend rehearsals in New York for a play during the shooting of the shower sequence, keen to spare the actor, considered 'excessively shy around women', any embarrassment.

Psycho proved both blessing and curse for Perkins, whose Hollywood career went into permanent decline after the film, although he was still given worthwhile parts in Europe; he reprised the role three times, and even directed *Psycho 3* (1986), as well as starring in more lurid psycho-killer films like *Pretty Poison* (Noel Black, 1968), *Crimes of Passion* (Ken Russell, 1984) and *Edge of Sanity* (Gérard Kikoïne, 1989). As far as he was concerned, as he claimed late in his career, 'I am Norman Bates.'

For the part of Marion Crane, Eva Marie Saint (*North by Northwest*), Hope Lange and even Lana Turner were among the actresses considered, before Janet Leigh got the part. Leigh was a wholesome star compared to Turner, with a heavily publicised marriage to 50s pin-up Tony Curtis, making her lingerie shots and the shower sequence even more shocking for contemporary viewers. Leigh, mother of scream queen Jamie Lee Curtis (see **CASTING, Halloween**), co-starred with her daughter in John Carpenter's *The Fog* (1980) and *Halloween H2O* (Steve Miner, 1998).

For Lila Crane Hitchcock chose Vera Miles, whom he had attempted to groom as a new Grace Kelly until her independent streak had made him give up in despair. Having recently had her head shaved for *Five Branded Women* (Martin Ritt, 1960), she was given an unflattering wig to wear. Sam Loomis was played by John Gavin, a bland Universal contract player who the director privately referred to as 'the stiff' following the lack of erotic tension between Gavin and Leigh; a slight resemblance between Gavin and Perkins was exaggerated in the film through lighting and the use of profile shots of each actor. The part of Caroline, Marion's office colleague, is played by Patricia Hitchcock, the director's daughter.

Hitchcock mischievously announced to the press that Judith Anderson and Helen Hayes were under consideration to play Mrs Bates, and was promptly deluged by requests from actresses keen to play the part. Norman's mother – voice and body – ended up being played by a number of people, with the voices of two women and one man spliced together to give her importunate whines an uncanny edge.

PRODUCTION: *Psycho* had more in common with the TV series *Alfred Hitchcock Presents* than the director's cinema career: the look would be very similar to an episode of the series, and Hitchcock would use most of his TV crew to make the film, although he also brought on board George Tomasini, his film editor, Bernard Herrmann for the music and Saul Bass for the title sequence and storyboards for the murders of Marion and Arbogast.

The cast and crew were sworn to secrecy over the film, which was referred to as 'Wimpy' in all in-house communication, and many of the cast members were unaware of the film's ending, having been given only those parts of the script containing their dialogue. As Paramount refused to allow the film to be shot on one of their lots, Hitchcock used a Universal-International studio lot, and maintained a closed set most of the time; studio publicists were barred from the set, and had to make do with images fed to them by the director, including one of him sitting in a chair marked 'Mrs Bates'.

The shooting was scheduled to last 30 days, with the director having worked the shots out meticulously beforehand. 50mm lenses were used, which on the 35mm cameras of the day gave the closest approximation to human vision available, grounding the theme of voyeurism in the film at the most basic level.

Of the shooting time, a week was given to the shower sequence – 70 camera set-ups for 45 seconds of footage – in which the staccato editing of a series of relatively benign shots gives the impression of savage violence. The film would feature a couple of other taboo-breakers too – Leigh in her lingerie, for instance, and the shot of a toilet flushing, an act previously unseen in mainstream Hollywood cinema – but nothing would have prepared audiences for the devastating shock of the shower murder.

Leigh wore moleskin covers to cover her nudity while shooting, and a body double was also used, although in the final edit she only appears when Norman rolls up the body in a plastic sheet. According to Leigh, the director himself wielded the knife, which had a retractable blade, as he knew exactly where he wanted it to go. The knife is never actually seen penetrating flesh, although the suggestion is so strong that some viewers swore they had seen a stabbing, and rumours of a prosthetic torso persist to this day.

The sequence was not only shocking but titillating. When the initial cut was sent to the MPAA (Motion Picture Association of America), they demanded that the nudity be removed from the sequence: Hitchcock simply repackaged the film and sent it back, whereupon it was accepted. There is also some controversy over who actually shot the sequence: Saul Bass, who storyboarded it, credits himself with having shot it as well, although Hitchcock denied such claims, and other cast and crew members support the director's authorship of the scene.

The director played up the fact that the film had essentially two acts, and kept the actors for each in separate camps. He viewed Lila and Sam as 'mere figures' to tidy up the loose ends of the mystery, rather than interesting characters in their own right: our sympathies lie with Marion and then with Norman, who is, even on repeat viewings, a sympathetic character. As ever, the director enjoyed manipulating the audience to make it empathise with a killer: when Marion's car is sinking in the swamp but hits a snag, our hearts stop for Norman.

The film finally wrapped on 1 February 1960, nine days over schedule: the director had had flu, which had slowed proceedings down. The crew remained on the lot to shoot three trailers.

The director was uncertain about the ending of the film, which has a skull superimposed over Perkins' face: it was eventually printed and distributed in two versions, one with the skull and one without. In fact he appears to have been uncertain that the film was fit for theatrical distribution at all; according to Bernard Herrmann he briefly considered editing it down for an episode of *Alfred Hitchcock Presents*.

SOUNDTRACK: Bernard Herrmann's shrieking score wasn't what the director initially had in mind for the film. He'd been toying with the idea of having a minimal soundtrack, with silence for scenes such as the shower murder; he would later develop the idea for *The Birds*, which has no conventional score at all. But when Herrmann, who had worked with Hitchcock on the director's last five films, suggested a score solely for strings, the director bit. Herrmann's aim was to match the director's mono-chrome visuals: 'In using only strings, I felt that I was able to complement the black-and-white photography of the film with a black-and-white sound.'

Hitchcock was most impressed by Herrmann's 'screaming violins', and did the unheard-of, for this parsimonious director: he doubled the composer's salary. The impact of the score, among Herrmann's most memorable, is immeasurable, with the dissonant noises keeping the audience's nerves on edge throughout the film, and its influence can be felt everywhere from Pino Donaggio's violin stings in *Carrie* (Brian de Palma, 1976) to Howard Shore's early Cronenberg soundtracks.

For the sound of the shower stabbing, Hitchcock asked his researchers to experiment with a selection of melons, and finally settled on a casaba as having the right kind of fleshy tone.

'IT'S ONLY A MOVIE ... ONLY A MOVIE ...': Hitchcock bought the rights to the title design of *Psycho*'s book cover, which used a cracked lettering that would feature heavily on posters for the film. The posters also featured shots of Leigh in her lingerie – the first explicitly suggestive shots of a star to advertise a mainstream Hollywood film – and Vera Miles and Anthony Perkins stifling screams.

There were no advance screenings for critics, and the film was booked nationally into thousands of cinemas following its pre-release engagement in two New York cinemas: if word of mouth was to spoil the shock ending, or bad reviews to put audiences off, Hitchcock wanted as many takings first as possible.

The advertisements for the film stressed that 'No one . . . BUT NO ONE . . . will be admitted to the theater after the start of each performance of Psycho'. A similar message had been used for some of the director's other films, but while there it was purely advisory, this time it was a contractual prerequisite for any exhibitor showing the film.

At the time it was normal for people to wander in and out of cinemas at will, regardless of a feature's starting time, and *Psycho* has been recognised as an important film in 'training' audiences to behave as they do today. The director was able to turn this inconvenience into a powerful marketing gimmick, advising cinema owners to hire security guards to keep audiences in line.

Of the three trailers, one reinforced the policy that nobody should be admitted after the start of the film, another featured the director saying 'Please don't tell the ending. It's the only one we have', and the third had Hitchcock, a household figure from his introductions to *Alfred Hitchcock Presents,* taking the viewer on a guided tour around the Bates house; it gave enough details of the plot to spur the viewer's interest, and showed a woman – who turned out to be Vera Miles, not Janet Leigh – screaming in a shower stall. No actual footage from the film features in the trailers.

RELEASE: Nobody was prepared for just how successful *Psycho* was. The film shattered attendance records everywhere it was shown, with well-publicised faintings and walk-outs adding to the furore surrounding its release; and crucially, audiences weren't giving away the ending.

Paramount, having expected the director's grubby little film to bomb, were amazed, and pumped money into promoting it. Hitchcock, who would usually move on to his next project fairly promptly, carried on promoting the film around the world; after having made at least one film almost every year since the start of his career in 1927, it took three years before his next film came out.

Audiences screamed so loudly during and after the shower sequence that the director asked for prints to be recalled so that the sound could be remixed to take into account their response; Paramount refused. Audiences also laughed, just as loudly, with some viewers treating the film as a particularly sadistic comedy. There are undoubtedly moments of black humour, with lines like 'Mother's not herself today' anticipating the quips of later screen killers such as *A Nightmare on Elm Street*'s (Wes Craven, 1984) Freddy Krueger. But according to Anthony Perkins, the response confused the director, who was 'confused, at first, incredulous second, and despondent third'.

The director's despondent mood must surely have been lifted by the film's box-office takings: $9.5 million from its first 13,000 cinema engagements, and an international gross of $6 million over the same period, earning the director $15 million personally from the first year of its release. Only *Ben Hur* (William Wyler, 1959) had made more money in the USA, and *Psycho* had been made for a fraction of the cost.

As well as the predictable talk from pulpit and psychiatrist's office of banning the film, *Psycho* was also allegedly cited by two murderers as having influenced them: 19-year-old Leroy Pinkowski, who stabbed a 14-year-old to death, and 29-year-old Henry Adolph Busch, who murdered three elderly women. The director was dismissive of such reports, maintaining that he was a chronicler rather than a shaper of human behaviour.

He gave similarly short shrift to members of the public who claimed that they had been so traumatised by the shower sequence that they were now unable to take showers: to one man who protested that his daughter now suffered from this phobia, Hitchcock suggested that she be dry cleaned.

The film was nominated for four Oscars: Best Director, Best Supporting Actress (Janet Leigh), Cinematography (John Russell) and Art Direction (Robert Clatworthy and Joseph Hurley); it won none. This may have been as much due to Hitchcock's refusal to play the industry game as for any other reason, and the director sent a message to Anthony Perkins after the actor failed to secure even a nomination: 'I am ashamed of your fellow actors.'

While *Psycho* has since been critically acclaimed – in an American Film Institute poll in 2001 it was voted the greatest thriller of all time – at the time most critics were horrified. The poor reviews may have come in part from critics' resentment at having to watch the film with the general public; the reviewer for *Time* was convinced he'd seen 'one of the messiest, most nauseating murders ever filmed', while the *New York Times'* Bosley Crowther described the film as 'A blot on an honorable career'.

But Crowther was among many critics to quickly revise his position, ranking the film as one of the ten best released in 1960; and other American critics, such as Andrew Sarris, writing in the *Village Voice*, liked it from the start, considering it 'the first American movie since *Touch of Evil* to stand in the same creative rank as the great European films'.

Critics in the UK, where two scenes were cut – one of Norman washing blood off his hands and six frames of Mother attacking Arbogast – were scathing, and it took the French critics to give the film the acclaim it deserved on its European release; a review in *Cahiers du Cinéma* maintained that 'Every scene is a lesson in direction by its precision, its sharpness, its efficacy, but also its beauty.'

CRITICAL EYE: Since its release *Psycho* has been dissected minutely and endlessly, with several books and countless essays devoted to its study. Critical responses tend to fall into two camps, with the film viewed as either radical or reactionary: critical of patriarchy or deeply misogynistic. Robin Wood's influential studies take the former view: for him horror is a potentially radical genre whose 'true subject is the struggle for recognition of all that our civilization represses or oppresses', and *Psycho* marks a break with horror tradition by keeping the repressed in the family, the fundamental institution of American life, rather than displacing it onto alien forms. Wood argues that the film redefines horror as both American and familial, as well as conferring 'on the horror film something of the dignity that *Stagecoach* conferred on the western': horror was now a semi-respectable genre, a valuable area of study.

Barbara Creed is among the critics contesting Wood's position. For her the Bates family is not normal: here, crucially, the father is absent, and the mother overbearing, and the film reaffirms rather than criticises the patriarchal family. For Creed the film hinges on patriarchal fears of women in general, and of the mother in particular: in the absence of a father, the mother is not kept in her 'proper' place, and Norman is prevented from performing the separation from her essential to entry into patriarchal culture. The patriarchal family is seen as a model of health and normality, while a dominant mother is dangerous and abnormal.

Peter Biskind takes a similar tack in *Seeing is Believing: How Hollywood Taught Us to Stop Worrying and Love the Fifties*. For him *Psycho* is a deeply reactionary film, attacking new models of masculinity and femininity: Norman is a parody of Dr Spock's ideal of the sensitive man, his feminine identification presented as pathological and dangerous. The film also attacks strong women: Marion's theft of the money is a threat to patriarchal authority, for which she must be punished.

But Hitchcock's attitude to gender is both fluid and ambiguous, which is what allows *Psycho* to support such disparate readings. Mrs Bates – at least as Norman remembers her – is hardly a model of Spock rearing: rather than a sensitive liberal, she is a tyrannical conservative, taunting Norman for not being enough of a man while refusing to allow him to indulge his sexual curiosity. And Norman's mother isn't entirely to blame for stunting her son's development: if anything Norman doesn't want to grow up, and feels threatened by his mother's attraction to other men. There is no evidence, in fact, that Mrs Bates is to blame for Norman's condition at all: she is solely seen as a construct of Norman's mind, which makes the view of the film as an attack on matriarchal families difficult to sustain.

And if the film is a reactionary defence of patriarchal families, it's a very flimsy one, as the patriarchal families shown in the film are equally flawed. Cassidy is buying a house for his daughter, who is 'getting married away from me', and his resentful language and tone suggest that he is using his money to exert a continued influence on her life; he also flirts with Marion, despite being a married man.

Marion is hardly a threat to the patriarchy: she only takes Cassidy's money so that she can reaffirm the traditional values of marriage. The money is, in any case, undeclared profits that the viewer senses Cassidy can afford to lose – not a crime that deserves quite such extreme punishment – and during her conversation with Norman she decides to take the money back. She doesn't use her sexuality to get her own way, or flirt with Norman; while he peeps at her she is unaware of his gaze, and Hitchcock described the shower scene to Leigh as 'a baptism, a taking away of the torment from her mind. Marion became a virgin again.'

Throughout the film the viewer is pushed towards identifying with Norman, and seeing his problems as related to those of the other characters: Marion, for instance, is oppressed by the memory of her dead mother, while Sam cannot escape the debts left by his dead father. Norman is presented in a sympathetic light, as being either unaware of his murderous impulses or bullied by his mother; and after Marion's death Norman is our only real point of identification, the other characters being bland and featureless.

This identification serves to implicate the viewer in Norman's actions: like him, the audience too are voyeurs, peering in through the window at the start of the film to see Sam and Marion half-dressed. The theme of surveillance – also explored at length in Hitchcock's *Rear Window* (1954) – is taken further: Marion's office is fronted by large windows, so that anyone can gaze at her; Cassidy leers at her; she is scrutinised at length by a policeman and a used-car salesman before Norman peeps at her; and the stuffed birds in Norman's parlour hold her in their unblinking gaze. She has even internalised the idea of surveillance, imagining various voices upbraiding her as she drives out of Phoenix; voices that also serve as a hint of schizophrenia, drawing the parallels between Norman and the others still closer.

The encouragement to identify with Norman is part of the film's sustained attack on audience expectations. Any cosy ideas about the past, or rural America, being a safe refuge from the impersonality of modern city life, were shattered: the past, symbolised by the Bates Motel, empty since the highway moved away, or Norman's room, filled with decaying children's toys, is corrupt and degenerate; and away from the city no one can hear you scream.

INDUSTRY IMPACT: The success of *Psycho* predictably ensured that a run of imitations followed. Ironically enough, many came from the directors and studios whose low-budget success the director had tried to emulate: William Castle made *Homicidal* (1961), *Strait-Jacket* (1964) and *I Saw What You Did* (1965), all of which took elements from *Psycho* while aping Hitchcock's gimmicky marketing strategy; and Hammer released a stream of thrillers with names like *Paranoiac* (Freddie Francis, 1963), *Maniac* (Michael Carreras, 1963) and *Hysteria* (Freddie Francis, 1965), most of which returned to *Diabolique*'s 'all a plot' story rather than the Bates world. The best of these are probably *Taste of Fear* (Seth Holt, 1961) and the Richard Matheson-scripted *Fanatic* (Silvio Narizzano, 1965), which exploited *Psycho*'s suggestion of a psychotic old woman by having just that as its villain, a theme inspired also by Robert Aldrich's shockers *Whatever Happened to Baby Jane?* (1962) and *Hush, Hush, Sweet Charlotte* (1964).

If *Psycho* cemented Hitchcock's position as one of Hollywood's leading directors, Michael Powell's *Peeping Tom*, released the same year, had the opposite effect: the film was quickly taken out of circulation after appalled reviews, and Powell's film career effectively ended.

The film features Carl Boehm as Mark, a professional photographer and cameraman who kills women with a camera tripod while filming their deaths: a mirror is fixed to the tripod, so that the women can view their own faces as they die. Mark's father, a psychologist, had experimented on the boy as part of his research into fear and voyeurism; Mark has now 'become' his father, and ends the film by ritually killing himself.

Peeping Tom shares many themes with *Psycho*, although its lurid Eastmancolor gives it a sordid atmosphere that is at times far more shocking: both films feature sympathetic psychotics with jobs; both explore the relationship between cinema and voyeurism; both feature psychoanalysis as a key theme; and both focus on dysfunctional families – in *Psycho* an absent father and domineering mother, in *Peeping Tom* an absent mother and domineering father.

Both films have also been seen as marking a shift in portrayals of madness, from 'mad' to 'psychotic': gone are the rolling eyes and grandiose boasts of a Peter Lorre, replaced here by a surface normality. If the 'madman' occupies a different universe, the psychotic is firmly in this one, and may not even know of his psychosis. But the break is far from complete: many of the films following Hitchcock and Powell presented madness in the melodramatic model, even if they did, along with these films, conceptualise it as 'caused'.

More recently, Brian de Palma has carved a career out of Hitchcock 'homages', returning to *Psycho*'s theme of a transvestite killer in *Dressed to Kill* (1980), which also reworks the shower scene, while Adrian Lyne's bunny-boiling crowd-pleaser *Fatal Attraction* (1987) takes the basic model of *Psycho* – blonde menaced by a psycho with a knife – and reverses it to feature a blonde psycho with a knife. *Psycho* also inspired two sequels, a remake and a prequel: but while *Psycho 2* (Richard Franklin, 1983) has an intriguing script and another superb performance from Perkins, none of the original film's successors have matched its power, with Gus Van Sant's 1998 virtually shot-for-shot remake the definition of redundant filmmaking.

The set-piece murders of *Psycho* and *Peeping Tom* also provided the blueprint for the slasher genre's obsession with the aesthetics of murder (see **ORIGINS AND INSPIRATION, Halloween**), while other films inspired by the Ed Gein case include *Deranged* (Jeff Gillen and Alan Ormsby, 1974), **The Texas Chain Saw Massacre** and *Ed Gein* (Chuck Parello, 2000).

FINAL WORD: The modern viewer doesn't have to look very hard to find faults in *Psycho*. The film is uneven, its magnificently engaging first half out of kilter with the drab remainder, and Norman looks ridiculous rather than terrifying in his Mother outfit today. But the film's tricks have filtered so far into modern consciousness that it can be easy to forget just how powerful the film was on its release.

Psycho was, simply, an assault on the audience. Hitchcock noted in the margin of the shooting script for the shower scene: 'The slashing. An impression of a knife slashing, as if tearing at the very screen, ripping the film', and if the murder of the heroine, while taking a purifying shower after repenting of her crime, wasn't shocking enough in its subversion of audience expectation, the shot of Mrs Bates's mummified head swinging into view finished most viewers off. In these jolting moments *Psycho* was a harbinger of the social unease of the 1960s, a revelation that no assumptions were safe, that no boundaries would be left unchallenged.

THINGS THAT GO BUMP IN THE NIGHT

The Haunting (1963)

'You may not believe in ghosts but you cannot deny terror'

USA, MGM, b/w, 107 mins

Directed by Robert Wise
Screenplay by Nelson Gidding, from Shirley Jackson's novel
The Haunting of Hill House
Associate producer: Denis Johnson
Producer: Robert Wise
Original Music by Humphrey Searle
Cinematography by Davis Boulton
Film Editing by Ernest Walter
Production Design: Elliot Scott
Set Decoration: John Jarvis
Costume Design: Mary Quant
Assistant Director: David Tomblin
Special Effects: Tom Howard

CAST: Julie Harris (*Eleanor Lance*), Claire Bloom (*Theodora*), Richard Johnson (*Dr John Markway*), Russ Tamblyn (*Luke Sanderson*), Fay Compton (*Mrs Sanderson*), Rosalie Crutchley (*Mrs Dudley*), Lois Maxwell (*Grace Markway*), Valentine Dyall

(*Mr Dudley*), Diane Clare (*Carrie Fredericks*), Ronald Adam
(*Eldridge Harper*)

SYNOPSIS: Hill House has a nasty past of murder, infanticide
and suicide, and both wives of the original owner, Hugh Crain,
died there. Parapsychologist Dr John Markway is given permission by its owner to investigate the house, on condition that
the owner's nephew, Luke, keeps an eye on the researchers:
Markway is taking two unmarried women to assist him.

One is Eleanor Lance, who is keen to run away from her former
life, having looked after an invalid mother for most of her adult
years. She is the first to arrive. The caretaker and maid warn her
of the house's malign qualities, but she gets a friendlier reception
from Theodora, Markway's other assistant.

After wandering around the house, they meet Markway and
then Luke. At dinner Markway reveals he wants to prove the
existence of the supernatural; Theo is there because of her ESP
abilities, and Eleanor because of poltergeist phenomena that had
been associated with her as a teenager. That night Eleanor and
Theodora are woken up by a loud banging; the men hear nothing,
having gone outside to look for what sounded like a dog.

Next day Luke finds 'Help Eleanor Come Home' written on the
wall. Eleanor is upset, and Theo teases her about her growing
attachment to Markway. They take a tour around the house,
seeing the conservatory and library, which Eleanor is unable to
enter. Markway wants to send Eleanor home, but she refuses – he
asks Theo to move into her room.

Markway finds a cold spot in front of the nursery, according to
him the heart of the house. That night Eleanor hears laughter and
voices, and complains of Theo holding her hand too tightly; but
Theo is on the other side of the room.

Mrs Markway arrives to take John home, telling him journalists
have found out about his experiment. He refuses to go, so she
insists on staying – and sleeping in the nursery. The others sleep
together downstairs, and see the door bulge after a furious
hammering; Eleanor runs to the nursery, but Mrs Markway has
gone. Eleanor goes to the library and climbs the fragile spiral
staircase; when she sees Mrs Markway's startled face appear in a
skylight she faints.

Markway insists that Eleanor leaves, and helps her pack. She
wants to stay, but drives off without Luke, who was to accom-

pany her. She loses control of the car, and sees a ghostly figure run across the road, before crashing into a tree, precisely where the first Mrs Crain died. The figure was Mrs Markway, who had been roaming confused and lost around the grounds.

ORIGINS AND INSPIRATION: Ghost stories don't always have to feature a ghost. Their remit is often more an exploration of unusual psychic states than the supernatural, and in their focus on the unseen and unknown they have been traditionally better served by literature than film. Perhaps this is why neither the silent cinema nor Universal's wave of horror classics embraced the ghost as they did other gothic figures; even *The Old Dark House* (1932) wasn't haunted, and on the rare occasions that ghosts appeared in Hollywood before the 1940s, they served much the same function as the devil – comic relief in light entertainment – or were confined to *Scooby Doo*-style thrillers like *The Ghost Breaker* (Alfred E Green, 1922), where the supernatural elements are explained away in the final reel.

1944 saw the release of the first serious American ghost film, *The Uninvited* (Lewis Allen), in which a brother and sister stay in a haunted house on the Cornish coast; the British film industry responded with a portmanteau ghost film, Ealing's *Dead of Night* (1945). The Ealing film is almost sunk by a gruellingly bad comic episode, but two others – one featuring a haunted mirror and the other a sinister ventriloquist's dummy – are genuinely chilling, and the final sequence, in which the central character is assailed by figures from each story, has an authentic nightmare logic.

These early ghost films established two broad genre conventions: ghosts are predominantly English and boast literary origins. *Dead of Night* featured adaptations of stories by HG Wells and EF Benson, while Robert Aickman worked on the film as a story adviser, and many later ghost films also wore their literary credentials on their sleeve.

If the ghost story is the respectable end of the disreputable horror genre for the literary establishment, so professing a liking for ghost films like *The Innocents* (1961) or *The Haunting* is more culturally acceptable than being a fan of **The Texas Chain Saw Massacre** or **Cannibal Holocaust**; where most modern horror works through excess, the more successful ghost films are models of restraint.

Restraint was not part of William Castle's vocabulary for his two haunted house movies, *House on Haunted Hill* (1958) and

Thirteen Ghosts (1960, see **ORIGINS AND INSPIRATION, Evil Dead 2**), but Jack Clayton's *The Innocents* was an altogether statelier affair, and returned to the ghost story's literary origins. Set and shot in England, the screenplay for this adaptation of Henry James's *The Turn of the Screw* was written by Truman Capote and William Archibald, and the film was beautifully shot in stark black and white by Freddie Francis, director of *The Skull* (1965) and *Tales from the Crypt* (1972) for Amicus and numerous Hammer films.

Here governess Miss Giddens (Deborah Kerr) is sent to a country house, Bly, to look after a boy and girl, Miles and Flora, who have been effectively abandoned by their uncle. Miss Giddens becomes convinced that the ghosts of the former governess and valet have possessed the children, and events unfold from her perspective, but she is clearly an untrustworthy narrator – a devout spinster, so obsessed by the idea of innocence corrupted that she finally takes matters into her own hands, with appalling consequences.

The film has been criticised for dispensing with some of the ambiguity of James's novella – here the ghosts are strongly intimated to be products of Miss Giddens' mind – but it is still a touchstone for many of the themes and techniques that informed later horror films. The use of a potentially unbalanced woman as the central viewpoint figure foreshadows both *The Haunting* and **Rosemary's Baby**, with the corresponding ambiguity foregrounded in the latter film; and Miss Giddens is similar in other respects to *The Haunting*'s Eleanor (the governess is also a spinster who has until now lived only with her family and has an unconsummated desire for a dominant man, the uncle) and Polanski's Rosemary, who like her suffers from religious and sexual guilt leading, perhaps, to full-blown supernatural paranoia.

The children here are also influential, with Martin Stephens (Miles) reprising his chilling performance as one of the alien children of *Village of the Damned* (Wolf Rilla, 1960) – they are, at least as seen through Miss Giddens's eyes, genuinely creepy, informing the ghost–child relationships of the better modern hauntings, *The Sixth Sense* (M Knight Shyamalan, 1999), *The Others* (Alejandro Amenábar, 2001) and *The Devil's Backbone/El Espinazo del Diablo* (Guillermo del Toro, 2001).

Shirley Jackson's novel *The Haunting of Hill House*, published in 1959, was a critical and commercial success; Stephen King points out in *Danse Macabre* that it is the only horror novel of the century to enjoy a broad and unapologetic critical acceptance. After seeing it reviewed in *Time*, director Robert Wise read the novel, which terrified him. He passed it to screenwriter Nelson Gidding, with whom he had worked on *I Want to Live!* (1958); Gidding also enjoyed it, and started working on a screenplay.

Halfway through writing it, he was struck by the idea that the novel was not about the supernatural at all, but was rather the record of Eleanor's mental collapse. When he and Wise visited Jackson to discuss the project, Gidding asked if this had been her intention: it hadn't, she told him, but she liked the idea. And had she considered any other title for the novel? Only one – *The Haunting*.

Gidding decided to retain some ambiguity over the supernatural phenomena – not to show the audience very much at all – and tightened the scale of Jackson's novel: the back story and the number of characters were reduced, and almost all of the action would now take place inside the house, providing a claustrophobic atmosphere guaranteed to turn the screw on characters and audience alike.

Wise owed MGM one more film under his current contract, and approached them with the idea. They liked it, but weren't prepared to budget it as highly as he wanted, so on a business trip to London he pitched it to the MGM studios at Borehamwood. They promised him a budget of $1.1 million: *The Haunting* remained set in New England, but was shot in the UK.

DIRECTOR: Robert Wise began an auspicious Hollywood career by working as a sound-effects editor in the mid-30s, before moving on to edit classics like *The Hunchback of Notre Dame* (1939) and *Citizen Kane* (1941), although he can take less pride in agreeing to butcher Welles's *The Magnificent Ambersons* (1942).

His career as director began under the aegis of Val Lewton, a producer hired by RKO in the 40s to make low-budget horror movies with lurid audience-tested titles like *Cat People* (Jacques Tourneur, 1942) and *I Walked with a Zombie* (Jacques Tourneur, 1943). The resulting films – which also include *The Seventh Victim* (Mark Robson, 1943), *Bedlam* (Mark Robson, 1946), *Isle of the Dead* (Mark Robson, 1945) and *The Leopard Man* (Jacques Tourneur, 1943) – were more like tight psychological thrillers than horror films, although they take periodic chills from their play on the fear of the unknown and the tension between atavistic superstition and modern rationality. Entirely unlike other 40s horror films, they represent something of an aberration in the development of the genre, but they did introduce a technique often imitated in later horror films, the 'bus', named after a scene involving a bus in *Cat People* which builds up tension for a false scare; slasher films often swiftly followed these (the broken window scene in **Halloween,** for instance) with a real scare as the killer leaps into action.

It is a mark of Lewton's influence that these films – helmed by a variety of talented directors – look and feel similar; it is a further tribute to the producer that his alumni directors went on to use his sense of understatement to devastating effect on later films. Two of the best Lewton-produced films are Jacques Tourneur's *Cat People* and *I Walked with a Zombie* (see **ORIGINS AND INSPIRATION, Night of the Living Dead**), and Tourneur returned to Lewton territory with *Night of the Demon* (1958, see **ORIGINS AND INSPIRATION, Rosemary's Baby**). Similarly *The Haunting* is Wise's Lewton tribute, its ambiguity, refusal to show the audience very much and its subtle use of sound to build atmosphere recalling his Lewton films, *Curse of the Cat People* (1944) and *The Body Snatcher* (1945).

The former is a ghost story of sorts, although its ghosts are more clearly the products of a child's imaginary world than the angry spirits of *The Haunting*. Despite featuring some of the same characters, this was not really a sequel to Tourneur's earlier film, nor indeed a horror film, but rather a sensitive portrayal of the imaginative realm of childhood, its only moment of terror stemming from a recounting of the legend of the Headless Horseman.

The Body Snatcher was closer to traditional horror fare, being an adaptation of RL Stevenson's story about Burke and Hare, 'resurrectionists' who supplied Edinburgh's medical community with corpses – some killed to order. While marred by a saccharine subplot about a crippled child, it benefited from one of Karloff's finest performances, and developed a strong sense of unease from the ambiguous relationship between Karloff and the doctor who employs him.

While still at RKO, Wise directed *A Game of Death* (1945), a remake of *The Most Dangerous Game* (Irving Pichel and Ernest

B Schoedsack, 1932), then returned to the realm of the fantastic with the SF classic *The Day the Earth Stood Still* (1951) and became one of Hollywood's A-list directors with *West Side Story* (1961). The director followed *The Haunting* with *The Sound of Music* (1965), which comes across at times as a grotesque parody of *The Innocents*, and later directed the paranoid classic *The Andromeda Strain* (1971), a less successful return to the under-stated ghost story with *Audrey Rose* (1977), and *Star Trek: The Motion Picture* (1979), his last major film.

CASTING: Richard Johnson, on contract to MGM, was working with the RSC during the shoot, and appeared in an adaptation of Aldous Huxley's *The Devils* in the evening while working on *The Haunting* during the day. He was once considered for the part of James Bond, but turned the role down, and felt that Sean Connery made a better choice. But Lois Maxwell, who played Mrs Markway, was only too happy to jump on the Bond bandwagon: she became Moneypenny.

Russ Tamblyn was also on contract to the studio, which forced him to reconsider after he initially rejected the role of the 'jerky' Luke. Eventually Tamblyn was happy with his part, as his character provides the only arc from sceptic to believer in the film, although at times he does seem to have wandered in from a different set. He was the only member of the cast to have anything like a career in genre cinema, starring early on in George Pal's *Tom Thumb* (1958) and *The Wonderful World of the Brothers Grimm* (1962), alongside more mainstream films like *West Side Story*, and later on he popped up in everything from Japanese monster extravaganza *War of the Gargantuas* (Ishirô Honda, 1966) to Dennis Hopper's neglected *The Last Movie* (1971). He also had a recurring role in David Lynch's *Twin Peaks*, albeit barely recognisable under his beard, as psychiatrist Dr Lawrence Jacobi.

Wise had seen Harris on stage, and felt her perfect for the part of Eleanor. She did not enjoy the shoot: while Johnson, Bloom and Tamblyn got on well, going out for dinner and spending time together off set, Harris spent all of her time alone and often in tears, feeling isolated and unhappy. She felt that the others didn't take the film as seriously as she did, but her depression was interpreted by her colleagues as an attempt to get into character: whatever the case, the performance is magnificent.

Harris refused to talk to Bloom on set, accentuating a tension that is clearly visible on screen, and Bloom was deeply upset by the rift until Harris visited her after the shoot had finished and apologised: she told Bloom that she hadn't been able to talk to her during the film because their characters had hated each other so much.

PRODUCTION: The house used in *The Haunting* is Ettington Park near Stratford-on-Avon; it is now a hotel. Only the exteriors were shot there, with infrared film providing an unnaturally high degree of contrast; the interiors were built on set at Borehamwood studios. Ettington Park was also used in *The Watcher in the Woods* (John Hough, 1980), and featured in a BBC documentary about ghosts; the house is reputed to be haunted, and Russ Tamblyn claims to have had a ghostly experience there while working on the film.

Although it runs against the 'old dark house' tradition, being well appointed and brightly lit, with few dark corners, the production design for the interiors is richly gothic and disturbingly overwrought: according to Richard Johnson it contributed to a subdued atmosphere on set. The sets also have ceilings, which adds to the sense of claustrophobia: this is a rarity in set design, as ceilings are usually left off to enable easier lighting.

The spiral staircase in the library was built specifically for the film, and had a cable running through its hollow centre; when tightened, the staircase was stable, but when loosened it would shake around. The handrail was used as a dolly for a handheld camera, and the shot that revolves up the staircase at dizzying speed was simply the result of reversing an earlier shot from the camera sliding down.

Wise felt that black and white worked best for the story, although he met with some resistance from the studio, and *The Haunting* was the last film he shot in monochrome. He also used experimental lenses to make the hallways look 'a little crazy': he was sent a 28mm test lens from Panavision which was considered a failure as it distorted the image. The company only allowed him to use the lens on condition that he sign a letter accepting full responsibility for the distorted effect.

The memorable effect of the door bulging towards the end of the film simply involved a props man pushing various objects against the other side of the laminated wood; it is the only instance of anything supernatural actually seen in the film, which relies more on sound and lighting for effect.

One sequence was cut before the film's release: originally an early scene had Theo writing 'I hate you' in lipstick on a mirror before yelling to a woman in a car, a more forceful statement of lesbianism than any in the film. But Wise finally thought it too overstated, and preferred the implied lesbianism that remains – Theo's repeated references to 'sisters', and Eleanor's accusation that she is 'one of nature's mistakes', as well as Theo's angry rebuff of Luke's advances.

SOUNDTRACK: What is unseen is not necessarily unheard, and *The Haunting* benefits enormously from the judicious use of sound. Jackson's novel describes the disturbing noises that assault the house's inhabitants with uncanny precision, and Wise uses his experience as a sound editor to transfer these flawlessly to the film's soundtrack, with each layer of lurching, creaking, blowing, muttering and clanging overlaying the next until they are joined by atonal horn blares and string shrieks at the film's crescendos. Stephen King describes the film as 'the world's first radio horror movie', an apt description of the density of the soundtrack. Yet some of the scariest scenes are played out in near silence, and Wise's film carefully allows tension to build between the climaxes.

Eleanor's point of view is forcefully presented with an echoey voiceover narration, signposted by a whimsical melody that takes on more sinister associations throughout the film; occasionally her stream of consciousness masks other dialogue, fixing the viewer ever deeper in her unsettled mind. The voiceover – much of which is taken verbatim from the novel – recalls **Psycho** as one of the film's influences: both feature female protagonists' internal monologues as they drive cars after having committed 'crimes' (Eleanor takes the car she shares with her sister without permission); in both, central characters have had personality-defining relationships with domineering mothers; and in both atonal, shrieking strings are used to add an almost unbearable degree of tension to the soundtrack.

RELEASE: The film's virtues were not readily apparent to contemporary reviewers and audiences, and it was only a modest success. *Monthly Film Bulletin* found that 'the mysterious noises themselves are quite pleasingly chilling – though at one point unfortunately reminiscent of a flushing toilet – but Wise's camera is so determinedly zooming in and out to make sure one knows that the girls are scared ... that all subtlety is banished'; while *Variety* was more damning, finding that 'all this production savvy has been squandered on a screen yarn that hardly merits, and cannot support, such artistic bulk'.

Part of the film's relatively chilly reception may have come from the fact that Eleanor, the principal viewpoint character, does not encourage audience identification. But *The Haunting* has acquired a reputation of being one of the scariest films ever made – Pauline Kael rates it as the best ghost story on film – over the subsequent years.

CRITICAL EYE: According to Dr Markway, Hill House is deranged. The house is personified using a number of techniques: in dialogue, its windows are referred to as eyes, and the nursery as the heart of the house; faces on doorknobs and, more subtly, in the wallpaper, give the impression that it is watching the inhabitants; and the roving camera, swooping over Eleanor from high vantage points and at one point even flattening her against a balcony, along with repeated edits juxtaposing her with various views of the house's interior, suggest its conscious malevolence.

As Markway tells us, there are no right angles in the house; all of the mirrors are set at a slight tilt, and the use of off-kilter camera angles and rapid edits further suggest the house's instability. Eleanor notes early on that Hill House is like a maze, and indeed it is impossible to accurately conceive its spatial configuration; traditional film grammar, which has characters exiting to the left of the frame to enter to the right in a different room, is not followed here; there is never a view from any of the windows, and nor is there any possibility of orientation through directional natural light. This is a schizophrenic's sense of space.

Time is similarly fractured, with the theme of repetition and doubling marking Hill House's resistance to its linear bounds: if the house is haunted by anything, it seems to be events. Both Eleanor and Abigail's companion ignored their elderly charges' knocks on the night of their deaths; and Eleanor dies in the same place as the first Mrs Crain, and in much the same way – all that is seen of the first Mrs Crain in the film's prologue is an arm dangling from an overturned carriage, and the final view of Eleanor is identical. Eleanor repeats actions and words throughout the film, bending backwards over a balcony twice and in one jarring scene running towards the camera, which swings away at the last moment to reveal that she is running towards a mirror: perhaps what Eleanor most fears at Hill House is herself.

Such parallels are never explored or explained in any depth, but remain deliberately ambiguous. The relationships between Eleanor and Abigail's companion, or between Eleanor and Theo, are vague and understated: the viewer is left to fill in the gaps, and to wonder why Theo feeds Eleanor sinister lines like 'It wants you, Nell', or 'You haven't the ghost of a chance'. Even the house's most direct communication with its guests, the writing on the wall, is ambiguous – HELP ELEANOR COME HOME can be read in two ways – and it is never clear whether the house is really haunted or whether Eleanor is the source of events, as with the poltergeist phenomena following her father's death.

In a way it's a false dichotomy: part of the film's power is the way it blurs the line between internal and external, presenting Eleanor's psyche as increasingly subsumed into the house. The film doesn't, however, support a *Repulsion*-style reading (see **DIRECTOR, Rosemary's Baby**), with the events taking place only in Eleanor's diseased mind: both prologue and ending occur away from her viewpoint, showing the house's haunted history and Luke, the former sceptic, accepting the supernatural.

INDUSTRY IMPACT: *The Haunting*, one of the first big-budget horror films, did not spark a boom in cinematic ghosts: its restraint and ambiguity seemed at odds with the genre's increasing reliance on explicit sex and violence, even if the immensely successful **Rosemary's Baby** gave it a nod, and when **Night of the Living Dead** opened the floodgates to a new breed of nihilistic gore films, the art of the restrained supernatural horror film seemed dead.

Most American ghost films of the 1970s were either incomprehensible (*Burnt Offerings*, Dan Curtis, 1976) or dull and lifeless (*Ghost Story*, Stephen Weeks, 1977); perhaps the decade's most effective hauntings were being shot by the BBC for TV broadcast. Jonathan Miller's 1968 *Omnibus* production of MR James's *Whistle and I'll Come To You* kickstarted the BBC's ghost run, and was soon followed by a series of Christmas ghost stories; it remains, along with *Night of the Demon*, the best James adaptation, an absurdist 16mm nightmare that plays like *Fawlty Towers* on a bad trip.

Also from the BBC was 1972's *The Stone Tape*, a Nigel Kneale-scripted film pitting a team of scientists against a malevolent ghost, much in the vein of the later, less successful British feature *The Legend of Hell House* (John Hough, 1973); and *Ghostwatch*, a mock documentary broadcast on Halloween in 1992, which despite the presence of such bland TV stalwarts as Michael Parkinson and Sarah Greene managed to terrify viewers so much that it prompted a barrage of complaints and has never since been repeated.

Meanwhile American ghost fans unimpressed by turkeys like *The Amityville Horror* (Stuart Rosenberg, 1979) had to wait for Stanley Kubrick's *The Shining* (1980) for a haunting of any distinction. The film was keenly anticipated: a major-league, ferociously independent director adapting one of Stephen King's best novels, with Jack Nicholson, then at the peak of his profession, in the starring role.

But when the film was finally released after three years' tinkering, critics and audiences were bemused. It's not hard to see why: for all that the Overlook is one of the most impressive haunted houses ever created, its endless corridors, vast spaces and demented interior design giving the sense of an eerie alien intelligence closer to *2001* (Stanley Kubrick, 1968) than most other horror films, the performances and pacing are finally too overwrought to maintain the high pitch of tension reached in the first forty minutes. After that, Nicholson's eyebrow-wriggling cartoon psycho sends the tone lurching into high camp for much of the rest of the film, although it does still feature one of the best ever 'no exit' scenes, as Shelley Duvall attempts to flee her husband's axe by climbing through a bathroom window that's just a little too small.

The soundtrack, too, although impressive enough in small doses, is finally too relentless to carry our fear; the Overlook owes more than a little to Hill House, with Kubrick screening *The Haunting* several times in pre-production and Jack Torrance joining the hotel's ghosts just as Eleanor's spirit remains in Hill House, but the film would have benefited from more of Wise's subtlety and a more measured pace. The Overlook's hauntings are too flashy, finally, to terrify, and although the film improves on repeated viewings – how far is Danny responsible for what happens? – its primary accomplishments, apart from its technical innovation and set design, are to present a harrowing picture of domestic violence, with real terror in the alcoholic father's violent rampages and the son's withdrawal from a hostile world.

The Steven Spielberg-produced *Poltergeist* (Tobe Hooper, 1982) set the tone for most American hauntings to follow, regrettably ditching the lure of the unseen in favour of effects-heavy spectral extravaganzas. It's only a short step from this supernatural version of *Close Encounters of the Third Kind* (Steven Spielberg, 1977) – whatever unique talent director Tobe Hooper possesses bleached out by backlit effects and overly cute children – to *Ghostbusters* (Ivan Reitman, 1984), and the temptation to use that big bag of CGI tricks proved too much for Peter Jackson's comedy-horror misfire *The Frighteners* (1996) and the makers of redundant remakes of *The Haunting, The Haunting of Hill House* (Jan de Bont, 1999), *Thir13en Ghosts* (Steve Beck, 2001) and *Ghost Ship* (Steve Beck, 2002) to resist.

More restrained, more interesting and, tellingly, far more commercially successful was *The Blair Witch Project* (Daniel Myrick and Eduardo Sánchez, 1999), a mock vérité account of the making of a documentary that goes horribly wrong. Although the film is highly derivative – *The Last Broadcast* (Stefan Avalos and Lance Weiler, 1998) and **Cannibal Holocaust** were there first – it is at least a partial success, returning to a fear of the unseen and unknown, relying on sound more than vision and retaining a degree of ambiguity – the audience doesn't, finally, know what has happened to the filmmakers – non-existent in most contemporary genre cinema. The film finally folds under the weight of its own hype, and repeat viewings are more likely to generate irritation than fear, but the filmmakers' effective torture of their cast, who allegedly didn't know what was going on during filming, is an object lesson for aspiring filmmakers to put their characters through the mill.

Ghost movies were big business for a while at the turn of the millennium, with a couple of major studio releases breaking away from an over-reliance on CGI. *The Sixth Sense* (1999) delivered a couple of genuine scares with its richly moody atmosphere, slowly building up tension to an effective tearjerker finale, but here the ghost story is used in the service of a studied conservatism rather than ambiguity, and the slightly hokey twist at the end prevents it from holding up to repeat viewing. *The Others* (2001) falls into the same trap, and is even more derivative, coming across as equal parts *The Innocents* (1961) and *Carnival of Souls* (Herk Harvey,

1962), but it too has some effective scares, and generates an atmosphere of non-specific unease rarely attempted nowadays outside a David Lynch film.

The Others, although it looks like a Hollywood production, was shot principally in Spain by a Spanish director and crew, and only part-financed by Hollywood money. Another Spanish ghost film came out the same year, the slickly entertaining *The Devil's Backbone/El Espinazo del Diablo*; but the ghost here, although impressive, is not finally the blood-curdling kind, and the film's principal focus is less the supernatural or psychic unease than the Spanish Civil War.

Still, given the ropiness of most mainstream Hollywood phantoms, horror fans – and more specifically fans of ghost films – have got used to looking away from the US for their icy chills. One country, in particular, has a culture of ghost stories that rivals or exceeds that of any Anglophone nation, and has recently been exporting its modern twists on old stories with considerable success – Japan (see **Ring/Ringu**).

FINAL WORD: *The Haunting*'s success relies upon its exploration of the unknown. As Markway points out, it is this – rather than the threat of physical pain or death – that is the source of terror here: 'Unknown. That's the key word – unknown. When we become involved in a supernatural event, we're scared out of our wits just because it's unknown.' By refusing to resolve the film's many ambiguities, or to show the audience any direct ghostly manifestations beyond a bending door, Wise forces our imaginations to fill the space with our own ghastly fears. The choice of black and white over colour is important here, as even from the start the viewer is thus given an incomplete picture; but the tremendous power of suggestion in scaring an audience sadly seems to have passed by the makers of extravagant ($80 million) flops like the 1999 remake.

ZOMBIE GUT-MUNCHERS

Night of the Living Dead (1968)

'They keep coming back in a bloodthirsty lust for HUMAN FLESH!'

aka Night of Anubis/Night of the Flesheaters

USA, Image Ten, b/w, 96 mins

Directed by George A Romero
Writing Credits (in alphabetical order): George A Romero,
John A Russo
Produced by Karl Hardman and Russell Streiner
Cinematography by George A Romero
Film Editing by George A Romero and John A Russo
Special Make-up Effects: Vincent J Guastini
Make-up Artist: Karl Hardman
Electronic Sound Effects: Karl Hardman
Sound Engineer: Gary Streiner
Special Effects: Tony Pantanello
Special Effects: Regis Survinski
Stunt Coordinator: Jacqueline Streiner
Assistant Camera: S William Hinzman
Script Coordinator: Jacqueline Streiner

CAST: Duane Jones (*Ben*), Judith O'Dea (*Barbra*), Karl Hardman (*Harry Cooper*), Marilyn Eastman (*Helen Cooper/Bug-eating Zombie*), Keith Wayne (*Tom*), Judith Ridley (*Judy*), Russ Streiner (*Johnny*), Kyra Schon (*Karen Cooper/Upstairs Body*), Charles Craig (*Newscaster/Ghoul*), S William Hinzman (*Cemetery Ghoul* [as Bill Heinzman]), George Kosana (*Sheriff McClelland*), Frank Doak (*Scientist*), Bill 'Chilly Billy' Cardille (*Field Reporter*), Mark Ricci (*Washington Scientist*), Lee Hartman (*Ghoul/News Reporter*), A C McDonald, Samuel R Solito, Jack Givens, R J Ricci, Paula Richards, John Simpson, Herbert Summer, Richard Ricci, William Burchinal, Ross Harris, Al Croft, Jason Richards, Dave James, Sharon Carroll, William Mogush, Steve Hutsko, Joann Michaels, Phillip Smith, Ella Mae Smith, Randy Burr (*Ghouls*)

SYNOPSIS: John and Barbra visit their father's grave in a cemetery a few hundred miles from Pittsburgh. After being teased by John, Barbra is attacked by a man; John wrestles him off, but is killed. Barbra runs to the car, crashes it and makes her way to a nearby house, where she meets Ben. She is traumatised and falls into a catatonic stupor; Ben boards up the windows and doors.

The radio tells them that the authorities are bewildered, and that ghouls are eating their victims; Ben discovers that the ghouls are afraid of fire, and finds a gun and food. Two men emerge from the basement, Tom and Harry; inconsistencies in Harry's story about why he didn't come up to help earlier makes Ben distrust him.

More ghouls attack, and only a bullet in the head seems to stop them. Tom's girlfriend Judy is also downstairs, along with Harry's wife, Helen, and their daughter Karen, who has been bitten by a ghoul. Harry thinks the cellar is the safest place to hide, but Ben insists they should stay upstairs; when Harry's wife hears the TV the others have found she wants to go upstairs too.

Civil-defence rescue stations have been set up, and a scientific explanation for the catastrophe is hinted at. Only one thing is clear: bodies of the dead must be burned or otherwise disposed of to prevent their returning to life.

Ben and Tom go out for a nearby truck, while Harry throws Molotov cocktails from the house to distract the ghouls. Judy races out to join Tom, but as they try to refuel the truck petrol is splashed on it, and it explodes, killing them.

Ben runs back to the house, but Harry doesn't let him in, so Ben kicks the door down and punches him. The power is cut off, and as Ben tries to barricade the doors and windows, Harry snatches the gun; Ben knocks it from his hands and shoots him. Harry crawls down to the basement, where he is partially eaten by his now undead daughter – the ghoul's bite is contagious. Karen then stabs her mother repeatedly with a trowel.

Barbra helps Ben, but when she sees John among the ghouls she is taken by him. Overwhelmed, Ben hides in the basement, where he shoots the undead Harry and his wife in the head.

The next morning, a posse of riflemen draws closer. Ben leaves the basement and peers out of the window; he is shot dead, and his body is burned on a pyre.

ORIGINS AND INSPIRATION: Raising the dead has long been a central horror theme, with Frankenstein's Monster providing one of the genre's most enduring archetypes and Cesare's somnambulist in *The Cabinet of Dr Caligari* (1919), all staring black-rimmed eyes and striding gait, rising from his coffin to kill at Caligari's command. Yet zombies, unlike many other horror staples, are cinema monsters, without literary origins; their only written sources are in folkloric studies like 1929's *The Magic Island*, and before Romero they drew heavily on Haitian beliefs, usually being black slave labour found in the Caribbean, not necessarily dead and certainly not about to eat you.

After the publication of *The Magic Island*, a New York stage production, 1932's *Zombie*, catapulted the walking dead into the limelight. *White Zombie* (1932), directed and produced by the Halperin brothers, capitalised on this surge of interest, borrowing sets (*Frankenstein*, *Dracula*), crew (make-up man Jack Pierce) and cast (Bela Lugosi) from Universal films for the screen zombie's debut in a minimally budgeted but unique 'poverty row' horror film. Lugosi plays Murder Legendre, white ruler of a veritable army of Haitian zombies which are created through the use of a drug that simulates death, and apparently controlled by Lugosi's piercing gaze. When Romero saw the film, he was terrified by an idea it didn't explore: what if the zombies were uncontrollable?

The Halperins tried unsuccessfully to repeat the film's success with a 1936 sequel, *Revolt of the Zombies*, in which zombie soldiers are created in Cambodia. The military theme was continued in *King of the Zombies* (Jean Yarbrough, 1941) and *Revenge of the Zombies* (Steve Sekely, 1943), which featured mad Axis scientists trying to use zombies for world domination.

Jacques Tourneur's *I Walked with a Zombie* (1941) is by far the best of these early zombie films, a Val Lewton production that transplants the plot of *Jane Eyre* to the Caribbean with a surprisingly modern psychological realism and a number of Lewton's trademark suggestively chilling sequences, including a famous night walk through the plantations. It also retains Lewton's characteristic ambiguity regarding the supernatural: if the woman purported to be a zombie is probably mentally ill, what is the audience to make of the goggle-eyed Carrefour?

Hammer's *Plague of the Zombies* (John Gilling, 1966) continues the theme of the exploitation of cheap labour with poor white villagers being turned into zombies for use as slaves in 19th-century Cornwall. Among its highlights is a dream sequence in which zombies, now visibly rotting corpses, emerge from their graves: the zombie's status as the walking, decaying dead was finally made clear.

While this scene may have influenced Romero, it's principally non-zombie films that are the true precursors to the look and feel of *Night*. Romero has acknowledged his debt to Herk Harvey's *Carnival of Souls* (1962), a weirdly poetic film about a woman who appears to survive a car accident, featuring crowds of white-faced ghouls running around with outstretched arms. The film plays like a carny sideshow version of *Repulsion* (Roman Polanski, 1965) – whose grasping hands also influenced *Night* – or a bargain-basement Lynch or Franju, but has an eeriness and trash vitality all its own.

The siege on the house is foreshadowed by Hitchcock's *The Birds* (1963), with which it shares boarded-up doors and windows and an explicit relationship between the attacks and unresolved tensions between the characters, while the look of the zombies is anticipated by *Invisible Invaders* (Edward L Cahn, 1959), in which invisible aliens revive white-faced corpses, and *The Last Man on Earth/L'Ultimo Uomo della Terra* (Ubaldo Ragona and Sidney Salkow, 1964), an adaptation of Richard Matheson's apocalyptic *I Am Legend* in which Vincent Price's house is besieged at night by the undead.

The film's other influences include *Frankenstein* (1931) and the Universal monster movies in general – several camera angles resemble Whale's tilts, the zombies tend to move like Karloff's Monster, and Johnny at the start of the film teases Barbra by imitating Karloff's voice – and the independent gore films made by Herschell Gordon Lewis (see **ORIGINS AND INSPIRATION**, **Evil Dead 2**), precursors to Romero's on-screen gut-munching.

Another key influence was EC Comics. The company began to publish horror comics in the 1950s, and their titles – which included *The Haunt of Fear*, *Tales from the Crypt* and *The Vault of Horror* – quickly became notorious for their explicit gore, occasionally acute stabs at social commentary and ghoulish humour. They also featured the living dead fairly frequently, thereby providing not only a style template but also content for the film, and often had ethnically diverse protagonists, a rarity in their day. Romero has consciously expressed a debt to the comics, not least by directing *Creepshow*, an explicit tribute, in 1982.

The undead are never referred to as zombies in *Night*: they are 'ghouls', conflated with cannibal figures of that name that had never really caught the public's imagination, despite appearing in several 30s movies. Here, for the first time, they were liberated from the shackles of a master – nobody was in control – and could only be stopped by destroying the brain stem, a rewriting of zombie mythology that went on to define almost every zombie film to come.

Romero, John Russo and Russell Streiner ran The Latent Image, a small Pittsburgh-based film production company specialising in making TV ads for local companies. Disheartened by working on ephemeral products for fickle employers, the three friends decided to pool their money and persuade others to invest in a low-budget feature – and the most effective film they could do for the money would be a horror film.

The exact authorship of *Night* is a thorny issue, which later led to protracted legal battles between Russo and Romero over who owned the rights to the name and concept. Romero appears to have originated the idea, having written an unpublished story called *Anubis* about a zombie-driven apocalypse, structured in three parts that correspond roughly to his three *Dead* films; but Russo wrote the bulk of the script, and the dialogue for Harry and Helen Cooper in the basement sequences was written by Marilyn Eastman, who plays Helen.

Having raised money from friends and local businesses – $300 from each investor, to the tune of around $114,000 – they set up a new company, Image Ten, to produce the film.

DIRECTOR: Romero was born in New York but moved to Pittsburgh as a student, to study art, design and drama. He'd already shot a couple of early shorts in New York, and soon after graduating he moved into TV production; even after the success of *Night* he continued to work extensively in television.

His efforts to break away from the horror genre have been largely unsuccessful, and the director has professed some disappointment that he has been unable to use the genre as a springboard to other material. The three films that followed *Night*, *There's Always Vanilla* (1972), *Jack's Wife* (1973), re-edited by the distributor and released as *Season of the Witch*, and *The Crazies* (1973) were all critical and commercial flops, although the latter bears several close similarities to the *Dead* saga. All were edited, photographed and scripted by Romero as well, apart from *There's Always Vanilla,* which was written by Rudolph J Ricci.

Romero directed sports pieces for TV to pay the bills before returning to horror with his favourite feature, perhaps the best revisionist vampire film, *Martin* (1977). This marked Romero's first association with special-effects maestro Tom Savini, whose work would provide *Fangoria* with centrespreads for many years to come, and demonstrated the director's reluctance to take the supernatural at face value; rather than recycling vampire lore for a cheap and easy exploitation film, *Martin* attempts, as critic Tony Williams puts it, to:

> stimulate its audiences into questioning the very origins of the fantastic and move them towards investigating the more relevant oppressive material causes of everyday existence which rely upon the concealing devices of superstition, fantasy and custom for their very existence.

Is the eponymous protagonist a vampire or a disturbed teenager, force-fed vampire legends by an insane family and endless Universal re-runs? He has no time for fangs, preferring instead to use a syringe and a straight razor, and takes time out from his job as delivery boy to become a star on a late-night radio chat show. The supernatural has no place in his world, and he plays against the grain of the vampire as egotistical or sexually potent, being a shy and virginal teenager. In the end it is irrelevant whether the viewer believes Martin to be a vampire or not: his host thinks he is, and drives a stake through his heart, believing him guilty of a murder he did not commit.

1979 saw the release of *Dawn of the Dead*, which Romero again scripted and co-edited as well as directed; Italian director Dario Argento (**Deep Red**) helped finance the film, and re-edited it for his domestic market. If at the end of *Night* the living appeared to have the upper hand over the zombies, by *Dawn* containment has failed, and civilisation fatally crumbled. What will the dead do when there is no more room in hell? Go shopping. Where *Night* comments on Vietnam, the civil rights movement and family tensions, *Dawn* focuses on consumerism and adult relationships, both heterosexual couples and male 'buddies', as a couple (Fran and Steve) and two SWAT members (Roger and Peter) take refuge from the zombies in a shopping mall.

The undead are creatures of instinct, returning to the mall to indulge atavistic desires for luxury goods; their numbers include a Hare Krishna and a nun, demonstrating that such desires existed in all walks of life. But the human characters are no less instinctual, gleefully running around trying on fur coats and eating caviar; eventually they manage to dispose of all the zombies in the mall, and only then does the futility of their consumption become apparent, and their relationships begin to falter. Ironically the mall is more fascinating to the three men than to Fran, who is the first to recognise what is useful to the group, watering plants and learning to fly the helicopter while the others take photos that can never be developed and cash that can buy nothing; finally their ennui is broken by a raid on the mall by a marauding gang of bikers.

If *Night* is nihilistic and bleak, *Dawn* offers some hope of salvation: here Peter and Fran, who cooperate and learn to shed the values of a defunct society, survive at the end, a reversal of the grim ending of Romero's first film, which had by now become a horror commonplace. *Dawn* plays more like an action picture than a horror film, with Peter using martial arts on a few zombies and much of the characters' time spent improvising *A-Team*-style solutions to their predicament; the music, too, foregrounds the comic elements of scenes that could be played for straight tension, prefiguring the 'splatstick' of films like **Evil Dead 2**. But horror fans had little reason to be disappointed, especially with Savini's lurid effects – limbs are ripped off, machetes buried in heads and bikers torn apart in what was probably the grisliest finale of any film to date, and *Dawn* marked the birth of a new wave of gore films. The film was remade, surprisingly well, in 2003, as Hollywood horror returned to its 70s glory days, and the remake even spawned a British spoof, *Shaun of the Dead* (Edgar Wright, 2004).

Romero followed it with a more personal project, *Knightriders* (1981), an Arthurian biker picture that flopped at the box office, and the Stephen King-scripted *Creepshow*, a portmanteau tribute to EC Comics that didn't measure up to the director's other work.

Day of the Dead was released in 1985, and remains the last of Romero's zombie films to date. His original idea was to create a world in which the living and the dead had come to terms, and trained zombie armies fought wars for human communities living underground; by the end the living-dead plague would have passed, and a fragile new community would be established. This version was budgeted at $6.5 million, but it would be near-impossible for an unrated film, as *Day*'s violence would make it, to recoup these costs; reluctant to cut back on the gore or to strip down the script, Romero instead turned back the clock to an earlier period in the zombie mythos.

Day is set on a subterranean military base, where a scientific project to help deal with the zombies is taken over by the military. Again Romero focuses on outsiders – the central figure is Sarah, a woman who is portrayed in neither overtly sexual nor fashionably gun-toting style, and her allies are a Jamaican, an Irishman and, briefly, a Hispanic man. By now there is no doubt that the zombies have overrun the humans; the community in the film knows of no other human groups.

In tone *Day* is, like *Dawn*, closer to action than horror, although it has a grimly claustrophobic feel leavened only by some grotesque scientific experiments. The zombies here are more spectacularly decayed than in the previous films, and the grisly experiments performed on them by Dr Logan (dubbed 'Frankenstein' by the soldiers) show how far Savini's effects work had come. Logan learns that the zombies do not need food; they are acting on pure instinct, and he takes it upon himself to train them, in a parody of parent–child nurturing.

The Frankenstein reference highlights the film's debt to Universal horror: Logan's pet project, Bub, is like a successful version of Frankenstein's Monster, with his chains and the monochrome laboratory – all the better to highlight the gory effects – recalling

Whale's films. The ending here seems even more optimistic than *Dawn*'s: the military are eviscerated in splashy detail while our three heroes escape to a sunny beach. Although Sarah still finds it difficult to dispense with old values – the final scene has her marking the days off in a calendar – she has realised that the military base's storage of tax returns and immigration records is futile; the others, meanwhile, have dispensed with their respective crutches of gun and hipflask.

But *Day* flopped at the box office, too serious for audiences delighting in the gory farces of *Return of the Living Dead* (Dan O'Bannon) and *Re-Animator* (Stuart Gordon), released the same year. Since then Romero's output has foundered: *Monkey Shines* (1988) was his first major literary adaptation, and the first of his films to be partly financed by a major studio. While this ambiguous tale of mad science and a murderous monkey has interesting sequences, it is perhaps predictably fatally flawed by studio interference.

For *Two Evil Eyes* (1990) Romero teamed up with Dario Argento, each adapting an Edgar Allan Poe story. Romero's is *The Facts in the Case of M Valdemar*, but its TV-movie blandness only shows how much less comfortable the director is with supernatural rather than SF-based horror stories. *The Dark Half* (1993), an adaptation of a Stephen King novel, was similarly disappointing – King's novels about writing have been adapted more successfully before (*The Shining* (1980), *Misery* (Rob Reiner, 1990)), and this was ultimately a confused and redundant take on recursive horror.

2000 saw the barely released *Bruiser*: a confirmed conformist who works for a lifestyle magazine wakes up faceless one day and takes the opportunity to revenge himself on those he feels have wronged him. Romero has referred to this as his take on **Eyes Without a Face**, but few reviewers have favoured such lofty comparisons.

CASTING: The only two professional actors in the film were Judith O'Dea (Barbra) and Duane Jones (Ben). Romero insists that the fact that Jones is an African-American was purely coincidental, and indeed it is never acknowledged in the film; he is, however, the first African-American lead in a horror film, and the first African-American lead in any feature not to have a romantic interest. The part was rewritten after Jones auditioned, changed from its original conception as a crude and uneducated truck driver to a more intelligent and thoughtful character, reflecting Jones's education. He was *Night*'s only actor to have much of a career in film, appearing in genre fare like *Ganja and Hess* (Bill Gunn and Fima Noveck, 1972), *Vampires* (Len Anthony, 1986) and *Fright House* (Len Anthony, 1989), although S William Hinzman capitalised on his fame as the cemetery ghoul to make his own zombie movie, *Flesheater* (1988).

PRODUCTION: The film's working title was *Monster Flick*, and it was shot between June and December 1967. The filmmakers kept costs down by using a house that was due to be demolished (although as it had no basement, those scenes had to be shot in the editing studio) and a predominantly amateur cast, both of which added to the film's vérité style. Most of the zombies were friends from the advertising business, who thought it would be fun to stagger around in facepaint, gnawing on a few bones: they were paid $1 and given a T-shirt saying 'I was a zombie on *Night of the Living Dead*' for their troubles.

One investor was a butcher, who provided various entrails for the cannibal scenes (although the blood is Bosco chocolate syrup); and other investors doubled up as both cast and crew members. S William Hinzman is the first zombie seen, and also worked as assistant cameraman; Karl Hardman, who played Harry Cooper, also selected the music, as well as providing the electronic effects; while Marilyn Eastman (Helen Cooper) was responsible for the make-up, as well as doubling as an insect-eating ghoul.

The television reporter, Bill Cardille, was in fact a local television reporter who hosted a horror movie show as well as occasionally presenting the news; and the rifle-toting posse at the end of the film was made up of locals who were only too happy to be filmed with their guns. The use of non-actors adds to the verisimilitude of the story, with the cheap black and white film stock – apparently Romero had the option to shoot in colour, but felt that monochrome suited the story better – recalling newsreel footage: even after the advent of colour TV, events on screen still looked more convincing in black and white.

One of the most important innovations of the film was to present explicit gore in a realistic style. As Romero explains:

> There was no MPAA or Rating Board at that point, so there was no panel of experts that were issuing dictates or

reviewing films saying you can leave this in but you have to take that out. But there was this unwritten law which came from over the course of years which said you had to sort of stand back and be polite and just show the shadow and not show the knife entering flesh. I just didn't know why. I guess from having been weaned on EC comic books and things like that I thought why not do it like that, and why hasn't anyone done it. I didn't think so much as we were breaking down barriers as why didn't anyone do it this way?

When the film was completed, Image Ten had considerable difficulty finding a distributor. Some were upset by the gore; Columbia was interested, but put off by the fact that it was black and white; and AIP wanted a happy ending. Finally the film was picked up by the Walter Reade Organization for distribution.

SOUNDTRACK: The music was taken from the Capital film music library, a subsidiary of Hardman Associates, which was run by Karl Hardman (Harry Cooper). He selected a range of music for Romero to choose from, and was also responsible for the electronic effects, which add more to the atmosphere – one particularly effective moment has Helen Cooper's screams looped and echoed – than the stock music. The release fee for the music was $1,500.

'IT'S ONLY A MOVIE ... ONLY A MOVIE ...': The Walter Reade Organization offered a $50,000 insurance policy against anyone dying of a heart attack while watching the film, in a stunt worthy of William Castle.

RELEASE: The film premiered at the Filton Theatre in Pittsburgh, and was met with a standing ovation. Unswayed by such a response, the distributors released the film on a double bill with *Dr Who and the Daleks* (Gordon Flemyng, 1965), a particularly crass piece of programming.

Most critics savaged the film on its release. Roger Ebert, in an article written for the *Chicago Sun-Times* but more widely read on its republication in *Reader's Digest*, attacked it as a bad influence on children, further confirming its links to EC Comics; while *Variety* found it 'casts serious aspersions on the integrity of its makers, distrib Walter Reade, the film industry as a whole and exhibs who book the pic, as well as raising doubts about the future of the regional film movement and the moral health of filmgoers who cheerfully opt for unrelieved sadism'.

One of the few positive reviews came from *The Village Voice*'s Richard McGuinness, who praised its 'crudely accomplished but spontaneous effect', its 'manic overacting . . . the actors' frenzies . . . are of an enthusiasm rarely seen in films but here look simply like reasonable responses to the circumstances', and a plot that 'is unrestrained and incorrigibly kills all the characters in what, near the end, becomes an avalanche of atrocities'.

The filmmakers weren't bothered by the predominantly bad reviews: the film was doing excellent business on the drive-in circuit, its reputation as a truly shocking horror picture spreading quickly by word of mouth; even in Continental Europe it was doing brisk business, and was reported by the *Wall Street Journal* to be the top money-making film in Europe in the year of its release.

But if it was a runaway success, they weren't seeing the spoils: the distributors were ill-equipped to deal with demand for the film, and 'ripped us off', according to Romero. Worse still, when the title was changed to *Night of the Living Dead* the copyright notice was accidentally left off, meaning that the film was considered public domain. The director eventually sanctioned the release of a colourised version simply in the hope that some of the original filmmakers would make some money from it.

Still, the savage attacks from some critics brought the film to the attention of others who had less conservative tastes, and it was quick to receive a critical rehabilitation. *Sight and Sound* ranked it among the year's top ten films, and Romero was invited to present it at New York's Museum of Modern Art as part of a series dedicated to the work of important new directors; even Ebert was able to describe *Last House on the Left* (Wes Craven, 1972) a couple of years later as 'a neglected American horror exploitation masterpiece on a par with *Night of the Living Dead*'. More recently, critic Carol Clover has referred to it as sparking her interest in horror films, and describes it as 'one of the great American films'.

CRITICAL EYE: Much of *Night*'s power comes from its clean break with genre conventions. Horror traditionally featured a normal, ordered universe disrupted by an irrational force that was then defeated by the forces of conservatism: the family, romantic love, science, the police/army, decisive behaviour or religion. But Pittsburgh is, according to Romero, a 'no bullshit' city, and *Night* is a no bullshit film. Each of the traditional horror film's reassurances is redundant in the face of the zombie menace:

- The family unit is entirely dysfunctional. Mrs Cooper despises her husband, and only stays with him for the sake of their daughter; and Johnny and Barbra resent the chore of visiting their father's grave. Family ties are even dangerous: Helen's love for her daughter stops her from running when Karen advances with a trowel, and Barbra's return to action is cut off by the sight of her reanimated brother.
- Tom and Judy, whose puppy love would in most previous horror films ensure their survival, end up providing freshly cooked meat for the zombie hordes, and Judy's romantic insistence on joining Tom is one of the factors that leads to their death.
- Scientists can only advise the survivors to dispose of their dead dispassionately. There's a suggestion that scientific endeavour is to blame, in the *Quatermass*-style reference to radiation brought back by an Explorer satellite; this is not repeated in the subsequent *Dead* films, but fits Romero's characteristic anti-authoritarian slant – here the authorities are probably to blame for the catastrophe.
- The police posse picks off Ben at the end, just when the audience thinks he might be saved. The sheriff boasts of having killed others who may well have been human; in fact the gunmen kill anyone they see who is not with them. The media don't help much either, and *Night* is one of the first films to explore the dubious role they play in a crisis.
- Decisive behaviour: Ben's plan to stay upstairs ends in death and disaster, and he eventually cowers in the basement he had previously described as a 'death trap'. His macho posturing and competition with Harry also endanger the whole group; while the zombies are united in their quest for food, the humans squabble and threaten one another. Barbra emerges from her catatonic state only to become more fresh meat: there is no reward for good behaviour here, and everyone dies.
- Religion: John maintains early on that there is little point in going to church, and the events of the film seem to back him

up. Although the zombies can be seen as a perverse interpretation of Christian resurrection doctrine, religious paraphernalia just adds one more danger to the environment, with John cracking his head on a tombstone; and nobody even bothers raising a crucifix against the ghouls, which are soon seen more along the lines of a natural disaster, compared by Tom to a flood.

The look of the film plays against the audience's expectations of what a cheap horror film should deliver, with its resolutely non-gothic graveyard and explicit references to the heritage of Universal horror it is about to turn on its head. The man the viewer might expect to be the film's hero is killed in the first five minutes, while its apparent heroine lapses into catatonia, an unexpectedly realistic reaction to events.

The film has been widely interpreted as a comment on the Civil Rights struggle and the Vietnam War, both at the forefront of the American public's consciousness in 1968. The all-white cracker posse at the end of the film recalls a lynch mob in its appearance, and a platoon of soldiers in its laconic banter while shooting anything that moves; it's impossible not to associate such hand-held black and white imagery, or the grainy stills of Ben's corpse being tossed onto a pyre, with the newsreel footage – of Kent State, Vietnam and the protest movement – burning its way into the American psyche at the time.

But while, according to Professor Adam Lowenstein, 'these images tell the . . . painful truth about those struggles in a way that not many films of the time or since have been able to', if this was all the film had to offer it should by now have lost its relevance and power. Yet it still packs a punch, with the film's satirical content harnessed less to specific social issues than to an incisive critique of human behaviour.

Night generates a range of fears – from primal anxieties about the return of the dead, the correct disposal of corpses, being eaten and parricide, to the modern potential horrors of everyday objects and relationships. But unlike most previous horror films, rather than attempting to resolve these fears it surrenders to and even wallows in them. The film has no intention of reassuring its audience; its political message is subversion and its logic is that of the nightmare, with a build-up of claustrophobia and tension marked by its downward movement and increasingly fast editing, culminating in the false dawn of the film's shocking ending. The possibility of salvation here leads only to death.

The zombies themselves have been seen to represent variously the waste inherent in consumer society, the psychic numbing of nuclear anxiety, and guilt over occupying a privileged economic position at the expense of others, mixed with fear that such a situation won't last. They come from all walks of life, reflecting contemporary fears of mass unemployment – in a recessionary climate nobody's job was safe.

Romero's comments seem to support such a view – 'Zombies are the real lower-class citizens of the monster world and that's why I like them' – and by the time of *Day* scientists are trying to train the zombies to work for them. But the director has also said of the zombie that 'He was us'. A radio broadcast in *Night* describes the zombies as 'ordinary looking (people) in a state of trance', recalling both Barbra's catatonia and, perhaps, the audience's apathy in continuing to accept a corrupt and morally defunct system. Romero's zombies often appear far more sympathetic than his human characters, and both act on instinct, the humans redundantly consuming luxury goods or jockeying for position just as zombies with no stomachs continue to snap feebly at human flesh.

Most people, throughout the *Dead* films, stick to the worthless values of a dying world, but for some the zombie apocalypse may offer an opportunity to start again; while this fragile optimism is lacking in *Night*, it redeems the grimness of its sequels, and suggests that even if the belief in something better seems futile, it is finally the only thing worth fighting for.

INDUSTRY IMPACT: *Night* marks the birth of modern horror, making it one of the most influential genre films. The brutal tone of 70s shockers like Wes Craven's *The Last House on the Left* (1972), **The Texas Chain Saw Massacre**, and David Cronenberg's *Shivers* (1975) and *Rabid* (1977) owes much to *Night*, with the latter two films also indebted to it for its imagery and apocalyptic feel. These films are also, like Romero's, regional independents, and *Night* heralded a new wave of anti-Hollywood filmmaking; as Quentin Tarantino has argued, without Romero you probably wouldn't have Steven Soderbergh.

As for the film's content, it was followed by a rash of inferior tales of the walking dead; among the best were Bob Clark's *Dead of Night* (1974), a Vietnam-era spin on WW Jacobs' *The*

Monkey's Paw; Amando de Ossorio's dream-like *Blind Dead* series (1971–5); and Jorge Grau's *The Living Dead at the Manchester Morgue* (1974), which saw shambling flesh-eaters in the Lake District, of all places.

The release of *Dawn* gave new blood to Italian exploitation cinema, with Lucio Fulci's films (*Zombie Flesheaters/Zombie/Zombi 2* (1979), *City of the Living Dead/The Gates of Hell/Paura nella città dei morti viventi* (1980), *The Beyond/L'aldilà* (1981)) heralding a golden age for fans of gorily inept zombie movies, with six Italian gut-munchers produced in 1980 alone.

Legal wrangles between Russo and Romero over *Night*'s ownership resulted in Russo being given the rights to use 'living dead' while Romero could use 'dead'; Russo and director Dan O'Bannon made a spoofy sequel to Romero's film with *Return of the Living Dead* (1985), which itself spawned two sequels and tapped in to a regrettable public taste for zombie parody. Most of the spoofs clogging up video shelves during the 80s defined everything bad about the decade's horror, being unintelligent, unfunny and unconvincing, although some (see **Evil Dead 2**) were gleefully excessive enough for sick laughs.

Russo also shot new scenes for a 'director's cut' of *Night* released in 1999, which Romero had nothing to do with; this should not be confused with the 1993 remake, scripted by Romero and directed by Tom Savini, which provided some effective twists on the original film.

Zombies continued to be favourites with low-budget filmmakers, and films like *The Video Dead* (Robert Scott, 1987), *Shatter Dead* (Scooter McCrae, 1993) and *Meat Market* (Brian Clement, 2000) were heavily indebted to Romero, while Japanese audiences couldn't get enough of the flesh-eating shamblers, with films ranging from the recursive (*Stacy*, Naoyuki Tomomatsu, 2001) to the comic (*Wild Zero*, Tetsuro Takeuchi, 2000) and ultra-stylish (*Versus*, Ryuhei Kitamura, 2000).

Wes Craven's *The Serpent and the Rainbow* (1988) was a rare post-Romero excursion into voodoo lore, but perhaps the most compelling recent addition to the zombie canon has been Michele Soavi's astonishing *Dellamorte Dellamore/Cemetery Man* (1994), which mixes the zombie rom-com theme of the late 80s and early 90s (*Deadly Friend* (Wes Craven, 1986), *Return of the Living Dead 3* (Brain Yuzna, 1993)) with surreal flights of fancy for one of the most impressive genre films of the decade.

FINAL WORD: If **Psycho** brought the horror movie home to the American heartland, *Night* didn't even have the distancing effect of the gothic Bates house; and if **Rosemary's Baby** shares *Night*'s bleak ending, there's always the reassuring suggestion that maybe it's all in Rosemary's mind. But here there is no escape. *Night* takes place on the night of the first Sunday of autumn, heralding a new era of nihilistic, bleak and savage horror – the genre would never be the same again.

SATANIC CINEMA

Rosemary's Baby (1968)

'Pray for Rosemary's Baby'

USA, Paramount/William Castle Enterprises, colour, 137 mins

Screenplay by Roman Polanski, based on the novel by Ira Levin
Directed by Roman Polanski
Producer: William Castle
Director of Photography: William Fraker
Production Designer: Richard Sylbert
Art Director: Joel Schiller
Costumes: Anthea Sylbert
Editors: Sam O'Steen, Bob Wyman
Music: Krystof Komeda
Assistant Director: Daniel J McCauley
Sound: Harold Lewis
Associate Producer: Dona Holloway

CAST: Mia Farrow (*Rosemary Woodhouse*), John Cassavetes (*Guy Woodhouse*), Ruth Gordon (*Minnie Castevet*), Sidney Blackmer (*Roman Castevet*), Maurice Evans (*Hutch*), Ralph

Bellamy (*Dr Sapirstein*), Angela Dorian (*Terry*), Patsy Kelly (*Laura-Louise*), Elisha Cook (*Mr Nicklas*), Emmaline Henry (*Elise Dunstan*), Marianne Gordon (*Joan Jellicoe*), Philip Leeds (*Dr Shand*), Charles Grodin (*Dr Hill*), Hope Summers (*Mrs Gilmore*), Wende Wagner (*Tiger*), William Castle (*Man Outside Telephone Booth*)

SYNOPSIS: Rosemary Woodhouse and her actor husband Guy move into an apartment in the Bramford, a New York townhouse, despite its history of witchcraft and Satanism.

Rosemary meets Terry, who lives with the Castevets, and admires her good-luck charm. Later Terry jumps out of the Castevets' window and dies. Minnie Castevet visits Rosemary, and invites the couple over for dinner. Guy is reluctant, another actor having secured the part he wanted in a play, but soon warms to Roman Castevet, and plans to visit again. Next day Minnie gives Rosemary Terry's good-luck charm, which Rosemary puts in a box.

The actor who'd won Guy's part goes blind, allowing him to take it. Later Guy apologises to Rosemary for his self-centredness: he wants to have a child, and has planned the timing meticulously.

They have a romantic dinner, and Minnie brings round a chocolate pudding. Rosemary's tastes chalky, and she covertly throws most of it away. But then she feels dizzy, passes out and has a dream in which she is raped by a demon.

Next morning she is covered in scratches, and Guy tells her he couldn't wait. She becomes pregnant, and goes to Dr Hill, an obstetrician recommended by friends. The Castevets arrange for her to see Dr Sapirstein, a more famous doctor.

Rosemary puts the good-luck charm on, and is advised by Sapirstein to drink a herbal mixture prepared by Minnie. She is in pain, and losing weight, but Sapirstein tells her not to worry. Rosemary's former landlord and friend Hutch comes round and is alarmed by her appearance; when he leaves, after running into Roman and Guy, he has lost a glove. Later he calls Rosemary and tells her he wants to see her. She keeps the appointment, but Hutch doesn't show up; he's in a coma.

Rosemary invites her old friends round for a party. They tell her to see Dr Hill for a second opinion on her pain; but Guy refuses to pay. The baby starts moving, and the pain goes.

Hutch dies. At his funeral, Rosemary is given a book he'd bought her. She discovers that Roman Castevet is the son of black magician Adrian Marcato, and believes that a coven of witches wants to sacrifice her child. Guy destroys the book, but Sapirstein reassures her that Roman is very ill and going on holiday.

Rosemary, believing that Guy is part of the coven, packs her bags and leaves, going to Dr Sapirstein then, suspicious of Sapirstein, to Dr Hill. The doctor calls Sapirstein and Guy, who come to pick her up. She escapes, but is soon sedated and goes into labour.

When she comes to, Sapirstein tells Rosemary her baby has died. She doesn't believe him. She stops taking her sedatives, and finds the coven gathered around the baby in the Castevets' flat. She is alarmed by his eyes, and is told by Roman that he is the devil's son. He asks her to mother the child and, responding to the baby's wails, she begins to rock the cradle.

ORIGINS AND INSPIRATION: The devil has had a privileged part to play on screen since the birth of cinema. Early innovator Méliès returned frequently to the Mephistophelian theme in his late 19th century inauguration of fantastic cinema, while the many film versions of *The Student of Prague/Der Student von Prag*, *The Golem/Der Golem* and *Faust* – notably Murnau's 1926 film – kept the subject at the forefront of the silent cinema era.

Since then the devil has become one of the principal archetypes of film, popping up in everything from comedy (*Bedazzled*, 1967) to hardcore porn (*The Devil in Miss Jones*, 1972). While his principal occupation in Hollywood fare was to provide light entertainment in Faustian comedies, a few films had a more authentic whiff of brimstone: 1934's *The Black Cat* (Edgar G Ulmer) pitted Bela Lugosi against Boris Karloff, high priest of a Satanic cult; and the Val Lewton-produced *The Seventh Victim* (Mark Robson, 1943) provided the template for many Satanic films to follow, by bringing devil worship into contemporary urban life and surrounding it with sceptics who are eventually forced to admit that witchcraft works.

The film has a group of modern-day Satanists pursuing ex-member Jacqueline Gibson (Jean Brooks) to her suicide, and its New York setting, its focus on the illusory nature of appearances and its mundane portrayal of devil worship anticipate *Rosemary's Baby*. Indeed its screenwriter Dewitt Bodeen, who attended a meeting of Satanists as part of his research, later recalled that his hosts 'were exactly like the devil worshippers in *Rosemary's Baby*.

It was even in the same neighbourhood on the West Side that they used in that film ... They were mostly old people and they were casting these spells while they knitted and crocheted.'

Jacques Tourneur, another Lewton alumnus, directed *Night of the Demon* (US: *Curse of the Demon*) in 1958. Loosely adapted from MR James's story *Casting the Runes*, this classic of understated horror benefited from some Crowleyan touches in the depiction of its villain, Karswell, but suffered from the producer's insistence that its monster should take up more screen time: the close-ups of the rubbery creature seems inserted from another film entirely, and are a crude violation of the film's carefully constructed atmosphere of dread menace.

In Britain, 1961's *Night of the Eagle* (Sidney Hayers; US: *Burn, Witch, Burn*) returned to *Night of the Demon* territory with a sceptic who is forced to believe; the plot anticipates Polanski's film with the roles reversed, by having Norman Taylor's wife Tansy using magic to further his career. He rejects the idea and discards her magical paraphernalia, with disastrous results.

Hammer invested its later vampire films with diabolical content, and dealt more explicitly with the themes of witchcraft and Satanism in the Nigel Kneale-scripted *The Witches* (Cyril Frankel, 1966) and 1967's *The Devil Rides Out*. The latter, one of Hammer's best, was adapted from Dennis Wheatley's novel of the dark forces underlying English conservatism by Richard Matheson, and had an inventive and convincing script; the direction by Terence Fisher is also taut and tense, and the casting of Christopher Lee and Charles Gray in the lead roles of the Duc de Richleau and Mocata is impeccable. Mocata, all steely gaze and impeccable manners, resembles a younger, more uptight version of Adrian Marcato, as well as sharing Crowleyan qualities with *Night of the Demon*'s Karswell: the devil, here, takes pains to receive only the finest representation.

By the time Ira Levin wrote *Rosemary's Baby*, a diabolical renaissance was in full swing. The Rolling Stones had released *Their Satanic Majesties Request*, and it had become fashionable in hipper circles to dabble in the occult and other esoteric belief systems. The key drive for many in the late 60s was personal development, and magic's concentration on imagination and willpower, allied with an LSD-inspired severing of ties with consensus reality and a distrust of conventional religion, meant that the black arts held a powerful appeal. After all, as these films demonstrated, magic worked, and brought the user into contact with a more profound reality.

Hitchcock was agent Martin Bridt's first choice for the film options to *Rosemary's Baby*, then being circulated in proof form, but when the director declined – whether due to his Catholicism or fear of being typecast as a horror director is unknown – William Castle, the low-rent showman responsible for gimmicky shockers like *The Tingler* (1959), snapped them up for $150,000, three weeks before the book was published.

Castle was under contract to Paramount, and took the proofs to the studio's head of production, Robert Evans. Castle wanted to direct the film, but Evans had another director in mind: Roman Polanski, whose *Repulsion* (1965), another tale of a young woman's isolation and paranoia, he'd recently seen. Castle was offered a deal as producer, receiving $250,000 and 50 per cent of the film's profits, and Evans contacted Polanski. Worried that the Polish director might not want to do another horror movie after *Repulsion* (1965) and *Dance of the Vampires/The Fearless Vampire Killers* (1967), he told Polanski, a keen skier, that he wanted to discuss *Downhill Racer*, a skiing film that was eventually helmed by Michael Ritchie; at the meeting he gave the director the proofs for *Rosemary's Baby* to look over.

Polanski loved the book, even if the film would necessarily be 'less personal, because it is not something that interested me before someone else knew about it'. He insisted on writing the script himself, and after three weeks in seclusion came up with a 260-page first draft; he then whittled this down with the help of Richard Sylbert, the film's art director. Most of the dialogue in the script was lifted directly from the novel, and it stayed very close to the novel's structure; the only major change was in the character of Minnie Castevet, in the novel a large and jolly woman, rather than the small, acerbic New Yorker of the film.

It was to be Polanski's first Hollywood film, and he had a commensurate pay cheque of $150,000 to write and direct, with no option on the profits.

DIRECTOR: Polanski's film career began when he was a student in his native Poland, acting in a few films by Andrzej Wajda and then spending five years at the State Film College, Lodz. In 1962 he made his first (and, to date, only) Polish feature, *Knife in the*

Water/Nóz w wodzie (1962), working on the scenario with Jerzy Skolimowski, who was later to film Robert Graves's *The Shout* (1979).

Knife in the Water was seen in England by producer Gene Gutowski, who invited the director to make *Repulsion*, his first English-language film, and *Cul-de-Sac* (1966), an absurdist comedy of manners. Polanski worked on the scripts for both films, and the former bore some similarities to *Rosemary's Baby*: in it Carol (Catherine Deneuve), a Belgian living in South Kensington, suffers a mental breakdown triggered by sexual fear. The action is largely restricted to her flat, and focuses almost exclusively on her subjective viewpoint, with the audience seeing her hallucinations. Several stylistic touches anticipate the later film – the jarring use of bells, the central character gazing at her distorted reflection, a monotonous piano practice in the background, ticking clocks and a door hidden behind furniture – and the themes of loneliness, madness and isolation are common to both films.

Yet *Repulsion* is altogether more claustrophobic, its moody monochrome photography producing a more powerful sense of alienation than the rich colours of *Rosemary's Baby*, and being leavened by none of its humour. Carol is far from a sympathetic protagonist, twitchy from the outset and soon homicidal, even towards one of the film's few sympathetic characters, and there is no exploration of the reasons for her schizophrenia, except for a suggestion of abuse in a family photo shown at the end. Deneuve's unflinchingly honest and convincing portrayal of schizophrenia, and the atmosphere of seedy hopelessness that pervades the film, make it a difficult experience to enjoy, and it is perhaps no surprise that Polanski turned to comedy for his next film.

But *Dance of the Vampires* (1967), a spoofy celebration of Hammer-style vampire films, was a critical and commercial flop, especially in the US where it was cut by twenty minutes, retitled and given a cartoon prologue. Polanski's requests to have his name removed from the film were turned down, and it has since become something of a cult favourite, richly gothic in a way rarely equalled by the films it parodies.

For *Rosemary's Baby* Polanski was the first filmmaker from behind the Iron Curtain to direct a Hollywood feature; it was also the first time he'd worked on a story by another writer, and his first film to have a full release in the UK.

Following the film's success Polanski was feted as the hottest new director in town, and was bombarded with scripts for new occult and supernatural thrillers, all of which he rejected. His next feature, a bloody *Macbeth* (1971), proved an expensive commercial failure, although it is one of the finest Shakespeare adaptations on film, and the follow-up, *What?* (1973), remains rarely seen even today. Polanski's wife Sharon Tate had been murdered by members of the Manson Family in 1969, and critics began to pay more attention to the director's stormy personal life – a process aided by the director's love of the limelight, although he would doubtless have preferred anonymity during his 1977 arrest for the statutory rape of a thirteen-year-old – than his films.

After the critically acclaimed *Chinatown* in 1974, Polanski made the third film in a loose trilogy of paranoid chillers, *The Tenant* (1976). In this adaptation of Roland Topor's novel he plays the lead character, Trelkovsky, who on moving into a new apartment becomes convinced that his neighbours are attempting to drive him mad by forcing him into the persona of the previous tenant, a woman who attempted suicide by throwing herself out of a window. Nosy neighbours feature heavily in *Repulsion* and *Rosemary's Baby* too, with the hitherto isolated protagonists surrounded at the end by curious faces, and here, as in the other films, the accent is on subjective experience, and the action mostly confined to a single location. *The Tenant* veers closer to the absurdist comedy of *Knife in the Water* and *Cul-de-Sac* (Roman Polanski, 1966) than his other genre films, and while it contains some genuinely disturbing scenes – Trelkovsky's first attempt at suicide fails, so he drags his broken body up the stairs to try again – its atmosphere of chilling ambiguity is marred by a shot that reveals his insanity.

Polanski's professed admiration for horror films, especially *Peeping Tom* (1960) and **The Haunting**, is understandable here, as his paranoid films mix the former's focus on voyeurism with the latter's anthropomorphised environments. He has stated that 'What I like is an extremely realistic setting in which there is something that does not fit with the real. That is what gives an atmosphere'; mundane objects take on sinister properties in his films, with a palpable menace generated by such prosaic sounds as the ticking of a clock or the whirring of an air conditioner.

Among the director's favourite writers are Pinter, Kafka and Beckett. Their key themes, isolation and claustrophobia, also feature heavily in Polanski's work, with a tight core of characters generally restricted to a single location; and the director has stated that he wants to make a film with one character alone. Human solitude is unavoidable in the corrupt societies of Polanski's world; the only workable communities are those that are given over to 'evil', such as the society of vampires in *Dance of the Vampires* or the Satanists of *Rosemary's Baby*. Perhaps because of this, in all of Polanski's genre films 'evil' triumphs.

Polanski returned to the horror genre with 1999's *The Ninth Gate*, by far the most interesting of the rash of millennial apocalypse films. In this eminently literary work, a reaction against the hyperactive film editing inspired by MTV and video games, Johnny Depp plays Dean Corso, a book detective on the trail of a grimoire with engravings by the devil himself. Polanski plays with genre convention, making the devil an attractive woman whose offer is genuinely liberating; Corso's story arc from sceptic to believer leads him not to fight Satanism but to embrace it; Satanists are pitted against each other, rather than working as a single community; and the overblown rituals familiar from other films are mocked as useless. While the film suffered from a lukewarm box-office response, it represents one of the most interesting and authentic portrayals of Satanism on screen.

CASTING: Polanski teamed up with artists to sketch the look of the characters he wanted – their faces, build and clothes – and the production team started looking for suitable actors for him. The director was keen to work with old Hollywood actors, and many familiar faces were cast against type: the building superintendent, for instance, was played by Elisha Cook, more familiar to audiences as a low-rent hoodlum, and the Satanists were all played by friendly character actors, a subversion of expectations that was also evident in the pink titles, which suggest a female child.

Polanski was seeing Sharon Tate, and hoped that somebody would nominate her for the part of Rosemary. Nobody did, although she does appear in an uncredited cameo during Rosemary's party for her old friends. Tate's friend Tuesday Weld was also favoured by the director, but Paramount had their eyes on Mia Farrow, star of TV's *Peyton Place*. When Polanski met her he was impressed by the star's vulnerability, although she looked nothing like the 'robust, healthy, all-American girl' he'd pictured

Rosemary as. Farrow went on to star in a few other genre pictures, including *Blind Terror* (1971) and *Full Circle* (1977), before joining Woody Allen's repertory team.

Polanski showed the script to his friend Warren Beatty, who rejected the part of Guy; Robert Redford was interested, and was Sylbert's favourite for the role – 'what we wanted was a matinee idol' – but Paramount was about to sue him; and Jack Nicholson was interested, but Polanski felt at the time that he was too little known. Finally director John Cassavetes (*Shadows* (1960), *A Woman Under the Influence* (1974)) suggested himself for the part to Castle, and Polanski agreed.

The director and Cassavetes did not get on well on set, partly because the actor wanted more freedom than Polanski was prepared to give. Mia Farrow also thought Polanski demanding in his insistence that the actors do things his way, but felt he 'inspired awe because he always seemed to know exactly what he was doing'. The relationship between Polanski and Cassavetes deteriorated to the point that Polanski was dismissive of his fellow director's films in interviews, and pointed out that he had not hired Cassavetes for his ability to act, but simply to play himself; Guy is, by any standards, a wholly unsympathetic character.

Cassavetes took his revenge in an interview with *Look* magazine after the film's release: 'Ask him why he's so obsessed by the bloody and gruesome, behaving like some kid in a candy store.' But the actor himself returned to the bloody and gruesome a few more times, being blown limb from limb by Amy Irving's psychic rage in *The Fury* (1978) and tracking down a demon rapist in *The Incubus* (1981).

Producer William Castle has a cameo, as the man who alarms Rosemary outside a phone booth; and Tony Curtis is uncredited as the voice of the actor who goes blind.

PRODUCTION: The film was scheduled for a 50-day shoot, with two weeks' location shooting in New York City and the rest of the film shot in LA. By the end of the first week, Polanski was a week behind schedule, and soon the studio began to panic. But Robert Evans loved the rushes, and persuaded the money men to relax. Farrow's husband Frank Sinatra was also dismayed by the overrun, as she had been scheduled to star with him in *The Detective* (1968); he asked her to leave the shoot, and when she refused he sent a lawyer to deliver divorce papers. This came as an unexpected blow, and Farrow's anxiety over the divorce is visible in her performance. The film finally finished four weeks over schedule, and $400,000 over the $1.9 million budget.

Polanski's perfectionism and attention to detail were the principal reasons why the production overran. This was a period film – albeit of a period just two years previous, 1965 – and the director wanted every detail perfect. Farrow's skirts grow gradually shorter as the film progresses, as short skirts were coming into fashion in 1965, and events such as the visit of the Pope and *Time*'s publication of an issue entitled 'Is God Dead?' feature prominently.

For the dream sequence, the opening scene was shot on a $150,000 yacht at Playa del Ray marina near Santa Monica, and Polanski had also ordered a copy of part of the Sistine Chapel ceiling made, down to the faded colours and cracks, which took craftsmen six weeks. The director drew on his bad experience with LSD for the tone of the sequence, although ironically acidheads enjoyed the scene, and the film became a favoured psychedelic accompaniment for the headstrong.

Polanski, an agnostic, preferred to retain some ambiguity in the film – even down to the final scene – and to give it a subjective focus that meant 'The entire story, as seen through her eyes, could have been a chain of only superficially sinister coincidences, a product of her feverish fancies.' He was influenced in this by reading Professor RL Gregory's *Eye and Brain: The Psychology of Seeing*, which argues that we see far less than we think, and that our ideas about reality are based on earlier perceptions distorted by faulty memory. The power of suggestion in the film worked well: many in the audience were convinced they had seen the baby's cloven hooves and tail, when all that is shown is a near-subliminal shot of two catlike eyes; and when the TV version debuted on ABC, there were reports that the censor had cut scenes featuring the baby. There never were any in the first place.

Predictably for a film with such a theme, what happened during the production has since been shrouded in rumour. Anton La Vey, founder of the Church of Satan, has claimed that he was employed to play the devil in the rape scene as well as to provide technical advice; but crew members deny this, and point out that actor Clay Tanner wore the devil outfit. Further rumours suggested that this was a cursed production, pointing to composer Komeda's death, the uremic poisoning of William Castle and Sharon Tate's murder as somehow connected to the film. Castle, ever the showman, seems to have been the principal motivator behind these rumours, which Polanski – a firm sceptic regarding the supernatural – rejected. Exteriors for the Bramford were, however, shot at the Dakota, a reputedly haunted apartment block in New York outside which John Lennon was shot in December 1980.

SOUNDTRACK: Polish composer Krystof Komeda wrote the scores for all of Polanski's films up to *Rosemary's Baby*, except for *Repulsion*. Originally trained as a doctor, Komeda was also an enthusiastic jazz musician who composed in his spare time; it was Polanski who persuaded him to take up composing full-time. Shortly after the film was released Komeda injured his head in a fall, and died from a brain aneurysm in April 1969.

The memorable lullaby that is the film's signature tune is hummed by an uncredited Mia Farrow, and captures the film's ambiguous mood perfectly with its sense of unease underlying a saccharine sweetness.

'IT'S ONLY A MOVIE . . . ONLY A MOVIE . . .': Posters for the film bore the slogan 'Pray for Rosemary's Baby' so boldly that some filmgoers mistook this for the film's title. Audiences had been warmed up by the huge success of Ira Levin's novel; the hardback stayed on the *New York Times*' bestseller list for 41 weeks.

RELEASE: The film was an outstanding success, grossing over $30 million, which made it one of the first horror blockbusters. Its box office probably wasn't hurt by the moral controversy over the film: the BBFC cut fifteen seconds from the rape sequence, because of 'elements of kinky sex associated with black magic', and although they didn't go quite as far as some religious groups who viewed the film as the work of the devil, the National Catholic Office for Motion Pictures in the US gave it a 'C' (condemned rating): '. . . because of several scenes of nudity [and] the perverted use which the film makes of fundamental Christian beliefs, especially the events surrounding the birth of Christ, and its mockery of religious persons and practices. The very technical excellence of the film serves to intensify its defamatory nature.'

They have a point: the film mocks organised religion throughout, with Hutch's story of the Trench sisters' cannibalism equated with Christian ritual and the final scenes a parody of the birth of Christ, Rosemary clad in the blue of the Virgin Mary as she greets a foreigner bearing gifts. Perhaps Polanski had hoped that the portrayal of the key Satanists as Jewish would fit Catholic tastes; whatever the case, it's ironic that this feminist Catholic film should have been created by two Jewish men, Levin and Polanski. Some Satanists were said to have embraced the film as a celebration of Satanism, although this doesn't seem to have been Polanski's aim: 'evil' triumphs in almost all of the director's films, and here the Satanists are hardly presented as attractive, even if witchcraft does, to Rosemary's eyes at least, work.

Catholic disapproval did not prevent the film from being nominated for two Oscars: Best Adapted Screenplay and Best Supporting Actress for Ruth Gordon; but it didn't win either of the awards.

Contemporary reviewers tended to enjoy the film but were disappointed that a director so talented had turned his hand to such ephemeral fare: The *New Yorker* noted that 'The film is very proficient, but all the same what's it for?' while Stanley Kaufman in *New Republic* felt it did not match the standards set by *Knife in the Water*, with the director now more a 'manufacturer of intelligent thrillers, clever and insubstantial'; *Monthly Film Bulletin* was one of the few magazines to give it an unapologetically favourable review, feeling that the film 'triumphantly confirms the promise of [Polanski's] early work'.

CRITICAL EYE: Critical views of the film since its release have focused on its ambiguity. Some see the events weighted heavily in favour of Rosemary's perception, while others argue that the conspiracy is a projection of mental illness; Polanski is on record as saying that he wanted both readings to be possible.

The film would work dramatically without any reference to Satanism; it is Rosemary's fears of pregnancy – and, to a lesser degree, her lapsed Catholicism and related sexual guilt – that drive the narrative. Her fears of her changing body shape are foregrounded by idealised representations of the body, such as a nude statue seen with her in several shots, and her isolation, illness and sense of impotence are not uncommon early reactions to pregnancy.

Indeed the film can be seen as a case study of prepartum psychosis, a form of temporary psychosis related to pregnancy that is characterised by actions like running away from home and infanticidal urges – the shift from Rosemary's initial protective-ness to her sense of the baby as diabolical fits this reading – and a range of disturbed biological functions.

The final scene seems to confirm Rosemary's fears, but the audience is still seeing events from her viewpoint: perhaps the pills she's been hiding after giving birth are anti-psychotics, prescribed after her shock at a still birth. When she enters the Castevets' apartment to find her child, the view is heavily distorted, recalling the relationship between distorted perspective and mental illness in *Repulsion*.

But why should she imagine a Satanic conspiracy? The tension between her Catholic guilt and sexual urges may have led her to fantasise a demonic rapist, both erotic reward and punishment; as Ernest Jones, in his study *On the Nightmare*, puts it, 'Sometimes voluptuous feelings are coupled with those of angst, especially with women, who often believe that the night fiend has copulated with them.'

Yet her husband, neighbours and doctors *do* conspire to take control over her life, whether Satanic or not – the explicitly non-Satanic Dr Hill, after all, still aids the conspirators. The symbolically named Guy plans her pregnancy down to the last detail, choosing the date and noting her missed period; his shiftiness around his pregnant wife can be understood as male unease about female reproduction, rather than further evidence that she is carrying the devil's spawn. Even her friends treat her differently, more as a pregnancy than a person, adding to her sense of isolation.

The film plays consciously on fears of male control of the female reproductive process: the Pill had been introduced at the start of the decade, revolutionising female biology, but its original hormone levels were soon considered dangerously high; and the Thalidomide scandal of the early 60s proved that many women's anxieties about male science were well grounded. It would not have been too much of a step for women to identify with Rosemary when she is bullied into drinking a noxious cocktail against her fears of what it will do to her, and decisions about her pregnancy are taken away from her at every stage.

Rosemary's impotence is clearest in the way she changes physically. With her pregnancy she becomes infantilised herself, as shown by her boyish haircut, her inability to distinguish between fantasy and reality, and a shift in perspective that has the apartment looming larger and larger in the background while the outside world seems more and more threatening. And as the audience sees the world through Rosemary's eyes, it goes through the same process, similarly unable to distinguish the imaginary from the real.

INDUSTRY IMPACT: *Rosemary's Baby* predictably inspired a series of lesser devil-worship films. One of the best was *Blood on Satan's Claw* (Piers Haggard, 1971), a British period piece with an authentically pagan flavour; but tastes for historical occult films had been superseded by Michael Reeves's bleak *Witchfinder General* (1968), which presented belief in witches as superstition, and witch-hunts as excuses for sadism rather than opportunities for vanquishing evil.

Robin Hardy's peculiarly resonant gem *The Wicker Man* (1973) follows a number of *Rosemary's Baby*'s themes in having a coven – here a group of pagans led by Christopher Lee in drag – presumed to practise ritual sacrifice; policeman Neil Howie (Edward Woodward), a staunch and virginal Christian, travels to the island of Summerisle off the west coast of Scotland to investigate the reported disappearance of a young girl. It eventually transpires that Howie, convinced that he is unearthing a pagan conspiracy, has been doing exactly what the islanders want him to all along, much as Rosemary is convinced the Satanists want to sacrifice her child, and in her protectiveness plays right into their hands.

American treatments of devil worship tended more towards the formulaic, with *The Mephisto Waltz* (Paul Wendkos, 1971) an inferior take on *Rosemary's Baby* in which a young husband is taken under the wing of an older man with a malign Satanic influence, of which the young man's wife is justly suspicious; and even the presence of Ruth Gordon in the 1976 TV movie *Look What's Happened to Rosemary's Baby* couldn't add any sparks to this lifeless sequel.

An intermittently interesting subgenre of devil-worship films came with news of the Manson Family murders, as misunderstandings of the Family's eschatological beliefs led to a rash of hairy hippy Satanist films like 1970's *I Drink Your Blood* (David E Durston). But the devil movie would only see a mainstream success on the scale of *Rosemary's Baby* again with 1974's soup-spraying piece of lurid Catholic propaganda, **The Exorcist.**

Rosemary's Baby's more interesting relatives are films that deal with its non-Satanic themes of pregnancy, nosy neighbours and paranoia. Fears of pregnancy and demonic children inform films from the sublime (David Cronenberg's *The Brood* (1979)) to the ridiculous (*And Now the Screaming Starts!* (Roy Ward Baker, 1973), *It's Alive!* (Larry Cohen, 1974)) and plain disturbing (*Eraserhead* (David Lynch, 1976)), while Spanish director Alex de la Iglesia's deliriously entertaining *La Comunidad* (2000), if not properly a horror film, owes much to Polanski's exploration of neighbours from hell.

The sense of paranoia and unease that runs through *Rosemary's Baby* was soon to become a commonplace of Hollywood cinema, and was itself foreshadowed by John Frankenheimer's *The Manchurian Candidate* (1962) and *Seven Days in May* (1964); Watergate only confirmed what the 60s generation had long suspected, and political conspiracy thrillers became a staple of 70s Hollywood cinema.

FINAL WORD: Part of *Rosemary's Baby*'s enduring appeal is the way that pregnancy and Satanism are not its only concerns: one of its coups is to present its evil in a milieu that is less one of realism than of the TV sitcom world of the 50s and 60s, and the film plays at times like a particularly twisted episode of *Bewitched*. Guy is a TV actor, crassly concerned with the placement of his ad, while the Satanists are parodies of the exaggerated normalcy of sitcom characters, drinking endless cups of Lipton's tea in their grotesque leisurewear, with their noses buried in the *Reader's Digest* when they aren't summoning Satan. Polanski pushed the novel's soap-opera qualities into the foreground, and turned it into a candy-coloured pastiche in which, as in **Don't Look Now**, the ludicrousness of the threat actually adds to its horror; as Richard Sylbert has pointed out, the film 'opens like a Doris Day movie. That's the whole point.'

POSSESSION

The Exorcist (1973)

'Somewhere between science and superstition, there is another world. The world of darkness.'

USA, Warner Bros. Inc/Hoya Productions Inc, colour, 122 mins

Directed by William Friedkin
Executive Producer: Noel Marshall
Producer: William Peter Blatty
Associate Producer: David Salven
First Assistant Director: Terrence A Donnelly
Screenplay: William Peter Blatty (based on his own novel)
Director of Photography: Owen Roizman (Iraq Sequences: Billy Williams)
Supervising Editor: Jordan Leondopoulos
Editors: Evan Lottman, Norman Gay (Iraq Sequences: Bud Smith)
Production Manager: Bill Malley
Special Effects: Marcel Vercoutere
Optical Effects: Marv Ystrom
Make-up Artist: Dick Smith

Title Design: Dan Perri
Music: 'Kanon for Orchestra', 'Tape Cello Concerto', 'String
Quartet (1960)', 'Polymorphia', 'The Devils of Loudun' by
Krzysztof Penderecki; 'Fantasia for Strings' by Hans Werner
Henze; 'Threnody 1: Night of the Electric Insects' by George
Crumb; 'Fliessend, ausserst Zart' from 'Five Pieces for
Orchestra, Op. 10' by Anton Webern; 'From the wind harp'
by Beginnings; 'Tubular Bells' by Mike Oldfield; 'Study No.
1', 'Study No. 2' by David Borden
Additional Music: Jack Nitzsche
Sound: Chris Newman (Iraq Sequences: Jean-Louis
Ducarmé)
Special Sound Effects: Ron Nagle, Doc Siegel, Gonzalo
Gavira, Bob Fine
Technical Advisers: Reverend John Nicola, SJ, Reverend
Thomas Bermingham, SJ, Reverend William O'Malley, SJ,
Norman E Chase, MD, Herbert E Walker, MD, Arthur I
Snyder, MD

CAST: Ellen Burstyn (*Chris MacNeil*), Max von Sydow (*Father Merrin, S J*), Lee J Cobb (*Lt William Kinderman*), Kitty Winn (*Sharon Spencer*), Jack MacGowran (*Burke Dennings*), Jason Miller (*Father Damien Karras, SJ*), Linda Blair (*Regan MacNeil*), Reverend William O'Malley, SJ (*Father Dyer, SJ*), Barton Heyman (*Dr Klein*), Pete Masterton (*Clinic Director*), Rudolf Schündler (*Karl*), Gina Petrushka (*Willie*), Robert Symonds (*Dr Tanney*), Arthur Storch (*Psychiatrist*), Reverend Thomas Bermingham, SJ (*President of University*), Vasiliki Maliaros (*Karras' Mother*), Titos Vandis (*Karras' Uncle*), Wallace Rooney (*Bishop*), Ron Faber (*Assistant Director*), Donna Mitchell (*Mary Jo Perrin*), Roy Cooper (*Jesuit Deacon*), Robert Gerringer (*Senator*), Mercedes McCambridge (*Voice of the Demon*)

SYNOPSIS: At an archaeological dig in Nineveh, Iraq, Father Merrin discovers a small carving of a demon, and tells his host he must return to the US.

In Georgetown, Washington, single mother Chris MacNeil hears sounds in the attic, and asks Karl, one of her housekeepers, to investigate. She is an actress, currently working on a film about student revolt called *Crash Course*.

Father Karras, a local Jesuit priest who is experiencing a crisis of faith, visits his mother in a New York slum. Later she is taken to a psychiatric hospital, where Karras visits her and is criticised by her brother for not being able to pay for private care; he is a trained psychiatrist, and could have taken a better-paid job. A church statue is defiled with oversized breasts and a phallus.

MacNeil's daughter Regan has been using a Ouija board. At a dinner party she urinates on the floor and tells a guest he will die soon. Her bed then shakes violently, even with both Regan and Chris on it.

Regan is subjected to a series of medical tests. The doctors visit her at home, but even after seeing her thrashing on the bed and talking in a guttural growl, they try to find a physical explanation.

Crash Course's director Burke Dennings is killed. His body is found at the foot of the stairs outside MacNeil's house, his head turned around. He had visited Regan before his death, and her window was wide open. A psychiatrist hypnotises Regan and is attacked. Doctors explain to MacNeil that the suggestive ritual of an exorcism might help her daughter, who apparently believes herself to be possessed by the devil.

Lt Kinderman quizzes Karras about Dennings's death and the defilement of the church. Kinderman finds one of Regan's sculptures at the foot of the stairs, and interviews MacNeil. Chris then sees her daughter masturbating with a crucifix and her head turning around, which prompts her to approach Karras for an exorcism. Karras is reluctant, but tests Regan and records her demon voices. On her belly appear the words 'Help me', and he is taunted with having neglected his mother. Karras approaches his Jesuit employers, who agree to an exorcism but recommend that Father Merrin, who has performed one before, preside.

Merrin refuses to hear Karras's psychological explanations or the history of the case, and proceeds immediately with the exorcism. This time Regan's head spins all the way around, she levitates from the bed and the statue of the demon seen earlier in Iraq appears in the bedroom. Karras is told by Merrin to leave, but returns later to find the priest dead, and attacks Regan, telling the demon to take him. He is duly possessed, but retains enough control to hurl himself from the window and fall down the stairs, killing himself.

Regan recovers and remembers nothing of her possession; the family moves away.

ORIGINS AND INSPIRATION: In 1949 William Peter Blatty, then a junior at the Jesuitical Georgetown University, read in the *Washington Post* of the Mt Rainier exorcism case. The incident involved a fourteen-year-old boy who had experimented with a Ouija board before apparently becoming possessed by the devil. Or at least that's what some Catholic priests thought, and they successfully exorcised him after several failed attempts; a Church inquiry later found that it was probably a case of hysteria with mild telekinetic effects, but to the young Blatty it was evidence of the devil's existence – and thus of God, angels and heaven.

Years later, after his career as a comedy writer – he co-scripted the Inspector Clouseau spoof *A Shot in the Dark* (Blake Edwards, 1964) among other films – had begun to founder, he thought of the story as a possible lead into new territories. He approached the exorcists involved, planning to write a factual case history, but was asked not to: the family had no desire to revisit this part of their history. But Father Bowdern, one of the priests involved, agreed to help him research a novel loosely inspired by the events, rather than a case history, on condition that he change the gender of the possessed youth to a girl, to further protect the family from unwanted publicity. *The Exorcist* was born.

Blatty finished the first draft of the novel in the summer of 1970, and showed it to his neighbour Shirley MacLaine, the inspiration for the character of Chris MacNeil. MacLaine took it to producer Lew Grade, with whom she had a film deal, but Grade, unimpressed, made only a low offer for the film rights.

MacLaine later starred in *The Possession of Joel Delaney* (Waris Hussein, 1972), a more interesting and convincing film than its blockbusting successor. Here the characters are more finely drawn, the tone more downbeat and ambiguous, and the Catholic imagery replaced by a Puerto Rican Santeria portrayed as both more mundane and more imaginatively rich than its Christian counterpart. The possession of a young man by his dead friend requires less of a leap of faith than the devil possessing Regan, and the terrorisation of the children at the end of the film easily matches anything in *The Exorcist* for nastiness, as a young boy is made to strip and dance while his sister eats dog food from a bowl: crucially, the audience feels for these vulnerable children, far more than it ever will for the entertainingly offensive Regan.

The hardcover rights to Blatty's novel were picked up by Harper and Row, who asked for a 'less obvious' conclusion; Blatty obliged, discarding Regan's original explanation of events that previously closed the book. During negotiations with the publisher, producer Paul Monash offered Blatty $400,000 for a six-month option to film the book, and promptly sold the option to Warner Bros for a reported $641,000, after several other studios passed; but the studio dropped Monash after Blatty showed that the producer was demanding unauthorised changes to the story. Blatty now took the mantle of producer, and wrote the first draft screenplay.

Various directors were approached, including Stanley Kubrick, Arthur Penn, John Boorman and Mike Nichols, all of whom turned the project down. Blatty felt the director should be agnostic, and not a Catholic, and favoured the Jewish William Friedkin, whose rudeness over another Blatty property had demonstrated an independence of spirit that impressed the writer – so much so that they'd already discussed working together on Blatty's next project, *The Ninth Configuration* (William Peter Blatty, 1980). Friedkin also had a background in documentary filmmaking, which Blatty felt could add to the realism necessary to suspend audience disbelief.

Warner Bros were initially reluctant – Friedkin had a reputation as a difficult director to work with – but were swayed by the critical and commercial success of *The French Connection* (1971) and Blatty's threat of legal action. By now the novel was a bestseller.

Friedkin was approached, and leapt at the chance, receiving $325,000 and a percentage of the film's profits. He and Blatty had much in common, not least the fact that both had been inordinately attached to their mothers, who had recently died. Still, he was so unimpressed by Blatty's first draft of the script that he refused to work from it, highlighting passages in the novel instead; Blatty reluctantly agreed to write a second draft, reducing various subplots and the role of Lt Kinderman.

DIRECTOR: Friedkin was born in Chicago, where he directed documentaries for TV before moving to the West Coast. There he worked on *Alfred Hitchcock Presents*, then directed four feature films in quick succession, including *The Night They Raided Minsky's* (1968); after *The Boys in the Band* (1970), Friedkin was reportedly advised by Howard Hawks to make more straightforward, unambiguously entertaining films, which led to *The French Connection* (1971), a fact-based thriller in a documentary style that avoided the self-conscious artiness of his earlier films and swept the board at that year's Oscars.

Friedkin never returned to the dizzy commercial heights of this film or *The Exorcist*. His next feature, *Sorcerer* (1977), a remake of Clouzot's *The Wages of Fear/Le Salaire de la Peur* (1952), was an expensive flop, and while thrillers like *The Brink's Job* (1979), *Cruising* (1980) and *To Live and Die in LA* (1985) have their fans, they did little to revitalise his career.

Friedkin returned to horror with *The Guardian* (1990), a silly story of a tree-worshipping nanny that has intermittent scares and allowed the director to fulfil his desire to work with tree stumps (see **PRODUCTION**), and he later attempted a car-chasing thriller comeback with *Jade* (1995), but neither these nor his more recent directorial efforts have lived up to his earlier promise.

CASTING: Blatty had hopes for Brando or Jack Nicholson as Father Karras, but Friedkin was worried that stars of such magnitude would overshadow his director credit, and perhaps work against the film's documentary style; he favoured non-stars in the key roles. Karras was Jason Miller's first part in a feature film; the actor, who had once trained to be a Jesuit priest, also appeared in *The Ninth Configuration*, and was 'Patient X' in *The Exorcist III* (William Peter Blatty, 1990).

Max von Sydow brought a dignity to the proceedings, but refused to countenance Friedkin's lofty claims of serious statements for the film. Von Sydow is perhaps best known for his appearances in many of Ingmar Bergman's best films, including *The Seventh Seal/Det Sjunde inseglet* (1958); his other genre-related appearances include *The Night Visitor* (László Benedek, 1971), *The Exorcist II: The Heretic* (John Boorman, 1977), *Deathwatch/La Mort en Direct* (Bertrand Tavernier, 1980), *Needful Things* (Fraser Clarke Heston, 1993) and Dario Argento's *Sleepless/Nonhosonno* (2001).

Jack MacGowran had previously appeared in Polanski's *Cul-de-Sac* (1966) and *Dance of the Vampires* (1967), as well as several more mainstream films; and Ellen Burstyn agreed to her only genre role, which had already been turned down by Jane Fonda, on the condition that she didn't have to lie by saying the scripted line 'I believe in the devil!'

Linda Blair's mother brought her in to test for Regan after the twelve-year-old's agency had overlooked her in favour of thirty others. It's not a role every mother would want to see her daughter in, and legend has it that Friedkin gave her the role after they talked about 'jerking off'; but Blair denies this, and maintains that during the crucifix masturbation she had no idea what she was doing.

Blair had several death threats after the film's release, and Warner Bros hired bodyguards to protect her for six months; she was also dogged by rumours that she had been somehow damaged during the making of the film, or that she or her parents had Satanist associations. While she received an Oscar nomination for her part, and owes her fame to the film, she maintains that her association with the role made it near impossible for her to get parts in major films. Instead she appeared in *Exorcist II: The Heretic* (1977), which nobody was ever going to get an Oscar for, and a string of low-budget exploitation films including *Hell Night* (Tom DeSimone, 1981), *Chained Heat* (Lutz Schaarwächter, 1983) and *Witchcraft* (Rob Spera, 1988). She reprised her Regan role in the pointless spoof *Repossessed* (Bob Logan, 1990), and has most recently been improving her prospects of breaking into serious territory with *The Blair Witch Project* (Scott LaRose, 1999) and *Cyber Meltdown* (Mary Case, 2004).

The Exorcist also features two cameos: the nurse who comes into the office after the arteriogram is Linda Blair's mother; and Blatty appears as the producer of *Crash Course*, seen briefly talking to Burke Dennings.

PRODUCTION: Shooting began on 14 August 1972, and lasted fifteen months. The production ran into problems from the start: as the US had no diplomatic relations with Iraq at the time Friedkin had to take an all-British crew overseas to film the prologue, and was only allowed to shoot there on condition that the team taught Iraqi filmmakers how to make fake blood, as well as training them in other film techniques. The director also quickly demonstrated where his difficult reputation came from: he let production designer John Robert Lloyd go after finding that he didn't like the sets for the MacNeil home, putting production back six weeks, and spent an inordinate amount of time over shots that to everyone else seemed non-essential.

Blatty, as producer, initially hung around the sets and at one point even 'fired' Friedkin, although he didn't expect the director to take it seriously; but Friedkin returned to the studio with an army of lawyers, leading Blatty to take a more hands-off production approach. The costs duly rocketed.

Friedkin had decided that for added realism he wanted the exorcism effects to be created mechanically, rather than using optical effects (the only non-mechanical effect in the film is the shot of Regan projectile vomiting). So the interiors of the MacNeil house were built at New York's Ceco Studios, with the real house in Georgetown used only for exteriors: Regan's bedroom had false walls for fork-lifting the bed, false ceilings for piano-wire levitations and air-vented windows to give the cold atmosphere in which the actors' breath is visible. For the exorcism sequence the entire room was enclosed and refrigerated, dropping the temperature well below freezing; cameras and contact lenses froze, and one day it even snowed indoors on set.

Friedkin had little time for the actors – he once claimed that 'I'd rather work with tree stumps than actors' – and preferred to focus on technical features like lenses and effects. He stopped at nothing to get the cast to react in the way he wanted, routinely using guns to startle them, and slapped Father William O'Malley to add intensity to his performance as he administered the last rites to the dying Karras.

More seriously, the health of both Linda Blair and Ellen Burstyn was compromised in special-effects scenes. A mould was made of Blair's body for the sequence where she is pulled back and forth on the bed; the rig came loose during shooting, and Blair's screams of 'Stop it! It hurts!' are genuine; she required back treatment afterwards. Similarly, in the scene where Chris is thrown across the room after witnessing the crucifix masturbation, Burstyn landed painfully on her back, despite having asked not to be pulled so hard; Friedkin, who routinely filmed the actors unaware, zeroed in on her pain and used the shot. Another genuine actor reaction came when Jason Miller takes a spurt of pea soup – used, rather unconvincingly, for Regan's vomit – in the face; it hadn't been planned, and wasn't expected.

Dick Smith constructed a dummy for the head-turning sequences, which he tested by driving it around New York City, turning a few pedestrians' heads too. Blatty was unhappy with these physical impossibilities, telling Friedkin 'supernatural doesn't mean impossible', but they turned out to be a major crowd-pleaser, as did the crucifix masturbation, perhaps the film's biggest draw for curious audiences. The effect of the head-turning scenes is enhanced by their positioning – the first comes immediately after the crucifix masturbation, from which the audience would still be reeling, and the second has the face of Blair's body double, Eileen Dietz in 'Captain Howdy' make-up, superimposed onto the dummy's face.

This demon face is shown clearly in two shots in the original cut, one during Karras's dream and the other during the exorcism itself; it comes from a make-up test done on Dietz but considered unsuitable for Regan. It is probably these near-subliminal shots that led to the rumours of subliminal demonic imagery permeating the film: evangelist Billy Graham later even argued that the prints of the film themselves were inhabited by a demon.

Dietz, 25 at the time of shooting, eventually took legal action against Friedkin and Warner Bros, upset by the director's publicity-friendly boast that no doubles were used in the film. Dietz was actually also used for rear views of Regan in the crucifix masturbation and the attacks on doctors; another body double was contortionist Linda Hager, hired for the infamous 'spider walk' sequence that was cut from the final edit. It's easy to see why the sequence was removed: the effect is unconvincing, and it spoils the structure of the film, providing a double climax (on top of the death of Burke) and making the use of a psychiatrist in the next sequence entirely redundant – therapy clearly isn't going to help now.

Both Friedkin and Blatty were happy to lose this scene, but after endorsing the initial 140-minute edit, Blatty was barred from post-production as Friedkin worked to bring the film in at around the two-hour mark. Blatty was upset by these further cuts, which include more medical tests, leading to a gap in logic when MacNeil tells Regan to keep taking her pills – what pills? – more of the film's theological content and a happy ending between Kinderman and Father Dyer; Friedkin felt that this was anticlimactic, but its omission led many to feel that the devil had triumphed by the end of the film.

Warner Bros. were predictably upset by the massive cost and time overruns, but were impressed enough by the rushes not to shut the production down. Friedkin blamed the overruns on a cursed set, and told journalists that 'There are strange images and visions that showed up on film that were never planned.' He cited various incidents to support the claim, much as William Castle had for **Rosemary's Baby**: Jack McGowran died shortly after the completion of his role, while Max von Sydow's brother died on the day the actor arrived for filming. A statue of Pazuzu, the demon seen in Iraq, went missing en route to the Middle East and turned up two weeks later in Hong Kong; and the set inexplicably burned down. While the story made for good publicity, most of the cast refused to believe in a curse, pointing out that over a fifteen-month shoot many accidents are likely to happen.

Friedkin, keen perhaps to bolster the film's publicity further, even asked Father Bermingham, who played the university president and acted as a technical adviser on the film, to exorcise the set; Bermingham refused, as he didn't want to panic cast and crew. Bermingham, who only agreed to work on the film on condition that it took its subject matter seriously, unlike **Rosemary's Baby**, wasn't the only Jesuit priest employed for technical advice: others advised Friedkin to beef up the obscenity of Regan's rants – and can take full responsibility for lines like 'Your mother sucks cocks in Hell' – and reportedly supplied him with a tape of a 'real' exorcism for the sound of the demonic voices.

SOUNDTRACK: The original score for the film was written by Lalo Schifrin, but Friedkin hated this 'fuckin' marimba music' so much that he threw the tape reels into the street and refused to use any of it. Instead a mixture of existing pieces was used, ranging from the shivery dissonance of Penderecki's modern classical works to Mike Oldfield's 'Tubular Bells'; the string music that plays over the closing credits is written by Jack Nitzsche, who worked with Friedkin again on *Cruising*, as well as scoring John Carpenter's *Starman* (1984).

But the music isn't the principal focus of the film's soundtrack. Much like **The Haunting**, *The Exorcist* uses sound as an essential tool in its mission to terrify the audience. The music itself tends to be unobtrusive, mixed low in the sound production to add an air of unease without distracting from the story; conversely, mundane sounds like a doorbell or telephone ringing are amplified to shatter the silence and startle the audience. Aural motifs are also repeated throughout the film, adding to its fatalist feel: the clanging of the dig in Iraq is repeated in the possession sequences, while the chanting of the priests during the exorcism sounds increasingly desperate after each repetition.

The sounds of the demon's activities came from various sources: Friedkin employed Gonzalo Gavira, who had done the sound for Jodorowsky's psychedelic western *El Topo* (1970), to improvise in front of a microphone while watching the film, and his twisting of a leather wallet was used for the head-turning sound; and Ron Nagle spent two weeks recording animal sounds, including angry bees, fighting dogs, caged hamsters and pigs in a slaughterhouse, all of which found their way into the multilayered mix of the demon's voice.

But the voice principally belonged to Mercedes McCambridge, an actress who had struck Friedkin as having suitably guttural tones once he'd rejected Blair's voice after extensive pre-production sound work. McCambridge worked hard in the role, swallowing and regurgitating raw eggs, smoking endless cigarettes and falling off the wagon to drink heavily for the part. Although she felt it unnecessary, she was also physically restrained, like Regan, while recording.

When Friedkin claimed that Blair had had no stand-ins during the film, McCambridge was furious – she had provided all the demon voices – and took legal action, which prevented the release of a soundtrack album featuring some of her dialogue. She was eventually credited on all but thirty prints of the film.

'IT'S ONLY A MOVIE ... ONLY A MOVIE ...': *The Exorcist* fever spread principally by word of mouth, with some audiences intrigued by Friedkin's outlandish claims of curses. The director had also misled journalists over the film's special effects, claiming that Blair had performed the vomiting scenes herself, and that the levitation had been achieved using a magnetic field.

RELEASE: Warner Bros were confused by the film, and didn't preview it for fear of causing offence. It opened in just thirty cinemas, where it played exclusively for six months. But the conservative release pattern, which could have killed off other potential blockbusters, did nothing to stop the film turning into a phenomenon, and it remains the highest-grossing horror film of all time.

Friedkin was stunned by the hysterical response, which had audiences fainting and vomiting – cinemas had kitty litter waiting to clean up after nauseous patrons – and ushers resigning rather than expose themselves to yet more screenings, as well as a smattering of heart attacks and miscarriages. In Berkeley one viewer attacked the screen in a misguided attempt to 'get the demon', and according to the *Toronto Medical Post* four women had to be confined to psychiatric care after seeing the film. Friedkin briefly considered recalling and re-editing the film, perhaps in response to the disturbing reactions, but was dissuaded by a studio executive.

The Catholic Church was besieged by requests for exorcisms, and while it advised scepticism over these cases, some high-ranking officials still supported the film, which the *Catholic Times* regarded as profoundly spiritual. But others were less impressed, joining the ranks of doctors and psychiatrists warning audiences of the dangers of the film; even one of its technical advisors said that it shouldn't have been released because of the danger of hysteria.

A new clinical condition known as 'cinematic neurosis' was recognised, in which disturbing films exposed psychiatric problems in people with no history of mental illness: *The Exorcist* was the first film to have had such a widespread neurotic audience response. Part of its power in this respect was seen to be its depiction of a disturbed childhood, recalling unresolved youthful anxieties; although many of those affected were men, adolescent girls were considered most at risk as they, much like many critics, were liable to interpret the film in terms of menstrual panic.

The film was also blamed for a range of criminal and suicidal acts, including one murder in the UK: in October 1974 a teenager who'd killed a nine-year-old girl told York Crown Court that watching the film had made him do it.

The furore was helped by the perceived leniency of the censors. In the US the MPAA had given it an R rating, allowing children to see the film with parental approval, but public pressure forced a reconsideration and a shift to a 17 certificate. In the UK the film was passed uncut with an X certificate but was still picketed by the Christian 'Festival of Light', and was later unavailable on home video for fourteen years.

The film was also banned in Tunisia in 1975, on the grounds that it presented 'unjustified propaganda in favour of Christianity', a view not shared by Evangelical groups in the US, who saw it as demonstrably Satanic. The Academy Award board took a more robust view, nominating the film for ten Oscars, although it won only two, one for Best Sound and the other, bizarrely, for Best Adapted Screenplay.

But reviewers tended to dislike the film. Tom Milne in *Monthly Film Bulletin* described it as 'no more nor less than a blood-and-thunder horror film, foundering heavily on the rocks of pretension'; and Pauline Kael hated it, particularly scathing in her rejection of Blatty and Friedkin's claims to have made a serious film – as she pointed out, there is no encouragement to sympathise with Regan's plight, and the moral absolutes of the film are a step back from the ambiguity explored by other New Hollywood directors.

The Exorcist was still playing in cinemas two years after its release, and grossed $160 million before it played out. Such money – from a genre that had been considered the province of low-budget players and low-income audiences – changed the nature of the industry forever.

CRITICAL EYE: While Friedkin has explicitly rejected any interpretation other than a surface reading of the film, some audiences had other ideas – didn't Regan represent the rebellious youth of the day? – and the film's preoccupations reveal perhaps more than the director intended.

Friedkin quotes the idea that the film is a misogynistic homosexual fantasy in which two men conspire to torture a young woman back to an Edenic state of non-sexual innocence as an example of a ludicrous critical interpretation of the film. Yet if the homosexual angle seems far-fetched, the rest of this interpretation is broadly valid: men *do* conspire to torture Regan throughout the film, whether they are doctors, Jesuit priests or indeed Friedkin himself; and its misogyny can be seen not only in its demonisation of female puberty but also in the other female characters – Chris and Mrs Karras, as well as Regan, make demands of Karras that leave him more vulnerable to the devil. There's even an implicit suggestion that Chris's status as single mother is somehow to blame for Regan's possession: Captain Howdy is uncomfortably close in name to Regan's father, Howard.

As one of the many exaggerated poles in the film – other contrasts include light and dark, noise and silence, movement and stillness – Regan at the outset seems a very immature twelve-year-old, her interests more like those of a younger child. But Chris is afraid of her budding sexuality, pointing to a picture of the two of them and complaining that 'It's not even a good picture of you. You look so *mature*.' And Regan's possession is marked in explicitly sexual terms: demonic evil is equated with female masturbation and an inventive line in saucy insults, with Regan at one point literally rubbing her mother's face in her newfound sexuality.

And these actions account for most of the devil's bag of tricks – he can also levitate, move furniture around and drop the temperature, but that's about it. Such pettiness – especially after the grand opening sequence – is compounded by the fact that the devil chooses a twelve-year-old girl, rather than, say, a politician or high-ranking banker, to possess. So why has the devil set his sights so low? Because, on one level, the film is a return to the hoary horror theme of the threat of female sexuality; but where other films respond to this in a more equivocal way, mixing lust with fear and often siding implicitly with their monsters, *The Exorcist* dispenses with any ambiguity, returning to a medieval Judeao-Christian view of women and in the process inadvertently exploring the idea that the control of women's bodies is one of organised religion's central concerns.

Another reason why Regan is possessed is that a more powerful victim might distract attention from the central focus of the film, which is after all titled *The Exorcist*: Karras's crisis of faith. Rather than a character of audience empathy or sympathy, Regan is little more than a tool allowing Karras to redeem himself, providing the evidence that allows him to choose between his conflicting secular and spiritual beliefs.

Of course, the devil has not only possessed Regan; he is blamed for a wide range of social ills, with a general moral breakdown signposted by images of slums, overcrowded mental hospitals, homeless drunks and Karras's crisis of faith. His presence is felt everywhere – from Iraq and Africa (where Merrin had performed a previous exorcism) to Washington.

Science and rationality can't help: Merrin refuses, twice, to listen to Karras's psychological explanations of Regan's predicament, and the medical procedures inflicted on her are among the film's most horrific scenes, the doctors' hollow promises toppling Christian theology from its usual position of vain hopefulness.

Early on Chris is seen acting in a film about student revolt, in which she tells the students that 'If you want to effect any change you have to do it within the system.' This reactionary message informs the entire film, advocating a turn away from the moral ambiguity of the late 60s and a return to moral absolutes and simplicity that anticipates the Reaganite conservatism of the 80s. The devil has here lost his position as symbol of rebellion, and the audience no longer has to concern itself with social ills: they are the product of Satanic forces, and can be conquered by faith.

The film tells the viewer that he should not seek to change the world, like the misguided students, but rather to distrust rebellion, change, unconventionality and, indeed, the body. It is not only sexuality that is demonised within the film: virtually all other bodily functions are used to show the depths of Regan's abjection, and the film revels in the idea that the body is itself somehow sinful, shameful and undignified. Part of its assault on the viewer is the message that, through his bodily functions, he is not so very far from Regan's vile behaviour. As Merrin tells Karras, in a scene cut before the film's release, the devil's aim is to confront them with their own bestial nature. And yet for all that humour was clearly far from Friedkin and Blatty's minds, there's something entertaining about Regan's endless spewing, a projection of shared toilet-training rage and resentment: when she vomits on a smug priest, she seems almost sympathetic in her steadfast refusal to follow basic rules of hygiene and etiquette.

INDUSTRY IMPACT: *The Exorcist* was followed by a series of rip-offs, including a blaxploitation picture (*Abby*, William Girdler, 1974) whose makers were sued by Warner Bros for breach of copyright. Catholic countries like Italy and Spain churned out the highest number, with only *The Antichrist/ L'Antichristo* (1974) reaching any level of distinction, while some of the more interesting takes on the film came from the adult film industry, with *The Sexorcist/L'Ossessa* (Mario Gariazzo, 1974) and *Angel Above, Devil Below* (1975) turning its sexual repression on its head by revelling in repeated masturbation sequences. The film's international success also spawned copies from Bollywood (*Jadu Tona/Black Magic*, Ravikant Nagaich, 1977) to Turkey (*Seytan/Satan*, Metin Erksan, 1974), and kickstarted the Hong Kong horror-movie industry, proving globally that horror could be a phenomenal financial success.

The Omen (Richard Donner, 1976) was the next blockbusting demonic film, providing a Protestant take on *The Exorcist*'s Catholic propaganda with a fundamentalist apocalyptic message that was followed by its own international imitations; but the film's basic themes owed more to **Rosemary's Baby** than *The Exorcist*, and future Satanic films similarly harked back to pre-*Exorcist* fare.

Hammer tried to leap on the Satanic bandwagon with the embarrassing *To the Devil . . . a Daughter* (1976), one of the final nails in the studio's coffin, and John Boorman's *The Exorcist II: The Heretic* (1977) was just as poorly received. It does have its moments, and its ambiguity is welcome after the reductivist theology of *The Exorcist*, but its occasional Burroughsian reality slips cannot redeem its confused plot and hammy acting.

Damien: the Omen II (Don Taylor, 1978) sparked off a new wave of films about young people with psychic powers (see **INDUSTRY IMPACT, Don't Look Now**), and its set-piece deaths – including one memorably under the ice of a frozen lake – made it by far the most entertaining film of the trilogy, with *The Final Conflict – The Omen III* (Graham Baker, 1981) providing an anticlimactic conclusion.

The Blatty-directed *The Exorcist III* was a disappointing addition to the serial-killer genre clogging up cinemas, and it wasn't alone in equating Satanism and serial murder. Alex de la Iglesia's *Day of the Beast/El Dia de la Bestia* (1995) was far better, a welcome return to a subversive slant on the devil, and the end of the millennium brought Roman Polanski back to the genre, with *The Ninth Gate* (1999, see **DIRECTOR, Rosemary's Baby**) going head to head with Arnie's hamfisted tale of Satanic pregnancy *End of Days* (Peter Hyams, 1999).

The Exorcist was re-released on its 25th anniversary in the UK, the departure of chairman James Ferman prompting the BBFC to grant it a certificate; and just a year later a re-edited version of the film, 'The Version You've Never Seen', was released. This featured a devastating remixed soundtrack; a substantially extended opening sequence in Northern Iraq; more scenes on Regan being tested in hospital before the priests are called in; the restoration of the infamous 'spider walk' sequence; more of the 'Captain Howdy' face; a discussion between Karras and Merrin during the exorcism; and the happy ending between Lt Kinderman and Father Dyer.

FINAL WORD: The main influence of *The Exorcist* was in what it showed, breaking a number of taboos over the content permissible on screen, and how it showed it: most horror films would from now on be driven by special effects. Audiences were probably more shocked than scared by the film, and disgust became a principal feature in post-*Exorcist* horror: disgust that, crucially, focused on the body.

In this respect *The Exorcist* is a key film in the development of body horror (see **ORIGINS AND INSPIRATION, The Fly**), sharing with Cronenberg's early films an insistence on explicit and spectacular views of bodily revolt; that the body horror in the film is more important to its success than its supernatural elements is demonstrated by the fact that while body horror came, along with the slasher film, to characterise the genre through the next two decades, supernatural horror films were thin on the ground.

Whatever the film's message, and despite the flabbiness of some earlier scenes, its dour simplicity does lend it a certain power, and it skilfully manipulates the audience with an inexorable build-up to its grim conclusion. Still, the 1999 voting of the film as 'The scariest movie of all time' reveals either that audiences haven't seen very many scary movies, or that Friedkin's bludgeon-like directing is the only way to get through to contemporary TV-dulled senses.

PSYCHIC TERRORS

Don't Look Now (1973)

'Pass the warning'

**GB/Italy Casey Productions/Eldorado Films, colour,
110 mins**

Directed by Nicolas Roeg
Executive Producer: Anthony B Unger
Producer: Peter Katz
Associate Producer: Federico Mueller
Assistant Director: Francesco Cinieri
Screenplay: Allan Scott, Chris Bryant, based on the short
story by Daphne du Maurier
Photography: Anthony Richmond
Editor: Graeme Clifford
Art Director: Giovanni Soccol
Music: Pino Donaggio
Sound editor: Rodney Holland

CAST: Julie Christie (*Laura Baxter*), Donald Sutherland (*John Baxter*), Hilary Mason (*Heather*), Clelia Matania (*Wendy*), Massimo Serato (*Bishop Barbarrigo*), Renato Scarpa (*Inspector Longhi*), Giorgio Trestini (*Workman*), Leopoldo Trieste (*Hotel*

Manager), David Tree (*Anthony Babbage*), Ann Rye (*Mandy Babbage*), Nicholas Salter (*Johnny Baxter*), Sharon Williams (*Christine Baxter*), Bruno Cattaneo (*Detective Sabbione*), Adelina Poerio (*Dwarf*)

SYNOPSIS: After their daughter Christine's death by drowning, which John Baxter has foreseen yet been unable to prevent, he and his wife Laura go to Venice. He throws himself into his work of restoring a cathedral, and she meets two Scottish sisters, one of whom, the blind and apparently psychic Heather, tells her that her daughter is well and happy in the spirit world. John is reluctant to believe this, but finds his wife far happier, although she faints in a restaurant after meeting the women. There has been a string of murders in Venice.

Laura meets the women again, and is told that John is also psychic, even if he resists the knowledge. They reluctantly agree to conduct a séance for her. John refuses to join them, and gets drunk at a nearby café; but then he tries to look through the keyhole of their room and is mistaken for a Peeping Tom.

Heather warns Laura that John should leave Venice immediately, but John responds angrily to the warning. That night the headmaster of their son's school calls: Johnny has been injured during a fire drill. Laura leaves for England, convinced this is the event Heather had warned her about. John almost falls to his death in the cathedral, and feels in turn that this ties in with the warning: he prepares to leave Venice, but sees a boat carrying Laura and the two women. Confused, he goes first to his hotel, which is now closed, then to the police. The police then follow him as he searches for and finds the women's hotel, but they have moved because of a Peeping Tom.

He calls the school and is surprised to speak to his wife, who is soon returning to Venice. The police have now arrested Heather, and John picks her up from the station to take her back to her hotel. When she starts having a fit he leaves, although her request not to let him go makes Wendy run after him. Shortly afterwards Laura arrives, and is sent after John. John has spotted a small figure in a red coat, just like his daughter used to wear, several times before: now he chases it into a ruined palazzo, locking the gates behind him. He seems to think the figure is a child – perhaps even the ghost of his daughter – but it is a murderous dwarf, who kills him. John's vision of Laura and the two women had been a premonition of his own funeral.

ORIGINS AND INSPIRATION: Mediums and psychics had featured in several films before *Don't Look Now*, although they were rarely central figures: *Blithe Spirit* (David Lean, 1945), *Night of the Demon* (1958), Hammer's *Hands of the Ripper* (1971) and *From Beyond the Grave* (Kevin Connor, 1973) featured genuine psychics, while charlatans appeared in *The Spiritualist* (Bernard Vorhaus, 1948), *The Medium* (Gian Carlo Menotti, 1951) and *Séance on a Wet Afternoon* (Bryan Forbes, 1964). All, with the exception of the medium in *Night of the Demon*, were female.

When producer Peter Katz sent Roeg Allan Scott and Chris Byrant's script for *Don't Look Now*, the director was impressed. He loved Daphne du Maurier's story in any case, especially the ending, and 'was looking for a story that ... would complete in some way, or continue in some way, a line of thought'. The film wouldn't be the clearest continuation of Roeg's first two features, *Performance* (1970) and *Walkabout* (1971), but it would share certain characteristics with them. The theme of expanded consciousness runs through all three films, from the heady mushroom transformations of *Performance* to the oblique information offered by *Don't Look Now*'s complex associational web; and another common feature is that their central characters either search for their identity or are pulled towards another identity, only to find the price they pay for its discovery is death.

Various changes were made from the original story. There Christine dies of meningitis, and Johnny gets appendicitis; the screenplay introduces the idea of accidents – in turn raising the question of fate – in Christine's drowning and Johnny's injury during fire drill, and these changes also relate to the film's themes of water and well-intentioned plans going awry.

The colour scheme of the story was changed too, with a reversal of du Maurier's blue for Christine and red for Laura; this is especially relevant in the light of another change, that to John's profession of art historian, with a professional interest in colour gradations. The entire film would be dominated by red and blue tones, a melding of fire and water.

In the short story, the Baxters travel to Venice on holiday, while in the screenplay John is restoring a cathedral there. This not only makes the screenplay's other changes more plausible – Venice is an unlikely holiday destination if your child has recently drowned – but introduces the themes of authenticity, fakery and religious and artistic decadence, as John discovers that the mosaics he is restoring are fake. And finally, while du Maurier's story begins in a Venice restaurant, the screenplay begins with Christine's drowning, encouraging the audience to identify much further with the Baxters' grief.

But du Maurier's story was not the only source material; the film would also reflect Roeg's interest in the writings of JW Dunne, whose *An Experiment with Time* posits the idea that the experience of linear time is entirely illusory. According to the director:

> I think we get messages or warnings that we try to resist . . . There's no such thing as seeing into the future because the future is already here. A premonition is just a way of confirming something you know. And I think film is the perfect medium to show this paradox. It's a time machine.

DIRECTOR: Nicolas Roeg entered the film industry in the late 1940s and worked his way up to being a camera operator in the late 1950s. He progressed to 2nd unit photography for David Lean's *Lawrence of Arabia* (1962) before receiving a director of photography credit on films like Roger Corman's *The Masque of the Red Death* (1964), probably Corman's finest Poe adaptation, and Truffaut's *Fahrenheit 451* (1967).

His first directing credit was shared with Donald Cammell, later to helm *Demon Seed* (1977) and the superior psycho thriller *White of the Eye* (1987). *Performance*'s elliptical *doppelgänger* tale of a vicious gangster (James Fox) who receives a personality makeover thanks to psilocybin mushrooms and rock musician Turner's (Mick Jagger) dressing-up box was shelved by Warner Bros for two years; the studio had assumed that with Jagger they were funding a star vehicle, rather than the gloriously chaotic paean to psychedelics that emerged.

The poor treatment of the film may have led Roeg to ensure that his next few films were more commercially viable: *Walkabout* featured a more linear narrative in its tale of brother and sister lost in the outback, alongside extensive nude shots of Jenny Agutter, while *Don't Look Now* was his first 'straight' genre vehicle. The film's themes – the supernatural, precognition and fate – provide the perfect context for Roeg's formal concerns, which include non-linear editing, looping structures of narrative time and the use of dense, multivalent symbol systems. It was also his greatest commercial success, attempts to use similar techniques in his next two films, an SF feature starring David Bowie (*The Man Who Fell to Earth*, 1976) and a psychological drama with Art Garfunkel (*Bad Timing*, 1980) finding less favour at the box office.

Roeg followed these with *Eureka* (1983), another case of bad timing: Jack McCann (Gene Hackman) hits his peak too early in life, and finds that there is nothing left for him to do except die. Despite being one of the director's richest films, it received almost universally hostile reviews and a poor commercial response; and since then Roeg has come close to fellow Briton Ken Russell in his fall from grace and apparent inability to return to previous form.

The director's next four films – *Insignificance* (1985), *Castaway* (1986), *Track 29* (1988) and *The Witches* (1990) – still have his idiosyncratic touch, but since then he has faltered more severely, with more TV work and fewer features during the 90s, although he did return to the realm of the supernatural with 1992's widely derided *Cold Heaven*.

CASTING: Although other actors were considered for the leads – principally real-life couple Robert Wagner and Natalie Wood – Roeg was adamant that he wanted Donald Sutherland and Julie Christie. Neither was initially available: Sutherland was working on another film and Christie was involved with the McGovern presidential campaign. But they too eventually slotted into place: McGovern was beaten by Nixon and Sutherland's film collapsed, leaving them free. Roeg liked the idea of having an English–American couple, who would never be entirely at home anywhere:

> I imagined him [John Baxter] as somebody who might have been a Rhodes scholar and had perhaps met [Laura's] brother at Oxford, so their families had been linked that way. I wanted to have them be almost golden people, so that it became rather like the incident at Chappaquiddick. Like the Kennedy family. They were unprepared in life. Most people are, aren't they?

Sutherland had his own ideas about the script, and thought the film should be more of a celebration of the positive potential of

ESP. Roeg didn't agree, but liked the actor's suggestion that he wear a wig, to fix him in audiences' minds more as 'John' than 'Donald Sutherland'.

The Canadian actor's long and successful film career has included a number of genre roles, from the Amicus portmanteau film *Dr Terror's House of Horrors* (1965) to Hammer's *Fanatic* (1965), *Invasion of the Body Snatchers* (Philip Kaufman, 1978), *The Rosary Murders* (Fred Walton, 1987) and *Buffy the Vampire Slayer* (Fran Rubel Kuzui, 1992).

Christie had worked with Roeg before: he'd filmed her in *Fahrenheit 451* and *Far From the Madding Crowd* (John Schlesinger, 1967). The director took the actress to a séance before they started filming *Don't Look Now*; they had been invited by the direct voice medium Leslie Flint, who was doing a session for some American parapsychologists. Flint told the group to 'uncross your legs', which Roeg later used in the film. Christie's other genre roles include the lead in *Demon Seed*.

PRODUCTION: Principal photography began in the UK in December 1972, broke off for Christmas, then resumed in January 1973 for seven weeks in Italy. The Baxters' Hertfordshire home actually belonged to David Tree, who played headmaster Anthony Babbage, and the white horse seen at the start of the film was intended as an augury of innocence before disaster: Roeg had seen one at an auspicious moment during the shooting of *Far From the Madding Crowd*, and later incorporated the figure into *The Man Who Fell to Earth*, *Bad Timing* and *Track 29*.

The drowning sequence proved difficult to shoot: Sharon Williams, who played Christine, was a good swimmer but refused to go underwater in the weedy pond; a neighbour's daughter was volunteered for the scene, again a good swimmer, but she balked at wearing the red mackintosh in the pond; and finally the scene was done in a water tank with a double, leaving Christine being played by three different girls.

Shooting in Venice was also problematic. The tides played havoc with the continuity, especially with Roeg's refusal to cheat by shooting fake reverse angles, and they also meant extra planning for shifting equipment. But other elements slotted into place uncannily easily. On the final day of a location recce Roeg and the location manager, who'd by then suggested building John's renovated church in a warehouse on the city outskirts, found a suitable church, Santo Nicola dei Mendici, which already had scaffolding in place as it was being renovated by the British 'Venice in Peril' charity. The Charlie Chaplin poster seen outside the church was there when the location was found, and soon Roeg found that he had 'got into a crazed groove about "let it be", the plot is all that is happening'.

Roeg, who never uses storyboards and disdains rehearsals, let his actors improvise in pursuit of allowing the film to follow a life of its own. The scene in the church where John plays with a light switch while Laura lights candles for Christine was improvised in preference to the wordy scene in the script, as were both the sex scene and the surrounding sequences of John and Laura preparing to go out. Roeg decided to shoot the sex scene when he realised that without it the couple would be seen almost perpetually arguing; with it, and its suggestions that this is the first time they have made love since their daughter's death, their closeness comes across all the more strongly, as well as adding a teasing suggestion that Laura may have become pregnant again.

Still, Christie found it difficult to shoot – there was little precedent for doing explicit sex scenes in mainstream films – and allowed Sutherland to take the lead. The scene is justly celebrated, although Roeg soon tired of being asked whether or not the actors had actually had sex, or fielding questions about extra footage being shot for a Continental version. Sutherland, by contrast, found his death the hardest scene to shoot: 'We shot the climax last and I knew I was going to die in it and I became literally convinced that I would die, and dying began to feel almost like a sexual rite.'

Roeg deliberately avoided showing the tourist side of Venice, focusing on the city's grimy alleyways and general aura of decay rather than the splendour of the skyline or the bustle of St Mark's Square. The producers, perhaps expecting more of a Venetian travelogue, were unimpressed by Roeg's vision of the city, and the director, worried that they might ruin the film in the edit, broke into the cutting room and removed four reels to prevent them from doing so.

SOUNDTRACK: 'It's so safe for me to walk ... the sound changes, you see, as you come to a canal and the echoes off the walls are so clear.' So Heather tells John Baxter, and the sound production of the film is rich and multilayered. There is actually very little music in the film, despite Pino Donaggio's memorable score: much of the tension is built up through the use of running footsteps echoing off walls, water bubbling and church bells ringing. Sounds contribute to the thematic doubling throughout the film: a cat's miaow is barely distinguishable from the baby's cries heard at the sisters' hotel room or the curious whimperings of the dwarf; the piano scales heard while John is followed by the police recall the halting playing of the film's signature at the start of the film; and Laura's scream at seeing Christine's body cuts sharply into the whine of a drill, mirroring Hitchcock's cut from scream to steam-train whistle in *The 39 Steps* (1935).

Don't Look Now was Donaggio's (credited as Donnagio) first major film score, and the composer is said to have been picked by the producer after being spotted on a gondola during location scouting in Venice. The composer went on to score films for Brian de Palma, contributing a haunting score for *Carrie* (1976) that recalls *Don't Look Now*, as well as *Dressed to Kill* (1980), *Blow Out* (1981), *Body Double* (1984) and *Raising Cain* (1992); he has also worked with Dario Argento, scoring *Two Evil Eyes/Due Occhi Diabolici* (1990), *Trauma* (1993) and the Argento-produced *The Sect/La Setta* (Michele Soavi, 1991); and Joe Dante, on *Piranha* (1978) and *The Howling* (1981).

RELEASE: Sectors of the British press tried to whip up a storm over the sex scene, but the film was passed uncut with an X certificate by the British censors, with none of the scandal of *Last Tango in Paris* (Bernardo Bertolucci, 1973) or the other films that gave the BBFC such a headache in the early 1970s. And most papers gave it good reviews, *The Times* even featuring it on the front page; the serious magazines also tended to like the film, considering it part of a loose trilogy with *Performance* and *Walkabout*; Tom Milne in *Sight and Sound* felt the films 'put Nicolas Roeg right up at the top as a film-maker', while Gordon Gow in *Films and Filming* found it 'a thriller of some depth'. Du Maurier was also impressed, and wrote to Roeg to congratulate him on having captured the emotions of John and Laura.

The film was rated R in the US, after Roeg removed nine frames of 'humping' footage, and was reviewed well there too. *Variety* noted that 'No matter what happens to this crackerjack chiller commercially – and the potential outlook is decidedly good – it should firmly establish Nicholas [*sic*] Roeg as the latest cult hero';

the *New Yorker* found it 'the fanciest, most carefully assembled enigma yet seen on the screen'; and even the *New York Times*'s Vincent Canby, who thought it a 'fragile soap bubble of a film . . . you may feel, as I did, that you've been had', acknowledged that Roeg got 'a great performance from Venice'.

CRITICAL EYE: The opening montage introduces all of the images and themes that will recur throughout the film. The titles appear over an image of a pond, its surface disturbed by rain; a pane of glass, like water a reflective surface, is broken by Johnny's bike, signifying the shattering of illusions but also danger. Mirrors feature strongly in the film, as does still water, either blinding from the glare of the sun or reflecting what lies above. But a reflection may not be quite what it seems; the dwarf mirrors Christine's image in the water, but she is the girl's inversion, old maniac rather than young innocent.

Water is everywhere: Christine drowns in the pond, and Laura, dressed for a funeral that may be Christine's or John's, leaves her home in the rain. Venice – a city whose alleyways seem endlessly to loop back on themselves – is slowly drowning, but is also a liminal zone, a borderland neither entirely water nor entirely land. The sense that the entire city is on the threshold of transformation is strengthened by the film's repeated images of bridges, doors and windows.

Early on John knocks a drink over onto a slide, causing a red stain to spread from a hooded figure in one of the pews – a figure that, the viewer later realises, will be the agent of his death. The shape of the stain is repeated in Christine's drowned body; Heather's brooch of a mermaid, creature of both land and water; a map of Venice; and the unfinished mosaic that John tries to restore, in itself a symbol of his partial understanding of the situation.

The beginning of the film mirrors the end, with Johnny and Laura separated from the main action, the son injured and the wife behind a barrier, while John runs to the aid of a red-cloaked figure, only to find death. Such doubling, seen also in John and Laura's slow-motion falls and the use of associative rather than linear editing, suggests a fatalistic view of the universe: that life is patterned, predestined.

Minor actions on John's part seem to bring about his fate: if he hadn't tried to spy on the sisters, they wouldn't have moved, and probably wouldn't have been arrested; if they hadn't been arrested, he would have met up with Laura, instead of encountering the dwarf. And if he hadn't closed a window in the restaurant, the other window wouldn't have opened and blown dust into Wendy's eye, prompting Laura to help her. Such chains of events recall convoluted comic sketches, and there is a strong sense of a cosmic joke being perpetrated on the characters: grotesquely, Christine's Action Man says 'Fall in!' before she does just that and drowns.

After meeting the sisters, Laura says, 'It's incredible. You can't change your course.' If events are predestined, what value does second sight have? If John had acknowledged his gift earlier, would he have been able to avoid his destiny – do clairvoyants see what *might* happen, rather than what *will* happen? It's not even clear who is psychic in the film: the bishop wakes up when John is murdered, while Laura appears to know exactly where he has gone when he leaves the sisters at the end. When does intuition become second sight? There is even the suggestion that the dwarf is psychic, as she shakes her head – presumably in response to John's assumption that she is a child, perhaps even Christine – before killing him; has she tricked him to his death through deliberately resembling his daughter?

Heather tells Laura that 'It's a curse as well as a gift', and certainly for John it comes as little help. He is aware of his daughter's drowning as it happens, but is powerless to prevent it; and he is persuaded to stay in Venice and meet his own death by a premonition of his funeral, which he fails to recognise as a vision. Perhaps he has been unconsciously willing his death all along, ravaged by guilt over the death of his daughter.

Although he has written a book entitled *Beyond the Fragile Geometry of Space*, and says 'Nothing is what it seems' before running to Christine, John cannot discard his rational belief system and embrace a broader consciousness, and sticks more closely to a later line, 'Seeing is believing'. It's not difficult to sympathise with him in this: his premonitions and visions provide a confusing jumble of information that he is unable to use in any case, and his failure to save Christine might have tainted his second sight with bad associations.

He is worried that for Laura such beliefs are dangerously irrational, and advises her to start taking her medication – it is never explained exactly what – again after the séance. In a way he's right to be concerned: Laura is credulous, exaggerating Heather's description of a 'shiny mac' to a 'shiny red mac' to convince John of her authenticity, and she takes only what she wants from Heather's warnings, insisting that Johnny's accident fulfils her prophecy when it is actually John who is in danger.

John's distrust of the sisters may come partly from their gender: they first speak to Laura in the women's toilet at the restaurant, a taboo zone for men, and can offer her the solace he cannot, so he feels excluded. Female sexuality is also brought to the fore in the séance, with Heather asking Laura 'Are your legs crossed?' before rubbing her skinny chest and crying out orgasmically.

But his main worry is that they are charlatans, preying on his wife's insecurities; that they are not authentic. The theme also underlies his work in the church: he is an atheist restoring a fake artwork in a monument to an afterlife he refuses to believe in, shoring up an illusion so that he does not have to face a broader truth. After he criticises the sisters in front of his wife, there is a shot of them cackling sinisterly: is this a projection from his fears?

Roeg refuses throughout to signpost exactly what kind of image the audience is seeing. Past, present and future are cut together, compressing space and time and presenting the viewer with the same riddle that faces John. It is unclear whether, as has been suggested, shots of Heather's milky eyes introduce a montage of images she 'sees'; and even the length of edits is no guide, with John's vision of the vaporetto carrying Laura and the sisters lasting longer than some shots that can safely be assumed to be of the present. This image destabilises everything the audience thinks it has understood about the film, and its meaning only becomes clear when it is repeated in the montage accompanying John's death.

The difficulty of interpreting signs is one of the film's central themes, with both vision and language increasingly unreliable throughout. John speaks some Italian, but as his confusion over Laura's whereabouts mounts, he seems to understand less and less, with long passages of untranslated Italian leaving the viewer equally in the dark. Even communicating in English is difficult: the phone call from Johnny's school opens with a bad connection and endless tentative 'hellos', and both Laura and John misinterpret Heather's predictions and warnings.

Roeg's refusal to lead the way, relying on an associative editing style that recalls memory rather than traditional narrative tech-

nique, both heightens our perceptions and increases our identification with the couple, adding to the vivid emotional impact of
the film. The viewer feels deeply for both John and Laura, the
incidental details of their preparation for going out or the
tenderness of their lovemaking fixing them as credible, sympathetic characters. Still more credible is the fact that neither is beyond
reproach: Laura at one point blames her husband for Christine's
death, while John chooses to lose himself in his work rather than
help his wife in her grief. But both are seeking for some means of
dealing with the tragedy of loss; both, ultimately, want their
daughter back.

In the cold melancholy of the film's setting – it is the end of the
season, the hotels are closing and the tourists are nowhere to be
seen – John has only Laura to turn to, another source of
resentment for her interest in the sisters. The other men he
approaches are all compromised in some way: the hotel manager
brandishes a comb like a flickknife; the police inspector seems to
have some sinister agenda of his own; and the bishop seems
altogether too worldly for his position, at one point even brushing
his hand against Laura's breast. There is a palpable sense of
closing in, of the confusion of being lost in a foreign culture, and
of John being watched, by the silent Venetians forever closing
shutters, by the policeman who follows him, by the medium and,
finally, by the dead.

INDUSTRY IMPACT: Roeg's vision of a Venice of doom and
decay influenced Brian de Palma's *Vertigo* rip-off *Obsession*
(1976) and Paul Schrader's *The Comfort of Strangers* (1990), and
the film's themes of a foreigner in Italy, untrustworthy perceptions
and murder mark it out as a close relative of the *giallo* (see
ORIGINS AND INSPIRATION, Deep Red). Its central image of
a brightly cloaked figure the audience is horrified to discover is not
a child also proved influential, recurring in Alfred Sole's excellent
psycho-thriller *Alice, Sweet Alice/Communion* (1976), David
Cronenberg's *The Brood* (1979) and Hideo Nakata's *Dark
Water/Honogurai mizu no soko kara* (2002).

But the film's most important influence was in initiating a wave
of psychic horror films. Brian de Palma's *Carrie* (1976), the first
and one of the best Stephen King adaptations, was the most
successful of these, an international hit that set the template for a
number of other films featuring young outsiders pushed to the

point of unleashing their psychic fury. De Palma returned to the theme with *The Fury* (1978), and other 'psicopath' films include *Psychic Killer* (Ray Danton, 1975), *Patrick* (Richard Franklin, 1978), *The Medusa Touch* (Jack Gold, 1978), *The Sender* (Roger Christian, 1982) and Stephen King's *Firestarter* (Mark L Lester, 1984); psychic links between killers and protagonists also proved popular, with the John Carpenter-scripted *Eyes of Laura Mars* (Irvin Kershner, 1978) starring Faye Dunaway as a photographer who has premonitions of a psychopath's killings, and the theme was continued in 1992's *Psychic* (George Mihalka).

The Dead Zone, filmed in 1983 by David Cronenberg, was another Stephen King adaptation, and the first time the director had worked on another writer's work. It came directly after the commercial disaster of *Videodrome* (1982), Cronenberg's most complex and rewarding film, and many fans were disappointed by this new direction, but *The Dead Zone* is still very much a Cronenberg film. The director was attracted to King's novel by the 'devil inside': although the viewer trusts that John Smith's visions – born out of a car crash that leaves him in a coma for five years – are authentic, there is always the suspicion that this is simply a mad assassin justifying his actions, as Smith prepares to kill politician Greg Stillson, convinced that he will eventually trigger a nuclear war. In its treatment of grief, its melancholic wintry feel and its exploration of a male protagonist's gift that is just as much a curse, it relates closely to *Don't Look Now*.

The director had dealt with the theme of psychic powers before, in 1981's *Scanners*. The film, which picks up the conspiracy/ telepathy ball badly fumbled by *The Fury*, plays like an early version of *X-Men* (Bryan Singer, 2000), with 'good' and 'bad' telepaths vying for control of their unique powers. The scanning power usually leaves its holders in the asylum unless they cope through sheer will power (Darryl Revok, the chief 'bad' scanner), art (Benjamin Pierce, a sculptor who lives inside a model of his own head), or Ephemerol, a drug that controls the symptoms but also caused the condition when given to pregnant women a generation before (Cameron Vale, the film's protagonist).

Cronenberg avoids any paranormal exploration of the scanners' powers in favour of an SF-based approach, with only the messy effects – our introduction to Revok comes with a show-stopping head explosion – marking this out as horror territory. Typically for the director's pre-*Videodrome* work, *Scanners* features a weak male lead; this is at least partly deliberate, with Vale a bland and credulous sap who swallows the corporate lies fed to him by the exploitative Dr Ruth wholesale. Our sympathies lie far more with Darryl Revok, whose fiery rhetoric eclipses Vale's pat responses as Revok attempts to wrest control of the scanners away from the sinister Consec organisation by any means necessary, recalling some 60s direct action radical.

More recently, *Final Destination* (James Wong, 2000) was a refreshing entry in the teen horror glut of the end of the millennium. Alex Browning's vision of a plane exploding saves the lives of a few fellow students but marks him out as a social pariah; the students have cheated death, but the grim reaper won't give up so easily. The film's best moments are its set-piece deaths, slapstick routines that play like souped-up versions of public-safety films: nowhere is safe, with danger lurking in every corner of the house. Its sequel, an immaculately choreographed motor-way pile-up aside, offered a less compelling version of the same story.

FINAL WORD: *Don't Look Now* offers more questions than it can answer, not only in terms of its wider themes of fate and free will but also in plot details. What is the true relationship between the dwarf and Christine? Why does John lock the gates behind him as he goes to his death? And why does he hesitate before diving in for his daughter? But these are less plot gaps than ambiguities adding to the richness of the narrative, Roeg's commitment to providing no easy answers making for an endless-ly fascinating film. *Don't Look Now* is many things: detective story, profoundly moving tale of loss, gothic mystery; but ultimately it is perhaps the finest tale of the supernatural ever told.

MEAT MOVIES

The Texas Chain Saw Massacre (1974)

'Who will survive and what will be left of them?'

USA, Vortex/Henkel/Hooper, colour, 80 mins

Producer/Director: Tobe Hooper
Story and Screenplay: Tobe Hooper, Kim Henkel
Executive Producer: Jay Parsley
Production Manager: Ronald Bozman
Cinematographer: Daniel Pearl
Editors: Sallye Richardson, Larry Carroll
Music Score: Tobe Hooper, Wayne Bell
Assistant Director: Sallye Richardson
Post Production Sound/Boom Man: Wayne Bell
Art Director: Robert A Burns
Grandfather's Make-up: WE Barnes
Make-up: Dorothy Pearl
Associate Producers: Kim Henkel, Richard Saenz
Songs: Roger Bartlett and Friends, Timberline Rose, Arkey
Blue, Los Cyclones

CAST: Marilyn Burns (*Sally*), Allen Danziger (*Jerry*), Paul A Partain (*Franklin*), William Vail (*Kirk*), Teri McMinn (*Pam*),

Edwin Neal (*Hitchhiker*), Jim Siedow (*Old Man* [more usually known as the 'Cook']), Gunnar Hansen (*Leatherface*), John Dugan (*Grandfather*), Robert Courtin (*Window Washer*), William Creamer (*Bearded Man*), John Henry Faulk (*Storyteller*), Jerry Green (*Cowboy*), Ed Guinn (*Cattle Truck Driver*), Joe Bill Hogan (*Drunk*), Perry Lorenz (*Pick-up Driver*), John Larroquette (*Narrator*)

SYNOPSIS: What we are about to see is based on a true story. Five young people are travelling around Texas in a van: Kirk, Pam, Jerry, Sally and her disabled brother Franklin. Pam reads their horoscopes, none of which are very encouraging. They pick up a hitchhiker, who explains that he and his family used to work at the slaughterhouse before they were mechanised out of a job. He cuts his hand, takes a photo of Franklin, burns it, then cuts Franklin before being kicked out and smearing blood on the side of the van.

They stop for gas but there isn't any; the gas-station proprietor does have sausages for sale, though. They look around a derelict house that used to belong to Franklin's father; Kirk and Pam go for a walk and find a neighbouring house, which they approach hoping for gas. Kirk goes inside and is promptly dispatched by a huge man with a sledgehammer, wearing an apron and a mask of human skin. Pam follows him inside, stumbles into a room filled with bone sculptures and chicken feathers, and is hung up on a meathook while the masked man, Leatherface, takes his chainsaw to Kirk's body.

Jerry looks for the missing couple, and finds Pam in a chest freezer, still alive. He in turn is killed with a sledgehammer. It is now dark, and Sally and Franklin go looking for the others.

Leatherface takes his chainsaw to Franklin then chases Sally through the woods. She takes refuge in the house where the others had been killed, and finds two apparently mummified corpses upstairs. As Leatherface saws the door down she jumps out of the window and runs, chased all the way, to the gas station. The proprietor calms her down, then beats her with a broomstick, puts her in a sack and drives her back to the house, picking up the hitchhiker on the way.

The hitchhiker and Leatherface fetch Grandpa, who is astonishingly still alive, from upstairs; he is revitalised by sucking on Sally's bleeding finger. She passes out, and when she wakes up finds that she is tied to a chair – it's dinner time. Grandpa is fetched to kill her with a sledgehammer, but is too weak to pull it off; after the first serious blow she manages to struggle free and jumps out of the window.

She runs to the road, chased by the hitchhiker who slashes her back with a knife; Leatherface and his chainsaw are not far behind. A lorry runs the hitchhiker over, and the driver throws a spanner at Leatherface; it knocks him down, and he cuts his leg with the chainsaw. Sally waves down a passing truck and is driven away, screaming as Leatherface dances with the saw.

ORIGINS AND INSPIRATION: Until the 1970s, cannibalism was not often depicted in horror films. *Dr X* (Michael Curtiz, 1932) and *Sweeney Todd, the Demon Barber of Fleet Street* (George King, 1936) are rare early examples of films featuring cannibals, but the act is never seen on screen: in the latter it is only hinted at as a means of disposing of Tod Slaughter's corpses, meat for the pie shop next door.

The prototype for the gore and slasher industries, HG Lewis's *Blood Feast* (1963) – like *Texas* the work of an independent Southern filmmaker – was similarly coy about its cannibal intentions: while there is limb-lopping and tongue-pulling a-plenty, no human flesh is ever actually consumed. *Tenderness of Wolves/ Zaerlichkeit Der Voelte* (1973), a film directed by Fassbinder protégé Ulli Lommel which deals with the true-life case of cannibal killer Fritz Haarman, also avoids flesh-eating imagery by making its protagonist more of a vampire, sucking on his victims' blood. Like Todd, Haarman sells cheap meat of dubious provenance on the black market, and the film is full of images of sausages and butchers' shops. Similarly, *Texas* only hinted at its characters' special taste in barbecues, although the theme was developed in its sequels.

The cannibals in these films appear none the worse physically for their dietary choices, and the first feral cannibal appeared in 1972's *Death Line* (US: *Raw Meat*). The film, directed by American Gary Sherman but set in London – principally in the tunnels around Russell Square tube station – featured a cannibal, listed as the 'Man' in the credits, preying on late stragglers on the underground. The Man is the descendant of workers – men and women – who were trapped when a tunnel collapsed in the 19th century; the company employing them couldn't afford to dig them out, and abandoned the project, leaving them to die.

The viewer is sympathetic to his plight: doubly so when his pregnant partner dies, leaving him alone, and when his first victim in the film is a seedy civil servant, whose death kicks off the police investigation. When he abducts the heroine towards the end, he is looking less for meat than for love, although to her boyfriend – intent on crushing his skull with a boot – the distinction probably doesn't matter. Despite his prodigious strength, the lack of five daily portions of fruit and vegetables has taken its toll, and he suffers from severe vitamin deficiency and a range of other ailments; his appearance is more convincingly feral than that of the mutant family of *The Hills Have Eyes* (Wes Craven, 1977), his speech reduced to a plaintive or angry 'Mind the doors!' With Donald Pleasence as an irreverent police inspector and a refreshingly sordid picture of London quite at odds with the establishment line, this gem is one of the best British horror films of the 1970s.

The idea for Hooper's knuckle-gnawing classic came to him one Christmas, when he found himself trapped in the hardware department of Montgomery Ward's by the throng of seasonal shoppers. Looking around, he saw a chainsaw, and realised there was one way he could make a quick exit – the broad outline of the film's plot and feel followed soon after.

Hooper had relatives in Wisconsin, who'd told him as a child tales of lampshades made of human skin and bone furniture, stories about Ed Gein (see **ORIGINS AND INSPIRATION, Psycho**), although Hooper claims not to have known the wayward artisan's name until after *Texas* was released. According to Kim Henkel, who co-wrote the script, a local case known as the 'Candyman murders' also influenced the film, directly inspiring the Cook's moral schizophrenia – he is far more concerned by the damage to the door than Leatherface's four murders; and Hooper himself cites EC Comics (see **ORIGINS AND INSPIRATION, Night of the Living Dead**) as the film's single most important influence. The ghoulish humour of the comics is certainly in evidence: while writing the script – known early on as *Saturn in Retrograde* then *Headcheese* – Hooper and Henkel treated many of the scenes as broad comedy.

Henkel was introduced to Bill ('Jay') Parsley, the film's chief financier, by ex-classmates Warren Skaaren and Ron Bozman. Skaaren, who later came up with the title of the film and constructed the corpse sculpture seen at the start, headed the newly founded Texas Film Commission, where Marilyn Burns worked. Burns was offered a part in the film, and she and Skaaren encouraged several local politicians to invest in the project as a tax shelter. The last thing they expected was for the film to actually succeed, and they were reportedly upset to be associated with such a sickening product.

Most of the cast and crew were friends of Hooper and Henkel, with the crew almost all graduates of the University of Texas, keen to get their first feature-film credit. Daniel Pearl, the DOP, was 23 and had just graduated from the university; he had shot plenty of hand-held camera footage and was chosen by Hooper not only for his availability at the price – cast and crew worked for a pittance, and saw little of even that – but his ability to shoot in a vérité style. Pearl also found a friend to part-finance the film, then budgeted at $80,000.

Robert Burns, who was responsible for the set design, had a tiny art budget to work with – $3000 including his salary – but collected various strange artefacts brought to him by friends, and made judicious use of a bucket of teeth and a pile of animal corpses dumped by a vet to construct the bone sculptures that go some way towards defining the film's look. He also experimented with various materials to get the look of Leatherface's mask, before settling on a model of fibreglass insulation in latex.

DIRECTOR: Hooper, after a childhood spent alternately at the cinema and with his nose in an EC comic, spent most of the 60s directing shorts, documentaries and adverts, before making his first feature, *Eggshells*, in 1969–70. This fragmentary hippy film won several awards at obscure festivals before vanishing, and put several of the key players in *Texas* together for the first time.

The director has yet to live up to the promise of his horror debut. In 1976 he made his first Hollywood film, *Eaten Alive*, but left before shooting was completed, citing disapproval of the nude shots he was asked to do. Still, for all its many flaws this tale of a hotel owner who feeds guests to his crocodile has an impressive EC Comics verve, and is one of Hooper's better efforts.

He was removed from his next two projects, and went on to direct the well-received TV mini-series of *Salem's Lot* (1979), then the crashingly dull *The Funhouse* (1981), during which he was approached by Steven Spielberg to direct *Poltergeist* (1982). The ghost movie took $76 million at the box office but its success was attributed to Spielberg – and certainly the film looks more like *Close Encounters* (1977) than *Texas* – with Hooper left out in the cold. A subsequent deal with Cannon resulted in three expensive flops: the intermittently entertaining *Lifeforce* (1985), an ill-advised remake of *Invaders from Mars* (1986) and the overblown gore comedy *The Texas Chainsaw Massacre 2* (1986).

Hooper's career has never really recovered, with control of his features routinely taken away by the studios: *Spontaneous Combustion* (1990), *Tobe Hooper's Night Terrors* (1993), *The Mangler* (1995) and *Crocodile* (2000) have few fans, and his remake of lesser 70s slasher *The Toolbox Murders* (2003) was barely released.

CASTING: Jim Siedow, the only professional actor in the film, was brought in to ensure a union deal, while Paul Partain had appeared in a supporting role in Sidney Lumet's *Lovin' Molly* (1974); none of the others had been in a commercial film before. Marilyn Burns went on to feature in *Eaten Alive*, then played Linda Kasabian in the Manson Family TV biopic *Helter Skelter* (Tom Gries, 1976) and was reunited with Edwin Neal in *Future-Kill* (Ronald W Moore, 1985). Gunnar Hansen capitalised on his familiarity with power tools in *Hollywood Chainsaw Hookers* (Fred Olen Ray, 1988), before moving on to more barrel-scraping video dreck.

Other cast members played even fewer genre roles after *Texas*: William Vail turned to set design after appearances in *Mausoleum* (Michael Dugan, 1983) and *Poltergeist*, Paul Partain appeared in the redneck Satanist road movie *Race with the Devil* (Jack Starrett, 1975), John Dugan popped up again in *The Return of the Texas Chainsaw Massacre* (Kim Henkel, 1994), and after a part in *The Texas Chainsaw Massacre 2*, Jim Siedow concentrated on his prolific theatre career.

PRODUCTION: Shooting began on 15 July 1973, and took around six weeks. While the director had a keen visual sense and knew what he wanted to film, his organisational skills were lacking, and Ron Bozman was responsible for making sure the shoot ran smoothly. Several scenes were improvised, and Hooper had to resist pressure from the producers to keep strictly to a shot list; if dialogue in the script didn't work, the actors ad-libbed, and the ruined house the characters visit first was written into the script when the filmmakers found it near the house they'd arranged to use for the family residence.

It was a tough shoot. Midsummer in Texas, with no air-conditioning, shooting between twelve and sixteen hours a day, meant that the cast's clothes and tempers deteriorated quickly. Just as well, then, that most of the shooting was done in the order it appears in the film. Particularly gruelling was the dinner scene: when John Dugan realised that his Grandpa make-up took around seven hours to put on, he insisted that all of his scenes around the dinner sequence be shot together, making for an exhausting 27-hour shoot.

Pearl and Hooper, shooting on 16mm that was later blown up to 35mm, had been warned that they should use the finest film stock available to keep the graininess of the blow-ups to a minimum; but this stock was very slow, and needed large amounts of light. So the dinner sequence, with the windows shut and blacked out (the scene takes place just before dawn) and large lights heating up the chicken sculpture and plates of rotting headcheese on the table, is remembered by most of the cast as the worst part of the shoot.

Gunnar Hansen was not allowed to wash his Leatherface outfit for fear that the colour might change, and by this point, as he'd worn it daily for almost four weeks, other cast members were avoiding him. The ostracism and 27-hour shoot took their toll: by the end of the scene he was barely able to differentiate himself from his part, and remembers thinking 'Kill the bitch' while the hitchhiker is taunting Sally. Disturbingly, he also cut Burns' hand with a knife for the scene where Grandpa sucks her finger, as the special effect wasn't working. Tellingly, by this point none of the crew batted an eyelid.

The reason why the violence in the film seems so realistic is that a lot of it *is* real, like this scene. Jim Siedow beat Edwin Neal with a hardwood stick, bruising him; the heads of both William Vail and Marilyn Burns were bruised and bloodied by the trick sledgehammer; Teri McMinn was genuinely in pain from the harness used to hang her on a meathook; and Marilyn Burns was really beaten by Siedow before she is put in a sack, and fainted when the scene was finished. Burns was also injured after the first jump through a window: a body-double was used for the shot of her leaping through the glass, but Burns had to jump from the roof so that they could shoot the landing properly; she landed badly and had a limp for the rest of the film.

There is only one gore effect, where Leatherface cuts himself in the leg with the chainsaw; according to Robert Burns Hooper had wanted more, including a shot of the meathook coming out of Pam's chest, but the art director put him off, arguing that graphic effects usually looked so fake that they actually distanced the viewer. Hooper, by contrast, claims that he avoided explicit violence after being told by the MPAA that if he didn't show any blood he'd get a PG rating for the film!

By the end of the shoot money was running low, and many of the cast and crew received percentages in Vortex, the company set up by Hooper and Henkel to produce the film, in lieu of pay; what they didn't know was that Vortex had never owned more than half the film, and had been selling off more of itself to continue production. The cast and crew points were eventually worth less than a quarter of what they'd originally imagined.

Editing and post-production were responsible for the principal cost overruns, and *Texas* eventually cost $125,000. Credited editor Larry Carroll was thrown off the film when it was clear that he didn't share Hooper's vision, and the director worked with Sallye Richardson to complete the edit at Hooper's house, having run out of money to rent space.

Finally, Hooper felt something was missing, and added the opening images: the crawl, which he imagined working like Orson Welles's notorious *War of the Worlds* broadcast; the corpse statues; and the sunspots, duly purchased from NASA. Most of the cast and crew had envisaged the film being at best a very minor success, and were astonished by the spirit evident in the final edit.

Hooper took the film around several distributors, but could find none to take it. Finally Bryanston Pictures, a shady distribution company with links to organised crime and cash to spare from the phenomenal success of *Deep Throat* (Gerard Damiano, 1972), agreed to distribute it, and appeared to offer a fair deal.

SOUNDTRACK: The sound design of *Texas* is flawless, and marks a move away from the dissonant strings that had characterised the genre since **Psycho** into a more interesting percussive realm. The film features a mixture of country songs heard on the radio, which are used as a counterpoint to the horrific visuals, and percussion-based music played by Hooper and Wayne Bell, from bassy rumbles through clanging cymbals to the stings that accompany the close-ups of Sally's eyes. Many sounds were slowed down or otherwise treated – the pig and cow noises came from Bell's father's voice – and much of the film is accompanied by the revving and whirring of the ever-present chainsaw.

'IT'S ONLY A MOVIE ... ONLY A MOVIE ...': The film's title, one of the most luridly effective in the history of horror, had the punters flocking to the screens, and made them think they'd seen much more than is actually shown. Bryanston's poster campaign, using lines like 'What happened is true. Now the motion picture that's just as real' and 'America's Most Bizarre and Brutal Crimes!', played on the idea that the film was based on a true story, and the distributors' occasionally inept blow-ups from 16mm only increased the graininess of the film, in keeping with its vérité qualities.

The fact that the filmmakers seemed to be slightly deranged themselves did nothing to harm the film's success either. Hooper was quoted in the Bryanston press notes as saying: 'It's a film about meat, about people who have gone beyond dealing with animal meat and rats and dogs and cats. Crazy retarded people going beyond the line between animal and human.'

RELEASE: The film opened on 11 October 1974 in the USA to withering reviews, of which one from the *Catholic Film Newsletter* is typical: 'Be prepared for a totally disgusting and, for many, literally nauseating experience ... a stream of unrelieved and explicit gore ... The film is sick, and so is any audience that enjoys it.'

That made for a lot of sick audiences: Bryanston's accounting methods left much to be desired, so precise box-office figures are unavailable, but in its first seven years the film grossed anywhere between $30 and $100 million. Its critical rehabilitation was rapid too, with the film being shown at the London Film Festival in 1975 and the Directors' Fortnight in Cannes in the same year, and being awarded the Jury's Special Prize at Avoriaz in 1976, as well as prizes at festivals in Trieste and Antwerp. Bryanston even took the film to the Museum of Modern Art in New York, then sent out a press release revealing what they'd done; and when New York reviewer Rex Reed, the first American newspaper reviewer to say he liked the film, gave it a positive review, others soon followed suit. *Texas* was hot news.

Still, it wasn't for everyone. Hooper has said that it took eight years to make the film (and thus him as a director) respectable, and it was routinely used to illustrate the sordid depths to which the horror genre had now sunk, as in the following memorable piece from *Harper's Magazine*:

> *The Texas Chain Saw Massacre* is a vile little piece of sick crap ... It is a particularly foul item in the currently developing hard-core pornography of murder, fundamentally a simple exploitation film designed to milk a few more bucks out of the throng of shuffling wretches who still gather ... in those dank caverns for the scab-picking of the human spirit ...

The BBFC, while they appreciated the film's quality, refused to certify it, although the GLC passed it for early cinema screenings. It remained uncertificated in the UK until 1999, 25 years after its first release.

Despite the film's commercial success, the filmmakers hardly saw any money from it. Bryanston appeared to withhold the considerable profits from them, and when they finally got around to suing the company, it was declared bankrupt. Many other companies made money out of *Texas*; most of the cast and crew received little more than a couple of hundred dollars.

CRITICAL EYE: Few films have come anywhere near matching *Texas*'s gruelling intensity. Many feature more horrific scenes or more gruesome effects – it's a remarkably bloodless film – but none approach its sheer relentlessness: from the moment Kirk steps inside the family's house, there is no let-up, nothing to distract our attention from the grimly claustrophobic events.

Time and space appear to loop back on themselves, with an authentic nightmare logic: when Leatherface chases Sally, he seems perpetually on the very brink of catching her, and when Sally first escapes, it is only to run back to her captors. This lack of control, a staple of bad dreams, is a key feature of the film. Neither Sally nor her friends can control or understand what happens to them; and nor can the Cook control his family, equally upset by the hitchhiker's graverobbing and Leatherface's treatment of their front door.

There is no explanation offered for what happens to the visitors – as punishment for trespassing it seems just a touch heavy-handed – but the repetition of portents and omens assures the viewer that these events are fated to happen. Pam reads from a book on astrology, and tells her friends that Saturn is in retrograde; the hitchhiker burns a photo of Franklin then smears what looks like some kind of symbol on the side of the van; and footage of sunspots fills the screen over the opening credits. According to Hooper: 'The structural puzzle pieces, the way it folds continuously back in on itself, and no matter where you're going it's the wrong place . . . that was influenced by my thinking about solar flares' and sunspots' reflecting behaviours.' Elsewhere he has suggested that the film is about 'a bad day – it's about a cosmically bad day'.

The film's nightmare logic is lent extra power through repetition: orbs including the sun, the moon, headlights and, horribly, eyes, fill the screen, and Sally jumps through a window twice, recalling the circular repetition of sleep paralysis. This is not the only instance of doubling in the film: the family is like a sick parody of the healthy group they kill, with Leatherface a grotesque mockery of the women and the hitchhiker as the family's Franklin – both of them blow raspberries, and Franklin wonders aloud whether he could cut himself like his slaughterhouse reflection. And as Kim Newman points out in *Nightmare Movies,* the family also parodies the nuclear family familiar from countless TV sitcoms: with the Cook (actually intended to be brother to Leatherface and the hitchhiker) as the long-suffering Dad, Leatherface as the busy housewife and the hitchhiker as the rebellious long-haired son.

Yet while undeniably monstrous, they are not entirely unsympathetic: their bone sculptures are inventive enough to demonstrate that they are intelligent and creative, and they take pride in their work. One of the film's many instances of absurd humour has the boastful description of Grandpa's killing abilities juxtaposed with his inability to successfully brain Sally.

This humour – which many missed on the release of the film – does little to lighten the tone, although it does add to the film's cartoon abundance of energy. Some of it just adds to the horror: when Sally's screams and tears are mocked by the hitchhiker, who mimes 'boo hoo hoo', the viewer is taken back to the worst childhood teasing, recalling early playground memories of despairing impotence.

The film's archetypal structure is borrowed from fairy tales: this isn't far from Hansel and Gretel, with its children lost in the woods who find an attractive house inhabited by a fiend who kidnaps and wants to eat them. But while fairy tales tend to serve the function of preparing children for the rigours of adult life, and thus present a positive face for all their often considerable violence, *Texas* inverts their traditional values and presents an apocalyptic vision of unremitting negativity.

There is no possibility of redemption here: all is dead, dry and dusty. The film's aesthetic is almost unique in this characteristically soggy genre; everything from the abundance of feathers to the endless bone sculptures and lack of blood gives the sense of dessication and sterility. There are no women in the family – save for one corpse, naturally mummified – and none of the men have any interest in sex: when Sally offers to 'do anything' for them all they can do is laugh. Women, or sex, would offer the possibility of regeneration; but this too is mocked in the film, the apparently dead Grandpa reviving on sucking Sally's blood. Here people are useful only as things, as meat to eat or bones to sit on, and the fairy-tale trope of the young usurping the old is turned on its head: here the old devour the young, and part of the film's power derives, in the words of critic Robin Wood, from 'the dead weight of the past crushing the life of the younger generation'.

Grandpa recalls **Psycho**'s Mrs Bates, ostensibly another aged country dweller resentful of young city folks' incursions onto her territory. The Bates Motel has been effectively put out of business by the construction of a new highway; similarly *Texas*'s family (named as the Sawyers – of course – in the first sequel) were made redundant when their local slaughterhouse was mechanised, and now make a living selling human sausages to unwary visitors.

The tension between town and country is extremely common in horror, and again relates to fairy tales with their classic trajectory of village to wood; in this sense *Texas* is related to other 'urbanoia' films like *Straw Dogs* (1971), *Deliverance* (John Boorman, 1972) and its more direct progeny *The Hills Have Eyes* (1977). Critic Carol Clover has identified the central thrust of these films in her influential study *Men, Women and Chainsaws*: the city has abused the countryside, and urban comfort comes at the expense of rural communities, whether the old silver mines in *Hills* that are now used for nuclear testing, or the dam that will soon flood the valley in *Deliverance* to provide extra electricity for the city. This fact is brought home to the city slickers on their rural jaunt, but is tempered by the realisation that the country folk are both morally and physically deficient – that they deserve whatever fate they suffer at the hands of the city.

This demonisation relies on their appearance – unkempt, and possibly even inbred, with dirty clothes and poor dental hygiene; their names – either they don't have them, or they use nicknames like 'Leatherface'; and their activities, which range from rape, whether of a woman (*I Spit on Your Grave* (1978), *Straw Dogs*) or a man (*Deliverance*), through cannibalism to, worst of all, unemployment. Rape and cannibalism are, respectively, sexual and dietary taboos, the transgression of which is routinely attributed to subjugated or colonised peoples: the place of the redskin as such cinema demons has largely been replaced by the redneck, although the feral family of *Hills* certainly appear, in their dress and dwelling at least, something of a throwback.

INDUSTRY IMPACT: The film's power lies less in its subject matter than its unrelieved intensity, and a nihilistic tone that aligns it with the other brutal shockers of the period, **Night of the Living Dead** and *Last House on the Left* (1972). Still, after Grandpa and family brought home the bacon, meat movies were churned out like sausage links, although few took from their inspiration anything more than the audacity of its title, with films like *3 on a Meathook* (William Girdler, 1972) and *The Drive-In Massacre* (Stu Segall, 1976) failing to live up to expectations.

Similarly disappointing were *Texas*'s three sequels, none of which came close to matching the original: *Part 3*, *Leatherface* (Jeff Burr, 1990), is probably the best of the bunch, with an endearingly psychotic child and Leatherface struggling with a Speak & Spell, although celebrity-spotters might prefer *Part 2* (Dennis Hopper wielding a chainsaw, 1986) or part 4, *The Return of the Texas Chainsaw Massacre* (starring Renée Zellweger and Matthew McConaughey, 1994). The original film was also pointlessly remade in 2003 by Marcus Nispel.

The Hills Have Eyes was a cut above any of these with its tale of an all-American family decimated by its feral counterpart out in the desert. Director Wes Craven makes good use of *Texas*'s art director for the look of the cannibal family – who, with two women, aren't nearly as menacing as *Texas*'s band – and gave Michael Berryman a career in playing leering bald psychos. But if

Texas is an influence on the film, *Hills* is more directly lifted from Craven's notorious debut, *Last House on the Left*, with which it shares its basic set-up of a civilised family driven to savage violence by its brutish mirror image. The reputation of *Last House* rests on its grim scenes of the torture, humiliation and murder of two teenage girls, but the impact of these is weakened by the film's ill-judged comic relief and an absurdly implausible storyline.

In the UK Pete Walker turned his attention away from sex comedies to make the downbeat but irreverently entertaining *Frightmare* (1974), replaying *Texas*'s mix of power tools and human meat with Sheila Keith as a demented old lady who won't be fobbed off with animal brains any longer.

Despite their close relationship, horror and comedy don't always mix well, and few of the cannibal comedies aiming to put filmgoers off their hot dogs managed to pull it off: *Motel Hell* (Kevin Connor, 1980) might have boasted some impressive imagery, but failed to live up to its human-farming premise, while Bob Balaban's *Parents* (1989), with its sitcom-perfect family whose son wonders where Mom keeps on finding leftovers, gave the right tone of sick laughs. Similarly successful was the Ed Gein biopic *Deranged* (1974), a far more entertaining and energetic film than the straighter *Ed Gein* (2000).

Gein was also the inspiration for the Buffalo Bill character in *The Silence of the Lambs* (1991), who shares his penchant for wearing the skin of his victims; Jonathan Demme's film also introduced a rare epicurean cannibal in Dr Hannibal Lecter, who showed that not all cannibals have to be feral savages (and we'll leave the 'savages' aspect to **Cannibal Holocaust**) – the practice might even be the pinnacle of good taste.

Antonia Bird's *Ravenous* (1999), which boasted the tagline 'You are what you eat', takes a similar tack, with its cannibals finding that human meat fills them not only with virility but also provides a rapid healing process. Cowardly Guy Pearce finds the strength to kill his enemies, while a characteristically psychotic Robert Carlyle draws enough energy from his forbidden diet to convince a group of strangers of his outrageously implausible story. The film, loosely inspired by the story of Alferd Packer, is slick and fun but entirely undisturbing, and could do with a transfusion from one of the darker Hong Kong takes on cannibalism, like *Bun Man: the Untold Story* (Danny Lee and Herman

Yau, 1992) or *Dr Lamb* (Danny Lee and Hin Sing 'Billy' Tang, 1992), also purportedly based on true stories.

Finally, probably the most telling influence of *Texas* is its introduction of the 'final girl' who survives the slaughter of her busload of teen friends. The last half-hour of the film focuses on Sally being chased by her tormentors but finally managing to escape; by the time of **Halloween**, this passive resistance had become active and would soon become highly conventionalised. But more on that later . . .

FINAL WORD: *Texas* remains one of the purest horror films ever made, and any sociopolitical readings of it pale against its true purpose: to terrify the audience. According to Hooper:

> The true monster itself is death. All the classic horror flicks – *Dracula*, *Frankenstein*, *Psycho* – have this in common. They have a unique way of getting inside you by setting up symbols that represent death: a graveyard, bones, flowers. If you put them in the proper order then you create the most important aura known as the creeps.

Texas gives you the creeps in spades.

MURDER ITALIAN-STYLE

Deep Red (1975)

'Flesh Ripped clean to the Bone ... And the Blood runs Red ...'

aka The Hatchet Murders (US theatrical re-release title), Suspiria Part 2 (Japanese English-language title)

Italy, Rizzoli Film and Salvatore Argento, colour, 130 mins
[Italian release]

Directed by Dario Argento
Executive Producer: Claudio Argento
Story and Screenplay: Dario Argento and Bernardino Zapponi
Director of Photography: Luigi Kuveiller
Music: Giorgio Gaslini, recorded by The Goblin
Editor: Franco Fraticelli
Art Director: Giuseppe Bassan
Assistant Director: Stefano Rolla
Special Effects: Germano Natali and Carlo Rambaldi

CAST: David Hemmings (*Marc Daly*), Daria Nicolodi (*Gianna Brezzi*), Gabriele Lavia (*Carlo*), Macha Meril (*Helga Ulmann*),

Eros Pagni (*Superintendent Calcabrini*), Giuliana Calandra (*Amanda Righetti*), Glauco Mauri (*Professor Giordani*), Clara Calamai (*Marta, Carlo's mother*), Piero Mazzinghi (*Mario Bardi*), Aldo Bonamano (*Carlo's Father*), Liana Del Balzo (*Elvira, Amanda's Housekeeper*), Vittorio Fanfoni (*Cop Taking Notes*), Dante Fioretti (*Police Photographer*), Geraldine Hooper (*Massimo Ricci*), Iacopo Mariani (*Young Carlo*), Furio Meniconi (*Rodi, Villa Varetaker*), Fulvio Mingozzi (*Agent Mingozzi*), Lorenzi Piani (*Fingerprint Cop*), Salvatore Puntillo (*Fabbroni, a Cop*), Piero Vida (*Hungry Cop*), Nicoletta Elmi (*Olga Rodi*)

SYNOPSIS: During the opening titles, a shadowy couple is seen struggling. There is a scream, then a child's feet are seen as a bloodied knife is picked up.

At a parapsychology conference in Rome Helga Ulmann demonstrates her telepathic powers, and senses a killer in the room. That night she is murdered. English jazz pianist Marc Daly, who has just left his drunk friend Carlo, is in the square beneath her window, and witnesses the murder. He races to her apartment, but sees only a black-raincoated figure walking away in the square.

The police interrogate him; he's sure he saw something in the apartment, but can't work out what. Journalist Gianna Brezzi arrives, and assumes Daly to be an eyewitness. Brezzi and Daly go to Ulmann's funeral, then have sex and argue about gender roles.

Daly, looking for Carlo, meets his mother, who sends him to Carlo's boyfriend's apartment. Carlo advises him to return to England, but Daly is becoming obsessed with the case. As he practises the piano later he is threatened by somebody in his apartment, who plays a children's tune on a tape player.

He tells Ulmann's colleagues about the tune, and it reminds one of them about a purportedly haunted house. Daly finds a book about the house in a library. Its author, Amanda Righetti, is scalded to death, but manages to write something in the steam on her bathroom wall before she dies. Daly visits the house and finds her body, then tells Ulmann's colleague Professor Giordani about her pointing finger; Giordani visits the house and finds out what she has written, then tries to call Daly, who is out.

Daly visits plant nurseries to track down the haunted house, as the garden features rare trees; when he finds it he is given permission to investigate by its caretaker. He discovers a wall painting of a murder hidden behind plaster.

Giordani is murdered at home, his teeth smashed out. Daly realises that there must be a hidden room in the haunted house, and finds a skeleton there. He is knocked unconscious but rescued by Brezzi; the house is set on fire. He recovers at the caretaker's house, and sees a picture drawn by the caretaker's daughter, Olga, that resembles the murder painting. Olga tells him that she copied it from a painting at her school, and he and Brezzi break into the school.

Brezzi hears a noise and is stabbed; Daly finds the picture, which is drawn by Carlo. Carlo threatens him with a gun, but the police arrive. Carlo escapes, only to be run over by a car. But Daly realises that Carlo couldn't have killed Ulmann, and returns to her apartment. There he is attacked by Carlo's mother, the killer he'd unwittingly spotted in a mirror on his first visit to the flat; her necklace catches in a lift shaft and she is decapitated.

ORIGINS AND INSPIRATION: Black leather gloves, straight razors, staring eyes and victims who've just stepped off a fashion shoot. The *giallo* (Italian for yellow) takes its name from the yellow covers of crime paperbacks published in Italy in the 1930s, principally whodunnits in the Agatha Christie or Sherlock Holmes mode, much as film noir refers to the French Série Noire and Fleuve Noir run of pulp crime paperbacks. As a film genre loosely identified by English-speaking audiences, the *giallo* is principally defined by its visual content, its storylines incorporating a range from gothic horror to crime melodrama while it returns to the same images and obsessions again and again.

The *giallo* has its roots in a number of sources: the themes of voyeurism and eyewitness from **Psycho**, *Rear Window* (1954) and *Peeping Tom* (1960), which also provided the template for the *giallo*'s plot construction around the graphic murders of a series of women; and the masked killers and sexual perversions of Germany's *krimis*, murder mysteries often based on the works of Edgar Wallace, which were mixed in the *giallo* with the police-procedural dramas popular on TV and a fetishistic attention to the aesthetics of violent death.

Mario Bava's *The Girl Who Knew Too Much/La ragazza che sapeva troppo* (US: *Evil Eye*, 1962) is widely credited as being the first *giallo* film, and explores a number of the themes that came to characterise the genre: an acknowledgement of its literary origins (Nora Davis reads a *giallo* on a plane at the start of the film); foreignness (the classic *giallo* protagonist is the foreigner in Italy); an exploration of voyeurism in the context of violent murder; an obsessive amateur detective; and a host of colourful red herrings and plot twists.

But it took Bava's second *giallo*, *Blood and Black Lace/Sei donne per l'assassino* (1964), to fix the genre conventions, with its focus on a masked, black-raincoated killer wreaking havoc among the beautiful models of a Rome fashion house. The *giallo* was now marked as a crossbreed between the horror and crime genres, with the film's murders exceeding anything in the other psycho-thrillers of the time in their stylishness, brutality and overt eroticism; as extravagant set-pieces melding beauty and death they were unmatched until Argento's startling debut *The Bird with the Crystal Plumage/L'uccello dalle plume di cristallo* (1970) six years later, and the film's use of colour and aggressively unnatural lighting also foreshadow Argento's supernatural chillers.

Bava continued to make *gialli*, alongside period gothic films (the magnificently stylised *Mask of Satan/Black Sunday/La Maschera del Demonio* (1960)), westerns (*The Road to Fort Alamo/La Strada per Forte Alamo* (1964)) and demented comic-book extravaganzas (*Danger Diabolik* (1967)), and had little to fear in the *giallo* arena from journeyman competitors like Umberto Lenzi. Still, none of his other *gialli* reached the dizzy heights of *Blood and Black Lace*; *Hatchet for the Honeymoon/Il rosso segno della follia* (1969) gave an ineffective nod to **Psycho**'s transvestite killer; while *5 Dolls for an August Moon/5 bambole per la luna d'agosto* (1970), inspired by Agatha Christie's *Ten Little Indians*, is principally memorable for its lurid set design and costumes, highlighting the camp appeal of many *gialli*, and its incomprehensible title, foreshadowing the outlandish monikers that followed Argento's debut. Only with *Twitch of the Death Nerve/Bay of Blood/Reazione a catena* (1971) did Bava return to anything like his previous *giallo* form, its graphic killings influencing the bodycount movies of *Friday the 13th*'s ilk, while its use of multiple murderers foreshadowed several Argento films.

But it took the success of the immensely stylish *The Bird with the Crystal Plumage* (Dario Argento, 1970) to kick off the golden age of the *giallo*. Sam Dalmas, an American in Rome, witnesses what he assumes to be an attack on a woman in an art gallery, and spends the rest of the film obsessively investigating the case;

but in the process he experiences a crisis of identity that soon became typical of Argento's male protagonists. While elsewhere the *giallo* characteristically focused on female hysteria and pathology, read in overtly psychoanalytic terms, *The Bird* set the stage for Argento's other *gialli* in featuring an exploration of masculinity through a naïve male protagonist, whose fragile worldview is shattered when he witnesses – and misinterprets – a violent event.

A key feature here is the unreliability of vision. Dalmas's assumptions about gender obscure the truth of what he saw, and while *The Girl Who Knew Too Much* had a similar twist, here 'whodunnit' matters less than the shattering of Dalmas's illusory ideas of gender and identity. Vision and eyes are central themes in other *gialli* too, featuring heavily in the films' titles – *Cold Eyes of Fear/Gli occhi freddi della paura* (1971), *Eyeball/Gatti rossi in un labirinto di vetro* (1974) – and occasionally graphically violated, as in Argento's *Opera* (1987).

The Bird's unprecedented international success led to a series of exotically titled *gialli*, not only from Italy (*Lizard in a Woman's Skin/Una lucertola con la pelle di donna* (Lucio Fulci, 1971), *The Black Belly of the Tarantula/La tarantola dal ventre nero* (Paolo Cavara, 1971), *Crimes of the Black Cat/Sette scialli di seta gialli* (Sergio Pastore, 1972)) but also Spain (*The Blue Eyes of the Broken Doll/Los ojos azules de la muneca rota* (Carlos Aured, 1973)). Argento himself followed it with two lesser *gialli*, *Cat O'Nine Tails/Il Gatto a nove code* (1971) and *Four Flies on Grey Velvet/Quattro mosche di velluto grigio* (1971), which are still more stylish than the competition, even if they don't quite match *The Bird* or *Deep Red*, his *giallo* masterpiece.

DIRECTOR: Argento's films straddle the rich border between European arthouse and exploitation, the films from his peak period (1975–85) appealing to critics and gorehounds alike; of the other directors in this book, only David Cronenberg has managed to sustain a combination of intellectual stimulation with visceral imagery so successfully. Argento's background as a film critic is important in this respect, as the director combines a familiarity with directors like Godard, Antonioni and Buñuel with a firm grasp of the mechanics of commercial filmmaking; and both directors have been recognised as outstanding visual stylists outside their fields, with Cronenberg directing an advert for Nike and Argento shooting not only a fashion show for Trussardi but also ads for Fiat and Johnson & Johnson.

The director has defined his influences in literary terms, pointing to the *gialli* of Agatha Christie, SS van Dine, John Dickson Carr and Cornell Woolrich, the thrillers of Boileau–Narcejac and Poe's fables as key loves; in cinematic terms he quotes German Expressionism, particularly the films of Lang and Murnau, as having had the most profound effect on his work.

He is often compared to Lang and Hitchcock, and shares something of the latter's public persona – he has directed a TV series, a kind of 'Dario Argento Presents' – and desire to make an audience identify with a killer: as well as **Psycho**, the finger-breaking scene in *Frenzy* (1972) is a clear precursor to the murderer's panicked near-capture in *Tenebrae* (1982) and grisly search for evidence in *Opera*. But while in both directors' films chaos lies beneath a fragile surface, their approaches towards its exposure are diametrically opposed: if Hitchcock's films are resolutely linear, Argento's are anything but.

Argento's non-linear logic comes partly from his writing technique: he claims to come up with his stories in a trance state, 'a little like that of the Surrealists, using automatic writing'. His unfettered imagination has led to predictable accusations of misogyny, which the director has not helped by identifying himself heavily with his killers; he has said that 'deep within me I love them', and the black-gloved, knife-wielding hands in many of his films are his own. He has also stated that: 'I like women, especially beautiful ones. If they have a good face and figure, I would much prefer to watch them being murdered than an ugly girl or a man. I certainly don't have to justify myself to anyone about this', and that 'I would probably make a pretty good murderer. In such an intense physical act like murder, between the victim and the murderer there is something sensual, something erotic deep down.'

Yet gender politics in horror are never as simple as they may at first seem, least of all in Argento's films, which routinely explore weak, unstable men shown up by strong, independent women. Indeed the leads in many of his films, most notably *Suspiria* (1977) and *Phenomena* (1985), are women, and Argento's primary concern seems less the murder of women than murder full stop: *Deep Red*, for one, sees the director happily dispatching people regardless of gender. Argento's work should also be seen in the wider context of Italian culture: opera, in particular, is filled with images of grotesque and violent death – often of young women – and the violence in Argento's films is often described as 'operatic'; it is no coincidence that two of his films have opera settings.

Almost all of the action in Argento's films happens indoors in urban settings: they may be set in photogenic cities (Rome, Milan, New York), but you'd never know it from the films themselves. Unlike many other *giallo* filmmakers, Argento avoids touristic establishing shots, and his focus on specific kinds of internal architecture means that his films exist in a kind of non-specific geographical space, a universe of high ceilings, overwrought furnishings and geometric order that provides the perfect back-drop for the perverted madness of his killers.

The director was born into a filmmaking family: his father was a film producer, his mother a photographer. He was a sickly child, given to long bouts of illness during which he devoured books, particularly Poe, and he grew up to become a film critic. The path from critic to director is well trodden, and Argento's first break in the movie business was working with Bernardo Bertolucci on the storyboards for Sergio Leone's *Once Upon a Time in the West* (1969); Argento has often been described as being to the thriller what Leone is to the western.

He wrote and sold several scripts then decided to try his hand at directing; his father Salvatore helped him finance the film, and *The Bird* was a resounding commercial success. After following it with two more *gialli*, Argento tired of the format and directed a little-seen comedy western, *Le cinque giornate/Five Days in Milan* (1973), which shares little in terms of style or content with his other work. The film failed to find an audience, and Argento returned to more familiar obsessions with *Deep Red*.

After considering adapting the works of HP Lovecraft, Argento took a different direction in the supernatural extravaganza of *Suspiria*, his most successful and best-known film. If Argento's *gialli* invite Freudian analysis, his supernatural works are explicit-ly Jungian, full of fire, water and Jungian archetypes. Co-written by his long-term partner Daria Nicolodi, whose occult beliefs provided the impetus for the film, *Suspiria* leaves narrative convention behind in its fantastically stylised exploration of witchcraft in a ballet school.

Using outmoded Technicolor stock, Argento creates a world of impossibly rich pinks and blues, saturated colours that wash over the baroque sets and grotesque murders; while it lacks the textual richness of *Deep Red*, it returns psycho-sexual excess to the fairy tale, its lysergic take on *Snow White* marking the director's most successful marriage of sound and vision yet, with Goblin's hisses and howls perfectly complementing the hallucinatory visuals.

Inferno (1980) continues the theme, but takes the set-piece murders from *Suspiria* further: here the entire film is a sequence of set-pieces, held together by the flimsiest of plots. If the film suffers from a weak male lead, it is still one of the most unique and sustained gothic visions ever created, and also showcases the director's sense of grotesque comedy: like the blind man killed by his own dog in *Suspiria*, a crippled bookshop owner here calls for help when he is attacked by rats, only to be hacked to death by a cleaver-wielding burger flipper.

Argento has failed to complete this prospective supernatural trilogy; *Tenebrae*, despite its name, was his return to the *giallo* format, allegedly inspired by the director's own brush with a stalker obsessed with *Suspiria*. Here a murderer stalks a Rome of blinding white modernist furnishings, splashed deep red as he kills 'sexual perverts' in ways inspired by an American writer's thrillers. The plot is typically audacious, and the look of the film, inspired by Andrej Zulawski's *Possession* (1981), provides some of the finest moments in Argento's films, even if the whole doesn't hang together as well as *Deep Red*.

Phenomena marks, for most, the end of the director's golden age, and is often considered his worst film. Donald Pleasence is clearly embarrassed to be delivering lines like 'it's perfectly normal for insects to be slightly telepathic' in his role as wheelchair-bound Scottish entomologist, but while the film is hobbled from the start by its insane plot of psychic insects roaming the Swiss countryside, some of the imagery is strange enough to make it worth a look, and perversely it's the director's personal favourite.

Opera, Argento's most lavish production to date, exaggerates the *giallo*'s obsession with eyes and looking as Betty, a young opera singer, has needles fixed under her eyes by a killer who forces her to watch him kill her boyfriend and costumier. The film is filled with images of eyes being violated – Daria Nicolodi is shot through the eye, and the killer has an eye pecked out and swallowed by a raven – and an SM aesthetic that pushes the connection between sex and violence further than any other Argento film. *Opera*'s ambiguous ending, with a crazed voice-over from Betty as she crawls around a field, alienated some of the director's fans, but it is in many ways the most full-throttle Argento film to date, hyperkinetic visuals married to an extravagantly weird storyline that constantly confounds our expectations.

After her messy end in *Opera*, Nicolodi refused to work with Argento again, and his work has foundered without a muse. 2 *Evil Eyes/Due occhi diabolici* (1990), a split film with George A Romero in which each adapted a Poe tale, is a mess, and *Trauma* (1993), Argento's first American production, was predictably compromised by studio involvement. It's an understandable bid for American success – despite the relatively popular *Deep Red* and *Suspiria*, Argento's subsequent films had been poorly treated by distributors, with *Tenebrae* recut and insultingly renamed *Unsane*, *Phenomena* recut as *Creepers*, and *Opera* not even released in America at all – but the film turned out to be a critical and commercial flop, and marked the director's only foray into the California sunshine.

Trauma did, however, mark Argento's daughter Asia's debut in one of his films; since then she has replaced Nicolodi as his muse, and has been treated similarly badly, although she is yet to be killed. The worst fate to befall her is probably her repeated rapes in *The Stendhal Syndrome/La sindrome di Stendhal* (1996), a confused meditation on one of Argento's favourite themes, the power of art to provoke violent responses.

But even this film looks like a masterpiece alongside the disastrous *The Phantom of the Opera/Il fantasma dell'opera* (1998), and it took *Sleepless/Nonhosonno* (2001) to provide a return to form for the director, with a *giallo* that replays the buried clue motif from *The Bird* and *Deep Red* and features some spectacularly brutal murders, although visually it pales beside the director's best work.

CASTING: Argento is routinely accused of paying far more attention to camera styling and set design than to the performances of his actors; the dubbing on most of his films doesn't help in this respect, and the curious are advised to seek out subtitled versions wherever possible.

But the actors in *Deep Red* are stronger than in his previous work: David Hemmings is one of Argento's few likeable and convincing male leads, and the film marks the first starring role for Daria Nicolodi.

The casting of Hemmings clearly recalls Antonioni's *Blow Up* (1966), the paradigm of the unsolvable mystery: there Hemmings plays Thomas, a photographer who believes he may have photographed a murder; but as he looks ever more closely at his photos, all he can see is grain, and the film uses the mystery format to explore, finally, the impossibility of knowledge.

Hemmings' other genre roles include *Eye of the Devil* (J Lee Thompson, 1967), *Fragment of Fear* (Richard C Sarafian, 1970), *Unman, Wittering and Zigo* (John Mackenzie, 1971) and *Thirst* (Rod Hardy, 1979), while as well as appearing in almost all of Argento's films from here until *Two Evil Eyes* – a broken ankle prevented her performing in *Suspiria* – Nicolodi also featured in Mario Bava's uneven *Shock* (1977) and Luigi Cozzi's *Paganini Horror* (1989).

Macha Meril was Renee in *Belle de Jour* (Luis Bunuel, 1967), and followed *Deep Red* with a part in the sleazy *Last House on the Left* (1972) rip-off *Late Night Trains/Night Train Murders/ L'ultimo treno della notte* (Aldo Lado, 1975) and Agnes Varda's devastating *Vagabond/Sans toit ni loi* (1985).

PRODUCTION: *Deep Red* was filmed from 9 September 1974 for 16 weeks on location in Turin and Rome, with interiors filmed at De Paolis Incir Studios. Argento originated the story, and the screenplay was written by Bernardo Zaponnini, who had also co-written Fellini's *Satyricon* (1970) and *Roma* (1972). Argento wanted a visceral response to the violence in the film, and decided to use painful incidents audiences could relate to; there are no gunshot wounds in *Deep Red*, as few audience members would have been shot, but many would have been scalded by boiling water (which kills Righetti), cut themselves on broken glass (like the broken window used to kill Ulmann) or knocked their teeth on a hard surface (Giordani). The strategy works: it's difficult to think of a murder scene as painful to watch as Giordani's jaw-bashing.

SOUNDTRACK: Music is associated with murder in *Deep Red* for both the killer and the audience. The killer plays a tape recording of a children's lullaby before each murder: as a professor of psychology suggests, the killer needs to re-create elements of a traumatic experience from their past – principally the association of music and violence – to kill again. Similarly, The Goblin's pounding jazz-rock score signals that the killer is close, and goes into overdrive once the set-piece murders have begun. The soundtrack's association between music and violence is so strong that the murders, impeccably choreographed show-stoppers, play like ultra-stylish rock videos, although they'd be unlikely to get heavy rotation on MTV.

Deep Red marked Argento's first work with The Goblin, elsewhere known as The Goblins or Goblin. On paper the band's music, which mixes elements of jazz, rock and funk with an inescapably 70s feel, shouldn't work in a horror film; it has no cinematic precedent, and seems designed less to scare or shock than to excite the viewer, a drum-roll for the excessively operatic act of violence to follow. While signature themes for a monster or killer are a staple of the horror genre, few other soundtracks invite the viewer to identify quite so much with the killer's glee.

The interplay between Argento's baroque visuals and Goblin's scores is one of the most memorable and distinctive features of his films, and the band went on to provide one of the genre's most innovative soundtracks in *Suspiria*. *Deep Red* foreshadows this, its hints of the later film's supernatural concerns mirrored in its sonic taster for *Suspiria*'s deafening 'Witch!'

The band also scored most of Argento's other films, as well as the Italian versions of Romero's *Martin* (1977) and *Dawn of the Dead* (1978) and exploitation favourites like Joe D'Amato's *Beyond the Darkness/Buio Omega* (1979), Luigi Cozzi's *Contamination* (1980), Bruno Mattei's *Zombie Creeping Flesh/Virus* (1981) and Michele Soavi's *The Church/La Chiesa* (1989).

RELEASE: Argento's film was one of his few successes in the US, but was not, by and large, well received in the press; in one of its only mainstream reviews, the *New York Times*'s Vincent Canby described Argento as 'simply a director of incomparable incompetence' in his knowledge of the rules of detective fiction.

The violence in this and other Argento films led to problems with censors in the UK, and the film was not readily available after 1983's Video Recordings Act (VRA). The current British DVD release cuts only a scene of Olga torturing two lizards, which renders her father's attacks incomprehensible.

CRITICAL EYE: *Deep Red*'s story is largely foreshadowed in *The Bird*: Marc, like Sam Dalmas, sees something he is unable to interpret correctly, and his obsessive investigation leads to a shattering of his naïve world-view. But the film goes far further than *The Bird* in its relentless non-linear twists and turns, and Argento misdirects the viewer at every opportunity.

Deep Red is full of red herrings and dead ends: the police feature in a number of scenes that demonstrate only their appetite for junk food; there are hints at a nature/nurture theme with Carlo as innocence corrupted and Olga born malign, which becomes irrelevant when the viewer learns that Carlo is not the killer; Carlo refers to a class conflict between himself and Marc, which is not only undeveloped but also essentially untrue, with Carlo's mother clearly comfortably off; and the hints of sexual perversion through images of black-rimmed eyes and leather gloves are clearly meant to direct the viewer's attention to the homosexual Carlo as the killer.

Argento uses visual techniques to misdirect the viewer too: shots of corridors draw the attention to the deepest point, although everything important happens halfway down; and film grammar is flagrantly disregarded, with shifts between omniscient and specific character viewpoints never signposted, and sometimes even segueing in the same shot. Argento's use of spatially disorienting pans, including the extreme close-ups of the killer's paraphernalia – knives, marbles and brightly coloured toys – further render point of view impossibly fragmented: the camera here has a mind of its own, roving restlessly over anything that takes its fancy, and often pausing on images that serve no narrative function whatsoever.

Part of Argento's aim here seems to be to bring home the unreliability of perception: the viewer watches as Marc, the 'eyewitness', repeatedly makes erroneous assumptions about what he has seen, and is invited not to trust his own perceptions either. The director also seems to be playing around with categories: nothing is quite what it seems, either in what's shown or the way it's done.

Marc's inability to understand what he has seen stems partly from his ideas about gender as fixed and immutable. At the most obvious level, he assumes that the killer is a man – an assumption the viewer may well make too: isn't the killer seen in the men's room at the start of the film? – but gender ambiguity and sexual unease haunt him throughout the film. Early on he hesitates before saying the word 'bordello', and he is teased by Brezzi about homosexuality; whatever his true tastes, he is clearly troubled by Carlo's boyfriend, who is actually played by a woman, foreshadowing the transsexual flashback figure in *Tenebrae*.

His ideas of the proper position of men and women are outmoded and chauvinistic: 'Women are delicate, fragile' while 'Men have the monopoly on intelligence'. But when Brezzi challenges him to an arm-wrestle she wins, despite his attempted cheat, and he becomes an object of ridicule in the broken passenger seat of her car. Argento has professed a liking for Sherlock Holmes, but Marc's bumbling investigation is closer to Watson, whatever progress he makes due only to a string of ludicrous coincidences; and just as Sam Dalmas fails to protect his girlfriend, Marc fails to protect Brezzi from being stabbed (although she survives – 'She is a strong woman', as the doctors tell him) and, again like Dalmas, he is rescued by his girlfriend from the killer.

The crack in the surface is a repeated image in Argento's films, a break in the characters' pattern of assumptions that they worry obsessively until they are overwhelmed by the chaos behind. Here Marc discovers a painting hidden behind a wall, and chips away at the plaster until he thinks he has revealed the image; but when he leaves, another piece of the plaster falls away, showing that he has seen only part of the picture. This concern with what lies behind surfaces is reflected in an obsession with surfaces themselves, from the microscopic exploration of texture in the film's close-ups to the jarring meeting of hard and soft in the deaths of Giordani and Carlo, as well as a pronounced focus on colour, particularly and unsurprisingly deep red, which is most audaciously evident in the pool of blood that reflects Marc's face at the end.

But surfaces never tell the whole story: much of the plot is driven by two-dimensional representations, which are almost always misinterpreted by the characters. Two images get the plot going: the reflection of Marta, which Marc mistakes for a painting; and the photo of Marc in the paper, along with the caption that he is an eyewitness to Helga Ulmann's murder. He is and he isn't: he does see Marta's face in the mirror, as do we, but it appears so briefly that neither Marc nor the viewer will know what it means; and he isn't introduced to Marta until later on in any case, so he couldn't have recognised her. It doesn't matter: the killer believes the caption, and tries to kill him.

The second half of the film is driven by the photo of 'The House of the Screaming Child', the picture Marc finds behind the wall, and the image drawn by Olga, a copy of one she'd found in the school archives. The narrative importance of these pictures pushes the bounds of credibility past breaking point. The photo of 'The House' is found only when a marginal figure refers to the legend of the haunting on hearing of the lullaby played by the killer: this is flight-thought association, a thought disorder characteristic of mania and schizophrenia, but nobody bats an eyelid when Marc acts on it, let alone when he actually discovers something at the house; and the clue provided by Olga's picture similarly defies narrative logic.

But then narrative logic was never one of the film's primary concerns: Argento is interested less in 'whodunnit' than in Marc's investigation into himself, the director's chaotic world inverting the standard model of detection. The wayward associational rules that govern Argento's universe also increase our identification with the killer, who appears to be the only character able to exercise any control: in a film intimately concerned with theatrics, the killer puts on the best displays, the extravagant murders models of order in the disorder around them. While the other characters are driven by reactions to representations, the killer is proactive and original: perhaps only the insane can make the most of an insane world.

But even the killer is finally subject to the whims of fate, her necklace caught in a lift shaft. Carlo's death similarly relies on a slapstick chain of coincidence and accident, as his foot is caught in a rope trailing from a rubbish truck, his head slams against a pavement, and when the truck drivers finally notice him and stop he is flattened by another car. The world is fraught with danger: Marc is saved by Marta's encounter with a lift, but he was struck by a falling windowpane earlier, and could easily have ended up like an early victim in *Suspiria*, impaled through head and chest by broken shards of glass.

The plot's reliance on coincidence to drive the plot foreshadows the full-blown supernatural extravaganzas of Argento's next two films. There are other hints of the supernatural here too: Ulmann is a telepath, and flinches back from her door being broken down seconds before it actually happens; and among the killer's knick-knacks is a woollen figure pricked with pins, like a voodoo doll. The previous tenant of 'The House of the Screaming Child', reportedly a haunted property, died in mysterious circumstances; does the lullaby heard by many in the house mean that Marta has been lurking there, and may thus be responsible for the tenant's death, or is something less prosaic to blame?

Finally, when Carlo tells Marc that he is responsible for the murders, the viewer realises not only that this may be true in a literal and obvious sense – if he hadn't begun his investigation, all the murders except Ulmann's may have been averted – but also that events around him foreshadow the murders. Marc is scalded by steam from a coffee machine in a bar, before Righetti meets her death by scalding; he jokes about the reason he became a pianist: 'My psychoanalyst says it was because subconsciously I hated my father. Pressing the keys was like smashing his teeth', and Giordani soon afterwards has his teeth smashed out.

There is a Hitchcockian transference of guilt here that is shared in the relationship between Marc and Carlo. Marc's sexual fear and gender instability are doubled in Carlo's unhappy homosexuality; both are professional pianists, at one point seen playing a duet in which each mirrors the other's part; Carlo, like Marc, is ineffectual, failing to kill Brezzi and threatening Marc with a gun he appears unable to use; and much as Carlo is defined by the primal trauma of seeing his mother kill his father, Marc cannot escape the hatred of his father he refers to jokingly early on.

Madness and guilt are too powerful in Argento's universe to be restricted to one character, but seem to spill out into the very atmosphere: by the time of *Tenebrae* (1982) the transference of guilt was so strong that the protagonist actually took on the role of killer himself.

INDUSTRY IMPACT: The *giallo*'s most obvious influence is on the slasher movie, with **Halloween** even reprising the knitting-needle defence from *Deep Red*; and while production of the *giallo* itself peaked in the 1970s, its style can be felt as far away as a film like *Perfect Blue* (Satoshi Kon, 1997), a Japanese manga exploration of Argento themes, and American 'erotic' thrillers like *Body Double* (Brian de Palma, 1984) and *Basic Instinct* (Paul Verhoeven, 1992).

As producer, Argento has fostered some interesting talent: Lamberto Bava's *Demons* (1985) and *Demons 2* (1986) are probably best avoided, but Michele Soavi's films represent some of the best recent genre material from Italy. His debut, *Stage-fright/Aquarius* (1987), is a slasher that shares with Argento's work a theatricality and a disarming use of sick humour, although it's hardly the ultra-stylish *giallo* some reports make it out to be; *The Church/La chiesa* (1989) is a messy gothic work with several spectacular set-pieces; while *The Sect/La setta* (1991) is tighter and again provides a showcase for Soavi's visual stylings, even if the plot is equal parts **Rosemary's Baby** and hippy Satanist schlock. Soavi's best film to date has been *Dellamorte Dellamore/Cemetery Man* (1994, see **INDUSTRY IMPACT, Night of the Living Dead**).

Argento's brand of theatrical violence informs much modern horror, although few directors have attempted to ape his style directly; but Argento-ish moments appear everywhere from Donald Cammell's superb desert psycho-thriller *White of the Eye* (1987), which opens with a close-up of an eye and a heavily stylised murder, to Alejandro Jodorowsky's *Santa Sangre* (1989), produced and co-written by Claudio Argento, which cross-breeds Argento-style murders with its director's uniquely surreal imagination.

FINAL WORD: *Deep Red* represents a break, stylistically, from Argento's previous *gialli*, being better financed, more stylish and more assured, and showcasing the spectacular murderous set-pieces upon which his reputation with horror fans largely rests. Argento brought to the genre a kinetic style and narrative audacity that few have matched, and *Deep Red* is the most concise and successful exploration of his obsessions, still packing a punch with its jaw-dropping bravura technique and show-stopping rock'n'roll murders.

STALK'N'SLASH, SLICE'N'DICE

Halloween (1978)

'The Night HE Came Home!'

USA, Compass International Pictures, colour, 91 mins

Directed by John Carpenter
Screenplay by John Carpenter and Debra Hill
Produced by Debra Hill
Executive Producers: Moustapha Akkad and Irwin Yablans
Associate Producer: Kool Lusby
Original Music by John Carpenter
Cinematography by Dean Cundey
Editors: Charles Bornstein, Tommy Wallace
Production Designer: Tommy Wallace
Assistant Director: Rick Wallace

CAST: Donald Pleasence (*Dr Samuel J Loomis*), Jamie Lee Curtis (*Laurie Strode*), Nancy Kyes [as Nancy Loomis] (*Annie Brackett*), PJ Soles (*Lynda*), Charles Cyphers (*Sheriff Leigh Brackett*), Kyle Richards (*Lindsey Wallace*), Brian Andrews (*Thomas 'Tommy' Doyle*), John Michael Graham (*Bob Simms*), Nancy Stephens (*Nurse Marion Chambers*), Arthur Malet (*Graveyard Keeper*), Mickey Yablans (*Richie*), Brent Le Page (*Lonnie Elamb*), Adam

Hollander (*Keith*), Robert Phalen (*Dr Terence Wynn*), Tony Moran (*Michael Audrey Myers Age 21*), Will Sandin (*Michael Audrey Myers Age 6*), Sandy Johnson (*Judith Margaret Myers*), David Kyle (*Judith's Boyfriend*), Peter Griffith (*Morgan Strode*), Nick Castle (*the Shape*)

SYNOPSIS: Haddonfield, Illinois, Halloween 1963. Michael Myers, a six-year-old boy, spies on his sister, then kills her after she's had sex with her boyfriend. Fifteen years later, Dr Sam Loomis is driven by a nurse to the asylum where Myers is held, planning to pick him up for a court date; but Myers escapes in the nurse's car.

Laurie Strode's father is selling the Myers's house. Accompanied by Tommy, a boy she babysits, Laurie puts the house key under the mat, and is seen by a shadowy figure inside. Afterwards she and Tommy are stalked; she tells her friends Lynda and Annie, but they think she is seeing things.

Loomis is certain Myers is heading for Haddonfield, but cannot convince the police; he finds a truck parked off-road en route, with Myers' hospital gown next to it and a body in the undergrowth. When he visits Judith Myers's grave, the headstone is missing.

Annie's father, the sheriff, is investigating the theft of a Halloween mask, some knives and rope. Loomis persuades him to go to the Myers' house, where they find the still-warm body of a dead animal. Loomis tells him that Myers is 'purely and simply – evil'.

That night Myers stalks Annie, who is babysitting a girl called Lindsey. Annie's boyfriend Paul phones her, and she drops Lindsey off with Laurie, who is babysitting Tommy in the house across the street, then prepares to drive to Paul's; but Myers is waiting in the car, and kills her.

Lynda and her boyfriend Bob arrive at the house where Annie was babysitting, and when they see no sign of her they have sex upstairs. Myers kills first Bob, then Lynda, while she's on the phone to Laurie. Laurie goes to the house to investigate, and finds Annie's body in bed with Judith's headstone; she then sees the bodies of Lynda and Bob, and runs out of the house after seeing Myers and falling down the stairs. A neighbour ignores her cries for help, and she returns to Tommy, locking the door only to find that a window is open.

When he attacks, she stabs Myers with a knitting needle, but he won't stay down; she hides in a closet, and stabs him with a coat hanger and then a knife when he breaks in; but even now he isn't dead. As they struggle, she pulls his mask off, and he is shot in the head and body by Loomis. But the body vanishes.

ORIGINS AND INSPIRATION: *Halloween* has the dubious distinction of kickstarting the disreputable cycle of slasher movies that dominated the genre during the early 80s and again, to a lesser degree, in the late 90s. The model wasn't entirely new: the killer's point of view (POV) shots that came to characterise the genre – *Halloween* opens with one of the best – have roots in the voyeuristic identification with a killer in **Psycho** and *Peeping Tom* (1960); the *giallo* (see **ORIGINS AND INSPIRATION, Deep Red**) provided another basic template; while the 'final girl' had appeared in **The Texas Chain Saw Massacre**, which also anticipated the slasher's busload of teens fresh to the slaughter.

The stripped-down slasher format – faceless psycho stalks women – had also been a staple of TV movies since the early 70s, with the British *Thriller* series providing endless spins on the format, while Carpenter's own TV movie *Someone's Watching Me!* (1978), which he finished two weeks before starting *Halloween*, showcased another strong female lead in Lauren Hutton.

Homicidal maniacs had stalked babysitters in theatrical releases before, notably William Castle's *I Saw What You Did* (1965) and Peter Collinson's *Fright* (1971); but the closest American cinema had come to the slasher was Bob Clark's *Black Christmas* (1975), which used a heavy-breathing subjective POV and some imaginatively fruity phone calls to terrorise a group of teens in a Canadian sorority house. Like *Halloween*, the film uses a holiday motif to good narrative effect, and benefits from well-rounded characters and an above-average cast, but its cryptic ending stopped it from being as popular or influential as Carpenter's film, and its shocks and scares are nowhere near as effective.

Independent producer Irwin Yablans liked John Carpenter's second film, *Assault on Precinct 13* (1976), and released it through his company, Turtle Releasing. The film, like Carpenter's first, *Dark Star* (1974), was not a success in the US, but did modestly well in the UK and was entered into European film festivals by an Englishman, Michael Myers. It was generally well received, and at a screening at the London Film Festival Carpenter and Debra Hill, his girlfriend at the time, met up with Yablans and Moustapha Akkad, a financier keen to break into the US film market.

Yablans had pitched an idea to Carpenter for *The Babysitter Murders*, essentially the outline for *Halloween*; Carpenter, who had nothing lined up after his current job, agreed, and together they sold the idea to Akkad. The financier was concerned by the low budget, tight schedule – Carpenter insisted he could make it in four weeks for $300,000, taking only $10,000 and 10 per cent of the profits to write, direct and score the film – and inexperienced crew, but was shamed into putting up the money when Yablans suggested that $300,000 was probably more than he was able to invest. Yablans came up with the title later – there had never been a film set on Halloween before, and this gave it a better name, a predefined atmosphere and a gimmicky releasing strategy for a traditionally quiet period in cinemas.

Carpenter wanted, and received, complete creative control of the film. Yablans agreed to the use of the widescreen Panavision format, an unusual touch in a low-budget film at the time, and the Panaglide camera, a recent innovation that allowed for far more convincing POV shots without the use of time-consuming dollies; but apart from telling the director he wanted regular shocks and a lack of explicit gore, he left the film to Carpenter and Hill, brought on board as producer.

Hill had been script supervisor on *Assault*, and co-wrote *Halloween* over three weeks with Carpenter: she supplied most of the girls' dialogue, having worked as a babysitter herself, while he was responsible for the Loomis dialogue and the positioning of Myers as a semi-mythic character, evil and unstoppable.

According to Carpenter, Yul Brynner's indestructible android killer in Michael Crichton's *Westworld* (1973) was an influence on Myers, while the idea for the mask came from **Eyes Without a Face**; the director had also, at college, been taken to a mental institution where he'd seen the staring eyes of a twelve-year-old schizophrenic boy, which provided the inspiration for Pleasence's dialogue about 'the devil's eyes'. Myers's mask was made in pre-production by Tommy Wallace, a Captain Kirk mask with the eyeholes widened, the eyebrows and sideburns taken off, the face spraypainted a bluish white and the hair teased out to wild effect.

The film was set in Haddonfield, Illinois, a non-existent town based on Hill's own hometown of Haddonfield, New Jersey, while most of the street names were taken from Carpenter's home town of Bowling Green, Kentucky, and the character names were either cinema in-jokes ('Dr Loomis' recalls Sam Loomis from **Psycho**) or taken from people Hill and Carpenter had known (Laurie Strode was one of Carpenter's ex-girlfriends).

DIRECTOR: 'I hate pretentious movies ... I suppose I've gone the other direction and just tried to have a good time and have the audience have a good time. Sometimes it's worked and sometimes it hasn't, you know?'

When John Carpenter was five, he went to a screening of *It Came from Outer Space* (1953), which kicked off a lifelong love of pulp movies. He began shooting his own films as a child, 8mm shorts with names like *Gorgo vs Godzilla*, and made longer films in high school.

After a year at Western Kentucky University Carpenter transferred to the University of Southern California's (USC) film programme. He didn't really fit in with the rest of the students, his love of genre product and Hollywood classics at odds with his generation's interest in social commitment. His favourite director was Howard Hawks, and he aspired to making westerns; a 40-minute film, 1970's *The Resurrection of Billy Bronco*, was a step in this direction, and won the college an Academy Award for best short.

After graduating, Carpenter spent four years with writer Dan O'Bannon (see **ORIGINS AND INSPIRATION, Alien**) expanding another short into the feature *Dark Star* (1974). The $60,000 film failed to receive distribution in the US, but it did get Carpenter an agent, and he soon managed to place a number of screenplays. Investors gave him $100,000 to make a second feature, *Assault on Precinct 13* (1976), a modern take on Howard Hawks' *Rio Bravo* (1959), and before and after *Halloween* he made two TV movies, *Someone's Watching You!* and *Elvis* (both 1978), which marked the start of a long-lasting working relationship with Kurt Russell.

The Fog (1980) features a Mr Machen telling ghost stories at the start, but it's far closer to Lovecraft territory, with its tale of seaside ghosts wreaking a terrible vengeance on a coastal community. While it makes great use of its locations, and is one of the few maritime ghost films to be even marginally successful, there are few surprises, and the more is seen of the seaweed-encrusted ghosts, the more they look like bargain-basement Dr Who monsters.

After reluctantly contributing to the first *Halloween* sequel, Carpenter directed the adolescent SF adventure *Escape from New York* (1981) and *The Thing* (1982). The latter may well be his finest moment (see **INDUSTRY IMPACT, Alien**), but its down-beat tone and ambiguous ending meant that it was not a commercial success.

His next feature, *Christine* (1983), disappointed genre fans by adding to the growing pile of cruddy Stephen King adaptations, and Carpenter moved away from horror for the SF romance *Starman* (1984) and the Hong Kong-style fantasy action picture *Big Trouble in Little China* (1986).

Prince of Darkness (1987) returned Carpenter to the Nigel Kneale world he had explored in the screenplay for *Halloween 3* (1983), and fared just as poorly; according to the director it was 'too intellectual for the audience', and the fight scenes in *They Live* (1988) ensured that it didn't share the same fate.

Since then Carpenter's output has been even patchier. *Memoirs of an Invisible Man* (1992) was an expensive flop, and *Village of the Damned* (1995) and *In the Mouth of Madness* (1995) similarly baffled audiences. But the latter is actually one of the director's better films, with an eerie Jonathan Carroll feel to its reality before it slips into a Lovecraftian rubber-monster limbo; and any film that references a writer as obscure as Robert Aickman deserves some credit. His most recent films lack even this feature's marginal interest: few apart from Carpenter himself thought *Escape from LA* (1996) an improvement on the original, and he finally realised his ambition to make a western (of sorts) with the unpleasant *Vampires* (1998) and *Ghosts of Mars* (2001).

CASTING: For the part of Laurie, Carpenter favoured young actress Annie Lockhart, but she turned the part down; Hill nominated Jamie Lee Curtis as an alternative, a Universal contract player fresh from a TV series, *Operation Petticoat*. The marketing angle was obvious: this was the daughter of Janet Leigh, who'd died so memorably in the mother of all psycho movies, and Carpenter was aware of a conscious debt to Hitchcock's films. Curtis was slightly concerned about being cast as a repressed, quiet character – she had been a cheerleader, and was in real life more like the other girls in the film – but she was delighted to be given the lead role.

After *Halloween*, Curtis became one of the most recognisable scream queens of the initial slasher run, appearing in *Terror Train* (Roger Spottiswoode, 1980) and *Prom Night* (Paul Lynch, 1980), but after the explicitly Hitchcockian *Road Games* (Richard Franklin, 1981) – her character's even called Hitch – she started to worry about being typecast, and shifted to comedy roles. Yet she always remained aware of her debt to Laurie Strode, and approached Miramax with the idea for *Halloween H20* (1998), as well as starring in *Halloween Resurrection* (Rick Rosenthal, 2002).

For Sam Loomis Carpenter wanted a name actor, someone the audience would be familiar with, and turned to British horror stars Peter Cushing and Christopher Lee; both turned the part down, and Yablans suggested Donald Pleasence. The actor initially rejected the role, but was encouraged to look again by his daughter, a fan of *Assault on Precinct 13*. He was a little alarmed by the portentous dialogue – 'I think it's a little melodramatic . . . but of course it's not intended to be *real*' – and took a flat fee for the part, rejecting a percentage offer as he didn't think much of the film's commercial potential.

Pleasence's reputation as a sinister character actor was sparked off by a 1960 stage production of Harold Pinter's *The Caretaker*, and bolstered in John Gilling's *The Flesh and the Fiends* (1959), *Circus of Horrors* (1960) and *Dr Crippen* (1962). He moved further away from leading-man roles with his cross-dressing routine in Polanski's *Cul-de-Sac* (1966), and after appearances as Blofeld in *You Only Live Twice* (Lewis Gilbert, 1967) and a tea-addicted police inspector in *Death Line* (1973), he was listed by *Variety* during the 80s as officially the busiest actor in the world.

He was happy to stay on board when the *Halloween* franchise took off, relishing the chance to play a good guy (albeit a twitchily obsessive one) rather than the usual villain; Carpenter also cast him against type in *Escape from New York* and *Prince of Darkness*.

Nancy Loomis was the wife of production designer Tommy Wallace, and Carpenter wrote the part of Lynda for PJ Soles, who he'd seen as a bitchy girl in *Carrie* (1976), another early entry in the modern teen horror stakes. Nick Castle, an old friend of Carpenter's, played 'the Shape', as the masked Myers character was later to be known, and was paid only $25 a day; when he asked Carpenter what his motivation was the director told him not to act at all, but Castle does add some eerie robotic touches of his own, notably his head tilt as he studies Bob's dead body.

PRODUCTION: The four-week shoot began in May 1978. Although set in the Midwest, the film was shot almost entirely in Southern California: the Myers house was in South Pasadena, and the Halloween street was in Hollywood, on Sunset Boulevard. Trying to make Southern California in the spring look like a Midwestern town in the autumn proved difficult; they tried to avoid shooting palm trees, although a few are visible early on in the film, and fake leaves were painted autumn colours and blown along the streets with a fan, then raked up for reuse in the next outdoor shots.

Apart from Donald Pleasence, who received $20,000 for a week's work, cast and crew were paid minimal wages, but everyone mucked in, and Carpenter remembers it as the most fun film he's worked on. Because of Pleasence's short availability, the film was shot out of sequence, and Carpenter supplied Curtis with a 'fear meter' that let her know how scared she was meant to be in each scene.

The murder of Judith Myers was shot last, with all of the crew working to redecorate the abandoned Myers house; and the long dolly shot that opens the film – it is actually broken up twice, although the edits are seamless – was inspired by Orson Welles's opening for *Touch of Evil* (1958), and was an audacious move for such a low-budget film. Due to the difficulty of working with children, Debra Hill, who had the smallest hands, held the knife during the POV shots.

Carpenter's use of the widescreen format added immensely to the film's success: his conception of the film was as a fairground ride, a ghost train, but it more closely resembles a pantomime with its 'he's behind you!' scares, encouraging the kind of audience participation that became a key part of the slasher's popularity.

SOUNDTRACK: Carpenter has written the scores for almost all of his films, and the importance of this soundtrack, which took three days to write, cannot be overestimated: the simple melody expertly builds up tension with variations on a theme during the first half of the film, but crucially leaves some of the scariest sequences in a near-unbearable silence. There's nothing new about it – Hill cites the children's lullaby in **Deep Red** as an inspiration, and the piano-note heartbeats are a clichéd device – but as with Carpenter's visual tricks, we're happy to give in to audience manipulation techniques that would seem crass in the hands of a lesser director.

The score uses a 5/4 signature, and was arranged by composer Don Wyman, who later worked on the soundtrack for *The Fog*. The director also formed a band with Tommy Wallace and Nick Castle, The Coupe Devilles, who played the song heard in the background when Laurie gets into Annie's car.

RELEASE: Yablans invited all of the major studios to distribute the film, but no representatives attended the preview screening. 4,000 prints were made by MGM as a favour to a crewmember, and Yablans took them around to individual cinemas, pitching the film directly. Carpenter, in turn, screened it at USC, but about a third of the audience walked out, and he was asked why he'd made such a sleazy, disreputable film. Critics at the Chicago Film Festival were kinder, and the film's success grew, slowly at first, until it finally took over $75 million on its original theatrical release, making it one of the most profitable independent films ever released.

Reviews were initially dismissive, but after one positive notice in *The Village Voice*, and the realisation that the film was fast becoming a major hit, many critics took a second look. *Monthly Film Bulletin* noted that despite the sexualised victims, the film had no agenda except to scare the audience: 'it cannot really be described at all in terms sociological or psychological. It is one of cinema's most perfectly engineered devices for saying "Boo!"' Pauline Kael, writing in the *New Yorker*, was more scathing, pouring scorn on its 'pitiful, amateurish script', but she granted that the film might satisfy 'part of the audience in a more basic, childish way than sophisticated horror pictures do'.

For the film's network TV premiere, additional scenes needed to be shot to fill NBC's running time. The two scenes featured Loomis describing how dangerous Myers was to incredulous colleagues, and Laurie telling Lynda that someone was watching her; the scenes are, remarkably, a seamless fit with the rest of the film.

CRITICAL EYE: Although *Halloween* has its share of audience groans – Laurie drops the knife twice, for no good reason – it's also filled with subtle touches that add to the atmosphere. The film's small town is closer to a Ray Bradbury creation than a real place, for all the babysitters' convincing dialogue, and the seasonal celebrations are alluded to without bludgeoning the audience. The background is filled with costumed children trick-or-treating, eerily glowing pumpkins and the suggestion that it's all – the shop robbery, the theft of the gravestone – some festive teenage prank; one of the simplest and most effective scenes has Laurie going to a neighbour for help, only to find the blinds closed against her and the lights turned out.

The bravura opening sequence has been seen by some commentators as 'explaining' Myers's psychosis: he has entirely misunderstood the primal scene of his sister having sex with her boyfriend, and carries out a grotesque imitation of the act with his phallic knife; the sexual activity (or prospective activity, for Annie) of the later victims sets them up for murder in the same way. But as we'll explore below, such an agenda was far from Carpenter's mind; and for anyone who's missed the point, the director gives Loomis – a deliriously fixated psychiatrist whose obsession with Myers is never fully explored – lines to explain the killer that deliberately avoid any Freudian analysis in favour of portentous mumblings about 'evil'.

INDUSTRY IMPACT: *Halloween* was cheap to make, requiring neither stars nor special effects, and immensely profitable. The point wasn't lost on film producers around the world, and a slew of slasher movies followed: from 1979, *Friday the 13th* (Sean S Cunningham), *Prom Night*, *Terror Train*; from 1980, *Bloody Valentine* (George Mihalka), *Night School* (Ken Hughes), *The Burning* (Tony Maylam); from 1981, *Friday the 13th Part 2* (Steve Miner), *Graduation Day* (Herb Freed), *Happy Birthday to Me* (J Lee Thompson), *Hell Night* (Tom DeSimone), *The Slayer* (JS Cardone), *The Prowler* (Joseph Zito); and so on. Most took their model more from *Friday the 13th* than *Halloween*, with graphic murders filmed with zero style, and were among the most formulaic films of any exploitation cycle, both in terms of production – they were almost invariably helmed by witless hacks and used no-name casts (although they got through so many obnoxious teens that a fair few stars got their first break in a slasher film) – and content.

The rules of the slasher, endlessly recycled but adhered to religiously, are as follows:

1. A traumatic event in the past creates a psychopathic killer.
2. The killer returns to the site of the event, usually on a specific date in the present that allows the makers to use a calendar motif in the title.
3. The killer stalks and graphically kills a group of obnoxious and stupid teens of both sexes, usually with some kind of blade, often a garden or farm implement.
4. A 'final girl' survives, usually boyish and often virginal, to thwart the killer, although he is never entirely vanquished.

Audiences for slasher films knew exactly what to expect, and participated in screenings, whooping and cheering when the killer struck and groaning as another prospective victim went for a walk in the woods. Scenarios were repetitive and unoriginal, and the films tended to recycle not only situations and characters but also shots and framing, with any inventive killings quickly appearing in other films; they were thus highly self-referential, making overtly recursive films such as *Scream* (Wes Craven, 1996), or spoofs from the slasher heyday like *Saturday the 14th* (Howard R Cohen, 1982), effectively pointless as comments on the genre.

While the psycho and serial killer movies that flanked the slasher and developed into one of the key mainstream Hollywood tropes of the 90s tended either to focus on police-procedural matters or to explore their killers' personalities, the slasher did neither. If the police appeared in a slasher film, they, like any other authority figures, were ineffectual, either ignoring teens' pleas for help or actively hiding information about the killer; and far from being given personalities, slasher killers were routinely kept off-screen, unidentified or masked, like the hockey-masked Jason of *Friday the 13th Part II* (Steve Miner, 1981) onwards, *Halloween*'s Shape or the Munch-masked killers of *Scream*.

Although it's built up to as a shock, it doesn't really matter who or what's under the Shape's mask: it could be anybody. As Loomis points out, he has no identity, but is an embodiment of evil, a force that cannot be stopped. Given the slasher's lack of personality or real identity, the standard accusation that the films rely on audience identification with the killer becomes problematic, even with the genre's heavy use of killer POV shots; and if and when the killer is finally exposed, his characteristic deformity, obesity or sexual inadequacy hardly invites empathy.

Our identification is probably closer to the 'final girl': she is presented from the start as the central character, both savvier and more resourceful than her peers, and camera POV tends to shift from the killer to her as the film progresses. If there are male hero types, they are usually cringing and impotent in the face of the threat, compared with her steadfast courage. It isn't that she lacks feminine characteristics – Jamie Lee Curtis was the 'scream queen' for a generation, after all – but rather that she alternates between masculine and feminine roles, equally adept at fleeing in terror and standing her ground.

Gender confusion tends to be at the heart of the relationship between slasher and 'final girl', underlying both the killer's pathology (*Dressed to Kill* (1980), **Psycho**) and the boyishness and gender-free name of the 'final girl'. But while gender slipperiness tends to be used for the killer as a shorthand explanation of psychosis, Carol Clover in *Men, Women and Chainsaws* argues that for the 'final girl' it is more often 'a kind of feint, a front through which the [male viewer] can simultaneously experience forbidden desires and disavow them on the grounds that the visible actor is, after all, a girl'. For Clover audience identification in horror is unstable, not only shifting between victim and killer and often encompassing both but also encouraging male audiences to identify with women on screen, both as victims, the eternal damsels in distress, and, increasingly, as victim-heroes.

Gender issues in slasher films, then, are more complicated than is suggested by the simple accusations of misogyny they often attract. While some films – Lucio Fulci's *The New York Ripper/ Lo Squartatore di New York* (1982) springs to mind – might warrant such criticism, others have a more ambivalent bias. It's important to remember that when the films first came out they were often used as date movies, and that the slasher boom was, perversely enough, the first exploitation trend to focus on women's lives, featuring a number of strong, independent female leads cast not just for their looks.

A related accusation routinely levelled at the slasher is that it has a reactionary sexual agenda. In *Halloween* the virginal Laurie survives, while the sexualised victims – Judith, Lynda and Bob have just had sex; Annie is in her underwear, on her way to pick up her boyfriend – die. Subsequent slashers like *Friday the 13th* (Sean S Cunningham, 1980) made the connection between sex and death even more explicit, with the homicidal Mrs Vorhees's anti-sex agenda coming from the fact that camp counsellors were having sex while her son purportedly drowned.

Yet such a message was not Carpenter's intention: he has jokingly apologised that 'I didn't mean to put an end to the sexual revolution!', but points out that the main reason why the teenagers in *Halloween* die is that they aren't paying attention. They are distracted, as teens generally are, by beer and sex: Laurie, with less on her mind, notices Myers, and is distinguished from her friends less by her virginity than her resourcefulness and quick-witted awareness of the threat. Crucially, Laurie is Myers's intended victim all along: the fact that she is virginal doesn't stop him from wanting or trying to kill her.

Although *Halloween*'s victims are predominantly female (if the truck driver is counted there are two men and three women killed), other slashers tended to kill in equal opportunity numbers. Death may come to the sexually active, but it also comes to the stupid: teens who, even when they know a killer is on the loose, decide to find a secluded spot to 'make out'. Such stupid characters, set up simply to suffer a grisly death, may demonstrate a callous disregard for humanity on the part of the filmmakers, but also account for some of the genre's success; as Stephen Thrower has pointed out, 'The *raison d'être* of the slasher film is to show the horrible (yet pleasing) death agonies of a busload of idiots ... Slash those teens and let me breathe!', and the victims of late-90s slashers seem even more deserving of their gruesome fates than their 80s counterparts.

More troublesome in some ways than the slasher's sexual agenda is its portrayal of the mentally ill as literal monsters. This has long been a problem with the related psycho-thriller genre – Pete Walker's *Schizo* (1976) came under fire from the mental-health organisation MIND for its equation of schizophrenia and violence – but at least the killers of films like **Psycho** and *Peeping Tom* (1960) were characterised as sympathetic and understandable in their psychoses. Slashers make no attempt to understand their killers, and nor do their directors – Carpenter's description of a schizophrenic boy's 'devil' eyes is crass at best.

But for many slashers the mentally ill tag is just a hook to hang the plot on. The killer tends to be closer to the supernatural than the insane: his indestructibility is ensured by a franchise's success, and in his on-screen actions he defies natural law. He can move with absolute silence, appearing and disappearing apparently at will; even the spaces he inhabits take on supernatural qualities, with familiar houses turning into darkened labyrinths and screams inaudible to others only a short distance away. The slasher's setting – always enclosed, usually rural or suburban – and formulaic conventions give it an unreal nature; even *Halloween*, which may look realistic at first, exists in the weird zone of empty streets, preppy teens and comfortable wealth later popularised by Wes Craven and the 90s teen-horror boom. The slasher may be the bogeyman, the figure from our nightmares, but these flat and unreal environments seem almost as disturbing.

Among the better original slashers are *Terror Train* (Roger Spottiswoode, 1980) and *Hell Night* (Tom DeSimone, 1981), which at least have high production values, the intermittently stylish *The House on Sorority Row* (Mark Rosman, 1983) and the tongue-in-cheek *The Slumber Party Massacre* (Amy Holden-Jones, 1982). A number of early slashers quickly became franchises, with *Halloween* spawning seven sequels: none, predictably enough, matched the original, and Carpenter and Hill bowed out after scripting *Halloween 3*, a sequel in name alone.

Halloween H2O (1998) stars both Jamie Lee Curtis and Janet Leigh, and has been the best received of Akkad's sequels. The financier overcame his initial reluctance to the *Halloween* concept when the cheques started coming in, and now drives the franchise, preventing scriptwriters from blowing up Myers or chopping off his head, which would make it difficult to bring him back: 'Everybody hates Michael Myers, but I want to keep him alive as long as I can.'

The *Friday the 13th* franchise has had no such qualms, ignoring encouraging titles like *Friday the 13th – The Final Chapter* (Joseph Zito, 1984) to resurrect Jason as a zombie and, finally, simply as an idea, pitted against his chief commercial rival Freddy Krueger in the ludicrous *Freddy vs Jason* (Ronny Yu, 2003).

Wes Craven's *A Nightmare on Elm Street* (1984) acknowledged the supernatural nature of the slasher by making him a dream demon, menacing the children of a lynch mob that had burned a razor-clawed child murderer to death. The film was an enormous hit, its mixture of effects-heavy set-pieces, wisecracking villain and grotesque pastel sets hitting a nerve with the moviegoing public: the film does contain one or two effective scares, but its atmosphere of silly, unthreatening fantasy typified the American product that dominated the field for the rest of the 1980s.

Much better was *Candyman* (Bernard Rose, 1992), which took Nancy's predicament from Craven's film far more seriously. Helen (Virginia Madsen) researches her urban legend thesis in a Chicago housing project plagued by the titular demonic ghost, but is framed for Candyman's murders; where understanding doctors coo over Nancy with high-tech tests as she shrieks about her dream demon coming to get her, Helen's situation is both more credible and far scarier, as everyone thinks she is insane. Even we're invited to question her version of events – is Candyman simply a figment of her imagination? – and the film's solid supporting characters and realistically decayed urban environment make a welcome change from the perfunctory characterisations and all-white, well-appointed suburbs more common to the genre.

Craven returned to the *Nightmare* franchise with part four, *Wes Craven's New Nightmare* (1994), a film-within-a-film that marked the director's dry run for *Scream*, his most successful take on the slasher film yet. *Scream*'s clever-clever self-referentiality is redundant given the conventions of the genre, but the film is effective enough as a slasher, manipulative jump cuts providing the necessary jolts and a few deft touches putting it ahead of the competition: Skeet Ulrich's psychotically exaggerated boyfriend whose girl won't put out, and some genuinely funny scenes featuring an uncredited Henry Winkler as the school principal expelling a couple of students. But *Scream*'s most lasting contribution to the slasher was simply to add a new level to teen obnoxiousness, genre familiarity providing another reason why these people have to die; and the film only flirts with real darkness inadvertently, through its smug superficiality and a tone that lurches from the genuinely unsettling to crass comedy.

Its massive success was followed by a series of substandard slashers that didn't even work on *Scream*'s level; the joke was definitely on the audience with films like *Scream*'s two sequels, *I Know What You Did Last Summer* (Jim Gillespie, 1997), *Urban*

Legend (Jamie Blanks, 1998) and *Valentine* (Jamie Blanks, 2001), this last a particularly insulting piece of dreck. *My Little Eye* (Marc Evans, 2002) was one of the few effectively nasty entries in the recent slasher boom, using its reality TV format to successful effect and providing a downbeat tone entirely at odds with the MTV gloss of its peers.

FINAL WORD: *Halloween* is not a message movie; it is designed purely and simply to scare the audience, and on this level, seen for the first time at least, it works remarkably well. The film is a step back from the gruelling tone of something like **The Texas Chain Saw Massacre**, aiming for a fun rollercoaster ride rather than a confrontational exercise in terror; but it pulls off its tricks with remarkable panache, making expert use of the Panavision format and distinguishing itself from the similar films that followed by featuring largely bloodless murders and generally likeable teens. For the slasher, it was downhill from here . . .

BACK TO THE FUTURE

Alien (1979)

'In space no one can hear you scream'

**GB/US, Brandywine/Ronald Shusett Productions, colour,
116 mins**

Directed by Ridley Scott
Story by Dan O'Bannon and Ronald Shusett
Screenplay by Dan O'Bannon
Produced by Gordon Carroll, David Giler and Walter Hill
Associate Producer: Ivor Powell
Executive Producer: Ronald Shusett
**Original Music by Jerry Goldsmith; soundtrack also features
extracts from 'Symphony No 2' by Howard Hanson and 'Eine
Kleine Nachtmusik' by Wolfgang Amadeus Mozart**
Director of Photography: Derek Vanlint
Editors: Terry Rawlings, Peter Weatherley
Production Designer: Michael Seymour
Art Director: Roger Christian, Leslie Dilley
Costume Design: John Mollo
Assistant Director: Raymond Becket, Steve Harding
Concept Artists: Ron Cobb, Chris Foss, Jean 'Moebius' Giraud

Visual Design Consultant: Dan O'Bannon
Special Effects Supervisor: Nick Allder
Small Alien Forms Co-designer and Maker: Roger Dicken
Alien designer: HR Giger
Alien Head Effects: Carlo Rambaldi
Director of Photography: Miniature Effects: Denys Ayling
Supervising Model Maker: Miniature Effects: Martin Bower

CAST: Tom Skerritt (*Dallas*), Sigourney Weaver (*Ripley*), Veronica Cartwright (*Lambert*), Harry Dean Stanton (*Brett*), John Hurt (*Kane*), Ian Holm (*Ash*), Yaphet Kotto (*Parker*), Bolaji Badejo (*Alien*), Helen Horton (*Mother* [voice])

SYNOPSIS: The crew of the Nostromo, a commercial towing vehicle, is woken up when Mother, the ship's computer, picks up what appears to be a distress signal. When they investigate, they find a derelict spacecraft and the body of one alien, as well as a large collection of eggs. Kane is attacked by something from an egg that fixes itself to his helmet; the others take him back on board, despite Ripley's protestations about following quarantine procedures.

The alien on Kane's face seems to be feeding him oxygen through a tube down his throat; it cannot be removed, choking him when they try to pull it off and spurting acid blood when they cut it. But eventually it comes off of its own accord, and dies. Kane has recovered, and the crew have a meal before going back into hypersleep for the journey home. Mid-meal, an alien bursts from Kane's chest and vanishes into the ship. As the others search for it, Brett is killed. They realise that it is using the airshafts, and Dallas, the ship's captain, looks for it with a flamethrower, only to meet the same fate.

Ripley is now acting captain, and tries to find out more about the alien from Mother. She discovers that the company employing them has rerouted the ship to pick up the alien, and that the crew is expendable. Ash, the ship's scientist, attacks her when she tries to tell Parker and Lambert, but Parker stops him. Ash is an android, and they shut him down after he tells them that the creature is essentially indestructible.

Ripley decides that they should blow up the ship. She prepares the shuttle, then goes back to look for the cat. The alien kills Parker and Lambert. Ripley manages to leave in the shuttle just before the ship blows up, but she is carrying an extra passenger: the alien. She puts on a space suit, straps herself into a chair and opens the airlock, sucking the alien out of the ship, then blasts him with the exhaust before going into hypersleep.

ORIGINS AND INSPIRATION: *Alien*'s roots lie in the SF/horror crossover of the 50s. Much has been made of the similarity between the film and *It! The Terror from Beyond Space* (Edward L Cahn, 1958), in which a blood-drinking Martian hides in a spacecraft's airshafts and slaughters astronauts; *It!*'s screenwriter, Jerome Bixby, later confessed that the inspiration for the film came from the Howard Hawks classic *The Thing from Another World* (1951, see **ORIGINS AND INSPIRATION, Invasion of the Body Snatchers**).

Them! (Gordon Douglas, 1954) features giant ants running amok in the dustbowls of the American Southwest; its mixture of cocoons, tunnels and flamethrowers informs the *Alien* films, although its impact is probably more visible in *Aliens* (James Cameron, 1986). *The Quatermass Xperiment* (1955) also explored the idea of contamination by an alien species with an unusual reproductive cycle, with an arrogant scientist whose thirst for knowledge puts the human race at risk. And *Alien* has a literary debt: science-fiction author AE van Vogt later brought a lawsuit against the makers of the film, claiming plagiarism of his 1939 story 'Discord in Scarlet'; the case was settled out of court.

The film's SF credentials are further fixed by its similarities to Mario Bava's *Planet of the Vampires/Terrore nello spazio* (1965), which featured a spaceship landing on an uncharted planet in response to a distress signal, only for its crew to be killed by aliens; and Stanley Kubrick's *2001* (1968), which took a rosier view of mankind's encounter with an alien lifeform. Kubrick's was the first film to explore the loneliness of space, and HAL was a clear inspiration for Mother; even the Nostromo's hexagonal doorways owe something to Donald Trumbull's designs for Kubrick's film, although *Alien*'s look is far dirtier than the clean antisepsis of *2001*. And *Star Wars* (George Lucas, 1977) and *Close Encounters of the Third Kind* (1977) had also demonstrated a new commercial and artistic potential for science fiction, even if their optimistic visions of galactic multi-ethnicity are turned on their heads in *Alien*'s gloomy anticipation of cross-species relationships.

But the film also has much in common with non-SF creature features: rumour has it that the script was pitched around Hollywood as '*Jaws* in Space', and the similarities between the two films are instructive. The ocean shares certain qualities with space, and both films have simple, stripped-down plots in which a corrupt organisation is at least partially responsible for the danger; the characterisations in both are purely functional; both feature Lewton-style 'buses'; and both wisely keep their creatures relatively unseen.

In 1970, Dan O'Bannon was a student in the graduate programme in film studies at USC. So was John Carpenter, who asked O'Bannon to help him make a short they then developed into a feature, *Dark Star* (1974). As well as acting in the film, an idiosyncratic SF comedy that featured an alien loose on a spacecraft, O'Bannon helped write the screenplay, edit the film and design the set and special effects. But when he asked Carpenter for a shared director credit Carpenter refused, and told O'Bannon he never wanted to work with him again.

O'Bannon, dismayed in any case by the poor audience response to the comedy in the film, decided he wanted to write a film that scared people. He met up with Ronald Shusett, a screenwriter who'd written the script for the Twiggy vehicle *W* (Richard Quine, 1974), to work on developing ideas for the films that eventually became *Total Recall* (Paul Verhoeven, 1990) and *Alien*.

Halfway through writing a script entitled *Memory*, O'Bannon was contacted by Alejandro Jodorowsky, who'd seen *Dark Star* and wanted O'Bannon to work on the effects for his film of *Dune*. Other members of the *Alien* team also worked on the film: Jean 'Moebius' Giraud, Ron Cobb and Chris Foss were hired to sketch out designs, and Swiss artist HR Giger was charged with creating the Harkonnen homeworld. But by 1977 *Dune* was dead, scuppered by its reported $20 million budget and Jodorowsky's idiosyncratic working practices; Dino de Laurentiis bought the film rights to the novel and David Lynch directed the film in 1984.

The collapse of *Dune* left many of its key players struggling to keep their heads above water. O'Bannon went to stay with Shusett and dug out *Memory*; inspired both by Giger's work and by the spider wasp, which lays its eggs in the abdomen of spiders, he came up with the chest-bursting sequence, but he was still having trouble finishing the script. Shusett reminded O'Bannon of another story he'd worked on briefly, featuring gremlins killing soldiers on a B17 during the Second World War; O'Bannon used this for the second half of the script, and renamed it *Star Beast*.

After giving the script a polish, Shusett took it to Hollywood matchmaker Mark Haggard, who made a deal with Brandywine, an independent production company run by Gordon Carroll, Walter Hill and David Giler. Hill and Giler tweaked the script further and got a development deal from 20th Century Fox, Hill's name, the audacious chest-bursting sequence and the success of *Star Wars* proving the property's biggest attractions for the studio. At the time Fox pictured a small film, with a budget of around $1 million, and O'Bannon probably saw himself as director (an ambition he finally fulfilled with the zombie comedy *Return of the Living Dead* (1985)); but Carroll had bigger ideas, imagining *Alien* less as *Dark Star 2* than a full-bore horror film.

Hill, who'd directed *The Driver* (1978), had numerous writing credits to his name, and a reputation for tough, no-nonsense scripts written in the present tense with scant regard for characters' motivations or background. He and Giler came up with the characters' names, changed the crew from all-male to five men and two women, and introduced a robot, Ash, who took many of Mother's lines. Fox's Alan Ladd Jr came up with the idea of making Ripley, the lead character, a woman, although with the resourceful 'final girls' of **The Texas Chain Saw Massacre** and **Halloween**, the figure was fast becoming a horror staple; still, it seemed to be casting against gender stereotype, as would the use of a male actor for Kane, the character who suffers an alien 'pregnancy'.

Carroll wanted Hill to direct, but Hill felt he didn't really know enough about SF or horror, and had his sights set on making a western. After several other directors, including Robert Aldrich, Peter Yates and Jack Clayton, were considered, Sandy Lieberson, head of European production for Fox, suggested Ridley Scott, whose first feature, *The Duellists* (1977), had attracted attention for its spectacular visuals. Scott had seen *Star Wars*, and felt that there was untapped potential in the SF genre; he read the script for *Alien* in 40 minutes and felt that 'it was more than a horror film, it is a film about *terror*'. He signed on as director, producing detailed storyboards that doubled the budget and ensuring that the film would be principally shot in the UK.

O'Bannon worked with Ron Cobb on developing a look for the spacecraft and characters. They wanted to give the film an unglamorous feel: the Nostromo should be slightly shabby, its crew more like long-haul truckers than heroic pioneers. Cobb and Chris Foss, known in the UK for his SF book-jacket paintings, worked up the designs for the spacecraft, and Moebius spent a few days working on set and costume design, although the look of the space suits came mainly from John Mollo, who'd worked with Cobb on *Star Wars*; other Lucas alumni including Roger Christian and Les Dilley were recruited to work on the film as art designers

O'Bannon's relationship with Brandywine deteriorated to the point where he was barred from the set during the shoot; Scott didn't help matters when he reportedly said that he preferred O'Bannon's original script to the Hill–Giler rewrite. O'Bannon was initially passed over for a writing credit, but when he went to the Writers' Guild for arbitration the story credit was given to him and Shusett, with Giler and Hill now credited as co-producers.

Giger came on board after other artists' sketches for the Alien proved unsatisfactory; when O'Bannon showed Scott samples of the artist's work, including one picture in his book *Necronomicon* that the director thought perfect for the Alien, Giger was hired to design not only the Alien but the planet they visit and the spacecraft, known in production as the Derelict, they find there: 'They asked me to design something which could not have been made by human beings . . . Everything I designed in the film used the idea of bones . . . I mixed up technical and organic things. I call this biomechanics.'

One lengthy sequence was cut out of the final script to keep costs down. In it the 'Space Jockey' (the dead alien found on the Derelict) has scratched a triangle in the dashboard in front of him; when the storm has calmed on the planet the crew see a pyramid on the horizon, and go to explore. A volunteer lowers himself through the hatch at the top, and finds a giant chamber filled with statues and hieroglyphics, designed to represent the Alien's reproductive cycle.

Scott was happy not to shoot the scene, but it represents an intriguing Lovecraftian angle not followed in the film or its sequels (Giger cites Lovecraft as a major inspiration, and the octopoid face hugger bears some relation to the writer's tentacled monstrosities): an exploration of the culture of the Aliens. Scott hoped that the film's sequel would 'explain what the Alien is and where it comes from', but such concerns were jettisoned in favour of high-octane action and, later in the saga, an exploration of the film's sexual subtext.

The groundwork for this was laid when Scott removed a scripted scene where Dallas and Ripley discuss having sex; this is understandable partly in the context of Scott's professed attitude to screen sex – 'Sex is boring unless you're doing it' – but also in setting up an environment where there is the potential for attraction between the Alien and Ripley.

DIRECTOR: Ridley Scott studied art and film at London's Royal College of Art before working as a set designer for the BBC. He began to direct for the broadcaster in the mid-60s, then left to work freelance, directing hundreds of advertisements before making his first feature, *The Duellists*. The film's extravagant visual style would become the director's trademark, reappearing in the hugely influential *Blade Runner* (1982), an adaptation of Philip K Dick's novel *Do Androids Dream of Electric Sheep?* that continued *Alien*'s exploration of humans' evolutionary position.

Hannibal (2001) was Scott's return to the horror genre, a disappointingly bland sequel to Jonathan Demme's *Silence of the Lambs* (1991) that confirmed that the director cares far more about the look of his films than their plot or acting. Scott and Sigourney Weaver have discussed plans to make a fifth and final instalment of the *Alien* saga, although nothing concrete has yet materialised; the scenario envisioned is said to be a journey to the Alien's home planet, exploring the Alien culture for the first time.

CASTING: The real star of *Alien* is the creature itself, and Scott took pains not to distract from this by making the film a celebrity vehicle. But he still spent a long time over the casting, and the ensemble team works perfectly, even with their shallow character-isations.

Sigourney Weaver had only had substantial roles in plays and an obscure Israeli film, *Madman* (Dan Cohen, 1978), before *Alien*; her 5'11" height had seen her passed over for other parts. When she tested for the film – hoping for Lambert rather than Ripley – Alan Ladd Jr asked all the women he could find at Fox what they thought of her for the lead; they liked the idea, and she was hired.

As an overzealous jobsworth, Ripley is initially an unattractive character, apparently inhumane in her insistence on quarantine procedures when Kane's life is at risk; as Scott put it, 'Sigourney was great because she has such a presence and authority as the officer who was most likely to irritate.' But she is resourceful and authoritative, discovering the Company's aims and taking charge when Dallas is killed; her love for the cat, Jones, which – in one of the film's less convincing sequences – she risks her life to save, shows a warmer side to her character which is developed in *Aliens*.

Ripley seems as essential a part of the *Alien* franchise as the Alien itself, with Weaver reprising the role in its three sequels; that she ends by having sex with a few Aliens (if only in scenes sadly excised from *Alien Resurrection* (1997)) is unsurprising given that Scott's film kickstarted her film career. The actress's other genre roles include *Ghostbusters* (1984) and the Hitchcockian serial-killer movie *Copycat* (Jon Amiel, 1995), and she was back in space for the spoof *Galaxy Quest* (Dean Parisot, 1999). She worked with Scott again on *1492: Conquest of Paradise* (1992), and also starred in Polanski's *Death and the Maiden* (1994).

Harry Dean Stanton's lugubrious features have livened up a wide range of leftfield films, from counterculture classics like *Two-Lane Blacktop* (Monte Hellman, 1971) to work from genre favourites John Carpenter (*Escape from New York* (1981), *Christine* (1983)) and David Lynch (*Wild at Heart* (1990), *Twin Peaks: Fire Walk with Me* (1992), *The Straight Story* (1999)).

Yaphet Kotto teamed up with Skerritt again for the *Death Wish*-inspired *Fighting Back* (Lewis Teague, 1982), as well as appearing in *Freddy's Dead: The Final Nightmare* (Rachel Talalay, 1991); Skerritt's other genre roles include *The Devil's Rain* (Robert Fuest, 1975), *Savage Harvest* (Robert E Collins, 1981), David Cronenberg's *The Dead Zone* (1983) and *Poltergeist III* (Gary Sherman, 1988).

The rest of the cast, with the exception of Bolaji Badejo, a 6'10" Nigerian art student recruited to wear the full-sized Alien costume after he ran into an agent in a London pub, are British born. Veronica Cartwright's genre appearances include *The Birds* (1963), *Invasion of the Body Snatchers* (1978), *Candyman II* (Bill Condon, 1995) and *Scary Movie 2* (Keenen Ivory Wayans, 2001), while John Hurt has starred in *The Ghoul* (Freddie Francis, 1974), *The Shout* (Jerzy Skolimowski, 1978) and *Lost Souls* (Janusz Kaminski, 2000).

Ian Holm's Ash is in a long tradition of English screen villains, from Charles Laughton to Anthony Hopkins. He brought many personal touches to the role, originating the early on-the-spot jog that suggests that all may not be quite as it seems and delivering lines of cod-scientific gibberish with style. His other genre roles include Terry Gilliam's *Time Bandits* (1981) and *Brazil* (1985), David Cronenberg's *The Naked Lunch* (1991) and *Existenz* (1999), *Mary Shelley's Frankenstein* (1994), *From Hell* (Albert Hughes and Alan Hughes, 2001) and Peter Jackson's *Lord of the Rings* trilogy.

PRODUCTION: Shooting began on 25 July 1978 and lasted for four weeks. The set for the Derelict was built at Bray, with a revolving chair for the Space Jockey that allowed reverse angles to be shot without building a complete set; the Nostromo sets were built at Shepperton, on four sound stages. Children were used in miniature space suits for the scene where the crew are first seen leaving the Nostromo on the alien planet, and when they find the Space Jockey, to make the sets look bigger.

Scott had a very developed idea of how he wanted the film to look, and screened Kubrick's *Dr Strangelove* (1964) to inspire the designers. Cobb's strategy was to make the Nostromo as functional as possible, and he used old aircraft parts to construct the bridge, which was deliberately built with a low ceiling for a claustrophobic feel. Three models for the ship were built: a twelve-inch version for medium and long shots, one four times that size for rear shots, to make the jet-burn look realistic, and a seven-ton rig used for early scenes on the planet's surface and the undocking sequence. At its peak, over 300 people were working on the film, which eventually cost $9 million.

Giger requested a large number of bones, which he mixed with Styrofoam for the first models of the creature and the Derelict. Three aliens were built: the face hugger, chest-burster and the full-size model. Giger designed all three and built the latter two with Carlo Rambaldi, later to build the tentacled lover of *Possession* (1981) and *ET* (Steven Spielberg, 1982), the more acceptable face of human–alien interaction; the face hugger was built by Roger Dicken under Giger's supervision.

Scott didn't want too much of the Alien seen at once, preferring only parts to be seen at any one time so that much of its appearance was left to the audience's imagination; many viewers were convinced that the creature grew larger and changed throughout the film, although there is only one full-sized model.

He also hoped to explore the Alien's limited life cycle, explaining that at the end:

> you see slime emanating from the Big Alien's body because we're trying to convey that maybe he's sealing himself in again, like in a cocoon. Also, by that point, he has to be provoked to attack, because he has to get on with his life cycle.

Apart from John Hurt, none of the cast had seen the chest-bursting alien before Kane's death was shot, and nobody was prepared for the amount of blood that came from the offal packed into Hurt's chest, least of all Veronica Cartwright, who took a heavy spray in the face. Animal organs were also used in the scene of the egg opening – the membrane on display is a cow's stomach lining, and the tentacle that whips out is a sheep's intestine – and the face-hugger autopsy, which used oysters and clams.

Scott controversially removed a scene towards the end of the film where Ripley finds Dallas and Brett in cocoons and incinerates them with a flamethrower; this explained more about the alien's reproductive cycle and its use of humans, but the director felt that it hurt the pacing of the film.

The titles were the work of graphic designers brought on board for the marketing artwork. Scott had wanted them to have a hieroglyphic feel, implying that the alien was from a sophisticated society; the lines that appear first also chalk up the alien's kills, one for each victim.

SOUNDTRACK: The film's soundtrack uses various disquieting sounds – from the high-pitched mechanoid squeaks of the 'dying' Ash to non-localised hums – to keep the audience uneasy, and Jerry Goldsmith's haunting orchestral score keeps the tension high even during the first forty minutes of the film. But Scott and Goldsmith disagreed over the use of the score, and many of the composer's cues were either rescored or moved, with the intended end-title sequence replaced by Howard Hanson's Symphony No. 2 (Romantic). The original score is available on a soundtrack album, and features as an isolated track on some of the DVD editions of the film.

Goldsmith was one of the hardest-working and most influential composers in the movie business, with over two hundred feature credits to his name, scored in a wide variety of styles. His genre films include *Seconds* (John Frankenheimer, 1966), *Planet of the Apes* (Franklin J Schaffner, 1968), *The Illustrated Man* (Jack Smight, 1969), *The Mephisto Waltz* (Paul Wendkos, 1971), *The Omen* (1976), *Poltergeist* (1982), *Psycho II* (1983), *Gremlins* (Joe Dante, 1984), *The Mummy* (Stephen Sommers, 1999) and *The Haunting* (1999); he worked with Scott again on *Legend* (1985), and also scored Polanski's *Chinatown* (1974).

'IT'S ONLY A MOVIE ... ONLY A MOVIE ...': Fox's marketing department experimented with a number of poster designs, including several with lettering by Giger, before settling on the lettering from the title sequence and the famous image of an egg opening.

Photos of the Alien itself were kept under wraps – the set had been closed, and the look of the creature was a well-kept secret – until the film's release, when a merchandising blitz began that hasn't really let up even today.

RELEASE: *Alien* had a conservative release pattern, possibly following concerns voiced by some Fox executives during previews that the film was too disturbing to succeed. It opened in just 91 cinemas in the US, with a broader national release a few weeks later; but its heavy television advertising and strong word of mouth made it the fourth highest grossing picture of the year, taking in $48.4 million by the end of 1979. It was nominated for two Oscars – art direction, which it lost to *All that Jazz* (Bob Fosse), and visual effects, which it won – but its reviews were mixed, partly from uncertainty over whether it was intended to be a horror or SF film.

Starburst's reviewer found it 'very annoying' and 'a botched job': 'as a science fiction film it's seriously flawed, but as a horror film it works perfectly'; and *Monthly Film Bulletin*, while recognising the 'commercial astuteness behind the recipe', was irritated by a 'moribund' plot and found ultimately that '*Alien* signified nothing very much – except, of course, at the box office.' *Sight & Sound* thought the film's 'spectacularly British xenophobia' reminiscent of Quatermass, and were impressed by the 'gorgeous, leisurely' visuals: 'beauty, ultimately, is what *Alien* brings to science fiction cinema.'

Various scenes were reinstated for the 2003 Director's Cut, particularly Ripley's discovery of Dallas and Brett in cocoons; the film also trimmed a few other scenes to maintain the pace, but makes no changes as substantial as those in the Director's Cut of *Blade Runner* (Ridley Scott, 1982).

CRITICAL EYE: 'It has absolutely no message. It works on a very visceral level and its only point is terror, and more terror.' Scott's take on the film clearly isn't shared by the academic establishment: *Alien* was the fifth most-assigned film in American science-fiction studies classes in 1997, and the series was matched only by *Blade Runner* in a recent count of academic publications about science-fiction films.

What these studies don't tend to pick up on is the various plot flaws of the film, although these haven't escaped the notice of other commentators, notably Kim Newman, who describes it as a 'dumb film'. The main criticism is that although Ripley repeatedly says 'We've got to stick together', the characters do anything but. Brett's lone search for Jones is often cited as an example of the film's implausibility, although to be fair he's being punished for having let the cat go in the first place and has no idea of the scale of the creature he's looking for; the separation of Ripley from Parker and Lambert towards the end seems harder to justify, and Ripley's return to the ship to look for the cat is both foolish and apparently out of character, put in more as a piece of misdirection – has the Alien infested the cat? – than a well thought-out plot point. But the film's pace, by now frenetic, glosses over these lacunae, its spectacular design distracting from the weaknesses of the plot.

A more serious criticism is that *Alien* is something of a missed opportunity: as David Cronenberg has pointed out, 'it had the potential to be incredibly complex and exciting and it chose the least strand that it could follow. It finally opted for the "monster chases girl" strand.'

But there are some ideas in the film: contemporary critics have tended to focus on its take on sex and gender, and given Giger's predilection for nightmarish erotic imagery it's no surprise to find a rich sexual subtext here. Yet the genderless Alien – both phallic in its full-grown form and vaginal in its face-hugger manifestation, invading hosts regardless of sex – is only half the story.

The film is full of birth imagery, with 'Mother' awakening the crew in a womblike chamber, representing a sterile, technological vision of birth in contrast to the messy alien chest-bursting. The

Nostromo's corridors also recall uterine passages, some dank and dripping with Alien slime, and Dallas's claustrophobic trip into the airshafts, with their cervical hatches, is a classic 'no exit' scene.

Much has been made of *Alien*'s play on human gender roles: it is Kane, a man, who is symbolically raped by the face-hugger and gives birth to the Alien, recalling what is according to Freud a common childhood misconception about pregnancy – that a mother is somehow impregnated through her mouth and gives birth from her stomach; and it is Ripley, a woman, who finally beats the Alien and survives. Yet for all that Ripley is a resourceful and independent heroine, Lambert plays down to gender stereotype by snivelling and sobbing her way weakly through the film, and even Ripley is finally portrayed stripping down to her underwear.

Scott's cynical take on this is that: '[the producers] kept saying, there's no sex in this movie. I said, well, you don't need any, but – there's a good opportunity here to have a little bit of, you know, hinted-at sexuality.' Weaver's own impression of the scene is more ambiguous, describing how the Alien would be intrigued to see her stripped down: 'It's just following its natural instinct to reproduce through whatever living things are around it.'

The sequence does humanise Ripley – throughout the film the Alien appears more organic than most of the human characters – and there is a slight hint of the sexual attraction between Ripley and the Alien that later in the series became a full-blown concern. This link exists between the Alien and the other characters too: the face-hugger attack has sexual overtones, as does the limb snaking up Lambert's leg before a cut to her screaming face.

Related to these fears of interspecies miscegenation are evolutionary anxieties: according to Ash the Alien is 'a perfect organism, its structural perfection ... matched only by its hostility'. Ironically, the description of the Alien as 'without remorse, conscience, morality ... a survivor' comes close to describing both Ripley and Parker, the strongest members of the crew. Ripley is the perfect Company Woman, following the quarantine rules by the book and even completing the captain's log at the end of the film; she is only redeemed as humane by the ludicrous act of going back for the cat, while Parker, who didn't want to respond to the distress call unless he was given more money, is redeemed by his selfless attack on the Alien, which he refuses to fire on for fear of hitting Lambert. Ripley, in the cold, emotionless state that allows her to survive where others (notably Lambert, crippled by emotion) do not, resembles not only the Alien but also the Company, another ruthless example of evolutionary success.

It is not only the Alien that threatens humans' positions on the evolutionary ladder: Ash, an android who is ironically portrayed as more humane than Ripley in letting Kane back on board, represents fears of replacement by machines; and, of course, he is also the ship scientist, fitting the film neatly in the classic horror tradition of distrust of science. Here the Alien should be killed, not studied, and common sense is more important than gathering knowledge; science is in the service of a corrupt organisation gathering the ultimate weapon for reasons that are never explored, and clearly doesn't have the best interests of the crew at heart.

INDUSTRY IMPACT: *Alien*'s cost meant that it was never going to spawn a cycle quite as relentless as the slasher, but many low-budget filmmakers gave it a game try. The film's immediate clones include *Contamination* (Luigi Cozzi, 1980), the endearingly crap *Inseminoid* (Norman J Warren, 1981), *The Intruder Within* (Peter Carter, 1981), *Galaxy of Terror* (Bruce D Clark, 1981) and the toothy monsters of *The Deadly Spawn* (Douglas McKeown, 1981); as Kim Newman has pointed out, 'With that kind of concentrated obnoxiousness falling weekly from the skies, Steven Spielberg's ET shouldn't have been surprised to find the generality of mankind unwilling to put out the welcome mat.'

Inseminoid and *Xtro* (Harry Bromley Davenport, 1983) make explicit *Alien*'s implicit rape, with the former's bug-eyed alien babies about as far from Giger's nightmare vision as it's possible to get; by contrast a tentacled monster featured in a consensual clinch with Isabelle Adjani in Andrej Zulawski's *Possession* (1981), a wildly excessive film about the break-up of a relationship that must have bewildered gorehounds who tracked it down on the basis of its inclusion in the banned list of the Director of Public Prosecutions (DPP). *Alien*'s sequels have similarly brought the subtext of Scott's film to the fore – Ripley and the Alien are symbolically linked in *Aliens* (1986), physically linked in *Alien³* (David Fincher, 1992), and by *Alien Resurrection* (Jean-Pierre Jeunet, 1997) Ripley *is* the Alien.

The film's spectacular special effects and visceral feel had more of an impact on the industry than any of its plot details, with 80s horror relied on to provide extraordinarily messy effects-laden set pieces. One of the few films to make truly inventive use of this remit was John Carpenter's *The Thing* (1982). Ostensibly a remake of *Alien*-inspiration *The Thing from Another World* (1951), Carpenter's film returned to John W Campbell's 1938 novella 'Who Goes There' for an alien that could imitate any lifeform, rather than resurrect the vegetable 'what-is-it' from the original film.

The Thing makes exceptional use of its Antarctic setting, whether through the bravura opening sequence of a dog being chased across the icy wastes or the cabin fever suffered by the members of the research team the alien assimilates one by one. The setting also adds to the film's melancholy atmosphere, and its icy sterility is contrasted throughout with the alien's freakishly chaotic transformations. The Thing may be able to imitate any living form, but it's imaginative enough not to go for anything dull: one of its victims' chests opens up, a giant vagina dentata that bites off a colleague's hands; and the severed head of another sprouts legs and walks off, prompting his colleague to voice exactly what the audience thinks: 'You gotta be fucking kidding.'

The film is an untoppable showcase for the advantages of mechanical effects over CGI, which has never been used so imaginatively, but for all its entertainingly grotesque transform-ations *The Thing*'s downbeat tone gave it a poor response at the box office. There are no jokes, no sense of parody, and no happy endings here: even at the start the arrival of the alien only deepens existing hostilities between the team members, who are clearly sick of each other's company, and the film ends with the final survivors slowly freezing to death, watching each other for any signs of transformation.

Finally, apart from influencing the look of countless rock videos for dodgy industrial bands, inspiring a run of substandard alien invasion films like *Predator* (John McTiernan, 1987) and *Species* (Roger Donaldson, 1995) and providing the template for *Event Horizon* (Paul WS Anderson, 1997), *Alien*'s most lasting impact on the film industry was in the character of Ellen Ripley, which took the 'final girl' of the slashers and gave her a big weapon: women finally got to blow stuff up as well.

FINAL WORD: *Alien* is, along with **Psycho, The Exorcist** and **Halloween,** one of the few horror films to become a major hit with mainstream audiences, but unlike these it still looks surprisingly good today. The murky atmospherics have helped Giger and Cobb's designs to stand the test of time – *Alien* looks in many ways more convincing than any of its sequels – and the chestbursting scene remains one of the most viscerally effective sequences in the history of horror.

We might agree with Cronenberg that the film plays it safe rather than exploring the broader range of the concept's possibilities; but its use of womb panic and birth anxiety is hardly formula fare, and Scott's pacing gives the film an urgency that leaves the viewer little room to wonder how it could have been done better. Space would never hold such convincing terrors again.

CONSUMING VIOLENCE

Cannibal Holocaust (1980)

'Those who filmed it were devoured alive by cannibals!'

Italy, FD Cinematographica, colour, 95 mins

Directed by Ruggero Deodato
Produced by Franco Palaggi and Franco Di Nunzio
Story and Screenplay: Gianfranco Clerici
Director of Photography: Sergio D'Offizi
Music Composed and Conducted by Riz Ortolani
Film Editor: Vincenzo Tomassi
Production Designer: Massimo Antonello Geleng
Assistant Directors: Salvatore Basile and Lamberto Bava
[credited for quota reasons: Bava did not work on this film]
Make-up: Massimo Giustini
Sound Engineer: Raul Montesanti

CAST: Robert Kerman (*Professor Harold Monroe*), Francesca Ciardi (*Faye Daniels*), Perry Pirkanen (*Jack Anders*), Luca Giorgio Barbareschi (*Mark Tomaso*), Salvatore Basile (*Felipe*), Ricardo Fuentes (*Chaco*), Gabriel Yorke (*Alan Yates*), Paolo Paoloni, Pio di Savoia, Luigina Rocchi, Lucia Costantini (*Woman Stoned for*

Adultery), Ruggero Deodato (*Man Sitting on Lawn Outside NY State University*)

SYNOPSIS: Four young American documentary filmmakers, led by Alan Yates, have been missing for two months in the Amazon basin. A rescue team, headed by NYU anthropologist Harold Monroe, is sent to find out what happened to them.

Soldiers capture a Yacumo warrior, who will lead Monroe's team into the jungle. Monroe also travels with a guide, Chaco, and his partner Miguel.

Chaco soon finds the corpse of Felipe, the documentary team's guide. They watch a Yacumo kill a woman in a ritual punishment for adultery, and follow him back to his village, using their warrior as bait. The Yacumo are scared by their arrival, but Miguel placates the chief with a flick-knife.

They find their first Yamamomo, the cannibal tribe sought by the Yates team, fighting with Shamatari warriors. They shoot some Shamatari and are welcomed by the Yamamomo; Monroe wins their trust and is shown the documentary team's corpses. The Yamamomo are reluctant to give away their film cans, but Monroe exchanges them for a tape recorder. The Yamamomo celebrate with a cannibal feast; Monroe and Chaco, professional to the end, dig in.

Back in Manhattan, Monroe is asked by a board of television executives to present Yates's footage as a documentary called 'The Green Inferno'. Monroe wants to see the footage first, and is shown an earlier Yates documentary, 'The Last Road to Hell', which features footage of African deaths. A TV executive assures him it is all faked.

Monroe meets the families of the dead filmmakers, none of whom mourn their passing. Back in the screening room, he and the board watch the 'Green Inferno' footage. The Yates team kill a turtle and eat it; their guide Felipe is bitten by a snake and dies after his leg is amputated.

They wound a Yacumo and follow him back to his village, where they stage a 'massacre of the Yacumo by the Yamamomo', shooting a pig then herding a group of Yacumo into a hut and burning it down. The TV executives are impressed.

After more atrocity footage is screened, Monroe says he wants nothing to do with the film, and shows the rest to the TV executives. The Yates team capture a Yamamomo girl and rape her; later they find a body impaled on a stake. The Yamamomo surround them, but the team are so excited by the footage that they carry on filming. Anders is speared and then shot dead by Yates and eaten by the Yamamomo; Faye is raped and decapitated; and Yates tries to run but is killed.

A TV executive tells the projectionist to burn the footage, but a crawl reveals that instead he sold it for around $250,000.

ORIGINS AND INSPIRATION: The Italian Third World cannibal cycle is almost unique in the country's exploitation film history in being a native form, rather than a rip-off of a successful American film. Although they take elements from *The Most Dangerous Game* (Irving Pichel and Ernest B Schoedsack, 1932), *A Man Called Horse* (Elliot Silverstein, 1970) and *Aguirre – The Wrath of God/Aguirre, der Zorn Gottes* (Werner Herzog, 1972), the films owe most to the mondo cycle, a series of sensationalistic documentaries that took their name from *Mondo Cane* (Paolo Cavara and Gualtiero Jacopetti, 1962). Mondo films were designed to shock and entertain Western audiences by depicting life in the developing world as 'savage' and 'uncivilised'; they characteristically mixed real and fake footage with misleading narration, and took a dubious gloss of authenticity from images of animal death, presented in demonstrations of 'wild nature' or strange tribal eating habits.

Umberto Lenzi's *Deep River Savages/Il paese del sesso selvagio* (1972) was the first film to apply the conventions of the mondo movie to an explicitly fictional form. A title card boasted of the authenticity of the story – a white man is captured by a tribe on the Thai/Burma border and is initiated into their ways – with rites 'portrayed as they are actually carried out'; and the film flanked its one scene of explicit cannibalism with animal-slaughter footage, in a cynical attempt to make its shoddy effects look more convincing.

Deodato's first cannibal film, *Last Cannibal World/L'ultimo mundo cannibale* (1976), followed in Lenzi's footsteps but racked everything up a notch, with the obligatory title card, more animal deaths and a grab-bag of gruelling cannibal scenes. Here Robert Harper lands on the island of Mindanao to visit an oil-prospecting party, but finds their camp abandoned; soon he and his companions are lost in the jungle, and are picked off one by one until Harper is captured after gorging on psychedelic mushrooms. He suffers various indignities, but soon befriends a native woman and escapes with her, although she is eventually tracked down and eaten. In a show of strength when cornered, Harper kills a cannibal and eats his entrails, after which he earns the tribe's respect and is allowed to leave.

After minor efforts from Joe D'Amato (*Emanuelle and the Last Cannibals* (1977)) and Sergio Martino (*Prisoner of the Cannibal God* (1978)), Deodato returned to the cannibal cycle. According to the director *Cannibal Holocaust* grew out of his anger with the press coverage of anarchist group the Red Brigade, an exploitative wallowing in footage of death and destruction presented 'in the public interest'; and he also intended it to be an attack on the mondo genre. Even from its title *Cannibal Holocaust* announced itself as brash and ballsy, a punk movie. Few other filmmakers would have wanted or been able to live up to the name, but Deodato succeeded in assaulting the audience with imagery so extreme that it shattered even the title's lurid expectations.

It wasn't the first film to criticise the mondo movie, although Deodato's sledgehammer rhetoric was a novelty: *The Wild Eye/L'occhio selvaggio* (1965), directed by *Mondo Cane*'s co-director Paolo Cavara, featured a cameraman who incited various acts of violence for his film; and Deodato's vision of filmmakers who kill for their art has its antecedents in both horror and mainstream cinema.

Sidney Lumet's *Network* (1976) was a biting satire of TV executives who will stop at nothing for higher ratings, and Paul Schrader's *Hardcore* (1979) featured George C Scott hoping not to find his daughter in a snuff movie. One of the richest explorations of the theme is *Peeping Tom* (1960, see **INDUSTRY IMPACT, Psycho**), while other films capitalised on news reports of snuff movies in the mid-70s to give their otherwise unremark-able films the commercial allure of the forbidden. The most notorious of these is *Snuff* (Michael Findlay and Roberta Findlay, 1976), actually a Manson-inspired film called *Slaughter* that had been made five years before and had languished on a distributor's shelf until its rank ineptitude could be turned to financial advantage. To justify its new title five minutes of footage were tacked on at the end, revealing that the rest was 'just a film' and showing the 'director' killing one of the actresses – who looked nothing like anyone in the previous film.

The publicity stunt worked better than the distributors could have hoped, adding a new bogeyman to the collective nightmare

– to date not one snuff movie (involving a murder committed for the express purpose of being filmed) has ever been found, although that hasn't stopped substantial media hysteria over the issue – and even giving it a location, with its tagline 'Filmed in South America . . . where life is CHEAP!'

DIRECTOR: Deodato's first break in the movie business came when he was asked to be third assistant director on Rossellini's *Il generale della rovere* (1959); he was uncredited, but became a much sought-after assistant director, working with gothic directors like Riccardo Freda and Anthony Margheriti. His first full directing credit came with *Phenomenal and the Treasure of Tutankamen/Fenomenal e il tesoro di Tutankamen* (1968), and since then he has plied his trade in any genre that has come to hand, from softcore porn to grisly slashers.

The director's misanthropist edge is first in evidence in the cop thriller *Live Like a Cop, Die Like a Man* (1976), and Deodato followed *Cannibal Holocaust*, which he regards as his best film – 'Even watching it today it is a masterpiece' – with *House on the Edge of the Park/La Casa sperduta nel parco* (1980), a bleak *Last House on the Left* (1972) rip-off that shared much of *Cannibal Holocaust*'s nastiness but none of its intelligence.

His genre films since then have tended to waste interesting casts: *Cut and Run/Inferno in Diretta* (1985) is probably the best, an Amazonian adventure movie that started off as a Wes Craven project; and *The Washing Machine* (1993) was twisted enough to be something of a return to form after the execrable *Bodycount/Camping del Terrore* (1986) and *Phantom of Death/Un delitto poco commune* (1988), although it's still a long way from the confrontational excesses of *Cannibal Holocaust*.

CASTING: The only professional actor in *Cannibal Holocaust* was Robert Kerman; as well as a bit part in Deodato's *Concorde Affair* (1979), Kerman was also a popular porn star in the 70s, operating under the name 'Robert Bolla', but he moved from one kind of meat movie to another a few more times, with *Eaten Alive/Mangiati Vivi!* (Umberto Lenzi, 1980) and *Cannibal Ferox/Make Them Die Slowly* (Umberto Lenzi, 1981) also to his credit.

The Yates team were all from the Actor's Studio in New York: this was Gabriel Yorke's only film, Ciardi also appeared in *Mosca Addio* (Mauro Bolognini, 1987) and Roger Vadim's *Safari* (1980),

Pirkanen turned up in *City of the Living Dead/Paura nella città* (Lucio Fulci, 1980) and had an uncredited part in *Cannibal Ferox*, while Barbareschi was reunited with Deodato for *Cut and Run*.

PRODUCTION: *Cannibal Holocaust* was financed principally by Deodato's German distributor, at the time buying his films unseen, and by Japanese investors, clearly convinced of the film's commercial potential in their territory: many mondo movies were shot with an eye on the Japanese market, and Deodato's film went on to do extremely well there.

The film was shot on location, with a base in Leticia in Colombia, near the borders of Brazil and Peru. Deodato maintains that the names of the tribes and their behaviour were accurately portrayed, and that the Yamamomo were indeed a cannibal tribe who devoured their enemies.

For the film's most shocking effect, the impaled woman sat on a small bicycle seat and was covered in fake blood, with a stake of balsa wood protruding from her mouth; and the woman in the abortion sequence really was pregnant, but the induced foetus is a doll. A sequence featuring a man tied to a log and used as piranha bait was shot but left out of the final edit, and appears on none of the prints in circulation.

SOUNDTRACK: *Cannibal Holocaust*'s familiarity with mondo conventions is shown not only with the title card but also the opening music, Riz Ortolani's cheesy listening fitting the travelogue footage of Amazonian jungle while apparently at odds with the film's uncompromising title; mondo movies characteristically used syrupy strings and inappropriately upbeat ballads to accompany their grim tours, with *Mondo Cane*'s 'More' reaching the top ten and being nominated for Best Song in the 1963 Oscars.

Later the soundtrack shifts, taken over by a memorably doom-laden string sequence that builds up to powerful crescendos, punctuated by synthesised stings; but occasionally it switches again, the cheesy intro music intruding in such jaw-droppingly inappropriate places as the Yates team's destruction of a Yacumo village. Deodato can't have been unaware of the effect of such jarring juxtapositions, and seems to be commenting on the uneasy relationship between screen violence and entertainment, which we'll return to later.

Ortolani is one of the busiest composers in Italian exploitation cinema, notably scoring *Mondo Cane* and the notorious *Africa Addio* (Gualtiero Jacopetti and Franco E Prosperi, 1966), Italian gothics like *The Virgin of Nuremberg/La Vergine di Norimberga* (Antonio Margheriti, 1963) and *The Castle of Blood/Danza macabre* (Antonio Margheriti, 1964), Lucio Fulci's *Don't Torture a Duckling/Non si sevizia un paperino* (1972), *House on the Edge of the Park*, Pupi Avati's *Zeder* (1983), various Tinto Brass movies and parts of Tarantino's *Kill Bill: Vol 1* (2003).

'IT'S ONLY A MOVIE . . . ONLY A MOVIE . . .': The marketing for *Cannibal Holocaust* relied on posters depicting confrontational images from the film, particularly one of a woman on a stake. Naturally these weren't to everyone's taste, and the campaign added fuel to the 'video nasty' fire in the UK during the early 80s.

RELEASE: *Cannibal Holocaust* was one of the most profitable Italian films of the 80s, making $20 million worldwide according to Deodato, of which $7 million was from Tokyo alone. Yet within weeks of its release in Italy, the film was withdrawn from circulation and banned after courts cited a law drafted to outlaw bullfighting, prohibiting the torture and killing of animals for entertainment.

Deodato defended himself in court several times, but the injunction stood for three years, during which he made no other films (*House on the Edge of the Park* had been made before *Cannibal Holocaust*'s release). Eventually the director was cleared of any charges and the film was re-released in a slightly trimmed form. Deodato could have been forgiven for not anticipating the legal furore over his film: real animal slaughter footage had been featured in films before, particularly in the cannibal cycle, and Umberto Lenzi's inferior rip-off *Cannibal Ferox* (1981), which sought to outdo Deodato's film in both real and prosthetic violence – a woman is hung by hooks through her breasts, and a man's penis is hacked off and eaten in front of him – was in free circulation while Deodato's was banned.

The film also came under fire in the UK, where complaints to the Advertising Standards Authority about the extreme imagery used on the packaging and posters were one of the contributory factors to the VRA. *Cannibal Holocaust* was among the 39 films deemed obscene by the DPP and banned, along with virtually any other film with the word 'cannibal' in the title. The film has since also been misinterpreted by several Trading Standards officers as a 'snuff' movie; a raid on a Birmingham comic fair in April 1993 that saw a copy confiscated from a dealer resulted in a newspaper report of 'the first known seizure in the city of a snuff video'. A truncated version has since been released in the UK, but the film remains banned in a number of territories, including West Germany and Australia.

Its fictional origins seem to have escaped others too. An ad for a screening at Detroit's Adams Theater screamed 'Savage! Terrifying! True! Those who filmed it were actually devoured by cannibals!', and a French magazine, *Photo*, ran a feature called 'Grand Guignol Cannibale', which suggested that 'men were really dismembered, beheaded, castrated and *mangiati vivi*!' in the film.

Most reviewers weren't so easily fooled, but attacked the film for its hypocritical attitude towards the violence it sought to condemn. *Variety* thought little of this 'patently phoney tale of cannibalism and the white man's mistreatment of native tribes', and condemned 'Deodato's inclusion of much extraneous gore effects and nudity, as well as the genre's usual (and disgusting) killing of animals on camera'. A reviewer for *Image et Son* noted that the 'rapes, feasts of raw flesh, gross shots of decomposing corpses, interminable flayings and diverse mutilations are depicted with a great luxuriance in sordid details to culminate in an apotheosis of voyeurism'; and along with others, *Cahiers du Cinéma* attacked the film's 'explicit racism'; while *Cinéma 81* noted that 'The anthropologist declares that it would be odious to show such films to the public, [but] what do you think the spectator is shown for the next hour and a half? The famous ignominious footage . . .'

CRITICAL EYE:

If you're bored by it, pretend it's real, but if you're excited by it, pretend it's fake.

The Incredible Torture Show

From the outset *Cannibal Holocaust* toys with the mondo movie's questionable claims to authenticity. It opens with a card telling the viewer that 'For the sake of authenticity, some scenes have been retained in their entirety', and ends with a crawl explaining that the projectionist ignored orders to destroy the footage and instead sold it on. The Yates team's disappearance is revealed through a news report, and 'The Last Road to Hell' contains authentic footage from African civil wars: here the mondo's misleading narration is turned on its head, with Monroe told that this was 'all a put-on'.

The Green Inferno footage constantly draws attention to its own technical shortcomings for a vérité style, with the use of hand-held cameras, scratched frames, soundtrack pops and lines from the projectionist like 'this shot's dark because the diaphragm setting in the camera is wrong ... there, now he's got it right' fixing it as more 'real' in the eyes of the audience. It doesn't seem to matter that much of the material is obviously unusable – often one member of the team is visibly clowning about in the background, and they spend an inordinate amount of time filming their own involvement in atrocities – or that, as David Kerekes and David Slater put it in *Killing For Culture*, 'a wavering tree branch or the ever reliable pop, start or film hiccup should occur always at the most technically advantageous moment': the footage is devastating.

The atrocities carried out by the Yates team – and the various punishments for adultery meted out by Yacumo and Yamamomo – seem convincing in their utter meanness, even if some of the effects are typically shoddy, and other images in the film are uniquely compelling: the **Texas Chain Saw Massacre**-style remains of the Yates team, the Yamamomo emerging from their tree homes, or the shocking image of the staked woman, all lend the film a power at odds with the occasionally inept acting and *mise en scène*. Indeed the finale is so apocalyptic that there is some confusion over who's actually being killed: a few plot synopses have Mark as the final victim, but it is actually Yates whose face bounces up and down in front of the camera; it can safely be assumed that Mark meets an equally grisly fate off screen.

The director has claimed that the film is a response to the Italian media's treatment of real-life violence in the late 70s, and the Yates team's violent actions recall criticisms levelled at several mondo filmmakers; Jacopetti and Prosperi, in particular, were accused of having colluded with mercenaries to stage killings for the camera in *Africa Addio* (1966), although the charges were eventually dropped. Yet Deodato has expressed an admiration for Jacopetti – 'His films were truly beautiful' – and made the Yates team American rather than Italian.

Still, an attack on the media's use of violence seems clear in the film: the real footage from 'The Last Road to Hell' appears shockingly bland when contrasted with the excessive spectacles of the fake Green Inferno, and Deodato seems to be pointing out that however an audience justifies its taste for violent imagery, finally it's only interested in sensational exhibitions, as the real footage here slips by almost unnoticed while the viewer waits expectantly for the next staged atrocity.

The most enduring criticism of Deodato's film is that it is guilty of the actions it seeks to condemn; it glories in elaborate displays of violence, Deodato's cast and crew do exactly the things for which the film criticises the Yates team, and it shares the Yates team's racist abuse of Yacumo and Yamamomo. The lingering shots of animal death, cheap shock tactics providing 'effects' far more realistic than the filmmakers could otherwise afford, are especially indefensible, Deodato's justification that all of the animals killed were eaten not only missing the point – the turtle sequence is particularly drawn out and horrible – but also untrue, as the snake and spider don't seem to contribute to any meals.

Yet the structure of the film goes some way towards answering the other criticisms. The positioning of the Monroe visit before the Yates footage might have prevented some critics from seeing the film's conservative message, but a closer look reveals that the two groups – Monroe's official party and Yates's cynical exploiters – behave in stark contrast to each other. Monroe is an anthropologist, and ensures that the Yacumo and Yamamomo are treated with respect: his team wait until they are invited into the villages, and defuse hostile situations with gifts. They may indulge in one of the few Western taboos not broken by the Yates party – cannibalism – but it is done in the context of acceptable exchange. They're not entirely blameless – they shoot a few Shamatari warriors to gain the Yacumos' respect, and Chaco resists Monroe's offers to help their guide carry the luggage – but compared to the Yates team they seem positively angelic.

Yates and his colleagues have no family ties and no sense of public/private boundaries, filming each other having sex, defecating and vomiting, even when they are asked not to. They intrude on the private moments of others too, filming a forced abortion and a woman's death throes, and set up 'atrocities' themselves, at one point even burning a Yacumo village down. If Monroe's group are prepared to honour patterns of exchange, the Yates team simply take what they want from the jungle; and in their greed to get the best footage, they are killed by Yamamomo whose cannibalism is a response to their unacceptable actions. They leave behind an atmosphere of fear and resentment – the Yacumos' uncharacteristic cannibalism at the start of the film is a ritual to chase the evil white men's spirits out of the jungle – and it is left to Monroe to build bridges, to reconstruct bonds of trust between the two communities.

INDUSTRY IMPACT: The least interesting of *Cannibal Holocaust*'s progeny are its purported sequels (at least two films carry the title *Cannibal Holocaust 2*, although neither has anything to do with Deodato's film) and the other films in the short-lived Italian cannibal cycle, *Eaten Alive!* (Umberto Lenzi, 1980), *Cannibal Ferox* and *Cannibal Apocalypse* (Antonio Margheriti, 1980), which share little of Deodato's intelligence.

As well as being the structural inspiration for films like *The Last Broadcast* (1998) and *The Blair Witch Project* (1999), *Cannibal Holocaust* has much in common with the confrontational cinema of the arthouse/horror fringe, being a gruelling experience comparable to Pasolini's *Salo* (1975), Agustín Villaronga's *In a Glass Cage* (1986) and Gaspar Noë's *Irreversible* (2002); but its most interesting relatives are the other genre films to explore the mechanics of film violence.

David Cronenberg's typically idiosyncratic entry, *Videodrome* (1982), started off when the director 'wanted to see what it would be like, in fact, if what the censors were saying would happen, did happen' – if images of violence had a direct and transformative effect on the viewer. The story follows Max Renn (James Woods), the buyer for Channel 83, a small outfit specialising in softcore sex and hardcore violence, as he searches for something harder than most of his suppliers can offer.

He's definitely interested when his assistant picks up Videodrome, a signal coming from Pittsburgh that features non-stop footage of women being tortured and killed against an electrified clay wall. But the Videodrome signal produces tumours, and the tumours make Max hallucinate – or is it the other way round? – as he becomes a pawn in a power battle between the evangelical

O'Blivions, celebrating the 'new flesh' caused by the tumours, and Spectacular Optical, a censorious organisation that wants to transmit Videodrome on Channel 83 and kill all of its 'sick' viewers. After his masochistic lover Nikki Brand (Debbie Harry) leaves him to audition for the show, his hallucinations take centre stage: the viewer sees only what Max sees, and shares his reality as he grows a vaginal slit in his stomach.

The first hour of the film is probably Cronenberg's finest work, an edgy exploration of masochism, voyeurism and control systems that features some of the most remarkable imagery ever to be distributed by a major studio; but the final scenes abandon any pretence at narrative, as Max is reprogrammed in a series of startling visual metaphors that ends with his death.

The Belgian *Man Bites Dog/C'est Arrivée Près de Chez Vous* (Rémy Belvaux and André Bonzel, 1992) is a remarkably polished student film following a documentary team making a film about a serial killer; far subtler and funnier than Deodato's film, it shares with it repeated literal and visual references to its documentary format, and involves its filmmakers in the killer's crimes, as they firstly help the affable Ben (co-producer Benoît Poelvoorde) dispose of bodies then shoot a rival documentary team following another killer.

Oliver Stone's *Natural Born Killers* (1994) couldn't be further from the Belgian film in its visual style, using a barrage of rapid edits and different film formats for its tale of serial killers turned celebrities. Entirely lacking the subtlety of *Man Bites Dog* in its hamfisted satire of the American consumption of suffering, it may be visually exhilarating, but like *Cannibal Holocaust* it's in many ways a perfect example of what it seeks to condemn.

Austrian director Michael Haneke's glacial explorations of the theme, *Benny's Video* (1992) and *Funny Games* (1997), are far more effective. In the first film Benny (Arno Frisch), a well-off teenager who tinkers endlessly with the video equipment in his bedroom, invites a girl back to his house only to kill her with a butcher's gun and record the entire event on video. When he shows the video to his parents, they perversely decide to protect him.

Frisch returns in *Funny Games*, as one of two young men tormenting a family on holiday on the shores of a lake. *Funny Games* is a more difficult film than its predecessor, being both more self-reflexive – Frisch (variously referred to as Paul, Jerry and Beavis in the film) repeatedly addresses the audience directly, asking them if the characters have had enough yet, and in one audacious scene rewinds the film – and more brutal.

If the young men, Peter and Paul, are unrealistic in their matching white outfits, emotionless game-playing and incessantly irritating banter, the pain of the victims is all too real. Haneke's aim seems to be to demonstrate that violence is not cathartic, or at least to deny any cathartic release within the film: the only violence seen is the shooting of Peter, which is immediately rewound and denied, and Haneke instead relies on long takes of family members sobbing in real emotional anguish.

The film works well as an astonishingly bleak psycho-thriller, which is presumably not exactly what Haneke intended. But if it is meant to be a critique of film violence in the cinematic mainstream it misses its audience, being a dour Austrian subtitled film unlikely to catch the attention of fans of action pictures; and if it is meant to attack horror it underestimates both many fans' 'endurance test' attitude towards confrontational films and some horror filmmakers' explicit concerns not to present violence as entertainment. As Michael Reeves wrote in defence of the downbeat tone of his *Witchfinder General* (1968): 'Violence is horrible, degrading and sordid. Insofar as one is going to show it on the screen at all, it should be presented as such – and the more people it shocks into sickened recognition of these facts the better.'

FINAL WORD: Deodato's approach is hardly subtle. *Cannibal Holocaust*'s TV executives are ludicrously overexcited, telling Monroe that 'People want sensation. The more you rape their senses, the happier they are', and the anthropologist's final line, 'I wonder who the real cannibals are?' brings the whole film back into the mondo sink it tries to comment on – and yet the film is still intelligent and effective in a way that subsequent entries in the cannibal cycle are not.

For all of the grey areas *Cannibal Holocaust* treads through – the repeated misogynistic scenes of punishment for adultery, based essentially on a dubious reading of Yacumo and Yamamomo sexual politics, vie with the scenes of animal slaughter for gratuitous shock value – it is an essential horror classic, a confrontational and marginal work that has lost none of its power in the 24 years since its release.

BODY HORROR

The Fly (1986)

'Be afraid. Be very afraid.'

USA, Brooksfilms, colour, 92 mins

Director: David Cronenberg
Producer: Stuart Cornfeld
**Screenplay: Charles Edward Pogue, David Cronenberg, from
a story by George Langelaan**
Cinematography: Mark Irwin
1st Assistant Director: John Board
Sound: Bryan Day
Editor: Ronald Sanders
Music: Howard Shore
Production Design: Carol Spier
The Fly **created and designed by Chris Walas Inc.**

CAST: Jeff Goldblum (*Seth Brundle*), Geena Davis (*Veronica Quaife*), John Getz (*Stathis Borans*), Joy Boushel (*Tawny*), Les Carlson (*Dr Cheevers*), George Chuvalo (*Marky*), Michael Copeman (*2nd Man in Bar*), David Cronenberg (*Gynaecologist*), Carol Lazare (*Nurse*), Shawn Hewitt (*Clerk*), Brent Myers (*Brundle Stunt Double*), Doron Kernerman and Romuald Vervin (*Gymnastic Doubles*)

SYNOPSIS: Scientist Seth Brundle meets journalist Veronica Quaife at a party, and invites her back to his lab to see what he's working on. He demonstrates his telepods – matter transmitters – for her, and she decides to run a story on him. He doesn't want her to, but her editor and ex-boyfriend at Particle Magazine, Stathis Borans, doesn't believe the story anyway. Seth offers her an exclusive, on condition that she wait until he can teleport organic objects.

Stathis's interest perks up when he does some research into Seth's background, but Veronica tells him she's not doing the story now. Seth tries teleporting a baboon, but the experiment fails. Still, it's an icebreaker for him and Veronica, and they have sex.

After experimenting with a teleported steak, he works on a change to the programme and experiments on another baboon, which survives. He and Veronica celebrate, but then she finds a dummy magazine cover Stathis has sent, threatening to expose the experiment.

She visits Stathis, and agrees to share information about the experiment with him. Seth realises they used to be a couple, gets drunk and teleports himself without realising that a fly is in the telepod with him. He is invigorated by the experience, and later encourages Veronica to try it; after marathon sex, she finds hairs in a wound on his back, and snips one off. She refuses to be teleported, so he goes looking for another partner.

At a bar he breaks another man's arm during an arm-wrestling contest then takes a woman ('Tawny') home. He puts himself through the telepods again then has sex with her, but she leaves when Veronica arrives. Veronica has tested the hairs, which appear to be of insect origin. He kicks her out, then checks the computer and finds that he has fused on a molecular-genetic level with a fly, becoming Brundlefly.

Four weeks later he calls Veronica, who goes to see him. He's now on crutches, and thinks that he has some kind of cancer. Stathis advises her not to go back – it might be contagious – but she returns to video him. He's walking on the ceiling, and feeling more positive about his transformation.

Veronica is pregnant, and dreams about giving birth to a giant maggot. Brundlefly finds that the only way to arrest the transformation is to fuse himself with another human. Veronica visits him but is unable to tell him about the pregnancy. Stathis arranges a midnight abortion, but Brundlefly breaks in and kidnaps her. She refuses to have the baby, so Brundlefly decides to fuse himself with her and their unborn child.

Stathis goes to Seth's lab with a shotgun but is attacked by Brundefly, who then prepares the fusion experiment. Stathis shoots the interlinking cable, and Brundlefly is fused with a telepod. He comes out and puts the shotgun to his head; Veronica shoots him dead.

ORIGINS AND INSPIRATION: The transformed body is one of horror's most enduring images, from ancient legends of wolfmen to the mild-mannered Dr Jekyll's savage alter ego Mr Hyde. Such tales mostly revolve around sexual repression and development: *The Wolf Man*'s (George Waggner, 1941) lycanthropy is a projection of Larry Talbot's sexual frustration in his relationship with Jenny Williams; Irena's fear of transformation in *Cat People* (1942) is figured in explicitly Freudian terms, with images of keys and speared cats repeated throughout the film; while *The Company of Wolves* (Neil Jordan, 1984) and *Ginger Snaps* (John Fawcett, 2000) both interpret lycanthropy as a metaphor for the onset of female puberty. *The Company of Wolves* is only, here, making explicit in a series of exquisite set-pieces what is coded in all fairy tales: the educational dramatisation for children of psychological crises of a sexual or familial nature.

Advances in technology meant that transformation scenes were very much to the fore in films from the late 70s and through the 80s: a rash of werewolf films took full advantage of the skills of make-up men like Rob Bottin and Rick Baker, with *The Howling* (Joe Dante, 1981) and *An American Werewolf in London* (John Landis, 1981) hinging on impressive effects sequences. And transformation didn't stop at a wolf snout: **The Exorcist** showed a barely pubescent girl turning into a demon, and *The Thing* (1982) could imitate any form imaginable, while David Cronenberg's explorations of the New Flesh demanded the coinage of a new phrase to describe them – body horror.

Body horror – which plays on fears of the body as monstrous and uncontrollable – is related to technology in two ways. Firstly, through the mechanics of representation: Cronenberg's early films, for instance, are showcases for effects technology as much as anything else; and secondly, through a sense that the body has become unstable and infinitely adaptable through science. The literary correlatives for this are the cyborgs and wetware obsessions of 80s cyberpunk and JG Ballard's psycho-sexual fusion of man and machine in *Crash*, but the idea also reflects real and subtler changes to the way we relate to our bodies.

Since the 80s an idealised vision of the human body has been formed by the advertising, entertainment and sex industries, in what critic Naomi Wolf has famously called the 'beauty myth': an aspirational body that cannot be obtained without technological intervention along the lines of plastic surgery and liposuction. What Wolf has described as the 'irresponsible medical experiments using desperate women as lab animals' recalls the mad scientists Cronenberg has resurrected from the early years of horror cinema – nine French women died during the initial liposuction trials.

But such innovations had at least the potential for more creative use: individuals have been able to change gender, a recurring theme in Cronenberg's work, and the 80s also saw a growing interest in body modification – through tattooing, piercing and scarification – in an apparent revolt against idealised and over-arching representations of the body beautiful.

The Fly (Kurt Neumann, 1958), adapted from a story by George Langelaan, tells the tale of a scientist who accidentally switches head and hand with a fly while experimenting with matter transmitters; after a futile search for the fly with his head, the scientist asks his wife to kill him by crushing his upper body with a hydraulic press. The film is talky and given a camp gloss by the presence of Vincent Price, but contains some startling images – Franju was said to be a fan, and the scientist's cloaked head recalls an Ernst print – and a degree of wilful perversity. But its message is finally deeply conservative, with the scientist destroying his matter transmitter before his death: there are some things man is not meant to know.

In 1984 Charles Edward Pogue (*Psycho III*) approached producer Stuart Cornfeld with a script for a remake, and Cornfeld – who'd previously put Mel Brooks and David Lynch together for *The Elephant Man* (1980) – sold the concept to Brooksfilms to produce and 20th Century Fox to release.

Preproduction was due to start in the UK in early 1985, with ad director Bob Bierman slated to direct and special effects from Chris Tucker (*Company of Wolves*); but a personal tragedy forced Bierman to back out, and Cornfeld approached Cronenberg, whose films he'd long admired. The director, who'd seen the original as a child and retained a nostalgic affection for the idea, had initiated an insect project of his own, 'Six Legs', for Universal – a comedy in which entomologists discover a Caribbean insect which is addictive when eaten – but had failed to get it off the ground. Since *The Dead Zone* (1983) he had been working for a year on a script by Dan O'Bannon and Ronald Shusett (see **Alien**) for *Total Recall* (1990), but after several rewrites he, Shusett and producer Di Laurentiis could not come to any agreement; so when Cornfeld approached him with *The Fly*, he accepted only on condition that he could rewrite the script extensively and shoot the film in Canada.

Cornfeld and Brooks were happy with this, and Cronenberg was inspired by some of Pogue's script, graphic material 'just like what I would have done'. What he didn't like was the characters and their attitudes – Pogue had retained the destruction of the teleporters, which Cronenberg thought was ridiculous, and also had the scientist unable to speak from relatively early in the film. Cronenberg wanted an articulate scientist who would rationalise what was happening to him throughout his transformation, and came up with new names and personalities for the key characters, as well as rewriting most of the dialogue.

DIRECTOR: Cronenberg has described his films as 'rehearsals or experiments rather than statements of belief', and 'experiments' gives us a good place to start. The director is the model mad scientist, creating sterile environments in which his experiments can run their course regardless of political or moral concerns; and he clearly has sympathy for the well-meaning tinkerers who unleash mayhem in his early films, distinguishing his resurrection of the mad scientist, a figure missing from most genre product of the 70s and 80s, from *Frankenstein*'s reactionary fear of science:

> The thing about man, the unique thing, is that he creates his own environment. It's in his nature to try to take control of it away from chance. So in a sense my doctors and scientists are all heroes. Essentially, they're symbolic of what every human tries to do when he brushes his teeth.

The scientists in *Shivers* (1975) and *Rabid* (1976) are catalysts for change, rather than the films' central focus: they take a back seat as their experiments go haywire and lead to widespread social chaos. But Cronenberg's focus soon shifted to the realm of the personal, and *The Fly* represents his most economical plot to date: Brundle the scientist initiates the experiment and Brundle the human suffers the consequences.

The director shares with William Burroughs, an important influence, an interest in systems of control, whether sexual (*Shivers, Rabid*), familial (*The Brood* (1979), *Scanners* (1980)) or even chemical (the addictions of *Scanners, Dead Ringers* (1988) and *Naked Lunch* (1991)). The sterile environment of Starliner Towers almost demands the savage outbreak of sexual energy in *Shivers*, and chaos is surely preferable to the corporate control of sinister institutions like Consec (*Scanners*) and Spectacular Optical (*Videodrome* (1982)); but Cronenberg remains profoundly ambivalent about his films' chaotic outbursts, and about the 60s programme of liberation as an end in itself. Stasis is not the answer – 'I think [the unconscious mind] must be interfered with despite the fact that the consequences are sometimes horrific. You have to live a life that balances between safety and disaster' – but perhaps, his films seem to say, some things *should* be repressed; if the unconscious is, to use filmmaker Guy Maddin's term, a 'roiling, furious, unforgiving and stinking realm', some control is necessary, to avoid the perceptual chaos of *Videodrome* or the undifferentiated lust of *Shivers*.

The battle site for control in Cronenberg's films is the body. The director's sense of death is profoundly physical, and the Cartesian mind/body split provides a profound source of horror for him – why should the mind die along with the body? His scientists, well-meaning innovators convinced that they can improve humanity through rational control of the body (with the exception of Dr Emil Hobbes in *Shivers*), represent the mind's side of the Cartesian split in attempting to deny the body its due; but the flesh revolts, colonies demanding independence in ways the mind cannot foresee.

The focus on the body has been married to developments in special-effects technology, providing the spectacular set pieces that made him a poster boy for the *Fangoria* generation and earned him the moniker 'Baron of Blood': Joe Blasco's bladder effects in *Shivers*, Nola Carveth biting into her external womb in *The Brood*, the show-stopping exploding head in *Scanners* and the hideous death by mutation of Barry Convex in *Videodrome* all kept horror's teen male market happy, providing the commercial success that has allowed the director to keep on following his own radical agenda.

Such 'gross-out' effects, along with what critics have often interpreted as a deep strain of sexual disgust running through his work, are for Cronenberg attempts to define a new aesthetics of the body. In the director's universe beauty is more than skin deep, and his films explore the relationship between internal and external – Nola Carveth's external womb, or Max Renn's vaginal stomach slit in *Videodrome*, are characteristic Cronenberg images. According to the director his attitude towards these displays is 'not disgust. It's fascination, but it's also a willingness to look at what is really there without flinching, and to say that this is what we're made of, as strange and as disgusting as it might seem at times', and in *Dead Ringers* Elliott is given one of the director's most oft-quoted lines: 'I've often thought there should be beauty contests for the insides of bodies – you know, best spleen, most perfectly developed kidneys.'

The director's wilful adoption of radical points of view also informs his ideas about disease. As a plaque on the wall of one of *Shivers*' doctors puts it, 'Sex is the invention of a clever venereal disease', and Brundle is stricken by a 'disease with a purpose'; Cronenberg has argued that 'perhaps some diseases perceived as diseases which destroy a well-functioning machine, in fact change the machine into a machine that does something else, and we have to figure out what it is that the machine now does'.

But this is a good example of the discrepancy many critics have pointed to between Cronenberg's articulate comments on his films and the experience of actually watching them. He has said of *Shivers* that 'I identify with the parasites', and argues that the film has a happy ending – the characters leaving Starliner Towers to infect the rest of the world look healthy and content – but it's undeniable that sex is presented as grotesque throughout the film: everything from incest to bestiality and paedophilia is at least hinted at, and 'normal' sexual relations seem impossible.

Similarly, the director's positive views on disease and transformation are rarely visible in the films themselves: most of them end in despair, even if there are hints of positive outcomes in *Scanners* and *Videodrome*, and no amount of rationalising on the part of Seth Brundle changes the fact that his transformation is monstrous and unstoppable. Cronenberg attributes his downbeat tone – he is one of the few directors in North America allowed the luxury of an unhappy ending – to a conscious avoidance of false optimism, a refusal to lie to the audience.

And yet for all their bleak endings, many of his films demonstrate a sense of humour and playfulness, an ecstatic energy feeding off the vicarious pleasure the viewer takes in the shattering of social convention. The parasite landing on an elderly lady's umbrella in *Shivers*, or Ron Mlodzik's disparaging comment on seeing Marilyn Chambers' injured body in *Rabid* – 'you'd think they could cover it up with a sheet' – show a playful self-awareness at odds with the director's sombre reputation; if *The Brood*, *Videodrome* and *The Dead Zone* have colder tones, *The Fly* allows Brundle to joke even as his body falls apart.

The director's sympathy for the agents of chaos and disruption is also clearly visible in his casting. The male leads of all his earlier films are weak characters who make for poor identification figures, and only when the central characters are both the agents of and sites for change does Cronenberg's skill as an actor's director come to the fore, with James Woods (*Videodrome*), Christopher Walken (*The Dead Zone*) and Jeremy Irons (*Dead Ringers*) doing career highlights with the director.

The director's first three features focused on women's bodies being experimented on by men, and Cronenberg has been criticised for his supposed womb envy or sexism. *The Brood* in particular has come under fire, most notably by critic Robin Wood, as a film favouring the oppression of women. The director has responded by pointing out that he has been attacked both for portraying women as sexually passive (*Shivers*) and predatory (*Rabid*); he's happy not to toe the party line, and points out that 'Someone who writes an anti-sexist tract is not going to write a great anything.' *Videodrome* was similarly criticised for its portrayal of Nikki Brand, a masochist who at one point burns her breast with a cigarette, but Cronenberg firmly believes that individual characters should not be taken to represent groups, and points out that 'to censor myself, to censor my fantasies, to censor my unconscious would devalue myself as a film-maker'.

For Cronenberg a focus on the sociopolitical interpretations of horror often misses the wider picture, the key concerns of death and separation: 'The appeal of horror is beyond politics. It's accessible to political criticism, but the appeal is very direct – right into the viscera, before it gets to the brain. And you don't have politics in the viscera.'

Gender roles in Cronenberg's films are far too complicated to invite criticisms of sexism or misogyny in any case. The commercial implications of his casting often escape critics, with the director struggling to finance *Rabid* because of its female lead; and since *Videodrome* Cronenberg has explored the kind of polymorphous perversity that characterised his first experimental features, *Stereo* (1969) and *Crimes of the Future* (1970), with many of his films involving the transformation of men into female forms: Max Renn's vaginal videoslit in *Videodrome*, for instance, Rene Gallimard's wilful ignorance of *M Butterfly*'s (1993) masculinity, or the explorations of bisexuality in *Dead Ringers* and *Crash* (1996).

Cronenberg was interested in both fiction and science from an early age, and enrolled in Toronto University to read biological sciences, but transferred after a few months to an English language and literature course. He wanted to be a novelist, and was heavily influenced by Burroughs and Nabokov, but felt hampered by his adoption of their styles. He dropped out of college and travelled around Europe; when he returned home the underground film movement had hit Toronto. He knew some of the filmmakers involved, and decided to try his hand, learning about the mechanics of filmmaking and shooting his first short, *Transfer*, in 1966, a seven-minute film featuring a psychiatrist and his patient in the middle of a field.

Along with several friends, he helped set up the Canadian Filmmakers' Co-operative, after the New York model, and made *From the Drain* in 1966. His first longer film, *Stereo* (1969), was partly funded by a Canada Council writing grant and was shown at several festivals: in its surgically created telepaths tested by scientists at the Canadian Academy for Erotic Enquiry it foreshadows several themes of the director's mature work.

After his second longer film, *Crimes of the Future* (1970), he decided to move into commercial filmmaking, and wrote the script for *Shivers* (see **INDUSTRY IMPACT, Invasion of the Body Snatchers**) in 1972. Resisting the dubious attractions of working south of the border (he has remained committed to making films in Canada throughout his career) he approached the Canadian Film Development Corporation (CFDC) for help financing the film. *Shivers* was a commercial success, but saw the first of many attacks from critics, with Robert Fulford's scathing condemnation ensuring that the CFDC could give the director's second feature only clandestine support.

Rabid (see **INDUSTRY IMPACT, Eyes Without a Face**) followed, like *Shivers* an apocalyptic vision of the breakdown of society through an explosion of sexual energy; the film's success led to a higher budget for the director's next two films, *Fast Company* (1979), an anomalous B-movie about racing-car drivers, and *The Brood*. The latter's exploration of the break-up of a relationship mirrored the failure of his first marriage, making it Cronenberg's most personal film to date; and it is often considered the director's first mature work, shifting the focus from the social to the personal and reducing the scale of the earlier films for the first of the director's increasingly claustrophobic settings. Yet the film's marketing as a horror/exploitation picture didn't help its sales, its bleak tone alienating many traditional horror fans while mainstream audiences gave it a wide berth; it was followed by *Scanners* (see **INDUSTRY IMPACT, Don't Look Now**), Cronenberg's purest SF film and an unusually optimistic entry.

Videodrome (see **INDUSTRY IMPACT, Cannibal Holocaust**) was his first film to be backed by major Hollywood distribution, but its uncompromising vision failed to find a market; disappointed by its lacklustre response the director moved for the first time to somebody else's work, with an adaptation of Stephen King's *The Dead Zone* (see **INDUSTRY IMPACT, Don't Look Now**).

The Fly in a sense marked the end of his involvement in the horror genre – his films were always ultimately *sui generis*, but toyed with horror themes and images, the director appreciating the wildness encouraged by the genre. He has never really tried to disassociate himself from horror, even as his films have become less genre-related, or to use it as a springboard to enter the mainstream – if anything he has followed commercial successes with more personal projects – but his later films tend to lack the humour and verve of his genre work.

Cronenberg then became his own producer with a project that had been gestating for six years – *Dead Ringers* (see **INDUSTRY IMPACT, Eyes Without a Face**) – and his subsequent films have been if anything still more idiosyncratic. *Naked*

Lunch, a surprisingly flat adaptation of Burroughs' unfilmable novel, failed to capture its emotional and visceral punch; the writer's influence is clearly visible throughout Cronenberg's work, and perversely other films he's made, particularly *Videodrome* and *Existenz* (1999), seem more Burroughsian.

M Butterfly reunited the director with *Dead Ringers*' Jeremy Irons, but was one of his few misfires, and *Crash* followed *Naked Lunch*'s model of a flatness verging on the ludicrous; again other films by the director seem closer to Ballard, with *Shivers* recalling the author's *High Rise*. *Existenz* was a return to form, an entertaining retread of *Videodrome*'s existential territory that is closer in spirit to Philip K Dick's shifting realities than any explicit Dick adaptation. The director's most recent film is another literary adaptation, Patrick McGrath's *Spider* (2002), an understated exploration of a schizophrenic's world.

CASTING: Cronenberg had always envisaged Goldblum and Davis, a real-life couple who had previously appeared together in *Transylvania 6500* (Rudy De Luca, 1985), in the lead roles. Cornfeld was initially reluctant, insisting that he look at other actresses and even offering the part of Brundle to Michael Keaton, but finally agreed. The couple's familiarity meant that the sex scenes were easy to shoot – in fact more explicit scenes were shot that did not end up in the film – but it was at first difficult for them to play convincing strangers, being too close to each other's mannerisms.

Jeff Goldblum seems to be already part-insect before even going through the telepod, full of twitches and tics and a peculiarly stop-start speech pattern; but his transformation into Brundlefly is astonishingly credible given the layers of make-up under which he had to work.

Goldblum, whose first feature-film appearance was in *Death Wish* (Michael Winner, 1974) as 'Freak #1', has appeared in several other genre films, including *Invasion of the Body Snatchers* (1978), *Mister Frost* (Phillipe Setbon, 1990) and *Jurassic Park* (Steven Spielberg, 1993); he also co-starred with Davis again in 1988's *Earth Girls are Easy* (Julien Temple). Davis appeared in *Beetlejuice* (Tim Burton, 1988), but is perhaps best known for Ridley Scott's *Thelma and Louise* (1991).

Cronenberg himself played the gynaecologist delivering Geena Davis's maggot baby, at her request – she didn't want a stranger in the part. The director also took a cameo role in *Shivers*, as well as appearing in *Nightbreed* (Clive Barker, 1990), *To Die For* (Gus Van Sant, 1995) and *Jason X* (James Isaac, 2001).

PRODUCTION: Production started in December 1985 in Canada, on sets constructed at the Kleinburg Studios north of Toronto. For the 72-day shoot Cronenberg surrounded himself with his usual crew: this was his sixth feature with Board, Irwin, Day, Spier and Sanders, and Chris Walas (*Gremlins*) replaced Tucker on special effects.

Shooting in Canada kept costs down, and Cronenberg brought the film in at under $11 million. The effects scenes were predictably the major expense, with many of the props, including the computer terminal, being built to work up to a certain level. Goldblum's final Brundlefly make-up took almost five hours to apply; earlier stages had been based on images of diseased bodies studied by Walas's team.

A coda was shot, in which Veronica dreams of giving birth to Brundle's butterfly child, but it was removed after test screenings showed that most audiences were unhappy with the leap from the tragic death of Brundlefly to a more easeful ending. Other sequences shot but cut in the final edit were a cat and baboon sent through the telepods, only for the fused creature to be beaten to death by Brundlefly; and a scene of Brundefly climbing on the exterior wall of his building, an insect limb emerging from his side.

SOUNDTRACK: Howard Shore's orchestral score opens with a sense of wonder familiar from other big-budget SF releases, but grows more doom-laden as Brundle's transformation takes over, and climaxes in a simple but powerful motif that emphasises the finality of the film's climax. Shore has scored all of Cronenberg's films since *The Brood*, apart from *The Dead Zone*; he was also the composer of choice for big-budget 90s psycho fare like *The Silence of the Lambs* (1991), *Single White Female* (Barbet Schroeder, 1992), *Se7en* (David Fincher, 1995) and *The Cell* (Tarsem Singh, 2000), as well as scoring *Ed Wood* (Tim Burton, 1994), *The Game* (David Fincher, 1997) and Peter Jackson's *Lord of the Rings* trilogy.

RELEASE: *The Fly* was Cronenberg's biggest box-office success to date, making more money than all of the director's previous films combined and receiving good reviews from tabloids and the quality press alike; *Sight & Sound* summed it up as 'Tightly paced, stylish acrobatics, cowgum gore'. Its virtues were also recognised by the industry: Chris Walas Inc was awarded the Oscar for Best Make-up in 1987.

CRITICAL EYE: *The Fly* plays with our expectations from the start. Brundle is aware of his relationship to the classic mad scientist, wearing five sets of the same clothes, Einstein-style, and hammering out melodramatic chords on his piano when Veronica visits him; when she tries to leave he refers to the telepods, only half-jokingly: 'You've already seen them. I can't let you leave alive.' Unlike the scientist in the original film, who takes pains to point out the socially beneficial uses of his invention – 'humanity need never want, nor fear, again!' – Brundle's attention, for all that his motion sickness may have driven his research, is fixed on the way it makes him feel. After going through the telepods he feels purged, finally 'realising [his] personal potential': rather than use his invention to transport vast quantities of grain to impoverished countries, as the scientist of the first film plans to, he looks for a woman to go through as well.

His evangelical fervour and demonstrations of physical strength recall another of *The Fly*'s relatives, the superhero story; his arm-wrestling contest in a bar is straight out of a Marvel Comics origins story, and he even talks about the 'dynamic duo' he could make with a willing partner. *The Fly* is *Spiderman*, done with a Wellsian flair; and Cronenberg's script isn't far from Wells's *The Invisible Man*, which again takes a central fantastic fact and puts it in an utterly credible environment, dealing with the mundane practicalities of invisibility much as Cronenberg shows Brundle-fly's increasing inability to perform normal human functions.

Ironically, as in *Dead Ringers*, the appearance of a woman makes the male protagonist's emotionally stunted life whole, but also catalyses his destruction. In neither film is this presented as the woman's fault: it is misinterpretations of her actions that lead to disaster. Here Seth gets drunk enough to make his fatal error because he thinks Veronica is having sex with her ex-boyfriend; and in *Dead Ringers* Beverly descends into prescription-drug limbo when he thinks Clare is having an affair. Far from being the villain of the piece, Veronica is *The Fly*'s most sympathetic character, lacking the arrogance and instability of the men, and in the most touching scene – and one that reportedly got more gasps of revulsion from audiences than the transformation or foot-melting sequences – demonstrates her love by hugging Brundlefly even as he falls apart in her arms.

There is an inevitability to both *The Fly* and *Dead Ringers* that recalls Greek tragedy, here helped by a claustrophobic atmosphere – most of the film, which Cronenberg has described as 'three people in a room', takes place in Brundle's lab – and the relationships between the characters. Borans seems interested in Veronica principally for her body, as mirrored in Brundle's attempt to fuse his body with hers. Both Brundle and Veronica struggle to maintain control over their bodies: Brundle with the metamorphosis changing him by the minute, and Veronica with not only Borans and Brundle but also the reluctant abortionist. Even Tawny's sexuality is controlled by other people (Cronenberg returned to the theme with the twin gynaecologists of *Dead Ringers*), access to her body being used as a pawn in a bet between two men.

Some critics have interpreted the transformation – explicitly figured as disease – as a metaphor for AIDS, although the director resists this reading. For him 'the film is a metaphor for ageing, a compression of any love affair that goes to the end of one of the lover's lives ... Every love story must end tragically.' Ageing is, like Brundle's condition, a continuous process of transformation, and is referred to explicitly, if in passing, by Veronica when she justifies her speed in telling Borans about Seth's experiment: 'I'm not getting any younger.' The theme gives an added poignancy to Veronica's decision to have an abortion: Brundle's only other means of cheating death is thus removed.

Brundle's transformation is so accelerated that his ideas always lag slightly behind his situation, although he tries to interpret the changes in a positive light. He refuses any treatment, keen not to become 'another tumourous bore', but documents his changes with scientific detachment leavened by a surprising degree of humour, videoing his idiosyncratic eating habits and keeping a museum of vestigial body parts, containing what appears to be a penis in a jar.

This constant mutation is one of the many factors distinguishing *The Fly* from other transformation narratives, and the fact that Brundle changes into an insect cannot be considered incidental. Insects are among the most alien species for higher mammals, although we live in such close proximity; our lineage separated from theirs before the Cambrian explosion, more than 600 million years ago. As Brundle points out, 'insects don't have politics', but what they do have is an adaptability and ability to transform that make them perfect vectors for Cronenberg's literalised metaphors.

Insects that pass through pupal metamorphosis have their bodies entirely broken down and re-formed in their transmutation from larval to mature stage, much as Brundle's telepods disintegrate and reintegrate matter, and the insect body, built on multiple repeated segments that can be altered or fused to create new structures, has a modular flexibility that leads it into the first rank of the Cronenbergian 'new flesh'. If humans are 'afraid to dive into the plasma pool', or unable to 'penetrate beyond society's sick, grey fear of the flesh', as Brundle accuses Veronica of being, insects have no such restrictions.

But becoming Brundlefly isn't the final transformation: Seth finally fuses with a telepod, recalling the man-machine hybrids of *Videodrome* or even *Fast Company* (1979), and anticipating *Crash* and the bio-ports of *Existenz*. Yet even now – after watching Brundlefly melt her ex-boyfriend's hand and ankle with insect vomit and nearly becoming fused with him herself – Veronica can hardly bring herself to pull the trigger of the shotgun the creature holds to its head, still recognising her lover under the layers of prosthetic effects.

INDUSTRY IMPACT: Although *The Fly* spawned a sequel, directed by Chris Walas, which jettisoned most of Cronenberg's ideas in favour of a concentration on gloopy effects, the director's influence has had its most interesting effects in Japan. The country has long had a cultural interest in transformation, as countless tales of shape-shifting ghosts and spirits attest, and Japanese fantastic cinema had previously embraced the theme in films ranging from *Attack of the Mushroom People/Matango* (Ishirô Honda, 1963), in which a shipwrecked group eat and turn into mushrooms, to *Guts of a Virgin/Shojo no Harawata* (Kazuo 'Gaira' Komizo, 1985), in which a rape victim mutates into a monster with a grotesquely oversized penis (with a mouth, naturally) she uses to kill one of the film's villains.

Evil Dead Trap/Shiryo no Wana (Toshiharu Ikeda, 1989) shows a definite Cronenberg influence in its tale of a TV hostess being sent a snuff video which seems to show her own torture and death; one male character at the end of the film even gives birth to an evil twin, recalling Cronenberg's gender-switching transformations. *Tetsuo* (Shinya Tsukamoto, 1990) uses *Videodrome*'s man-machine imagery for a stylised techno-nightmare that draws equally on David Lynch's *Eraserhead* (1976), although the central character's discovery of a metal spike emerging from his cheek is straight out of *The Fly*.

Organ (Kei Fujiwara, 1996) shares *Tetsuo*'s quality of surreal nightmare in its depiction of organ dealers and a host of multi-coloured bodily fluids – tellingly, both this and *Tetsuo* feature images of human cocoons, filtering *The Fly*'s insect concerns through their respective worlds of metal and meat – but probably the most delirious transformations of the new Japanese cinema are the snail people of *Uzumaki* (Kei Fujiwara, 2000). Here transformation is less, as has often been suggested, a metaphor for Japanese cultural instability and economic uncertainty, than a gloriously weird celebration of special-effects potential, closer to *From Beyond* (Stuart Gordon, 1986) than Cronenberg's body horror.

FINAL WORD: While *The Fly* isn't Cronenberg's best film – *Videodrome* and *Dead Ringers* are more likely contenders for the title – it is one of his tightest and most successful evocations of body horror, and marks a key turning point in the director's work, marrying his earlier reliance on effects-driven set pieces with real emotional warmth.

As Terrence Rafferty wrote in *Sight & Sound*, Cronenberg 'seems to have isolated, in remarkably potent form, the poignant monster form that runs through so many horror pictures', and it is this aspect of the relationship between Veronica and Seth, beyond the film's ideas or effects, that is its enduring legacy. *The Fly* is the genre's most moving love story.

HORROR COMICS

Evil Dead 2 (1987)

'Kiss Your Nerves Good-Bye!'

Alternative title: Evil Dead 2: Dead by Dawn

US, Renaissance Pictures, colour, 82 mins

Directed by Sam Raimi
Written by Sam Raimi and Scott Spiegel
Co-producer: Bruce Campbell
Executive Producers: Alex De Benedetti, Irvin Shapiro
Producer: Robert G Tapert
Music: Original Music by Joseph LoDuca; also features
uncredited excerpts from 'Danse Macabre, Op 40' by
Camille Saint-Saëns
Cinematography: Peter Deming
Editor: Kaye Davis
Art Director: Randy Bennett, Philip Duffin
Special Make-up Design and Creation: Mark Shostrom
Special Make-up Effects Unit Crew: Howard Berger, Robert
Kurtzman, Gregory Nicotero, Shannon Shea, Aaron Sims,
Bryant Tausek, Mike Trcic
First Assistant Director: Joseph Winogradoff

Supervising Sound Editor: David West
Stop-Motion Animation: Doug Beswick

CAST: Bruce Campbell (*Ashley 'Ash' J Williams*), Sarah Berry (*Annie Knowby*), Dan Hicks (*Jake*), Kassie Wesley (*Bobbie Joe*), Theodore Raimi (*Possessed Henrietta*), Denise Bixler (*Linda*), Richard Domeier (*Ed Getley*), John Peaks (*Professor Raymond Knowby*), Lou Hancock (*Henrietta Knowby*), Snowy Winters (*Dancer* [dance sequence]), Sid Abrams (*Fake Shemp*), Josh Becker (*Fake Shemp*), Scott Spiegel (*Fake Shemp*), Thomas Kidd (*Fake Shemp*), Mitch Cantor (*Fake Shemp*), Jenny Griffith (*Fake Shemp*), William Preston Robertson (*the Hand, the Dark Spirit, the Deer Head, the Enchanted Objects* [voice])

SYNOPSIS: Ash takes his girlfriend Linda to a cabin in the woods. There he finds a tape recording by Professor Knowby, describing his discovery of the Book of the Dead and reading out passages from it. Linda is possessed by a demon, and Ash decapitates her; then he too becomes possessed, although when the sun rises he reverts to normal.

Ash tries to drive away, but the bridge is down. Back at the cabin, he is attacked by Linda's headless body. When his hand is bitten by her head, it too becomes possessed and attacks him, so he saws it off with a chainsaw.

Meanwhile Knowby's daughter Annie is en route, with her boyfriend Ed; they are bringing her father missing pages from the Book of the Dead. When they find that the bridge is down, locals Jake and Bobbie Joe lead them to the cabin. Ash shoots at the door when he hears them, but is overpowered by Ed and Jake.

Annie sees the bloodied chainsaw and can't find her parents, so they lock Ash in the cellar, fearing the worst. But then they listen to the tape player, and find that the professor locked his possessed wife in the cellar; they only just manage to pull Ash out before he is killed by the demonic Henrietta. Ed turns into a demon and attacks Annie, but Ash hacks him to pieces.

The spirit of Professor Knowby appears, and tells them that the Book's missing pages reveal how to get rid of the demons. Bobbie Joe runs into the woods, and is attacked by trees; Jake takes Ash's gun, throws the missing pages in the cellar and forces the others outside to look for her. But Ash turns demonic again and attacks him; Annie hides in the house, and accidentally stabs Jake when he comes back. She tries to drag him into the house for safety, but he is pulled into the cellar and killed.

Ash turns back to normal and collects the missing pages from the cellar, but Henrietta savages him; he only manages to kill her when Annie distracts her with a lullaby. Annie reads from the missing pages, and the cabin is assaulted by trees and a huge demon face. She is stabbed by Ash's possessed hand, but finishes reading out the pages, and the tree demons are sucked into a vortex to another dimension. Unfortunately so is Ash. He is surrounded by people in armour who are just about to kill him when they are attacked by a demon and flee; Ash kills it with his shotgun and is hailed as their saviour.

ORIGINS AND INSPIRATION: As Alfred Hitchcock has pointed out, comedy and horror are Siamese twin genres, joined at the nervous laugh. Both defy easy categorisation, with an influence far broader than their respective genres; both have a visceral effect, relying on the balance between nervous tension and cathartic release; and both have an anarchic interest in the overthrow of order. As David Cronenberg has observed, 'We all need periodic releases from the tyranny of good taste.'

A direct line of ghoulish humour can be drawn from Jacobean revenge tragedy to EC Comics, and even early horror films parodied a form that had hardly been born, with James Whale's Universal gems (*The Old Dark House* (1932), *The Invisible Man* (1933), **Bride of Frankenstein**) displaying a deliciously mordant wit. But such sophistication didn't last for long: soon the only horror pictures Universal was making were parodies, unfunny Abbott and Costello vehicles that traded on the status of Frankenstein's monster, Dracula and the wolfman as cultural icons.

The birth of the teenager in the 50s gave new expression to these old forms in barely coded metaphors for puberty and the oncoming responsibilities of the adult world, as youths variously sprouted hair or fangs as they wondered why they couldn't get a date: *I Was a Teenage Werewolf* (Gene Fowler Jr, 1957) was the sideshow reflection of *Rebel Without a Cause* (Nicholas Ray, 1955), but didn't take itself nearly so seriously. And if the paranoid fantasies of the 50s (**Invasion of the Body Snatchers**) were played straight, many of the monster movies filling drive-ins through the decade were meant to be fun first and foremost: who could take films like *Attack of the Crab Monsters* (Roger Corman, 1957) or *Attack of the Giant Leeches* (Bernard A Kowalski, 1959) seriously?

Showmen like Roger Corman and William Castle tapped into the zeitgeist, with sick horror comedies like *A Bucket of Blood* (Corman, 1959) and a grab-bag of teen-friendly gimmicks: Castle's two haunted-house movies, *House on Haunted Hill* (1958) and *Thirteen Ghosts* (1960), used in-cinema effects like Emergo, 'more startling than 3-D!', in which a glow-in-the-dark skeleton was floated above the audience's heads on a pulley, or 'Illusion-O', a variation on 3-D glasses where audiences were given 'ghost viewers' and 'ghost removers' to defend against abject terror. But probably Castle's most famous effect was for *The Tingler* (1959): 'Percepto' involved electric vibrators attached to cinema seats, which trembled during a scene where the titular creature, a centipede-like manifestation of fear that can only be stopped by screaming, escaped in a cinema.

The late 50s also saw ghoulish fun embraced as a way of consuming horror. The first issue of Forrest J Ackerman's pun-filled *Famous Monsters of Filmland* was published in 1958, featuring sections like 'Fang Mail' and 'Readers' Die-jest', and influenced a generation of directors who, like Joe Dante (*Piranha* (1978), *The Howling* (1981), *Gremlins* (1984), *Matinee* (1993)), brought a love of demented 50s monster mayhem to their films. Meanwhile horror hosts like Vampira, Zacherley and Ghoulardi served as EC-style Cryptkeepers to square-eyed children around the US, introducing monster movies on local TV networks with their tongue firmly in cheek.

When Herschell Gordon Lewis and his partner David Friedman saw that the market for the nudie pictures they had been making in the early 60s was drying up, they tried to work out how they could make an impact as low-budget filmmakers. Which topics would sell best, cost least to shoot and be avoided by the major studios? It didn't take them long to come up with an answer: gore. Excessively violent images of tongues ripped out, limbs pulped, bodies dismembered – it didn't matter if the effects weren't convincing, as long as audiences were shocked.

1963's *Blood Feast* was the first gore film, and effectively redefined the horror genre with its tale of an Egyptian caterer, Fuad Ramses, attempting to invoke the goddess Ishtar through a feast of body parts. Astonishingly inept even by Lewis's estimation, like many zero-budget genre films it works best when viewed as a comedy; but it still pulled in the slack-jawed punters, and remains Lewis's most successful film even though his later work was technically more proficient, more intentionally funny and gorier.

2000 Maniacs (Herschell Gordon Lewis, 1964) showed the slow deaths of a group of Northern tourists visiting the South for a Civil War centennial; the same director's *Color Me Blood Red* (1965) followed a maniacal artist's search for the perfect shade of red; and *The Gruesome Twosome* (1967) ramped up the black humour with its mother and son team looking for fresh scalps for their wig business. His last two gore films were both sicker and more violent: showing a clear debt to the Grand Guignol, the Parisian theatre that had achieved widespread notoriety for its theatrical displays of limb-lopping by the mid-20s, *The Wizard of Gore* (1970) involved a stage musician inviting women to be sawn in half and have swords thrust down their throats; while with *The Gore Gore Girls* (1972) Lewis signed off with a flourish, showcasing the absurdly gory deaths of a series of strippers.

Vincent Price had featured so often in films by Corman and Castle that he can be considered the clown prince of a gentler era of horror comedy, but his best work didn't come until Douglas Hickox's 1973 *Theatre of Blood*. This British picture took its cue from the actor's two earlier *Dr Phibes* films, the first of which featured a series of murders modelled on the Pharaoh's ten Old Testament curses, for the most audacious run of gimmicky deaths yet.

Here Price plays an overblown Shakespearean actor, Edward Lionheart, who takes revenge on sniping critics by killing them in various Bard-inspired ways. The casting of Price, routinely criticised as a hammy actor himself, is only matched by the supporting cast, a roll call of Britain's finest character actors; and the comic touches of Lionheart's various disguises – most memorably as afroed gay haidresser – perfectly complement the surprisingly gory deaths of the critics, from Michael Hordern being stabbed to death by derelicts to Robert Morley being force-fed his poodles in a pie.

Later in the 70s horror parodies did brisk business: *Love at First Bite* (1979) was the highest-grossing vampire film ever released until *Bram Stoker's Dracula* (1992), and the classic gothic styles of Hammer and Universal were also parodied in Paul

Morrissey's *Blood for Dracula* (1974) and *Flesh for Frankenstein* (1973), Mel Brooks's *Young Frankenstein* (1974) and Roman Polanski's earlier *Dance of the Vampires* (1967).

Even the more harrowing offerings of the decade, grim assaults like **The Texas Chain Saw Massacre** or *Eraserhead* (1976), were shot through with black comedy, and *Dawn of the Dead* (1979) proved influential in its mix of social satire, gore and intermittent slapstick, but few films were prepared to go quite as far as *The Incredible Torture Show/Blood Sucking Freaks* (Joel M Reed, 1977). This astonishingly sleazy and tasteless film, equal parts HG Lewis and John Waters, mixed bad gore effects, SM stylings and a memorably deranged cast to queasily entertaining effect. The slender story involves Sardu and his dwarf sidekick Ralphus torturing naked women onstage for a jaded New York audience convinced it's all faked; it isn't, and Sardu keeps a cage full of crazed women downstairs for the white slave trade.

The film's so excessive on every level that it's difficult to take seriously, although that didn't stop it from being banned in the US after protests by Women Against Pornography, who responded poorly to images of women's hands and feet being chopped off and eyes gouged out; in one of the film's most shocking sequences an unhinged surgeon pulls a woman's teeth then shaves her head, drills into the skull and drinks her brains through a straw. Few protesters would have made it to the end, where the meat-happy slaves from the basement are released and kill Sardu and his cohorts; the final scene has one of the slaves about to chow down on a penis in a hot-dog bun.

In 1982 Frank Henenlotter's *Basket Case* was released, ushering in a new era of 'splatstick' with its messy but comical effects and cartoon energy. Henenlotter, whose love of trash cinema from nudie cuties to sex-education films leaves Tarantino's fanboy geekiness in the shade, started off making Super 8 films with names like *Lurid Women* – 'Out of the night they came ... crawling and drooling and making shameful noises' – before progressing to 16mm to tell the story of Duane's struggle to keep his grotesquely malformed Siamese twin brother, Belial, in his basket before he claws any more hapless victims to shreds.

Henenlotter's film, which has memorably been described as '*ET* as if written and directed by a psychopath', recalls American horror cinema's origins in freakshow culture, and shows a marked Tod Browning (*Freaks*, 1932) influence in its fascination with human oddities. The distributors, in the best carny tradition, slapped on a memorable tagline ('The tenant in Room 7 is very small, very twisted and very mad') and gave out surgical masks to viewers: 'Free surgical masks – to keep the blood off your face!', winning the film a place in trash lovers' hearts.

Another popular comedy-horror strand was kicked off with *Re-animator* in 1985, a far funnier and more inventive film than the other zombie comedy of the year, *Return of the Living Dead*. Directed by Stuart Gordon, produced by Brian Yuzna and very loosely based on a Lovecraft story, *Re-animator* introduced Jeffrey Combs as the roommate from hell, a medical student whose grisly experiments to raise the dead lead to splashy, effects-heavy and entertainingly over-the-top mayhem. Slickly produced and imaginatively gory, with art direction from **The Texas Chain Saw Massacre**'s Robert A Burns, the film was soon followed by *From Beyond* (1986), also ostensibly a Lovecraft adaptation. Marginally less gory but even more audacious in conception than its predecessor, this tale of a scientific experiment to contact beings from another dimension ended up with a bald Combs sucking out peoples' brains after his pineal gland emerges on a stalk, along with a host of sub-*Thing* transformations that mark some kind of tidemark in rubbery pre-CGI effects.

But probably the splashiest film to emerge from this gore-soaked era was Jim Muro's *Street Trash* (1987), a hilariously tasteless concoction of melting winos and unworkable necrophilia skits, very loosely based on Kurosawa's *Dodes'ka-den* (1970). Muro, who'd worked with Henenlotter on *Basket Case*, is an accomplished Steadicam operator, and his love for the device is clear in the film; sadly it's his only feature, and his career has long since left sick low-budget splatter for Steadicam work on major Hollywood features like *Titanic* (James Cameron, 1997). *Street Trash* may lack the production values of the Yuzna films, but for gross-out comedy and sheer inventiveness it's a hard act to follow.

Horror wasn't the only source of inspiration for these films, which often also drew on silent-comedy techniques – Raimi undercranking the camera in *Evil Dead 2*, and Bruce Campbell's mobile features and exaggerated physical humour, put the film squarely in the silent-movie tradition. Many also had a demented energy that had more in common with *The Muppet Show* than a slasher film, and the 'rubber monster' effects in *From Beyond* and *Evil Dead 2* involved extrapolations of Muppet technology.

Monty Python proved influential too, with the over-the-top skits in *The Holy Grail* (Terry Jones, 1975) and *The Meaning of Life* (Terry Jones, 1983) showing a similarly excessive shock dynamic – once violence went past a certain point, it was funny: *gore* was funny.

But even if they were in part a response to the dour and unimaginative run of slasher films that opened the 80s, horror comedies dominated the genre so much during the decade that many fans worried that downbeat horror had been pushed out of the market: *The Thing* (1982) had been replaced by *From Beyond*. And many horror comedies lacked the inventiveness of the best entries: anyone who's sat through a Troma production, one of the *House* films or something like *Spookies* (Thomas Doran and Brendan Faulkner, 1986) will find that the joke's definitely on them.

After leaving school Sam Raimi and Bob Tapert decided to try making a feature, and got jobs to save seed money, as well as approaching potential investors. They'd done some market research into what sold well, and realised that horror, still filling drive-ins across the country, was the best entry into the film industry. They shot a Super 8 short, 'Within the Woods', to demonstrate they could make a scary film, and pioneered the 'Ram-o-cam' – a camera strapped to the centre of a long plank, the weight of which evened out bumps in motion – as well as several scenes that would be repeated in the *Evil Dead* films.

Having raised $90,000, they set up a production company, Renaissance Pictures, and made *The Evil Dead* (Raimi, 1981). The film took the feel of a grim 70s shocker – the cabin looks like something out of **The Texas Chain Saw Massacre**, and the film's unity of space and time (it all takes place in and around the cabin, over one night) links it to horror's worst nightmares – and infused it with virtuoso technical innovation, a manic cartoon energy and a surreal imaginative flair. Despite Stephen King's description of the film as 'ferociously original', there's not much that hadn't been done before: the Book of the Dead draws on Lovecraft, and the demon make-up and multi-tracked voices are straight out of **The Exorcist**, but its gleefully deranged take on hackneyed horror tropes made it an instant classic. Raimi was just nineteen.

Not everyone was convinced: some of the investors were upset that Raimi seemed to have made a comedy, and American distributors stubbornly refused to stay awake during screenings. It took Palace, who picked the film up for UK distribution after a screening at the Cannes Film Festival and made it a hit in Britain, to get American distributors to notice the film, and it was soon released to rave reviews in the US.

In 1983 Irvin Shapiro, a Renaissance Pictures sales agent, suggested a sequel, and took out ads in trade papers announcing 'Evil Dead II: Army of Darkness'. Raimi was initially sceptical about the idea, but his interest perked up when his second feature, *Crimewave* (1985), flopped. His first draft of the script had a 13th-century medieval setting, but this eventually had to wait until the second sequel. He couldn't use clips from the first film as flashbacks to explain what had happened, because the rights to it had been sold to so many companies around the world that chasing them proved too much of a headache. Given that he now had to shoot extra footage covering the events of the first film, he scaled down the medieval aspect of the script, and when the project was finally budgeted at $3.75 million, he rewrote the script again, to leave only the very end set in the 13th century.

Financing, which eventually came from Dino Di Laurentiis's DEG, was not easy to find: both Universal and 20th Century Fox declined when offered the screenplay, and co-writers Raimi and Spiegel took out a full-page spread in *Variety* looking for investors. One point in its favour was that the screenplay was short: exposition is kept to a minimum, and dialogue pared down to single words like 'toolshed' and 'chainsaw', Raimi and Spiegel keen to return to a silent-movie style of visual comedy.

Never really a fan of horror films, Raimi had been concerned by complaints about the tree rape in the first film, and wanted to make the sequel less offensive, so he decided to replace some of the on-screen gore with laughs. The opening scenes would be a reprise of the first film, although as the filmmakers were unable to secure the original actress for Linda, this left many viewers confused by Ash's carefree return to the cabin where he'd endured 'the ultimate experience in gruelling terror' previously.

DIRECTOR: Sam Raimi started making Super 8 films with friends in his early teens in Michigan, charging a quarter for schoolmates to sit through *Three Stooges*-inspired comedies. Even in these early films he developed a kinetic, acrobatic camera style and love of violent physical humour, and while many other directors have attempted to create live-action cartoons – most notably the Coens in *Raising Arizona* (1987) – few have succeeded quite as well as Raimi at his best.

The director, whose style approaches some delirious marriage between *Road Runner* and martial-arts films, claims that none of his stylistic quirks are superfluous – 'I always go for the clearest, most comprehensible way of telling the story, and then I think, "How can I complement this to make it a little more exciting, juice it a little?" ' But mainstream success has seen him tone down his berserk cartoon energy, and his skills are best showcased in his earlier films, rather than the blander studio work.

After *The Evil Dead* he directed *Crimewave*, a live-action cartoon co-scripted by the Coen brothers that suffered from studio interference, although it's inventive and bizarre enough not to deserve its current obscurity. Raimi returned the favour by co-writing *The Hudsucker Proxy* (1994), and the brothers have also used several of their ex-flatmate's trademark camera pyrotechnics in their films.

After *Evil Dead 2* Raimi made the successful superhero picture *Darkman* (1990), his first major studio film; a still more slapstick *Evil Dead* sequel, *Army of Darkness* (1993), which followed the misadventures of Ash in a medieval world; and the entertaining Sharon Stone western *The Quick and the Dead* (1995).

Following excursions into TV fantasy and baseball drama (!), Raimi returned to genre film with *The Gift* (2000), a slick supernatural thriller set in the Deep South that showed uncharacteristic stylistic restraint; *Spider-Man* (2002), one of the best of the Marvel adaptations clogging up multiplexes at the beginning of the millennium, and its blockbuster sequel *Spider-Man 2* (2004).

CASTING: Bruce Campbell has worked with Raimi since their school days, which probably accounts for much of the delight the director evidently takes in torturing him. Campbell, whose most memorable qualities are a Desperate Dan chin and a pre-*Jackass* streak of exhibitionist masochism, has had his biggest screen roles in Raimi's films, although since having his scenes as 'Wedding Shemp' deleted from *The Quick and the Dead* (1995) he has only managed cameos in *Spider-Man* (2002) and its sequel. He has also worked with the Coen brothers, taking a small part in *The Hudsucker Proxy* (1994) and uncredited cameos as soap-opera actors in *Fargo* (1996) and *Intolerable Cruelty* (2003); John

Carpenter (*Escape from LA* (1996)) and William Lustig (*Maniac Cop* (1988)) provided other genre roles.

Dan Hicks appeared in *Darkman*, *Maniac Cop* and Wes Craven's *Wishmaster* (1997), and was reunited with Campbell in the Scott Spiegel-directed slasher *Intruder* (1998), which also featured Sam and Ted Raimi.

PRODUCTION: The film was shot in North Carolina from May to August 1986, with exteriors filmed in Wadesboro and the interior of the cabin built in a junior high-school gym hall in Wilmington. As DEG wanted an R-rated film, Raimi tried to use deep-red blood as little as possible, replacing it with black, blue and green fluids; but the ploy – which adds to the cartoony feel of the film – didn't work.

By all accounts it was an enjoyable shoot: members of the team routinely joked about ideas to Raimi, who then actually used them in the film, and some skits were lifted directly from the director's Super 8 shorts. Several ideas that were toyed with then discarded include the suggestion that everything had been in Ash's mind, and that a group of escaped convicts should accidentally dig up Linda's body.

Other scenes were shot but edited out of the film before release. When Linda's head falls into Ash's lap it originally wormed a four-foot tongue into his mouth; the scene was shot in reverse but Raimi was unhappy with Campbell's reverse-motion acting. When 'Evil Ed' is axed by Ash, there was a sequence showing him running around with half a head, as well as a shot of his body parts twitching on the floor; these may have been removed in an attempt to get an R rating. Another scene removed was from Ash's second possession, during which he stormed around the woods and ate a squirrel; and further shots of Henrietta in demon make-up were removed from the Knowby sequence at the start of the film.

Continuity proved to be a problem, with the entire film shot out of sequence; characters' clothes look variously less bloody or bloodier than they should throughout. Another difficulty came with the demonic white contact lenses: the actors couldn't see through them, and had to rehearse their movements extensively before filming.

The make-up for Raimi's brother Ted, who played the possessed Henrietta, was a full body suit that took around six hours to put on: towards the end of the film a white fluid can be seen dripping from her ear, a mixture of Raimi's sweat and talcum powder. The suit also split open, and the two halves can be seen baggily hanging apart as Henrietta flies around the room.

Bruce Campbell was also tortured on set; he did most of his own stunts (particularly the plate-breaking sequence, undercranked by Raimi for cartoon effect), and the director delighted in making already uncomfortable situations worse, poking branches at his star during his final car drive, as well as for the scene where he is hurled through the woods backwards.

The producers objected to Ash's being essentially alone for the first half-hour of the film, and to him sawing off his hand; they worried that now he would no longer be a credible identification figure for the audience. Campbell was more sanguine: 'It's great to torment the hero like that. It's just wonderful to be able to permanently alter your main character in some way. You have to show that he too is expendable.'

SOUNDTRACK: Joseph LoDuca's manic score perfectly re-creates the feel of old Warner Bros cartoons, with its quicksilver mood changes and quiet/loud dynamic perfectly mirroring Raimi's visuals. The sound effects are also endearingly over the top, with the 'Ram-o-Cam' chasing Ash with a sound like a plane taking off, mixed with slowed-down speech. There are subtler effects too: Ash's 'groovy', or the sound of him spinning the shotgun and blowing on the barrel, are unrealistically exaggerated, while the rocking-chair creak was digitally combined with a human scream to add an extra edge.

LoDuca also scored all of Raimi's other films up to *Darkman*, as well as Brian Yuzna's *Necronomicon* (1994), the French werewolf movie *Brotherhood of the Wolf/Le Pacte des Loups* (Christophe Gans, 2001) and TV series like *Hercules*, *Xena* and *American Gothic*.

RELEASE: *Evil Dead 2* was never submitted to the MPAA, as Raimi wouldn't agree to the cuts necessary for an R rating. As DEG wouldn't release X- or unrated films, a dummy distributor, Rosebud International, was set up, which was still able to use the distribution DEG had booked.

But the film fared poorly at the box office, despite receiving generally good reviews: Roger Ebert described it in the *Chicago*

Sun-Times as a 'sophisticated satire . . . the violence and gore are carried to such an extreme that they stop being disgusting and become surrealistic', while the *Washington Post* felt that 'everything is so Out There, so comedically exaggerated, that there's no way to take the film[s] seriously. Raimi and his crew certainly don't.'

Evil Dead 2 did marginally better in the US on video, but was a runaway success in Italy and Japan, and its reputation has grown since its initial release: it was ranked number one on *Spin Magazine*'s 1993 list of the 'Top 100 Films of the *Spin* Years'.

In the UK the film was released uncut for cinemas but had one scene – Ash's head being kicked as he lies on the ground – removed for the video release. It has since been restored.

CRITICAL EYE: Although *Evil Dead 2* is widely considered a special-effects showcase, some of the effects – especially the tree demons at the end – are unconvincing, and the film's real virtues lie elsewhere. Raimi is particularly deft at handling reality slippages, and a few scenes early in the film have an authentic nightmare quality, with Ash attacked by his mirror image before finding that he is strangling himself, or the genuinely disturbing sequence where everything in the cabin starts to laugh at him.

Time and space are elastic and untrustworthy, as befits a cartoon world: the clock stops in an impossible position and Ash's first day in the cabin passes with insane speed; the layout of the cabin defies logic, apparently maze-like and impossibly large as Ash is chased around it early in the film, and the trail to the cabin vanishes shortly after the arrival of the others. In Raimi's demented world nothing can be trusted – not even your own hand.

And the film profits from following the golden rule of exploitation cinema: nobody is safe. Most viewers will initially identify with Ash, but this identification will be strained when he saws his own hand off, and broken altogether when he is possessed; the ineffectual Ed looks like he might be a hero, but is soon hacked to pieces with an axe; Jake quickly proves a scurvy cretin; and Bobbie Jo loses our sympathy by panicking and running into the woods. That leaves just Annie, although some of her heroics – accidentally stabbing Jake, then dragging him to the 'safety' of the cellar door – are questionable. And her reward for creating the vortex that sucks the Deadites out of our world? A starring role in *CHUD II: Bud the Chud* (David Irving, 1989).

INDUSTRY IMPACT: In the same year that *Evil Dead 2* was filmed, New Zealander Peter Jackson made his debut feature, *Bad Taste*. Financed by the country's Film Commission, this gory slapstick comedy followed some very stupid New Zealanders as they tried to cope with an invasion of aliens intent on using humans as fast food. Mindless, excessive and a hit with gorehounds the world over, the film was soon followed by *Meet the Feebles* (1989), in which Jackson joined the dots between the Muppets and splatstick with a grim tale of sleaze-soaked puppets.

Jackson's third feature, *Brain Dead* (1992), is still the high-water mark in cinematic gore: as Raimi admitted after seeing the film, 'cannibal slapstick has seen its *Intolerance*', although Jackson's own estimation of it as 'just a total heap of mindless junk' is equally valid. This incredibly soggy story of a young man, Lionel, trying to keep up appearances with a cellar full of zombies, is irreverent, intermittently funny and very silly. The film's blood-drenched effects – at one point Lionel uses a lawnmower to dispose of wave after wave of undead – were amazingly passed uncut by the BBFC; perhaps they respected the hero's decision to turn a picture of the Queen to the wall before the carnage ensues.

Henenlotter's second feature, *Brain Damage*, also came out in 1987; drawing on his love of *The Tingler* (1959), Henenlotter wanted to make a new type of LSD film, and to further blur the boundaries between horror and comedy. If *Basket Case* is *Dead Ringers* (1988) played for sick laughs, *Brain Damage* makes friends with one of the turd parasites from *Shivers* (1975): its name is Elmer (as indelibly etched on any viewer's brain after watching the demented crooning of 'Elmer's Song') and it's tired of being middle-aged couple Morris and Martha's pet, so it escapes to offer their neighbour Brian injections of its euphoric, hallucinogenic and highly addictive parasite juice. The only thing it asks in return is a fresh supply of human brains. Since then Henenlotter has stayed in the comedy-horror field, with two *Basket Case* sequels and *Frankenhooker* (1990), although none of these have matched the dementia of his first two films.

Stuart Gordon and Brian Yuzna have also continued in the *Re-animator* vein, with varying degrees of success. Gordon's high points include *The Pit and the Pendulum* (1990) and *Dagon* (2001), a return to Lovecraft territory, while Yuzna made his directing debut with *Society* (1989) (see **INDUSTRY IMPACT,**

Invasion of the Body Snatchers), before going on to helm two disappointing *Re-animator* sequels and the third and best entry in the *Return of the Living Dead* series, as well as tapping a raw nerve with *The Dentist* (1996).

Most 90s mainstream genre entries have been tinged with parody to a degree, although some filmmakers could handle it better than others: Robert Rodriguez's *From Dusk Til Dawn* (1996) was a poor cousin to *Near Dark* (Kathryn Bigelow, 1987) in the vampire Western stakes, but Ronnie Yu, recruited from Hong Kong after the success of *The Bride with White Hair/Bai fa mo nu zhuan* (1993), was able to bring a cartoon edge to moribund franchises with *Bride of Chucky* (1998 – 'Chucky gets Lucky!) and *Freddy vs Jason* (2003).

FINAL WORD: *Evil Dead 2* is the perfect horror comic. Fun, inoffensive and entirely lacking in subtext, the film is only hampered by the irony of censorship: the adolescent audience who would enjoy this most are unable to see it legally in most territories. But it's still entertaining for adult viewers: if some of the humour wouldn't seem out of place in Peter Farrelly's 1994 moronathon *Dumb and Dumber* (Ash puts a copy of *A Farewell to Arms* on the bucket covering his severed hand), the sheer audacity of Raimi's technique, throwing everything from stop-motion animation to anamorphic distortion into the mix, brings the film out of the teen ghetto and fixes it as a delirious and hallucinatory horror classic.

SERIAL-KILLER CINEMA

Henry: Portrait of a Serial Killer (1989)

'Yeah, I killed my Mama . . .'

USA, Maljack Productions, colour, 82 mins

Directed by John McNaughton
Written by Richard Fire and John McNaughton
Produced by Lisa Dedmond, Steven A Jones, John McNaughton
Executive Producers: Malik B Ali, Waleed B Ali
Music by Ken Hale, Steven A Jones, Robert McNaughton
Original Songs by Mic Fabus
Director of Photography: Charlie Lieberman
Editor: Elena Maganini
Art Director: Rick Paul
First Assistant Director: Paul Chen
Special Make-up Effects Artist: Jeffrey Lyle Segal

CAST: Mary Demas (*Hooker* #1), Michael Rooker (*Henry*), Anne Bartoletti (*Waitress*), Elizabeth Kaden (*Dead Couple* [wife]), Ted Kaden (*Dead Couple* [husband]), Denise Sullivan (*Floating Woman*), Anita Ores (*Mall Shopper* #1), Megan Ores (*Mall Shopper* #2), Cheri Jones (*Mall Shopper* #3), Monica Anne

O'Malley (*Mall Victim*), Bruce Quist (*Husband*), Erzsebet Sziky (*Hitchhiker*), Tracy Arnold (*Becky*), Tom Towles (*Ottis*), David Katz (*Henry's Boss*), John Scafidi (*Kid #1 with Football*), Benjamen Passman (*Kid #2 with Football*), Flo Spink (*Woman in Cadillac*), Kurt Naebig (*High-school Jock*), Kristin Finger (*Hooker #2*), Lily Monkus (*Woman in Beauty Shop*), Ray Atherton (*Fence*), Eric Young (*Parole Officer*), Rick Paul (*Shooting Victim*), Peter Van Wagner (*Bum #1*), Tom McKearn (*Bum #2*), Frank Coranado (*Bum #3*), Lisa Temple (*Murdered Family* [wife]), Brian Graham (*Murdered Family* [husband]), Sean Ores (*Murdered Family* [son]), Pamela Fox (*Hairstylist*), Waleed B Ali (*Store Clerk*), Donna Dunlap (*Dog Walker*)

SYNOPSIS: 'This film is a fictional dramatization of certain events.' Henry drives around Chicago looking for victims. He works as an exterminator, and uses the equipment to trick a woman into letting him into the house. He is living with Ottis, a fellow ex-con whose sister Becky comes to stay: her marriage has broken up and she hopes to earn some money before she brings her daughter over as well.

Ottis works as a garage attendant, and sells weed on the side. He tells Becky that Henry killed his mother, and later Becky asks Henry if this is true. He says that it is: he killed her after she made him wear a dress and watch her having sex.

Becky gets a job, and models a T-shirt for the men; Ottis tries to kiss her, and is stopped by Henry. The men pick up two prostitutes, who Henry kills. Ottis is shocked, but Henry, realising his friend is only worried about getting caught, explains his philosophy of killing – 'it's you or them' – and tells him that he changes his MO each time and travels around the country constantly to stay ahead of the law.

Ottis kicks the TV in, and they go shopping for another one. A fence is repeatedly rude to them, so they kill him and take a TV and a video camera, which they use to film themselves around the house. Henry is resistant to Becky's amorous advances.

Ottis is punched in the face by a student weed buyer when he makes an unwelcome pass, and Henry stages a solo murder to help him get over his rage; they put their car bonnet up in an underpass and Ottis shoots the first person who stops to help.

Henry and Ottis watch a video of their murder of a family, during which Henry stops Ottis from having sex with the mother's corpse; Ottis then watches it again in slow motion. Later Ottis accidentally breaks the video camera as they drive around, and Henry kicks him out of the car after they argue; Henry then takes Becky out for a meal and Becky comes on to him hard back at the flat, until Ottis appears.

Henry goes out for a walk, and considers various potential victims before going home to find Ottis raping and throttling Becky. He kicks him off, but Ottis breaks a bottle over his head; Becky only stops her brother from killing Henry by stabbing him in the eye. Henry kills Ottis, saws up his body then drives off with Becky to dump the corpse-filled bin liners. They stay at a motel, where Henry tells Becky they can stay at his sister's ranch; she tells him she loves him; he tells her he loves her back.

The next morning Henry leaves the motel alone with a heavy suitcase, which he dumps on the roadside.

ORIGINS AND INSPIRATION: The serial killer, as chief bogeyman of the second half of the 20th century, has correspondingly been well documented on celluloid. Early avatars such as Bluebeard and Jack the Ripper lent their stories to numerous films, but the serial killer subgenre really began with Fritz Lang's *M* (1931), four decades before the FBI's Robert Ressler coined the term to describe the repeat stranger killers spreading mayhem throughout 70s America. *M* was the first horror film to entirely eliminate the element of fantasy from the genre, defining a subgenre that crossbred horror with crime, and anticipated later trends by basing its story on a true-life serial killer, Peter Kurten, the 'vampire of Dusseldorf'.

Early serial killers tended to look strange or monstrous, and were clearly outside the accepted social order; even *M* drew on Peter Lorre's bizarre features in its portrait of a killer clearly far different from you or I. It took the noir films of the 40s and 50s, like *Beware My Lovely* (Harry Horner, 1952), to give serial killers a normal appearance, and the focus of the killer's difference then shifted to his mental state.

The Invisible Man (1933) was the first film to posit mental illness as the cause of repeat murder, with Claude Rains giving a bravura turn as a cackling megalomaniac in a smoking jacket; and through the 1940s psychoanalysis was favoured as a model for unlocking killers' rationales, with mental illness conferring a diminished responsibility on the killers themselves.

Psycho and *Peeping Tom* (1960) were watershed films in the development of the subgenre: case studies that refused to concern themselves in the slightest with police procedure and gave their killers a sympathetic face. Norman and Mark are victims, whose compulsion to kill is their only form of self-expression; but if Mark's problems fall slightly short of full-blown psychosis, there was no doubt in the audience's mind of Norman's insanity, and a slew of case studies followed, populated by mad, unstoppable killers.

These tended, like **Psycho** and *Peeping Tom,* to avoid any focus on police investigations and to take an increasingly non-judgmental tone in the depiction of their killers. Many took their inspiration from real-life killers: Albert DeSalvo in *The Strangler* (Burt Topper, 1964) and *The Boston Strangler* (Richard Fleischer, 1968); Beck and Fernandez in *The Honeymoon Killers* (Leonard Kastle, 1970); Fritz Haarman in *Tenderness of the Wolves* (1973); Ed Gein in *Deranged* (1974); Donald Nielson in *The Black Panther* (Ian Merrick, 1977), a rare British case study; and Henry Lee Lucas in *Confessions of a Serial Killer* (Mark Blair, 1985), shot after McNaughton's film but released first.

If the films weren't based on true-life cases, they tended to stress bizarre methods of killing as gimmicks to ensure box-office success; guns were out, and more tactile weapons in. *The Toolbox Murders* (Dennis Donnelly, 1977) featured Cameron Mitchell taking nail guns and drills to his unfortunate victims' heads, and the power-tool theme continued in the early 80s as director Abel Ferrara played Reno, a struggling artist who finds that a portable electric drill helps him cope with financial pressures and noisy neighbours, in *The Driller Killer* (Abel Ferrara, 1980).

The period offered up some other irredeemably sleazy psychos who had British censors reaching for their scissors: Joe Spinell's sweaty, obese photographer in *Maniac* (William Lustig, 1980) scalps his victims for wigs to put on the mannequins surrounding his bed; Donny in *Don't Go in the House* (Joseph Ellison, 1980) burns his victims with a flamethrower; and the Vietnam vet killer in *Don't Answer the Phone* (Robert Hammer, 1980) – 'You'll want to take a shower after watching this', warns one guide – strangles his victims with a stocking filled with coins.

Some of these films, adjuncts to the slasher films popular at the time, mix softcore sex with hardcore violence, and come uncomfortably close to the rape porn of films like *Last Victim/Forced*

Entry (Jim Sotos, 1975) and *Scrapbook* (Eric Stance, 1999); but *Maniac* and *Don't Go in the House* are leavened by moments of bizarre and probably unintentional hilarity, the former bursting the bounds of credibility by having Caroline Munro fall for the shifty psycho and the latter dressing Donny in the finest disco threads for a night of dancing that inevitably ends in flambé mayhem.

When a deal to produce a video compilation of wrestling clips fell through, MPI Home Video's Waleed Ali offered John McNaughton the chance to shoot a horror film with the money saved, around $100,000. McNaughton, who'd been trying for years to set up a feature, leapt at the chance, but knew that for that budget he wouldn't be able to make an effects-based film.

One of his friends, a true-crime enthusiast who also worked at MPI, showed him a TV documentary on Henry Lee Lucas, a serial killer who at the time boasted of having killed over 300 people, although he later retracted his claims. McNaughton was horrified by the look of Lucas and his accomplice, Ottis Toole, but also felt that the killer had an 'off-centre charm; you could see how he could get close enough to people to accomplish this'. Although Henry constantly changes his story about how he killed his mother, his history is true to what Lucas told police: the real-life killer's mother had reportedly been a prostitute who put him in a dress and made him watch her have sex with clients, and his father had lost his legs in a railway accident.

McNaughton had worked with video before but not film, and had few contacts in Chicago, so he got in touch with his old friend Steve Jones, who directed animated adverts and was well connected in town. Jones introduced him to co-writer Richard Fire, who was involved with the Chicago Organic Theater Company, and the company also supplied two members of the cast, Tom Towles and Tracy Arnold.

McNaughton and Fire wanted to redefine the horror genre by introducing a human monster who would be neither redeemed nor vanquished by the end; the screenwriters decided that 'if horror films are intended to horrify, let's horrify . . . to the extreme', by removing any element of fantasy: according to McNaughton, 'The monster is indeed real, he walks among us in the world, from town to town – perhaps even yours – and he is waiting outside the cinema for his next victim to be chosen at random.'

The director had an exploitation movie in mind, but Fire thought more could be done with the concept, and is largely responsible for the thoughtfulness of the film; surprisingly, he also came up with the excessive imagery at the start, such as what British censor James Ferman described as the 'prurient and exploitative' shot of a dead woman with a bottle in her face. The videotaping of the family murder came from McNaughton, who was inspired by Thomas Harris's novel *Red Dragon*, in which the protagonist films his murders.

DIRECTOR: McNaughton trained in television production in college in Chicago but was unable to land a job in the industry after graduating. He travelled around the country for a few years, working in a factory, a carnival and a shipbuilder's before returning to Chicago to try to break into film or television again. He was working as a bartender (in a bar used as a location in *Henry*) when he met the Ali brothers, who ran a production company then known as Maljack, and later MPI; they hired projectors and public-domain film loops out to bars, and wanted to start producing films for the new home video market. Their friend Ray Atherton (who plays the fence in the film) had footage of gangsters that McNaughton was hired to put together for a video release, *Dealers in Death* (1984), which was narrated by Broderick Crawford.

The high profile of *Henry* as a censorship *cause célèbre* led to other work for the director, although he is evidently pained that it remains his best-known film; a video of *Henry*, shown to Martin Scorsese, was instrumental in landing McNaughton the job of directing *Mad Dog and Glory* (1993), starring Robert de Niro. He has not returned to genre work since 1991's sci-fi horror *The Borrower*, although the bank-robber picture *Normal Life* (1996) and the trashily entertaining neo-noir *Wild Things* (1998) use genre elements.

CASTING: Towles, who originally read for the part of Henry, had a background in improvisational comedy, and his 'buffoon' performance, in a set of fake gnarled teeth, accounts for much of what McNaughton describes as the film's comedic tone. *Henry* has been Arnold's only substantial film role; Towles played Harry Cooper in the 1990 remake of *Night of the Living Dead*, and his other genre appearances include Stuart Gordon's *The Pit and the Pendulum* (1990) and Rob Zombie's *House of 1000 Corpses*

(2003); he has also featured in several of McNaughton's other films and TV projects.

The director initially had trouble casting Henry; most of the local theatre types turned their noses up at the script, and one rejected the part when it was offered to him. McNaughton was considering casting an older man, who wouldn't have been able to carry off the romantic subplot with Becky, when a member of the make-up team recommended that he meet Rooker, who duly turned up for a test in character and terrified him. He was dressed almost exactly as he is in the film; only the shoes and socks were changed. Rooker was offered a part in a play at the prestigious Steppenwolf Theater at the same time, but opted for Henry instead, as it was a lead role, although he and the other leads received only $2000 for their work.

It was not something he would regret – Rooker has since appeared in big-budget mainstream productions like *JFK* (Oliver Stone, 1991) and *Cliffhanger* (Renny Harlin, 1993), as well as genre fare like Romero's *The Dark Half* (1993); he played another killer in *Sea of Love* (Harold Becker, 1989) and, ironically, the police officer in serial-killer film *The Bone Collector* (Phillip Noyce, 1999).

The use of unknown actors, while determined by the film's budget, also removes any of the sense of security the audience has with familiar star faces; the actors had a couple of weeks to rehearse before shooting began, developing a minimal, semi-improvisational style that looks astonishingly realistic considering their lack of experience, and adds considerably to the documentary feel.

PRODUCTION: McNaughton initially envisaged *Henry* as being shot in a documentary style, with a hand-held camera following a serial killer around for two weeks. But the original cinematographer, who was highly skilled in hand-held documentary work, left before production due to a prior commitment, and McNaughton selected Charlie Lieberman, who'd worked on documentary-style substance-abuse films, as his replacement. The film's style, involving carefully framed shots, a naturalistic tone and washed-out colours rather than hand-held camerawork, came from both McNaughton and Lieberman; the director had worked as a stills photographer on the streets of Chicago, and wanted to capture the city's gritty texture.

The script was written to the budget, which was finally around $125,000; McNaughton claims that if he'd had more money, the only thing he would have changed was the amount he paid cast and crew. As it was, the director had to call in favours from friends to use props and locations – all of the film is shot on location – for free, and as he couldn't afford to pay for any rights, anything seen on TV screens in the film was owned by MPI.

Henry was shot in 28 consecutive days in October and November 1985, with one day's shooting lasting an astonishing 23 hours. According to McNaughton it was a 'fun picture to make', although possibly not for the actor who played the mother in the home-invasion sequence, who reportedly went into shock afterwards.

The film was originally planned as a direct-to-video release from MPI, but when McNaughton and Fire watched the dailies they realised that the film could be distributed theatrically. The shooting title was simply *Henry*, but Waleed Ali pointed out that they needed something to mark it out from other *Henry*s littering video-shop racks, and so the distinctive name was born.

SOUNDTRACK: *Henry* benefits from an inventive use of sound; apart from the music itself, which features bassy chanting tones punctuated by dissonant piano and electric guitar riffs and heavy percussion, many of the ambient effects are treated and fed back into the mix. A car door slams shut with an echo when Henry and Ottis pick up the prostitutes, while lines of dialogue are mixed with the sounds of killing that accompany the still tableaux at the start of the film; this concentration on aural rather than visual information – only slow camera pans around the after-effects of Henry's rampages are seen here – makes the first murder the viewer actually witnesses far more powerful.

Other sounds are used too: percussive clangs offset the muffled shots and screams in the background as Henry tells Becky about killing his mother; during the murder of the fence the sound of a dentist's drill is buried in the soundtrack; and the filmmakers experimented with techniques like playing Arnold's screams backwards on the score, which was recorded at a studio run by born-again Christians who predictably found *Henry*'s content disturbing.

But not all of *Henry*'s sound effects were so sophisticated: a Styrofoam rubber cup was crunched near a microphone for the sound of a neck snapping, and a plastic sack was torn for the sound of Ottis's body being torn apart. The filmmakers also paid around $50 a song to use songs by local, unsigned bands to play on the radio.

'IT'S ONLY A MOVIE … ONLY A MOVIE …': New York-based painter and inveterate prankster Joe Coleman, described by McNaughton as 'visualis[ing] the world from the viewpoint of the criminally insane', arranged a video screening of the film in New York, where it was seen by Elliott Stein, and painted a promotional poster for use in the marketing. It was based on the bathroom-mirror sequence towards the end of the film, with Henry's face surrounded by Boschian hell creatures, images of the film's bloodied victims and lines of dialogue; perhaps inevitably, the poster was banned, and a still taken from the same scene was used instead.

RELEASE: McNaughton showed a rough cut of the film to the Ali brothers, who hated it. By the time the editing was completed MPI were convinced they had wasted $125,000, and shelved the film. But video copies were made and sent to various critics and production companies, and when the film was first screened in public, on a video projector at the Chicago Film Festival, it was championed by Rick Kogan of the *Chicago Tribune*, although many other critics found its apparent moral blankness abhorrent. When it was shown in New York, the *Village Voice*'s Elliott Stein wrote a long article praising it, but its biggest break came when documentary-maker Errol Morris (*The Thin Blue Line* (1988), *The Fog of War* (2004)) arranged for it to be shown at the 1989 Telluride Film Festival, where Robert Ebert was impressed by its 'brutal but honest' tone.

Atlantic wanted to distribute the film theatrically, but the MPAA would only pass it with an X certificate, a commercial kiss of death; they did not even recommend any cuts, viewing the film as irredeemable in its lack of moral condemnation. It was partly *Henry*'s censorship limbo that led to the introduction of the A (for adult) rating, and the film was eventually released unrated in the US in 1989.

In the UK Electric Pictures voluntarily cut a 38-second sequence from the beginning of the film (the woman with the bottled face) before submitting it to the BBFC in 1991; it was classified for theatrical release with a further 24 seconds cut from the home-invasion sequence, and later released on video with further trims to (and a rearrangement of) this scene and the fence's murder. The film was not released uncut in the UK until early 2003. British reviewers were divided over its virtues: Amy Taubin, in an article in *Sight & Sound*, derided it as 'blatantly misogynistic', although Kim Newman in a review in the same magazine found it 'challenging, uncomfortable and honourable'.

CRITICAL EYE: *Henry* is the most scrupulously realistic portrait of a serial murderer yet filmed. Like *The Driller Killer*, it grounds its killer in the grubbily low socio-economic milieu to which most serial killers belong: Henry has a low-paid, unstable job (as exterminator, which McNaughton admits is a 'rather heavy-handed metaphor'), lives in a shared apartment with little or no privacy and is illiterate. There is a hint of class assertion in his crimes – he kills a middle-class family – but this is not offered as a catch-all explanation, as he kills street prostitutes as well. His principal rationale for choosing victims seems to be whoever he can get away with, although all of his victims are white, accurately reflecting most serial killers' reluctance to cross racial boundaries.

The story of how Henry killed his abusive mother is told on three occasions, the details changing each time; the serial killer is here presented as arch fantasist, a man who reconstructs the past to fit the needs of the present. The details may change in Henry's mind because of his insistence on using a different MO for each killing, and a blankness that perhaps smears his memory of one victim into another; but even if the viewer accepts his tale of abuse (and McNaughton seems to want him to – these details are based on Lucas's case history) the director is careful not to present Henry as a victim. Even as he tells Ottis that 'it's you or them', Henry is presented as a cunning and resourceful survivor, travelling around the country to evade capture and using whatever comes to hand – including the exterminator kit he is encouraged to keep by his boss – in pursuit of his ends.

Henry appears to take little pleasure in his murders; he kills whenever he is forced to make an emotional response – whether angered or otherwise aroused – and his murders define him, filling the void of his character. But sexual inhibition seems to be an important factor in his need to kill; he is uncomfortable with Becky's advances, and resents Ottis's open displays of sexuality.

Ottis apparently views anyone – man, woman or close family – as a potential partner; it doesn't even matter to him if they're alive or dead. While Henry actively encourages Ottis's murders, starting him off with a relatively easy gun murder and watching with pleasure as he progresses to more tactile methods like strangulation and neck-breaking, he disapproves of Ottis's necrophiliac and incestuous urges. If Henry is a classic example of an organised killer, remaining calm and cold even while taking life, Ottis represents a disorganised killer, going into a gleeful frenzy during their bouts of mayhem; but the only criticism of his enthusiasm comes from Henry, whose lopsided morals present an impossible point of identification for the audience.

Ottis and Becky belong to the same socio-economic dead end as Henry, and their lives have been similarly shaped by their environments: Ottis is an ex-con who sells weed and eventually rapes his sister; Becky was abused by her father as a child, and is fleeing a broken marriage with her daughter left behind. There's a suggestion that Becky, who becomes more intrigued by Henry when she learns he killed his mother, might provide some form of redemption for him: when she comes on strong he does not flee or respond violently, but the moment is broken when a leering Ottis appears, shattering what little privacy the couple can hope for. Henry goes for a walk, clearly planning to kill someone, yet after considering two victims he returns home: have Becky's advances put him off killing again? But he finds Ottis raping Becky, and kills him, albeit arguably in self-defence.

There is an inevitability to this, when coupled with the studied avoidance of any explanation for Henry's crimes and the fact that he gets away at the end – the police are nowhere to be seen in the film – that represents an assault on the audience's expectations. Most serial killer films are informed by pop-psychology explanations of their killers' motives, but *Henry* recognises the ultimate futility of searching for such easy answers: Henry may kill partly to assert control over an environment in which he is otherwise impotent, but he also does it simply because he can.

A more direct attack on the audience comes with the infamous home-invasion sequence. This is carefully set up from the start: the first overt violence seen in the film comes when Henry and Ottis, goaded by an unpleasant fence, kill him in an overblown and theatrical style, stabbing him with a soldering iron, throttling him and smashing a TV over his head. Until then the violence had been suggested through the use of still tableaux of corpses and an aural tapestry of shots and screams; the audience's expectations have been built up for the TV scene, described by McNaughton as 'violence as entertainment – it's even funny'. The fence is so despicable that the audience finds itself empathising with Henry and enjoying the scene, which plays like a traditional action film set-up; no matter that the 'hero' here is Henry, and that murder is an unjustifiably strong reaction against rudeness.

The next killing, Ottis's murder of a good Samaritan who stops to help them with their car, sows the seeds of unease – in no sense is this character's death justified or entertaining – and shortly afterwards the viewer is presented with the home-invasion scene. This is shown on what the viewer initially takes to be a video viewfinder, assuming that he is witnessing the events in real time; but it slowly becomes apparent that it is on a TV, and the camera eventually tracks out and around to reveal Henry and Ottis watching the screen, consuming violence as entertainment just as the viewer had with the murder of the fence – Ottis even rewinds the tape to watch it in slow motion.

McNaughton's design, in presenting the classic model of screen violence as entertainment, then following it with a profoundly ugly scene of realistic violence, is devastatingly effective, especially in its implication of the viewer. And Robert Cettl, in his study of the subgenre, *Serial Killer Cinema*, suggests a further twist:

> Perhaps McNaughton intended to suggest that this is the audience's secret desire in watching serial-killer films – to get as close as possible to a recorded portion of the killer's actual acts, as opposed to mere representations of it. This encapsulates one end of the serial-killer film's stylistic spectrum – the deglamorising and intended demystifying docudrama portrait of 'authenticity'.

The scene is followed by one of broad comedy, in which Ottis breaks the video camera then argues with Henry. The lurch in tone from horror to comedy doesn't entirely work, although it's evident elsewhere as well: after the murder of Ottis, Becky says that they should call the police, prompting Henry's 'Not a good idea', and the final scene of the film, in which Henry leaves the motel with Becky in a case, is blackly parodic of the end of *Five Easy Pieces* (Bob Rafelson, 1970).

McNaughton feels that the comedic tone of the film, what he describes as 'the poetry of idiocy', helps to make the audience more uncomfortable through playing on conflicting emotions, but the film's naturalistic style means that the nightmare comedy that adds to the horror of **The Texas Chain Saw Massacre** or *Eraserhead* (1976) is here more likely to have the opposite effect, letting the audience off the hook. But this isn't a major criticism: most audiences will be too shell-shocked to laugh, and it may even help the documentary feel – comedy, after all, often rears its head in the most inappropriate situations.

Finally, *Henry* is the necessary corrective to the glut of films portraying serial killers as glamorous or superhuman individuals. *The Silence of the Lambs*' Dr Hannibal Lecter is almost an aspirational role model, highly educated and an inventive cook, but Henry represents the true banality of evil, boasting only a lack of empathy and a flatness of effect entirely at odds with any Nietszchean transcendence of morality. Some of the most powerful scenes in the film are subtle demonstrations of Henry's blankness: his meal of burger and chips after the murder of two prostitutes, and his offer to share with Ottis to restore their relationship, for instance; Ottis, naturally, accepts. Yet the viewer is encouraged to empathise with Henry, which the director describes as 'a very difficult position to be put into, but a useful one, I hope. For by attempting to understand and share the feelings of one so damaged and seemingly beyond redemption, we are forced to confront our shared capacity for evil.'

INDUSTRY IMPACT: The delay in *Henry*'s release meant that it came out in the US not long before Jonathan Demme's *The Silence of the Lambs* (1991), a film that did much to legitimise the serial-killer film and remove it from its low-budget origins. The critical and commercial success of Demme's film as a crossover hit – a horror film seen by non-horror audiences – led to a rash of big-budget serial killer vs profiler films, from *Se7en* (David Fincher, 1995) to *The Bone Collector* (Phillip Noyce, 1999), which tended to portray their killers as demonic or superhuman rather than exploring Henry's banal naturalism. The quickly tired formula involved theatrically arranged corpses, profilers who get too close to the killers they track and A-list casts, and despite the horror themes that propelled the films – violation of the body, madness and death – they were not sold as horror films at all, but rather as thrillers, their large budgets and police-procedural leanings differentiating them from grubbier fare such as the slasher or true-crime film.

Case studies in the *Henry* mould were thinner on the ground. A sequel, *Henry: Portrait of a Serial Killer 2 – Mask of Sanity* (Chuck Parello, 1998) essentially recapitulated the triangle of the first film, but failed in its attempt to replicate its docudrama feel and sorely missed the presence of Michael Rooker; and *Man Bites Dog* (1991, see **INDUSTRY IMPACT, Cannibal Holocaust**) was less concerned with serial murder than its depiction in the media.

Several other true-life serial killer films have been released: *Killer* (Tim Metcalfe, 1996) thought Carl Panzram wasn't such a bad guy after all, while *Dahmer* (David Jacobson, 2002), *Bundy* (Matthew Bright, 2002) and *Gacy* (Clive Saunders, 2003) are interesting principally in their unwitting comments on the American serial-killer industry. *Bundy* seems particularly reprehensible in its semi-comic treatment of a relatively recent case, inviting the viewer to laugh at one of the killer's bikini-clad victims stumbling as she tries to escape. More recently, the Eileen Wuornos biopic *Monster* (Patty Jenkins, 2003) has been touted as a harrowingly realistic study of serial murder, but no amount of cotton wool in Charlize Theron's cheeks can obscure the film's soap-opera mechanics.

The most interesting psycho case studies post-*Henry* have been, like McNaughton's film, borderline arthouse efforts. Lance Kerrigan's *Clean, Shaven* (1994) was a devastating portrait of a schizophrenic man (Peter Greene giving a performance of extraordinary intensity) who may or may not be a child killer, trying to get his daughter back from her adoptive family; the film's use of sound and a memorably horrific scene in which Greene trims his nails beyond the quick make this one of the most painfully compelling portrayals of madness on film.

German director Jorg Buttgereit's *Schramm* came out the same year, a substantial technical improvement on his overrated *Nekromantik* films; this intimate observation of a serial necrophile and killer came uncomfortably close to celebrating its protagonist's work as an attack on sexually moribund convention, taking it a step further than *Henry*'s deliberately non-judgmental tone, but at least it treated its subject with the heaviness missing from most Hollywood treatments.

FINAL WORD: *Henry*'s non-judgmental tone and lack of re-demption or punishment make it an easier film to admire than enjoy; few viewers will be prepared to test McNaughton's assertion that after five viewings it becomes a comedy, and perhaps that's as it should be. Serial murder may exert a heady fascination – witness the saturation media coverage of the phenomenon from the 1970s to the end of the century – but ultimately its study reveals only a void of meaningless slaughter. *Henry*'s recognition of the futility of 'explaining' serial murder almost cancels the film out – why, then, are we watching? – but in its cold, hard gaze at the true face of human monstrousness, its unflinching honesty and its brutally effective construction it is the last word in serial-killer cinema.

HAUNTED JAPAN

Ring/Ringu (1997)

Japan, Asmik Ace Entertainment, colour, 91 mins

Directed by Hideo Nakata
Screenplay by Hiroshi Takahashi, from Kôji Suzuki's novel
Ring
Produced by Shinya Kawai, Takenori Sento and Takashige
Ichise
Executive Producer: Masato Hara
Original Music by Kenji Kawai
Cinematography by Junichirô Hayashi
Production Design by Iwao Saito
Assistant Director: Kuni Risho
Sound: Yoshiya Obara
Special Effects: Hajime Matsumoto

CAST: Nanako Matsushima (*Reiko Asakawa*), Miki Nakatani (*Mai Takano*), Hiroyuki Sanada (*Ryuji Takayama*), Yuko Takeuchi (*Tomoko Oishi*), Hitomi Sato (*Masami Kurahashi*), Yoichi Numata (*Takashi Yamamura*), Yutaka Matsushige (*Yoshino*), Katsumi Muramatsu (*Koichi Asakawa*), Rikiya Otaka (*Yoichi Asakawa*), Masako (*Shizuko Yamamura*), Daisuke Ban (*Dr Ikuma Heihachiro*), Kiyoshi Risho (*Omiya the Cameraman*),

Yûrei Yanagi (Okazaki), Yôko Ôshima (*Reiko's Aunt*), Kiriko Shimizu (*Ryomi Oishi*), Rie Inou (*Sadako Yamamura*), Hiroyuki Watanabe (*Hayatsu*), Miwako Kaji (*Kazue Yamamura*), Yoko Kima, Asami Nagata (*Junior High Schoolgirls*), Keiko Yoshida, Yoshiko Matsumaru, Yoho Naose (*Senior High Schoolgirls*), Maki Ikeda (*Yoko Tsuji*), Takashi Takayama (*Takehiko Nomi*), Toshiliko Takeda (*Yamamura as a Teenager*), Chihiro Shirai (*Sadako as a Young Girl*), Mantarô Koichi (*Town Hall Moderator*), Shinkichi Noda, Kazufumi Nakai (*Press Representatives*)

SYNOPSIS: Teenage girls Tomoko and Masami discuss an urban legend about a cursed video: after watching it the viewer is warned by phone that he will die within a week. Tomoko has seen a similar film, and dies shortly afterwards, along with three of her friends. Tomoko's aunt, Reiko Asakawa, is a single mother and reporter doing a TV story on the popularity of the cursed video myth, and becomes suspicious after Tomoko and her friends die on the same day.

She discovers that they had stayed in a resort on the Izu peninsula, and finds a copy of the video they watched. She watches it herself, and enlists her ex-husband Ryuji Takayama's help in solving the mystery, copying the video and giving it to him to watch. Their son Yoichi also watches it, and claims that Tomoko told him to.

When they slow the tape down, they can hear a voice in a dialect from Oshima Island. They find out that an Oshima woman, Shizuko Yamamura, predicted a volcano eruption, which relates to the images on the video. Reiko takes Yoichi to stay with her father.

She and Ryuji visit Oshima and stay at an inn run by Shizuko's cousin's son. Ryuji, who has psychic powers, finds the room featured on the video and meets Shizuko's cousin. Through him they learn that a Professor Heihachiro had run tests on Shizuko's ESP in Tokyo; during a public demonstration in which she was branded a fraud, her daughter Sadako killed one of the journalists with her mind, after which Shizuko went crazy and committed suicide by throwing herself into the volcano.

They return to the cabin, suspecting that Sadako, who'd been taken away by the professor after Shizuko died, was buried there. Under the cabin they find a sealed well; as they pull the water out in buckets, Reiko finds Sadako's corpse and hugs it. Over a week has passed since Reiko saw the video, and they assume they are now safe.

But back at Ryuji's house Sadako climbs out of the TV, and Ryuji dies of fright. Reiko, visited by a ghostly figure, works out that the only reason she survived was that she copied the tape and showed it to someone within a week; she drives off to save her son and spread the video curse.

ORIGINS AND INSPIRATION: Japanese cinema has been haunted from its inception. Drawing on ancient folk tales and the kabuki and noh theatre gave filmmakers a set of familiar conventions and figures to play with, drawing on the Japanese love of refined technique to tell the same stories over and over again.

One of the most popular figures was the vengeful female ghost, related to the *hannya* (female demons) of ancient myth. For *Ring* Nakata drew on two famous tales: the Yotsuya Ghost Story, filmed over twenty times and based on a popular kabuki play in which Oiwa, a samurai's murdered wife, returns to haunt her killer; and Okiko, the story of a female servant killed and thrown down a well that she then haunts.

Most Japanese ghosts are, like these, far more purposeful than their Western counterparts, partly because they have more specific origins: they are the spirits of people who have died violently and missed the ceremony through which they would have met their ancestors; now they must wander the earth without rest.

In early Japanese cinema the spectral merely added atmosphere to stories like *The Great Bodhisattva Pass/Daibosatu Toge* (1935), but with Kenji Mizoguchi's *Ugetsu Monogatari* (*Tales of the Pale Moon after Rain*, 1953) phantoms took centre stage. This, the first Japanese ghost film to be distributed in the West, revealed that Eastern spectres were far from the flimsy chain-rattling wraiths Western audiences were used to; they were altogether more corporeal, and the theme of the ghostly lover, a phantom distillation of the Western *femme fatale*, recurred throughout Japanese cinema. Mizoguchi's film also demonstrated that unlike the West, where ghost stories were a subgenre of horror and thus considered the province of cheap exploitation films, in Japan they permeated the culture, and could be the subject of serious statements from respected filmmakers.

Less a horror film than a meditation on the themes of tradition and respect for the past, *Ugetsu Monogatari* tells the story of two potters, Tobei and Sanjuro, who leave their families in war-torn feudal Japan to search for better things. Tobei is obsessed with the idea of becoming a samurai, and manages to trick his way into being made a general before finding his wife, who'd been left destitute and raped by wandering samurai, working in a brothel. Sanjuro hungers for wealth, but while selling his wares he falls in love with a woman of noble birth, and enjoys an ecstatic affair until he discovers that she is a ghost. He travels home and is greeted by his wife, only to find that she too is dead; he returns to his wheel and kiln, still haunted by her presence.

This evocative and powerful film, widely regarded as one of the masterworks of world cinema, might be considered profoundly conservative in its message not to aspire to be anything other than what you are. Given the time of its production, it's not surprising that the film struck a chord in Japan: Sanjuro's ghostly lover is a literalised metaphor for false hopes and illusions, the spectre of victory that eluded the country in the Second World War. But the film's conservatism has a more humanist basis, allied with a sense of loss, a resonant harking back to a simpler past: Japan's programme of modernisation had been recent and swift, leaving many fearing that something vital had been left behind.

Others were more enthusiastic about change and industrialisation, and sought to actively suppress Japan's traditional culture. In the 1890s educator Tetsujiro Inoue had attempted to eradicate superstitious folkloric belief, and in the 1920s the State similarly suppressed the development of new religions: in both instances the past was seen as illogical and chaotic, a hurdle in the march towards modernisation. If *Ugetsu Monogatari* approached the past with reverence and nostalgia, other films characterised it as monstrous and vengeful, enraged by its repression and devastating in its eruption into the present.

The monstrous past was a popular theme in *kaidan* (strange tales) and *obake* (ghost stories), and featured in Masaki Kobayashi's *Kwaidan* (1964), an adaptation of four ghost stories by Lafcadio Hearn, a 19th-century English Orientalist who did much to publicise Japanese culture in the West. *Kwaidan* was the most expensive film shot in Japan to date, director Masaki Kobayashi's perfectionism – he insisted on painting all the sets himself – giving it a shooting time of over a year. International audiences were enthralled by its mixture of images from traditional Japanese painting and theatre, and the film won the Special Jury Prize at Cannes, although it was not a success in Japan.

In the first story, *Shadowings*, a samurai rejects his old life in order to advance socially, but finds that he detests his shrewish if rich wife, and cannot stop thinking about the woman he left behind. He returns to her, and they spend the night together: in the morning he realises he has slept with a corpse. The second story, *Yuki-Onna/Snow Woman*, also shows the past returning in supernatural form to wreak vengeance: a woodcutter meets a ghost on a wintry night and has his life spared on condition that he never speak of the encounter to anyone. Years later he tells his wife, a beautiful stranger with no family, about the snow woman, only to find that she and the ghost are one and the same.

Kwaidan is an exceptionally beautiful film, a masterpiece of set design and art direction, but all the attention has gone on the highly stylised environments, making the film strangely cold: unlike Mizoguchi's humanism, here the viewer cannot empathise with the characters, but only admire the theatrical displays.

Onibaba (Kaneto Shindô, 1964), a classic ghost story without a ghost, has one of the most atmospheric settings of any horror film, shot almost entirely among the waving reeds of a riverbank. A mother and her daughter-in-law make ends meet during a feudal war by killing wounded samurai, selling their armour and disposing of their bodies in a deep pit; but when the daughter-in-law meets another man, the mother fears the end of their partnership, and dresses in a demon mask to scare her off. It works for a while, but on a stormy night the lovers overcome their fear, and the mother-in-law finds her mask fixed to her face ... The film, boiling over with repressed eroticism, only flirts with horror through the devastating final moments, as the mother-in-law attempts to remove the mask, but this too comes from a vengeful past – the mask is stolen from a samurai who has been tricked into plunging to his death in the skeleton-filled pit.

The director of *Onibaba*, Kaneto Shindô, made a full-blown ghost film with 1968's *Kuroneko*, a version of the popular cat ghost story: here a woman and her mother-in-law are raped and murdered in 17th-century Japan, but are animated by a feline spirit and return to seduce passing samurai and suck their blood. Finally a warrior is sent to deal with them who turns out to be none other than the wife's former husband.

Although *Kwaidan* and *Onibaba* were the only *kaidan* of the 60s to reach Western audiences, studios like Toei, Daiei and Shintoho produced many other ghost films for the domestic market, released principally around July and August, the time of O-Bon, the festival of the dead.

Not all of them took the subtle approach of the popular exports: *Yokai Hyaku Monogatari* (*One Hundred Monsters*, Kimiyoshi Yasuda, 1968) mixed ghosts with rubbery monsters for an effects spectacular; and *Sweet Home* (Kiyoshi Kurosawa, 1989) used Dick Smith's (**The Exorcist**) talents for its *Poltergeist*-inspired tale of a film crew who visit an abandoned haunted house only to meet their deaths at the hands of an enraged ghost, in an early example of the modern Japanese cinema's resolutely contemporary hauntings.

Kôji Suzuki's novel *Ring* was published in 1991 and quickly became a bestseller. The novel is substantially different from Nakata's film: Kazuyuki Asakawa, its protagonist, is a married man, and his associate Ryuji Takayama is an unsavoury character who may be a rapist. The famous scene of Sadako climbing out of a TV screen is also missing from the book: Nakata has credited *Videodrome* (1982) for inspiring it.

But perhaps the biggest change is in the character of Sadako and the nature of the cursed video. In the novel Sadako is genetically a man, born with a syndrome that makes him appear outwardly female; and the video kills not through supernatural causes but a virus, which also accounts for the imperative to copy it and show it to other people.

The character of Shizuko Yamamura, Sadako's mother, was based on a real person, Chizuko Mifune. Word of Mifune's powers of extra-sensory perception, which had developed while practising meditation, spread throughout Japan in the early 1900s, and Tomokichi Fukurai, Assistant Professor of Psychology at Tokyo University, used her as a subject in his experiments on ESP.

After a public demonstration in 1910, in which Mifune was dismissed as a fraud, she committed suicide by swallowing poison. Undeterred, Fukurai (the inspiration for the character of Professor Heihachiro in the book and film) used another subject, Ikuko Nagao, who was said to have the ability to imprint images on film or other media through her will, a power known as *nensha*. She too was accused of being a fraud, and died after a strong fever. Fukurai still didn't give up, and took a third subject, a woman called Sadako Takahashi, who reportedly had both the powers of foresight and *nensha*. But the professor's standing never really recovered from the accusations of fraud, and in 1919 he left Tokyo University.

After Suzuki followed it with a sequel, *Rasen*, in 1995, *Ring* was adapted for a TV series featuring many of the actors who went on to appear in the films. The series was a runaway success in Japan, and as Suzuki's publisher Kadokawa was also a high-profile film producer, a cinema version of the story was widely anticipated as well. But nothing happened until Masato Hara's independent company Ace Pictures, which was better known for importing foreign arthouse pictures than making films itself, teamed up with Kadokawa and secured the film rights to the publisher's books.

Hara had seen Nakata's first film, *Joyuu-Rei/Ghost Actress/ Don't Look Up* (1996), and thought he'd be perfect for *Ring*; *Rasen* was to be filmed directly afterwards, by TV director Joji Ida, for a simultaneous release in 1998. Nakata read the book and watched the TV series, then spent six months working on the screenplay with Hiroshi Takahashi, who dispensed with the scientific explanations of the novel and changed the protagonists to an estranged couple, adding another degree of tension to the story.

The distorted photos of the people cursed by Sadako are based on *shinrei shashin*, or spirit photographs, in which the faces of ghosts are reportedly captured but appear blurred; they are a popular feature on Japanese Fortean TV shows, and recall Nagao's *nensha* techniques. According to Nakata the photos were also inspired by films like *Amityville 3-D* (Richard Fleischer, 1983) and *Ghost Story* (John Irvin, 1981), which featured a snapshot in which characters marked for death had distorted faces; and Takahashi introduced him to a better breed of ghost film, recommending **The Haunting** and *The Innocents* (1961) for tips on creating a palpable atmosphere of dread.

DIRECTOR: Nakata's love of film began when he moved to Tokyo from the countryside, watching by his estimation around 300 films a year as a student. After graduating he landed a job at Nikkatsu studios, perhaps best known in the West for producing 'roman porno' classics like Tanaka Noboru's *The True Story of Abe Sade/Jitsoroku Abe Sade* (1975) and Seijun Suzuki's startling yakuza films *Tokyo Drifter/Tôkyô nagaremono* (1966) and *Branded to Kill/Koroshi no rakunin* (1967).

He worked there as assistant director for seven years, then directed his first feature, *Ghost Actress* (1996), which was again scripted by Takahashi. Although reportedly missing the chills of Nakata's later genre work, it did feature a vengeful female ghost with long black hair, dressed in white – a dry run for Sadako.

Nakata returned to the *Ring* world with *Ring 2* in 1999 (see below). *Dark Water/Honogurai mizu no soko kara* (2002), his next horror film, was his most accomplished yet, another adaptation of a Kôji Suzuki novel that returned to *Ring*'s mixture of supernatural unease and familial tensions. Single mother Yoshimi Matsubara is fighting a battle for custody of her daughter with her ex-husband, and her case isn't helped when strange things happen in her new apartment – the water has hairs in it, and she can hear footsteps in the empty room above ...

The film's watery theme and yellow-raincoated phantom recall **Don't Look Now**, although it's closer in tone to *The Sixth Sense* (1999) in its occasionally mawkish conservatism; but the visuals are far more atmospheric than Shyamalan's film, Nakata's sinister sense of space well served by Matsubara's drab apartment block and the perpetual rain, and the ending is more unexpectedly downbeat than most Hollywood films could get away with. In Nakata's world ghosts exact a heavy price for the sins of the past, and they don't seem to care who pays.

At the time of writing Nakata is slated to direct the American *Ring 2*, currently in pre-production.

CASTING: Matsushima had appeared in the *Ring* TV series, and returned for *Ring 2*; Hiroyuki, a popular face in ninja and samurai films, also appeared in *Ring 2* and *Rasen*.

PRODUCTION: *Ring* cost around $1.5 million, and was shot over five weeks. Rie Inou, who played the adult Sadako, was heavily involved in developing the look of the character. She was a student of kabuki theatre, and used its technique of exaggerated movements to describe emotion for Sadako's jerkiness; the shot of her emerging from the well was shot in reverse motion, with Inou walking backwards.

SOUNDTRACK: Sound design in Japanese films tends to be stylish and innovative – *Ugetsu Monogatari*, *Kwaidan* and *Onibaba* all have strikingly evocative soundtracks and use techniques that didn't percolate down to Western cinema for years – and *Ring* is no exception. The film's oppressive soundtrack mixes detuned gong sounds and dense electronic soundscapes from Kenji Kawai with the skittery strings of Polish composer Krzysztof Penderecki, whose music was also used in *The Shining* (1980) and **The Exorcist**. Kawai, who had composed the soundtrack for *Ghost in the Shell/Kokaku Kidotai* (Mamoru Oshii, 1995), also went on to score *Ring 2*.

The composer worked closely with a sound technician, overseeing the sound design down to the smallest detail: according to Nakata 'they mixed four different qualities of phone sounds because they did not want them to sound like Hollywood phones!' The soundtrack had fifty tracks for Kawai's music and fifty for sound effects, and integrated them seamlessly: it's impossible to tell where the music stops and the effects begin.

Fairly typically for a recent Japanese film, the music lurches into sentimentality at times, such as when Reiko hugs Sadako's corpse; and the song that plays over the end credits should also be mentioned for being similarly awful, dodgy trance pop that seems to belong to a different film altogether.

'IT'S ONLY A MOVIE … ONLY A MOVIE …': Sadako quickly became a national celebrity, and was featured in several Sega attractions, a *Ring*-themed haunted house at Tobu Zoo in Saitama and merchandise including mugs and T-shirts.

RELEASE: *Ring* was the most successful horror film ever released in Japan, grossing over 1 billion yen, or around $15 million, with its co-released sequel *Rasen*; it also broke records in Hong Kong and Singapore. The sequel (otherwise known as *The Spiral*) performed terribly at the box office, and has only recently been released in an English-subtitled version.

The film's urban-legend theme fed back into reality when it was featured on *Unexplainable*, a popular Japanese TV show dealing with bizarre or occult events. It was suggested that Asakawa's apartment was actually haunted by the ghost of a young woman who'd committed suicide in the living room: when Reiko is standing on the balcony while Ryuji watches the video, she turns around and a girl's face – not Reiko's – can be seen reflected in the patio door.

The film went on to be an international hit, winning awards at film festivals in Brussels, Montreal and Pusan, and had its UK premiere at the Edinburgh Film Festival in 2000, along with *Ring 2* and Takashi Miike's *Audition/Odishon* (2000). British journalists were stunned by the energy of the new Japanese horror cinema, and although the film only played in a handful of cinemas it won accolades from the *Evening Standard* ('knuckle-biting terror'), the *News of the World* ('Go see it if you dare'), *Time Out* ('creepy, genuinely scary modern psycho-horror') and *Sight & Sound*, which warned that the final scene 'will scare the living hell out of you'.

CRITICAL EYE: Given the film's overwhelming success, it's surprising that so much of it doesn't really make sense. Nakata's murky, claustrophobic style extends to the confusing storyline, full of about turns and contradictions; widely reported as a successful melding of ancient Japanese myth and modern urban-legend horror, the film actually occupies a position entirely its own, a fever dream redeemed from utter incoherence by a handful of astonishingly creepy images.

The present in *Ring* is sterile and antiseptic, a rational world disturbed by a monstrous eruption from the past. Sadako was the subject of experiments carried out by a scientist unable to understand her, and was buried alive in a slimy, deep, dark well – a symbol for the irrational past, while the volcano referred to on the video is a clear image of that past's vengeful return. And the past is very particular about the forms it takes in the present: Sadako's repressed energy manifests itself in the trappings of the high-tech consumer society, whether through the distorted photos of her victims or the cursed video itself.

Yet the irrational is hardly restricted to her appearances in the film. Ryuji himself has psychic powers, and Reiko seems to develop some of her own over the course of the film, even though in her position as journalist she is aligned with the bullishly rational newsmen who prompted Shizuko's suicide.

Their investigation into the video is closer to **Deep Red**'s flight-thought association than standard models of detection. Reiko and Ryuji leap from one discovery to the next through intuition and ghostly visits: they are led by a hooded figure's hidden message to find out about the eruption of Mt Mihara, and soon unearth the story of Shizuko and Sadako. After their guess about the location of Sadako's body proves correct, Reiko hugs the corpse – an iconic image mixing the appeasement of the past with a close interlinking of sex and death – and we, like the heroes, think the nightmare is over. But Ryuji dies, and the hooded man again appears to Reiko, pointing to the video that she must copy if she is to save her son's life.

The entire Sadako/Shizuko back story is in a sense a colossal red herring, a discovery that makes absolutely no contribution to solving the problem of the cursed video. Other leads are suggested but not followed up – Ryuji cryptically announces that maybe Sadako's father wasn't human – and Nakata seems less interested in the logic of the plot than in infusing an atmosphere of dread into every environment in the film. As the director has stated in an interview:

> What I really intended to do is present the fearful side of nature itself ... I shot some scenes in Oshima where there was a very bad or unnatural feeling in the air. Or even in Washitsu [a Japanese-style room], where some rooms are very dark and have an eerie aspect in themselves.

The presence of the hooded man further confuses matters: the screenplay makes it clear that he is meant to be Ryuji, and Reiko herself calls out 'Ryuji' on his final appearance. He is seen three times: first in the video itself, with his hidden message; second in Asakawa's father's house, pointing towards Yoichi, who is already watching the video; and third when Reiko wonders why she survived and Ryuji died, when he points towards the copied video. But for the hooded man's first two appearances, Ryuji is still alive; so how could he be a character on the video? And does he appear on it to people who have had no actual contact with Ryuji? It's also unclear what the precise role of the figure is: he seems on first impression to be helping Reiko solve the mystery, but actually just pushes her towards copying the video and spreading the curse. Is he, like Tomoko, whose ghost encourages Yoichi to watch the video, a phantom in Sadako's employ – and one even before his death?

Ring manages to make a virtue of its logical flaws and inconsistencies through a pervasive eeriness: science cannot explain away the irrational, and some strange events simply have to be accepted. But while other Japanese ghost films provide a strategy for coping with the inexplicable, in a set of conventions and codes characteristically involving honour and honesty, at the end of *Ring* Reiko drives off to infect her father, a light smile playing on her lips, in a chilling reversal of the humanist statement of *Ugetsu Monogatari*.

INDUSTRY IMPACT: *Ring* was remade almost as soon as it had come out in Japan, as *The Ring Virus* (Dong-bin Kim, 1999) for the Korean market; the film is very close to the original, repeating it shot for shot at times.

After *Rasen* failed at the box office, Nakata and some of the original cast for *Ring* were asked to make an alternative sequel, *Ring 2*. Unlike the other *Ring* films, this was based on an original story by Nakata and Takahashi, rather than one of Suzuki's novels, and is even stranger than its predecessor, with a demented scientist attempting to draw Sadako's energy out of Yoichi by using a swimming pool and a selection of bizarre headpieces. But its nightmare images of a child Sadako moving her mother's mirror or scuttling up the side of the well hit the right spots, and the film was another success. A prequel made in 2000, *Ring 0: Birthday* (Norio Tsuruta), explained away the mysteries that had surrounded Sadako in the first two films, and was perhaps as a result far less interesting.

DreamWorks acquired the rights to remake *Ring* in 2001, with Gore Verbinski at the helm. Hollywood's track record of remaking foreign films was not encouraging: the disturbing Dutch feature *The Vanishing/Spoorloos* (1988) was remade in 1993 by the director, George Sluizer, for 20th Century Fox, with an unbelievable happy ending tacked on; Alejandro Amenábar's *Open Your Eyes/Abre Los Ojos* (1997) became a Tom Cruise vehicle with *Vanilla Sky* (Cameron Crowe, 2001); and the US distribution rights to the superb Danish psycho-thriller *Nightwatch* (1994) were snapped up by Miramax only for them to effectively lock the film away while the director, Ole Bornedal, shot a tepid remake in 1997 with Ewan McGregor and Nick Nolte. In many ways it's an appalling form of cultural colonialism: American remakes are sold back into the source countries, with distribution muscle often ensuring that the original films are quickly pushed out of the limelight. This happened with *The Ring*, otherwise a surprisingly effective film that respected the original's mood; it earned $135 million just in the US, and also eclipsed Nakata's film in Japan, grossing more by its third week than *Ring* had during its entire theatrical run.

Ring has heralded a new wave of Japanese horror, and from the mid-90s onwards the country's genre films have been released at a rate unseen since the 60s. Some of them, like *Ring*, deal with the effects of modern technology and the relationship between present and past – particularly Sion Sono's highly recommended *Suicide Club/Jisatsu Circle* (2002), or the films of Kiyoshi Kurosawa (*Kyua/Cure* (1997), *Karisuma/Charisma* (1999), *Kairo/Pulse* (2001)); while others took a fresh slant on hoary Western clichés like zombies (*Junk* (Gregory King, 2001), *Stacy* (Naoyuki Tomomatsu, 2001), the positively demented *Wild Zero* (Tetsuto Takeuchi, 2000)), or explored uniquely Japanese transformation fantasies (*Uzumaki*, 2000).

Possibly the most interesting director to emerge from the recent boom has been Takashi Miike, whose *Audition*, like *Ring*, made Western audiences sit up and pay attention to Japanese horror. This astonishingly prolific filmmaker (Miike has made over fifty films since 1991) revels in a kinetic anarchy whose only parallel in the West is early Sam Raimi. While best known for his yakuza films, Miike has worked in pretty much every field going, from pop-group promo (*Andromedia* (1998)) to demented claymation musical (*The Happiness of the Katakuris* (2002)); and his other genre-related film, *Ichi the Killer* (2001), is one of the most notorious releases of recent years, an exhilarating live-action comic about a meeting between the ultimate sadist and the ultimate masochist.

At his best Miike represents everything exhilarating about Japanese genre cinema – a shattering of convention, an embrace of high weirdness with no discernible narrative function and a bravura technical style that will leave your jaw on the floor. As Miike says, 'What good is life without adventure? We don't need a manual for making a movie.'

FINAL WORD: What strikes the deepest chord in *Ring* is the film's imagery, which lingers long after the confused narrative has faded away. *Ring* presents no explicit deaths at all, and not a drop of blood, but relies instead on simple yet effective sequences achieved with minimal effects: not only the infamous shot of

Sadako climbing out of a TV, but the subtler, equally creepy images of Shizuko's mirror moving back and forth, the public demonstration or the embrace of Sadako's corpse deep in the well.

But the film itself is less important than the way it has sparked off a renaissance in Japanese horror films and boosted overseas access to and interest in the country's genre material. This is something of a godsend to fans of Eastern horror whose copies of *Tetsuo* (1990) and *Tetsuo 2* (Shinya Tsukamoto, 1992) have been run into the ground, and for genre fans in general who are bored with vacuous mainstream American filler. Even if part of the appeal of these films comes through an unfamiliarity with Japanese genre conventions, there's enough variety of technique on display to ensure that the lure of the exotic won't pall for some time yet.

AFTERWORD

Horror has lost its teeth. US genre product today harks back to the golden age of the 70s, whether in homages like *Cabin Fever* (Eli Roth, 2002) and Rob Zombie's *House of 1000 Corpses* (2003), remakes of **The Texas Chain Saw Massacre** and *Dawn of the Dead* (1979), or re-releases of **The Exorcist** and **Alien**; but the political edginess and sense of real danger that characterised the decade's best offerings is long gone. British horror died an ugly death in the 80s, with *Hellraiser* (Clive Barker, 1987) providing an irritatingly trans-Atlantic swansong; and only in Japan can the genre be recognised as enjoying any kind of renaissance.

But a dearth of new material is made up for to a degree by the DVD revolution, which has brought us astonishing rarities like *Mill of the Stone Women* (Giorgio Ferroni, 1960) and Fernando Arrabal's films in spotless widescreen transfers; and a body of fan writing that peers ever more closely into the obscure crevices of world cinema for its genre fix.

Horror fandom has come a long way from *Fangoria*'s slavering admiration of effects maestros; magazines like Stephen Thrower's *Eyeball* and publishers like Harvey Fenton's FAB Press have married high production values and glossy publications with incisive and authoritative writing, providing definitive accounts of the works of directors like Mario Bava, Dario Argento and Ruggero Deodato.

One of the most important features of this trend has been to cast a wider net than horror fandom's earlier obsession with gore quotients: Alejandro Jodorowsky and José Mojica Marins are hardly genre directors in a strict sense, but both have a lot to offer horror fans, and genre appreciation is now likely to encompass the *fantastique* in all its crazed glory. For fans of imaginative, idiosyncratic, exhilarating and ballsy filmmaking, a far wider world has recently opened up, with copies of films like *Uzumaki* (2000) and *Evil Dead Trap* (1987) readily available on DVD in your local megastore, and a host of wild and woolly obscurities just a brief internet search away. Happy hunting!

SELECT BIBLIOGRAPHY

The following books, magazines and websites were used but not quoted from:

BOOKS

Brottman, Mikita, *Meat is Murder*, Creation Books, London, 1998

Brottman, Mikita, *Hollywood Hex – An Illustrated History of Cursed Movies*, Creation Books, London, 1999

Butler, Ivan, *The Cinema of Roman Polanski*, A Zwemmer Ltd, London, 1970

Creed, Barbara, *The Monstrous-Feminine – Film, Feminism, Psychoanalysis*, Routledge, London, 1993

Curtis, James, *James Whale*, The Scarecrow Press, Inc., Metuchen, NJ and London, 1982

Dendle, Peter, *The Zombie Movie Encyclopedia*, McFarland & Co, Jefferson, N Carolina, 2000

Dyson, Jeremy, *Bright Darkness – the Lost Art of the Supernatural Horror Film*, Cassell, London, 1997

Fenton, Harvey and Flint, David (eds), *Ten Years of Terror – British Horror Films of the 1970s*, FAB Press, Guildford, 2001

Gallant, Chris (ed), *Art of Darkness – the Cinema of Dario Argento*, FAB Press, Guildford, 2000

Grant, Michael (ed), *The Modern Fantastic – The Films of David Cronenberg*, Flicks Books, Trowbridge, 2000

Howarth, Troy, *The Haunted World of Mario Bava*, FAB Press, Guildford, 2002

Hutchings, Peter, *Hammer and Beyond*, Manchester University Press, 1993

Hutchings, Peter, *Terence Fisher*, Manchester University Press, 2001

Hutchings, Peter, *Dracula*, IB Tauris, 2003, London

Jancovich, Mark, *Rational Fears – American Horror in the 1950s*, Manchester University Press, Manchester, 1996

Jaworzyn, Stefan (ed), *Shock Xpress 1*, Titan, London, 1991

Jaworzyn, Stefan (ed), *Shock Xpress 2*, Titan, London, 1994

Jaworzyn, Stefan (ed), *Shock*, Titan, London, 1996

Jaworzyn, Stefan, *The Texas Chain Saw Companion*, Titan Books, London, 2003

Juno, Andrea and Vale, V (eds), *RE/SEARCH 10: Incredibly Strange Films*, San Francisco, 1986

Kerekes, David and Slater, David, *See No Evil – Banned Films and Video Controversy*, Critical Vision, Manchester, 2000

Kracauer, Siegfried, *From Caligari to Hitler, a Psychological History of the German Film*, Princeton University Press, Princeton, 1947 (this edn 1974)

Kuhn, Annette (ed), *Alien Zone: Cultural Theory and Contemporary Science Fiction Cinema*, Verso, London, 1990

LaValley, Al (ed), *Invasion of the Body Snatchers*, Rutgers University Press, New Brunswick and London, 1989

Manguel, Alberto, *Bride of Frankenstein*, BFI, London, 1997

Newman, Kim (ed), *The BFI Companion to Horror*, BFI, London

Schneider, Steven Jay (ed), *Fear Without Frontiers – Horror Cinema Across the Globe*, FAB Press, Godalming, 2003

Skal, David J, *The Monster Show*, Plexus Publishing Ltd, London, 1994

Sullivan, Jack (ed), *The Penguin Encyclopedia of Horror and the Supernatural*, Penguin, Harmondsworth, 1986

Thompson, Nathaniel (ed), *DVD Delirium vol 1*, FAB Press, Godalming, 2002

Thompson, Nathaniel (ed), *DVD Delirium vol 2*, FAB Press, Godalming, 2003

Thrower, Stephen (ed), *Eyeball Compendium*, FAB Press, Godalming, 2003

Tohill, Cathal and Tombs, Pete, *Immoral Tales: Sex and Horror Cinema in Europe 1956–1984*, Titan, London, 1995

Tombs, Pete, *Mondo Macabro: Weird and Wonderful Cinema Around the World*, Titan, London, 1997

Weldon, Michael, *The Psychotronic Encyclopedia of Film*, Ballantine Books, New York, 1983

MAGAZINES

Shock Xpress
Flesh & Blood
Eyeball
Shock Cinema
Uncut
Sight & Sound
Monthly Film Bulletin

WEBSITES

www.bbfc.co.uk
www.imdb.com

INDEX OF QUOTATIONS

10 'dashing, venturesome . . .', André Gide, quoted in *Murnau*, Lotte H Eisner, University of California Press, Berkeley; first published in English in 1973, Martin Secker & Warburg Ltd, London

12 'more of a soporific . . .', *New York Times*, 4 June 1929

13 'jumbled and confused', *Herald Tribune*, 4 June 1929

13 'Not since *Caligari* . . .', *New York Post*, June 1929

13 'Never again . . .', p.102, *The Haunted Screen*, Eisner

13 'It is crude, unsubtle . . .', p.35, *Horror Movies*, Carlos Clarens, Martin Secker & Warburg, London, 1968

13 'not as terrible . . .', pp.7–8, *The Journals of André Gide*, André Gide, journal entry, 27 February 1928, trans. Justin O'Brien, Alfred A Knopf, New York, 1949

Bride of Frankenstein

24 'it stinks . . .', Whale, quoted p.27, 'Production Background', Gregory W Mank, *The Bride of Frankenstein*, ed. Philip Riley, MagicImage Filmbooks, 1989

26 'After more than twenty . . .', Karloff, quoted p.21, *The Illustrated Frankenstein Movie Guide*, Stephen Jones, Titan Books, London, 1994

27 'idiots, half-wits . . .', Frye, quoted p.45, ibid.

27 'a weird, strange character! . . .', Lanchester, quoted p.45, ibid.

30 'subtleties of emotion . . .', reviews quoted in *The Films of Boris Karloff,* Richard Bojarski and Kenneth Beals, The Citadel Press, New York, 1974

30 'the breeding of monsters . . .', *Spectator*, 5 July 1935

Invasion of the Body Snatchers

38 'my favorite film . . .', p.178, *A Siegel Film,* Don Siegel, Faber & Faber, London, 1993

38 'when people suffer . . .', ibid.

38 'exposed what . . .', Siegel, quoted *Sight & Sound*, vol 2, # 8, p.39

39 'Well, I think . . .', 'Don Siegel on the Pod Society', Stuart M Kaminsky, in *Science Fiction Films*, ed. Thomas R Atkins, Monarch Film Studies, Simon and Schuster, New York, 1976

40 'One night . . .', p.184, Siegel, op. cit.

40 'bursting with pods', p.185, Siegel, op. cit.

60   'declared stance . . .', p.97, *The Complete Hammer Films Story*, Hunter

Eyes Without a Face
66   'The trouble with Clouzot . . .', Franju, quoted in Lowenstein, A. 'Films Without a Face: Shock Horror in the Cinema of Georges Franju', *Cinema Journal*, Summer 1998, vol 37, # 4, p.37
67   'I have always . . .', Franju, quoted p.18, *Franju*, Raymond Durgnat, Movie Magazine Limited, London, 1967
68   ' . . . the fantastic is above all realism . . .', pp.156–7, Franju, quoted in 'Plastic Surgery Disasters', Andy Black, *Necronomicon Book Three*, ed. Andy Black, Noir Publishing, Hereford, 1999
68   'It's an anguish film . . .', Franju, quoted p.83, *Franju*, Durgnat
68   'the most beautiful horror film', Franju, quoted p.24, ibid.
68   'Dr Thierry de Martel's . . .' Franju, quoted p.28, ibid.
69   'gives the unreal reality', Franju, quoted p.27, ibid.
69   'because the more tender . . .', Franju, quoted p.31, ibid.
70   'deliberately revolting', *Sunday Times*, 6 September 1959
70   'WHY did they let this film come in?', *Birmingham Evening Despatch*, 5 August 1960
70   'When a director . . .' *Monthly Film Bulletin*, March 1960, vol 27, # 3/4
70   'the spectators dropped like flies', B Gay-Lussac, 1960, *L'Express*, #456

71   'pleased and excited . . .', p.7, *I Lost it at the Movies*, Pauline Kael, Marion Boyars, London, 1994
71   'Even dubbed, *Eyes* . . .', ibid.
72   'ravaged by Genessier's familial egoism . . .', p.86, *Franju*, Durgnat

Psycho
84   'excessively shy . . .', p.109, *Alfred Hitchcock and the Making of Psycho*, Stephen Rebello, Marion Boyars, London, 1990
87   'In using only strings . . .', 'Herrmann, Hitchcock, and the Music of the Irrational', Royal D Brown, *Cinema Journal*, Spring 1982

123 'He was us', Romero, quoted on *Son of the Incredibly Strange Film Show*

Rosemary's Baby

128 'were exactly like . . .', Bodeen, quoted p.70, *The Satanic Screen – An Illustrated Guide to the Devil in Cinema 1896–1999*, Nikolas Schreck, Creation Books, London, 2000

130 'less personal . . .', Interview with Polanksi, Harrison Eagle, *Film Comment*, Autumn 1968

132 'What I like . . .', Interview with Polanski, Michel Delahaye and Jean André Freschi, *Cahiers du Cinema* (in English)

134 'what we wanted . . .', Sylbert, quoted in 'Rosemary's Baby – A Retrospective' on Paramount Region 2 DVD

134 'inspired awe . . .', p.227, *Repulsion*, Thomas Kiernan, NEL, London, 1982

134 'Ask him why . . .', Cassavetes, quoted p.57, *Polanski*, Barbara Leaming, Hamish Hamilton, London, 1982

135 'The entire story . . .', *Roman* by Polanski, p.228, Heinemann, London, 1984

137 'The film is very proficient . . .', p.56, ibid.

137 'manufacturer of intelligent thrillers . . .', Stanley Kaufman, *New Republic*, 15 June 1968

137 'triumphantly confirms . . .', *Monthly Film Bulletin*, May 1969, vol 36, # 424

138 'Sometimes voluptuous feelings . . .', p.46, *On the Nightmare*, Ernest Jones, Liveright, New York, 1971

140 'opens like a Doris Day movie . . .', Sylbert, quoted in 'Rosemary's Baby – A Retrospective'

The Exorcist

148 'I'd rather work . . .', Friedkin, quoted p.74, *William Friedkin: Films of Aberration, Possession and Reality*, Thomas D Clagett, Silman James Press, 2003

149 'supernatural doesn't . . .', Blatty, quoted p.67, *The Exorcist*, Mark Kermode, BFI Modern Classics, BFI, London, 1997

150 'There are strange images . . .', Friedkin, quoted p.34, 'The Curse that Hangs over *The Exorcist*', Benjamin Fort, *Castle of Frankenstein*, # 22, 1974

Deep Red

192 'a little like . . .', Argento, quoted p.228, *Broken Mirrors/Broken Minds*, Maitland McDonagh, Sun Tavern Fields, London, 1991

192 'deep within me . . .', Argento, quoted in *Dario Argento World of Horror* documentary

192 'I like women . . .', Argento, quoted p.54, *Stay out of the Shower*, William Schoell, Dembner, New York, 1985

192 'I would probably . . .', Argento, quoted *World of Horror*

197 'simply a director . . .', '*Deep Red* is a Bucket of Ax-Murder Cliches', Vincent Canby, *New York Times*, 10 June 1976

Halloween

207 'I hate pretentious movies . . .', Carpenter, quoted by Spence Abbott, IGN.com, 1996

208 'too intellectual . . .', Carpenter, quoted in Crew Filmographies, *Halloween* 25th anniversary DVD release

209 'I think it's a little melodramatic . . .', Pleasence, quoted in 'A Cut Above the Rest', documentary on *Halloween* 25th anniversary DVD release

211 'it cannot . . .', *Monthly Film Bulletin*, February 1979, vol 46, # 541

211 'pitiful, amateurish script', *New Yorker*, 19 February 1979

214 'a kind of feint . . .', p.18, *Men, Women and Chainsaws*, Carol J Clover, BFI London, 1992

215 'The *raison d'être* . . .', 'Pre-Postmodern Slasher Seeks Ironic Teen for "Meaningful" Termination', Stephen Thrower, p.9, *Flesh and Blood Compendium*, ed. Harvey Fenton, FAB Press, Godalming, 2003

216 'Everybody hates . . .', Akkad, quoted in *A Cut Above the Rest*

Alien

223 'it was more . . .', Ridley Scott, quoted p.8, *David Thomson on the Alien Quartet*, David Thomson, Bloomsbury, 1998, London

224 'They asked me . . .', HR Giger, quoted p.13, ibid.

224 'explain what . . .', Scott, quoted p.56, ibid.

225 'Sigourney was great . . .', Scott, director's DVD commentary, Alien Legacy edition

245 'wanted to see . . .', Cronenberg, quoted p.94, *Cronenberg on Cronenberg*, ed. Chris Rodley

247 'Violence is horrible . . .', *Listener*, 30 May 1968

The Fly

251 'irresponsible medical experiments . . .', p.236, *The Beauty Myth: How Images of Beauty are Used Against Women*, Naomi Wolf, William Morris & Co, New York, 1991

252 'just like . . .', p.40, *Starburst*, March 1987, No. 103, Vol 9, # 7

252 'rehearsals or experiments . . .', p.169, 'The Interview', William Beard & Piers Handling, *The Shape of Rage*, ed. Piers Handling, Academy of Canadian Cinema, Toronto, 1983

252 'The thing about man . . .', p.90, 'The Word, the Flesh and David Cronenberg', John Harkness, in ibid.

253 'I think [the unconscious mind] . . .', p.179, 'The Interview', Beard and Handling

253 'roiling, furious . . .', Guy Maddin, quoted p.13, 'The Saddest Filmmaker in the World', Kristine McKenna, *Arthur*, May 2001

254 'not disgust . . .', Cronenberg, quoted by A Billson, 'Cronenberg on Cronenberg: a Career in Stereo', *Monthly Film Bulletin*, January 1989, vol 56, # 660, p.5

254 'perhaps some diseases . . .', Cronenberg interviewed by Kim Newman, *Shock Xpress*, Summer 1987, vol 2, # 1

254 'I identify . . .', p.179, 'The Interview', Beard and Handling

255 'Someone who writes . . .', p.57, *Cronenberg on Cronenberg*, ed. Chris Rodley

255 'to censor myself . . .', p.14, *BFI Film Dossier 21: David Cronenberg*, ed. Wayne Drew

255 'The appeal of horror . . .', p.60, *Cronenberg on Cronenberg*, Rodley

260 'Tightly paced . . .', 'On Now', *Sight & Sound*, Winter 1986/87, vol 56, #1

261 'three people in a room', *Shock Xpress*, Newman

261 'the film is a metaphor . . .', p.125, *Cronenberg on Cronenberg*, Rodley

263 'seems to . . .', 'Out of the Blue', Terrence Rafferty, *Sight & Sound*, Winter 1986/7, vol 56, # 1

Ring/Ringu

302 'they mixed . . .', Nakata, quoted in 'The "Ring" Master', interview with Donato Totaro, 21 July 2000, www.offscreen.com

303 'knuckle-biting terror' and following press quotes taken from 'Press' page on Tartan's DVD release

303 'will scare . . .', 'Ring' review, *Sight & Sound*, September 2000, vol 10, # 9

304 'What I really intended . . .', Nakata, quoted in Totaro interview

306 'What good is life . . .', Miike, quoted p.309, *Agitator – The Cinema of Takashi Miike*, Tom Mes, FAB Press, Guilford, 2003

APPENDIX
RECOMMENDED DVD RELEASES

Nosferatu: BFI, Region 2 PAL

Bride of Frankenstein: Universal 2-disc set with *Frankenstein*, Region 2 PAL

Invasion of the Body Snatchers: Republic Pictures, Region 1 NTSC

Dracula: Warner Bros, Region 2 PAL, currently available only as part of a three-disc Hammer box set with *The Curse of Frankenstein* and *The Mummy*

Eyes Without a Face: TFI, Region 2 PAL. This edition, the only DVD release currently available, lacks English subtitles

Psycho: Universal, Region 1 NTSC; the Columbia PAL release is missing this edition's hour-long documentary

The Haunting: Warner Bros, Region 2 PAL

Night of the Living Dead: Elite 25th Anniversary or Tombstone Editions, Region 0 NTSC

Rosemary's Baby: Paramount, Region 2 PAL

The Exorcist: Warner Bros, Region 2 PAL. The first DVD release is the only one to carry the full original theatrical print; for the 25th Anniversary Edition Friedkin tweaked a number of sequences.

Don't Look Now: Studio Canal, Region 2 PAL

The Texas Chain Saw Massacre: Universal, Region 2 PAL

Deep Red: Anchor Bay, Region 1 NTSC

Halloween: Anchor Bay 25th Anniversary Edition, Region 2 PAL
Alien: 20th Century Fox 'Director's Cut' 2-disc set, Region 2 PAL
Cannibal Holocaust: EC Entertainment 2-disc set, Region 0 NTSC
The Fly: 20th Century Fox 2-disc set with *The Fly 2*, Region 2 PAL
Evil Dead 2: Momentum Pictures, Region 2 PAL
Henry: Portrait of a Serial Killer: Optimum, Region 2 PAL
Ring: DreamWorks, Region 1 NTSC

INDEX